The Turnings of Darkness and Light

THE TURNINGS OF DARKNESS AND LIGHT

Essays in Philosophical and Systematic Theology

KENNETH SURIN

Associate Professor and Director of
Undergraduate Studies, Department of Religion
Duke University, Durham, North Carolina

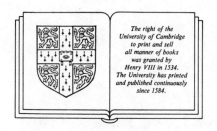

The right of the
University of Cambridge
to print and sell
all manner of books
was granted by
Henry VIII in 1534.
The University has printed
and published continuously
since 1584.

CAMBRIDGE UNIVERSITY PRESS

CAMBRIDGE

NEW YORK   NEW ROCHELLE   MELBOURNE   SYDNEY

Published by the Press Syndicate of the University of Cambridge
The Pitt Building, Trumpington Street, Cambridge CB2 1RP
32 East 57th Street, New York, NY 10022, USA
10 Stamford Road, Oakleigh, Melbourne 3166, Australia

© Cambridge University Press

First published 1989

Printed in Great Britain
at the University Press, Cambridge

British Library cataloguing in publication data
Surin, Kenneth, 1948–
The turnings of darkness and light:
essays in philosophical and systematic theology.
1. Christian theology.
I. Title.
230

Library of Congress cataloguing in publication data
Surin, Kenneth, 1948–
The turnings of darkness and light:
essays in philosophical and systematic theology /
Kenneth Surin.
p.   cm.
Bibliography.
Includes index.
ISBN 0 521 34159 0
1. Philosophical theology. I. Title.
BT40.S87 1988
230 – dc19

ISBN 0 521 34159 0

CE

For my mother, Joan Cecilia Surin

*and in memory of my father, George Joseph Surin (1910–1975),
and my brother, Patrick David Surin (1949–1953)*

Contents

While pursuing this context of syntax as a pivot for the turnings of darkness and light, I was startled to discover that the word *syntaxis* occurs in the title of a treatise by the second-century Greek astronomer, Ptolemy, whose geocentric view of the relations among the bodies in the solar system also deals with the question of what in the world turns around what. . . . Is there a relation between grammar and gravitation? Could the relations between clarity and obscurity really be as simple – or as complex – as night and day?

(Barbara Johnson, 'Poetry and Syntax' in *The Critical Difference: Essays in the Contemporary Rhetoric of Reading*, Baltimore: Johns Hopkins University Press, 1985, pp. 69–70)

Preface

The essays in this collection were written between 1974 and 1987. As will be evident from a cursory inspection of this book's contents, I have changed or modified my positions on a number of important issues. These changes have generally been the result of conversations and correspondence with many individuals. I am particularly grateful to John Hick, who has been unfailing in his kindness from the time I began my graduate studies under his supervision in 1972. Nearly every topic discussed in this book has featured on Hick's intellectual agenda at some stage, and although our disagreements are substantial, it would be impossible for me to deny that my own work has grown out of a strenuous engagement with various aspects of Hick's *oeuvre*. I am also indebted to the following for valuable discussions relating to one or more of the essays contained herein: Gavin D'Costa, David Ford, Stephen Fowl, Hans Frei, Stanley Hauerwas, Brian Hebblethwaite, C. T. Hughes III, Werner Jeanrond, Greg Jones, Nicholas Lash, Gerard Loughlin and Rowan Williams. I owe an even greater debt to John Milbank, who has been unfailingly effective as a conversation partner. Needless to say, my helpers are not responsible for any flaws that remain.

The writing of the previously unpublished essays in this collection was facilitated by a period of sabbatical leave spent as a visiting scholar at St Edmund's College, Cambridge, and the Faculty of Theology at Oxford. I am grateful to the Master and Fellows of St Edmund's for their hospitality, and also to Maurice Wiles for making possible my association with the Oxford Theology Faculty in the Trinity Term of 1986. I am also indebted to the library staff at my previous institution, the College of St Paul and St Mary, Cheltenham, who enabled me to benefit from their very efficient

inter-library loans system. But, as ever, my greatest debt is to
Fiona, my wife, who saw me through those bleaker moments which
today confront any British-based academic trying to do serious
work in a cultural and intellectual environment riven by the
prejudices of a philistine government. Our son, Alastair, and our
daughter, Rebecca, were born during the time when most of these
essays were being given their final form: their presence has forced
me to attend more fully to the futurological implications of any
lines of thought I happened to be pursuing.

Except for some minor stylistic changes, undertaken mainly to
ensure consistency from one essay to the next, I have chosen not to
revise these essays. My positions on a variety of issues have
changed markedly over the last decade or so, and any attempt at
real revision would have necessitated a wholesale rewriting.
Indeed, several essays would then have borne very little resemblance to their originals. Rather than do this, I have sought to
indicate in the appropriate endnotes where and how I have changed
my views. In general, those essays written and published since 1985
are most representative of my current positions.

As an undergraduate, I was trained to be a philosopher in the
analytic tradition. As a graduate student, I became interested in
what, in this tradition, passes as 'the philosophy of religion'. These
essays, especially the more recent ones, are (in part) an attempt to
extricate myself from the confines of the tradition which gave shape
to my earliest philosophical endeavours. This process has been slow
and uneven, something reflected in the substance and tone of these
essays. I am well aware that in some sense this process is still to be
completed. But it began around 1983, when, mainly as a result of a
year's close study of the work of Theodor Adorno, I became
convinced that the fundamental orientation of the analytic tradition
of philosophy was irremediably ahistorical and 'theoreticist' (in the
sense delineated by Marx in his 'Theses on Feuerbach'). The
analytical philosopher is not encouraged – in principle – to locate
his or her reflections in situations characterized by an irreducible
historical particularity. Even less is he or she taught to see that *all*
intellectual activities either address or evade, whether directly or
indirectly, *practical* problems within those situations. To have this
awareness, however, the philosopher needs to be able to describe
these situations and their historical genesis. Increasingly, therefore, I saw the need to draw on two exemplary accounts for the
resources to describe the 'operating conditions' not only of the kind
of theorizing I had previously been engaged in, but also of the

rather different modes of reflection that were now coming within my purview. The accounts in question were those of Karl Marx and Max Weber. At the same time, my interests were being drawn in a more recognizably 'theological' direction. Prompted by Nicholas Lash and Dewi Phillips, I began to appreciate the extent to which the 'philosophical theism' sponsored by analytical philosophy of religion bears hardly any relation to the strands of theological activity characteristically associated with Irenaeus, Athanasius, the Cappadocians, Augustine, Anselm and Aquinas (to cite but a few emblematic figures). This philosophical and theological reorient-ation shows itself most clearly in chapters 2, 3, 10, 11 and 12. The remaining essays are however fairly explicitly, though not always totally, wedded to 'philosophical theism' in one or other of its forms. I am well aware that, in consequence, there will be some who may regard the earlier essays as less unsatisfactory than the ones which happen to reflect my current views.

It is in the very nature of a collection like this that some repetition is unavoidable, especially when two or more essays have themes which overlap.

I am grateful to the editors and publishers for permission to reprint several chapters which have been published before or which were written for other occasions:

Chapter 1 was first printed in *The Journal of Theological Studies*, 32 (1981), 401–22. Reprinted by permission of the Oxford University Press.

Chapter 2 was first printed in *Modern Theology*, 2 (1986), 235–56. Reprinted by permission of Basil Blackwell.

Chapter 3 was prepared for a seminar of the 'D' Society, The Divinity School, University of Cambridge; and a conference on Religious Theories of Language at the University of Lancaster held in July 1986.

Chapter 4 was first printed in *The Scottish Journal of Theology*, 35 (1982), 97–115. Reprinted by permission of the Scottish Academic Press.

Chapter 5 was first printed in *The Harvard Theological Review*, 76 (1983), 225–47. Copyright 1983 by the President and Fellows of Harvard College.

Chapter 6 was first printed in *New Blackfriars*, 62 (1981), 521–32.

Chapter 7 was first printed in *New Blackfriars*, 64 (1983), 323–35.

Chapter 8 was first printed in *Neue Zeitschrift für Systematische Theologie und Religionsphilosophie*, 24 (1982), 131–49. Reprinted by permission of Walter de Gruyter.

Chapter 9 was first printed, in a briefer version, in *Religious Studies*, 19 (1983), 323–43. Reprinted by permission of the Cambridge University Press.

Chapter 10 was first printed in *Modern Theology*, 4 (1987), 187–209. Reprinted by permission of Basil Blackwell.

Chapter 11 was first printed in *The Journal of the American Academy of Religion*, 53 (1985), 383–410.

Chapter 12 was prepared for the Society for the Study of Theology Annual Conference, held at the University of Cambridge in April 1987.

Chapter 13 was first printed in *The International Journal for the Philosophy of Religion*, 16 (1984), 128–38.

Abbreviations

A David Burrell, *Aquinas: God and Action* (London: Routledge & Kegan Paul, 1979)

AB Dietrich Bonhoeffer, *Act and Being*, trans. Bernard Noble (London: Collins, 1962)

CD Karl Barth, *Church Dogmatics*, trans. G. W. Bromiley *et al.* (Edinburgh: T. & T. Clark, 1936–74)

CFH S. W. Sykes and J. P. Clayton, eds., *Christ, Faith and History: Cambridge Studies in Christology* (Cambridge: Cambridge University Press, 1972)

CG Jürgen Moltmann, *The Crucified God: The Cross of Christ as the Foundation and Criticism of Christian Theology*, trans. R. A. Wilson and John Bowden (London: SCM Press, 1974)

CI *Critical Inquiry*

CNS Sebastian Moore, *The Crucified Is No Stranger* (London: Darton, Longman & Todd, 1977)

COR John Hick and Brian Hebblethwaite, eds., *Christianity and Other Religions* (London: Collins/Fount, 1980)

CPR Immanuel Kant, *Critique of Pure Reason*, trans. Norman Kemp Smith (London: Macmillan, 1964)

CR Stanley Cavell, *The Claim of Reason: Wittgenstein, Skepticism, Morality and Tragedy* (Oxford: Oxford University Press, 1979)

DE Max Horkheimer and Theodor W. Adorno, *Dialectic of Enlightenment*, trans. John Cumming (London: Verso, 1979)

EGL John Hick, *Evil and the God of Love* (London: Macmillan, 1966)

FMW *From Max Weber: Essays in Sociology*, eds. H. H. Gerth and C. Wright Mills (London: Routledge & Kegan Paul, 1970)

GJC Walter Kasper, *The God of Jesus Christ*, trans. M. J. O'Connell (London: SCM Press, 1984)

GS G. W. H. Lampe, *God as Spirit: The Bampton Lectures, 1976* (Oxford: Clarendon Press, 1978)

SJT *The Scottish Journal of Theology*
ST St Thomas Aquinas, *Summa Theologiae*, the Blackfriars translation (London: Eyre & Spottiswoode, 1964–)
T *Telos*
Th *The Thomist*
TDB Nicholas Lash, *Theology on Dover Beach* (London: Darton, Longman & Todd, 1979)
TND George A. Lindbeck, *The Nature of Doctrine: Religion and Theology in a Postliberal Age* (London: SPCK, 1985)
TPE Kenneth Surin, *Theology and the Problem of Evil* (Oxford: Basil Blackwell, 1986)
WCA Ronald Gregor Smith, ed., *The World Come of Age: A Symposium on Dietrich Bonhoeffer* (London: Collins, 1967)
WK Rowan Williams, *The Wound of Knowledge: Christian Spirituality from the New Testament to St John of the Cross* (London: Darton, Longman & Todd, 1979)

1
Creation, revelation and the analogy theory

The heart of St Thomas Aquinas's views on the nature of language about God is his thesis that all assertions about God are to be construed analogically.[1] Aquinas offers this as one thesis, but it is fruitful to regard it as consisting of two separate claims: a *linguistic* subthesis, which provides for the formulation of analogy rules governing the meaning derivations of terms in natural language; and a *metaphysical* subthesis, designed to facilitate the application of these rules to theistic language, by expressing the truth (as Aquinas saw it) of the cosmological relation that exists between God and the objects of creation.[2] One of the main purposes of this essay will be to argue that the theology of revelation requires us to construe this relation between God and the world as an ontic (or ontological), and not a cosmological, relation. That is, the theology of revelation behoves us to construe the relation between God and the world as an 'isomorphism' of being, antecedent to any act of divine creation, and not as something which is the mere consequence of God's creative act (as would be the case in a cosmological relation).[3]

I Aquinas's two subtheses

(*AL*) Natural language has two analogy rules, one for 'attribution' and the other for 'proper proportionality', which specify that the instances of a term are analogues if they instantiate a semantic property (of the term in question) which conforms in its use to either or both of these rules.[4] In both these rules instances of the same term (the analogues) are applied to different objects (the analogates): they differ, however, in their mode of application. With regard to the first rule – the analogy of attribution – the property or attribute signified by the term in question really belongs to one, but not the other, of the objects. With regard to the second rule – the analogy of proper proportionality – both objects actually possess the property signified by the term in question. Aquinas uses the term 'health' to illustrate the way the first rule works. According to him, we can say both of a diet and a man that they are healthy, although the property *being healthy*, which is signified by the term 'health', actually belongs to the man only: in describing a diet as healthy we merely assert that it is the cause of health in the man.[5] Likewise, the term 'life' illustrates the way the second analogy rule works. When we assert of a man and an aspidistra that they both possess life, we mean that each of them is, in the literal sense of that term, *alive*. Or in scholastic terminology, the property signified by the analogous instances of a term is found formally in both of the analogates in question. At the same time, the analogy theorist wishes to qualify this rule by saying that the property is possessed in a mode commensurable with the 'degree of being' constitutive of the analogates in question. This qualification is standardly expressed in terms of the quasi-mathematical formula: 'the life of a man is to the essence of a man as the life of an aspidistra is to the essence of an aspidistra'.[6]

(*AM*) The similarity of *meaning* among the instances of a term, established by the two analogy rules, is connected with the similarity of the *things* possessing the property signified by that term. (Such a term will therefore be one that can be predicated of *both* God and the objects of creation; it thus signifies a property which can be ascribed, in a suitably qualified sense, to both God and such objects.)

Aquinas's account of the nature of theistic language hinges crucially on (*AM*), since he wants to say, essentially, that the terms of our language can have a theistic reference, and can be used to describe God in a suitably qualified sense, precisely because of the cosmological relation that exists between God and his creation. Accordingly, the cornerstone of Aquinas's analogy theory is his metaphysics of creation: without it the analogy theory remains a merely interesting and original theory about meaning derivation in ordinary language. That is, without the metaphysics of creation embodied in, or presupposed by, (*AM*), the analogy theory would be a truncated theory consisting solely of its linguistic component (*AL*), and as such it would not be a theory about sentences that purport to refer to, and to describe, God. It would not be a *theo*-logic. And since the present discussion is concerned with

Aquinas's theory from the point of view of its application to theistic language, our attention must focus on this metaphysics of creation, and its role in connecting Aquinas's two subtheses to form a general analogical theory of *theistic* language, i.e. a theo-logic.[7] But first we must dwell briefly on St Thomas's motivation for constructing such a theory. Aquinas believes he needs an analogical theory of theistic language because:

(a) If the predicate terms in God-statements are *completely equivocal* (that is, applied in totally different senses from the ones they possess when applied to mundane objects), then any inferences from statements about such objects to statements about God will be invalid, committing the fallacy of equivocation; and all God-statements will be cognitively non-significant, because we will not be able to explicate these statements in terms that are accessible to the experiences of creaturely objects. The outcome of equivocal predication is agnosticism, and this Aquinas finds totally unacceptable, since it goes against the basic presupposition of his theology that our natural cognitive powers can furnish us with evidence for the truth of theistic statements.

(b) If the predicate-terms in God-statements are *univocal* (that is, applied in the same senses as the ones they possess when applied to mundane objects), then our conception of God will be anthropomorphic, since our explications of God-statements will be derived solely from the experiences of creaturely objects. Aquinas contends that if we are to describe the transcendent Christian God, then our descriptions of him must designate him as a reality essentially different from anything encountered in our experience.

As a consequence of the constraints expressed in (a) and (b), the predicate terms in God-statements must be partly equivocal with regard to their counterpart terms in ordinary experience-describing statements. Aquinas holds that a systematic elucidation of the relation between God-statements and ordinary experience-describing statements must involve an analogy theory, and, moreover, that if we use such a theory, we shall preserve both the notion of God as an utterly transcendent being and the intelligibility of theistic discourse, and not rule out the possibility that human experience can provide some evidence for the truth of statements about God. His motivation, therefore, is to steer a course between the twin pitfalls of agnosticism and anthropomorphism.[8]

According to the analogy rule for attribution, we can call God by the names of his actions, because he is the cause of his actions. Thus, when we say that God is wisdom we merely assert that he causes wisdom to exist in the objects of his creation. The term 'God' is for Aquinas an abbreviated definite description or predicable general term (*nomen naturae*), signifying all the properties attributable to him by virtue of his being the Creator and Sustainer of the world. Three major problems are likely to arise in connection with the application of the rule for attribution.

Firstly, since Aquinas uses the existential arguments of the Five Ways to establish certain relations between God and the world, any objections to these arguments will immediately render the analogy theory suspect (with regard to its function as a theo-logic). Against this possible objection, James Ross has proposed that we can, for the sake of argument, either assume that there is reliable evidence for the existence of an entity which is First Cause, Cosmic Designer, etc., or accept as a matter of religious faith that such a Creator exists.[9] Ross's proposal, however, is almost certain to frustrate one of Aquinas's key objectives in formulating an analogy theory, viz. the preservation of the cognitive significance of theistic language. Aquinas's theory purports to be a theory of the *meaning* of theistic utterances, but it is also more than just a semantic theory. For in purporting to be such a theory it presupposes that certain correspondences can be established between the nature of God and the nature of creaturely objects – the theory cannot 'get off the ground' without these correspondences. However, as a necessary condition of establishing these correspondences, Aquinas has to assume that *true* statements can be made about God: if he cannot say anything about God that is true, then he cannot claim to have established any *valid* correspondences. Consequently, Aquinas's meaning-theory presupposes a theory of the truth of theistic statements as a condition of preserving the cognitive significance of these statements. Ross's proposal, by assuming the truth of theistic statements on purely 'fideistic' grounds, suffices to get Aquinas's theory off the ground, but only at the price of surrendering the principle that analogical language can express our cognitions of the objective reality that is God. For to uphold this 'objectivity principle' we have to accept that theistic statements can conform in principle to canons of truth, intelligibility, and rationality that are *extrinsic* to faith and its requirements, and this is precisely what the 'fideist' will not, or cannot, allow. Any formulation of the rule for attribution must respect this 'objectivity principle' if it is to accord with Aquinas's intentions in formulating the analogy theory.[10]

Secondly, it would seem obvious to that problematic creature –

the simple believer – that when we ascribe a property to God, e.g. wisdom, we mean just what we say, that is, that God is wise as an intrinsic part of his nature.

Thirdly, we know that Aquinas himself is not prepared to ascribe to God's essence all the properties of which he is the cause: he does not argue, for example, that God is a body because he creates creatures that are embodied. Aquinas, then, definitely does allow exceptions to the principle established by the analogy rule for attribution, i.e. the principle that we can call God by the names of his actions because he is the cause of his actions. This raises the obvious question of the criteria by which he allows exceptions to this principle, for if he has no such criteria he is open to the charge that he applies this analogy rule arbitrarily. And, moreover, the more exceptions he allows to this principle, the less informative the rule for attribution becomes. However, modern analogy theorists take this problem seriously, as they do the other difficulties we have just listed. Their standard manoeuvre at this juncture is to augment the rule for attribution with the rule for proper proportionality.[11]

The analogy rule for proper proportionality enables the analogy theorist to say that the attributes we ascribe to God actually inhere in him, but only in a manner appropriate to his essence. Thus, although God is wisdom, he is not wise in the way that human beings are wise: his wisdom corresponds to his self-subsistent being, and none of us is that kind of being. Unfortunately, the invocation of the rule for proper proportionality in this context only creates another difficulty for the analogy theorist, because Aquinas maintains that we cannot know God's essence (*ST*, I. 13. 1). That this contention of Aquinas's is inherently agnostic is obvious from the following passage of H. P. Owen's, a modern analogy theorist who follows Aquinas on this matter:

> We do not know God's essence. Therefore we cannot understand the manner in which his attributes belong to him. In any comparison between God and man we understand the analogue only in the human analogate. Its mode of being in the divine analogate is permanently hidden from us in this life. Hence there is not a complete comparison between our use of analogy in the finite realm and our use of it in religion. When we interpret another person's character by analogy with our own we can (to some extent at least) imaginatively 'enter' into his experience; for we are fellow members of the human species. But we cannot enter into God's experience; for we cannot share his Godhood (or *aseitas*). . . . Hence, though we can predicate personality of God we cannot understand its mode of being. We know *that* God is personal; but *how* he is personal we do not know. The doctrine

of analogy does not 'explain' his nature in the sense of 'making it plain' to our understanding. Rather it states a mystery which no human mind can pierce.[12]

This account of the *modus operandi* of the rule for proper proportionality is unacceptable for the following reasons.

Firstly, in asserting that the analogy theory 'states a mystery which no human mind can pierce', Owen, and Aquinas with him, seem to be going against a presupposition of the latter's theology we mentioned earlier, viz. that our natural cognitive powers can provide us with evidence for the truth of theistic statements. This presupposition lies behind Aquinas's espousal of the analogy theory, and to say that this theory 'states a mystery which no human mind can pierce', without qualifying this statement, is equivalent to saying that what this theory affirms or entails is beyond the compass of our natural cognitive powers. On this interpretation, Aquinas might as well abandon 'natural theology', and instead rely on God's grace to make known to us the truth of theistic statements.[13]

Secondly, mysteries are apt to be uninformative, and the generally uninformative character of the rule for proper proportionality is obvious. For what the rule does is to assert that a relational likeness exists between the way in which some creaturely attributes are proportioned to creaturely nature, and the way in which God's attributes are proportioned to his nature: it does not, however, provide for any *direct* comparisons between the two types of attributes. For, basically, in order to show that a relation of proportional similarity exists between two objects, we have to establish a relation of similarity between them in the first place. And we could not establish such a relation unless we have some antecedent knowledge of God's nature and attributes. This much was perceived by Berkeley, who said, 'You cannot argue from unknown attributes, or, which is the same thing, from attributes in an unknown sense.'[14] This antecedently required knowledge, however, cannot be provided by the rule for proper proportionality since it is presupposed by it. At this juncture, modern analogy theorists, e.g. Mascall and Owen, reverse the manoeuvre that they resort to when faced with difficulties apropos the other analogy rule (the rule for attribution): they now revert back to that rule as a means of circumventing their problems apropos the rule for proper proportionality.[15] The presumption made by the analogy theorist is that although the two analogy rules are insufficient when taken individually, they are mutually validating and sufficient when taken conjointly. This presumption is open to serious objection, not only because the rule for attribution has its own problems (as we have already indicated), but because it is question-begging in a quite serious way, and so cannot supplement the rule for proper proportionality in the way required by the analogy theorist. To see this we have only to consider the relation the rule for attribution has to the 'existential' arguments of the Five Ways. Aquinas (and Mascall, Owen and Ross, following him) use the Five Ways to establish that several relations exist between God and the world: (i) 'being moved by'; (ii) 'being efficiently caused by'; (iii) 'being conserved in existence by'; (iv) 'being excelled by'; and (v) 'being designed by'. These relations, we have seen, are required to operate the rule for attribution, but they are used in a different sense from their mundane uses, that is, they are used analogically. The analogical usage, however, cannot be interpreted in terms of the rule for attribution because this rule presupposes precisely such a usage. For the terms in the relations expressed by (i)–(v) have to be con-s. rued analogically, and yet (i)–(v) are required to operate the rule for attribution. Furthermore, as was pointed out above, Aquinas has to assume that true statements about God are possible before he can assert that (i)–(v) specify certain relations between God and the world. That is, he needs a theory of truth for theistic statements *before* he can account for their meaning, and this is incongruous: it is a philosophical commonplace that a statement has to be meaningful before it can be assigned a truth-value. It follows, *a fortiori*, that neither analogy rule can support the other in the way envisaged by the analogy theorists who resort to this manoeuvre.

To summarize the discussion so far: we have briefly examined each of Aquinas's analogy rules, and found them to be inadequate. We then examined the strategy – adopted by some modern analogy theorists (to wit, Owen and Mascall) – which purports to show that the two analogy rules, although individually insufficient, can be regarded as mutually supporting when taken conjointly. This strategy we found to be unworkable. The analogy theorist, if our arguments are correct, is faced with the crucial problem of providing a twofold basis for the operation of both analogy rules. With regard to the rule for attribution she has to demonstrate that it is possible for us to attribute the same property to both God and creaturely objects (albeit in a suitable qualified sense); and with regard to the rule for proper proportionality she has to establish that a relation of proportional similarity exists between God and such objects. Neither of these, we have argued, has been satisfactorily undertaken by Aquinas (seemingly), Mascall, or Owen. I want now to argue that this failure can be overcome if we adopt a rather different approach to analogy based on Aquinas's metaphysics of creation.

It was seen earlier that the crux of Aquinas's account of the nature of theistic language is the metaphysical subthesis (*AM*), and that Aquinas articulates this subthesis in terms of a cosmological relation that exists between God and the world. The alternative approach proposed here requires us to conceive of this as an ontic (or ontological), as opposed to a cosmological, relation between God and the world. Naturally, in so doing we are making a fairly radical departure from the traditional 'Thomist' conception of this relation: the alternative that we propose is almost certainly not one that Aquinas himself would have entertained. Nevertheless, its basic structure is firmly rooted in his theological system, and we have only to make it explicit.[16] Our approach will also have the advantage of enabling us to reconcile the *analogia entis* of Thomism with the *analogia fidei* of Karl Barth.[17] But before proceeding to do this, let us consider a noteworthy attempt to get round the problems we have just mentioned by adverting to the notion of the incarnation. The analogy theorists who make this attempt usually argue that since Jesus Christ is the ideal exemplar of the divine attributes, we can use Christ incarnate as the primary focus of analogical predication: terms that are used in mundane contexts are applicable to God precisely because in the person of Jesus of Nazareth God is present. To quote Michael Durrant, an analogy theorist who espouses this strategy:

> we must look, it seems, to the pattern of Jesus Christ himself, for Christians hold that in Christ we have an instance of infinite goodness, infinite wisdom, infinite mercy, etc. Having brought out what it is to say that Christ is infinitely good, wise, merciful, etc., we can bring out the contrasts and similarities with saying that a person is good, wise, merciful, etc. This is what needs to be done and, I contend, all that can be done.... Christ's actions of love to his disciples and followers are precisely instances of what is intended by the phrase 'infinite love', and some future investigation must reveal the differences and dissimilarities, likenesses and similarities, between the two concepts of 'love' – the love of persons and the love of Christ; love and infinite love. To assuage the sceptic, a trinitarian would also have to show the relation between 'good', 'merciful', 'wise', etc., when predicated of persons, and 'infinitely good', 'infinitely wise', 'infinitely merciful', etc., when asserted of the other members of the Trinity; but I do not see anything theoretically impossible about this once the programme has been worked out in the case of Jesus Christ.[18]

Durrant's programme, it seems to me, is fraught with the following difficulties:

1. It is not obvious that a trinitarian can 'assuage the sceptic' by showing that the desired relation exists between terms predicated of Jesus Christ and those predicated of the other members of the Trinity; for, quite simply, Jesus of Nazareth possesses certain properties that other members of the Trinity cannot be said to possess. Thus, for instance, the Christian analogy theorist must accept that Christ was tempted, but it is difficult to see how the Father and the Holy Spirit can be said to be susceptible to temptation, let alone in a way that bears an appropriate relation to the temptation of Christ. The very notion of Christ's incarnation makes a substantial, or even essential, difference to the properties that can be ascribed to him, and is bound therefore to differentiate him essentially from the other members of the Trinity. It may be possible to deny that the incarnation serves to differentiate Christ essentially from the other persons of the Trinity; such a denial, however, will saddle the analogy theorist with the following dilemma. On the one hand, if Christ's 'incarnational' properties do not serve to set him apart from the other members of the Trinity, then these properties must in principle be ascribable to them as well. But, as we have just seen, it is difficult to accept how one such property – viz. that of being tempted – can be ascribed to the other members of the Trinity, since they are commonly regarded in the orthodox Christian tradition as being insusceptible to desire (a necessary condition of being tempted). On the other hand, if Christ's 'incarnational' properties do set him apart from the other members of the Trinity, then the notion of Christ as the decisive locus of the *imago Dei* would be threatened, and we would be precluded from using the incarnated Christ as the primary focus of analogical predication. It would seem, therefore, that a trinitarian analogy theorist cannot meet the requirement that an appropriate relation be specified between terms predicated of Jesus Christ and those predicated of the other members of the Trinity. She can meet this requirement only if she is prepared to accept an attenuated conception of the incarnation, or else resort to the highly problematic Sabellian doctrine of *unus Deus – unus Spiritus – una substantia – una persona*. This she cannot do, for the incarnation is the nerve of her strategy, and she must at all costs preserve a sense in which the nature of Christ can be fully and properly expressed in ordinary experience-describing language. The God-man of Durrant's programme has to hover at a very precise (linguistic) point between

heaven and earth; and it is difficult to see how the other members of the Trinity can be made to hover at the same point without stirring up a philosophical and theological hornets' nest.[19]

2. The proponent of the 'incarnation strategy' must also face up to the following dilemma: is Christ, or is not Christ, a generically different kind of being from anything encountered in human experience? If he is such a being, then there would be no point of connection between the divine Christ and objects encountered in human experience, and we would not be able to ascribe to the 'godness' of the former any predicates describing the latter. Consequently, the advocate of this strategy is required to assume that the difference between the divine Christ and such objects is only a difference of *degree*, and not of kind, and so she has no alternative but to accept a 'degree' christology. And 'degree' christologies, as successive generations of theologians have noted, are open to very serious objections.[20]

3. It seems clear that in order to recognize Jesus Christ as the ideal exemplar of the divine attributes, we need to possess beforehand the concept of what it is for a being to be infinitely good, infinitely wise, infinitely merciful, etc. That is, we must already be able to recognize the differences involved in possessing these attributes in their finite and infinite modes, which amounts to saying that we need to establish a *prior* relation of proportional similarity between these modes of attribute possession. However, as we have already indicated, it is precisely in this respect that the analogy rule for proper proportionality is deficient; and since the 'incarnation strategy' presupposes the use of this broken-backed analogy rule, it cannot be used to remedy this flaw in the analogy theory.

For these reasons, then, we have to reject the strategy proposed by Durrant and those analogy theorists who advert to the notion of the incarnation – this strategy is profoundly problematic and another means of making the theory feasible must be sought. It was said earlier that Aquinas's metaphysics of creation (the subthesis (*AM*)) holds the key to any understanding of his analogy theory's function as a theo-logic (or that of any theory purporting to resemble his theory), and we have now reached a stage in our argument which requires this claim to be substantiated. It will be our submission that this metaphysics must take the form of an ontology for the *imago Dei* if the analogy theory is to be an adequate theory of statements *about* God. This will not only give us a theological legitimation of analogy, but will also pave the way for a possible *rapprochement* between Aquinas's analogy of being and Barth's analogy of faith.

II Aquinas's doctrine of creation

Aquinas's doctrine of creation is fairly deeply permeated by the neo-Platonic strands of thought he inherited from St Augustine.[21] Plato held the view that universals (or *Forms*) ought to function as paradigms for human and divine thought and action. Universals, according to Plato, are ideal examples of themselves, and because they are such ideal exemplars, they can function as human and divine paradigms.[22] This Platonic conception was taken over by Augustine, who modified it to accord with his specifically Christian understanding of the nature of creation.[23] For Plato's view that universals are independently existing entities, which God must imitate as closely as possible if he is to create well, is not one that is straightforwardly compatible with the Christian understanding of creation. Thus Augustine asserts that 'God was not fixing his gaze upon anything outside Himself to serve as a model when he made the things he has created, for such a view is blasphemous.'[24] Aquinas, who shares Augustine's abjuration of this aspect of Plato's doctrine, likewise asserts:

> since it seems alien to the Faith that the forms of things should subsist of themselves, outside things and without matter – as the Platonists held . . . – Augustine substituted in place of these Ideas which Plato posited the ideas of all creatures existing in the divine mind. All things are formed according to these. . . .
>
> (*ST*, I. 84. 5)

Both Augustine and Aquinas, then, reject the view that God creates by conforming his creative activity to an independently existing idea or set of ideas. Rather, for them God creates by conforming his creative activity to his *own* idea of what is created – God's ideas are the exemplars for his creative activity. Thus Augustine says of God's Ideas:

> The ideas are Original Forms or fixed and changeless patterns of things which have not been fashioned from the Forms themselves and consequently, being eternal and always the same, are contained in the Divine Mind. And while these themselves neither come to be nor cease to exist, it is maintained that, in accordance with them, everything is fashioned capable of having a beginning and an end, as well as whatever actually comes into or goes out of existence.[25]

Although Augustine and Aquinas agree that the Divine Ideas function as exemplars, they differ when it comes to spelling out the relation these Ideas have to God. (Both Augustine and Aquinas use the term 'Idea' as a technical term signifying these divine ideas which function as exemplars, and I shall capitalize 'Idea' whenever it is used in this technical sense.) Augustine identifies these Ideas with God's *concepts*, whereas Aquinas regards them as God's exemplary ideas in the *likeness* of which he creates things. The difference will become obvious only when we amplify Aquinas's views; for the moment, let us say that an idea is for Aquinas the *form* of the object created. To quote him:

> by 'Ideas' we understand the forms of other things, existing apart from the things themselves. Now the form of a thing having an existence apart from the thing itself, can have two functions: either to be an exemplar or pattern of the thing whose form it is said to be; or to be the principle of knowing that thing, in the sense in which the forms of knowable things are said to be in the knower. . . . Thus the form of a house already exists in the mind of the architect. This can be called the idea of the house because the architect intends to make the house to the pattern of the form which he has conceived in his mind. Now since the world is not made by chance, but is made by God acting as an intelligent agent . . . there must be in the divine mind a form, to the likeness of which the world is made; and that is what we mean by an Idea.[26]

Now, in trying to clarify the notion of what he means by an *idea*, Aquinas points out, *contra* Augustine, that it is not to be regarded as a concept (or intelligible species, in his terminology) by which we come to understand something, it is, rather, the very object of the intellect's understanding. Or as Gilson succinctly puts it, 'The idea is no longer that *by which* the intellect knows but *that which* the intellect knows and that by which the intelligent being can accomplish its work.'[27] An idea, in short, is something understood, in the likeness of which something is made.

Aquinas, since he upholds the doctrine of the divine simplicity, is constrained to say that all God's Ideas are identical with himself, from which it follows that everything is made in the likeness of himself. However, since nothing but God is in the *perfect* likeness of God, everything is but an imperfect imitation of God, each according to its own degree of being:

> divine wisdom holds the originals of all things, and these we have previously called the Ideas, that is the exemplary forms existing in the divine mind. And though they are many and various in the relation-

ship of things to them, nevertheless they are not really other than the divine essence proportionably to the manifold sharing of its likeness by diverse things. In this sense, therefore, God is the original exemplar of them all.[28]

Having undertaken the necessary task of outlining Aquinas's ontology of creation (i.e. the subthesis (AM)), we are now in a position to ground the analogy theory in this doctrine of God's creative act.

III Creation and analogy

According to this doctrine of God's creative act, all things are replicas of God, since they participate in the Divine Ideas which are identical with his essence. We are, so to speak, the *in re* transmutation of ideas that prior to such transmutation exist *in intellectu* in the divine mind. It is now possible to outline how the two analogy rules operate in the light of this doctrine. (In so doing we are certainly not restating what Aquinas *did* in fact say, nor are we stating what he *should* have said; rather, we are stating what he *could* have said, *if* he had used a different starting-point for the analogy theory.)

Where the rule for attribution is concerned, we are justified in applying to God terms that apply primarily to mundane objects because these objects are created by God in the likeness of the divine archetypal ideas (which are of course God himself). There is an 'isomorphism' of being between these objects and these archetypal ideas which are God himself, and this 'isomorphism' generates a relation of likeness or similarity between God and us. That is, God's essence and his work of creation are not generically different: as Eberhard Jüngel points out in a discussion of divine revelation, 'God's work and essence are not of two different kinds, it is ... impossible that the reality of God and the reality which owes its existence to God's work should be related to each other as two different ontological strata and even less that they should fall apart as two worlds separated through a χωρισμός (division)'.[29] It is this generic likeness between God and his creation which the analogy rule for attribution seeks to establish. At this point we must confront a possible objection that can be urged against this rendition of the rule for attribution. According to this objection, the very concept of analogy of attribution entails causal – or in this context, ontic – connection between God and his creation. But, the objection proceeds, in using the rule for attribution as a basis for applying to God terms that have their primary function in human discourse, are we not making an unwarranted move from using attribution in the context of ontic connection to making it a *rule* about language? How can we justify the transition from the context of ontology to the context of language? Our answer to this serious objection is derived from Barth. If we are to formulate a viable theo-logic, that is, a language of the world that is *about* God, we must at least aim for a language that is capable of expressing the reality of God. Quite simply, we must, in Barth's words, 'attempt to speak theological language' (*CD*, I/1, p. 341). But we can only speak theological language if we speak of God's revelation in this language; otherwise our language will consist solely of statements which infer the reality of God from the reality of the world. The God expressed in such language will be no more than a logical construction out of the reality of the world. The reality of God, as opposed to the reality of the world, must therefore be our primary focus if we are to speak theological language. The reality of God is expressed by God in his revelation of himself, and the language of the reality of God (theological language) must necessarily be the language of revelation. This is why Barth says that the language which is open to the reality of God must, 'as it were, be commandeered by revelation' (*CD*, I/1, p. 340). Now, the sphere of God's creation is his creation, and the language of the world can speak the truth about God precisely because it is the language of the world created by God, as Jüngel points out (cf. note 17 above). The language of the world can speak about God only because this language comes – via God's work of creation – from the being of God. The very language we use to speak about God is a gift of his grace, hence any language about God must be language of the connection between God and the world. All theological language is saturated by the being of God, and this is why attribution, while concerned specifically with the ontic connection between God and the human creature, is also a rule about human language (about God).[30] So, having overcome this objection, we can now reasonably uphold our rendition of the rule for attribution – namely, that we are justified in applying to God terms that apply primarily to mundane objects because there is an 'isomorphism' of being, established by Aquinas's metaphysics of creation, between God and such objects. We must now proceed to outline a version of the rule for proper proportionality, in the light of this metaphysics of creation.

The 'isomorphism' of being between God and the creature,

which stems from our participation in the divine essence, is necessarily flawed and distorted by our imperfect mode of participation in the divine essence. Consequently, the relation of similarity established by the rule for attribution is only one of *proportional* similarity. And this is exactly what the rule for proper proportionality is about.[31] If my arguments are correct, Aquinas's ontological conception of God's creative act can furnish us with an analogy theory that is a viable theo-logic, that is, a language that really is *about* God. But several questions remain, which we must address ourselves to, if our endeavours on Aquinas's behalf are to be fully justified. Are we now left with *two* analogy theories, one mediated by the cosmological doctrine of the Five Ways, and the other by the ontological doctrine of God's work of creation? Where does one version stand in relation to the other? Why does Aquinas only hint at the version of the analogy theory that we have just outlined? The answers to these questions, it seems to me, lie in the area of Aquinas's distinction between truths that are known by revelation (faith) and those that are naturally knowable (reason) (*ST*, I. 2. 2). Before discussing this distinction in any detail, let us say, provisionally, that Aquinas has both an explicit analogy theory, relating to his conception of truths that are naturally knowable, and an implicit analogy theory, relating to his conception of truths that are known by revelation. The former he chose to develop, the latter he did not (though he *could* have done so, had he chosen to, because the latter is implicit in his theological system).

For Aquinas, the goal of all knowledge is knowledge of God, but revelation gives us knowledge of God 'from above', from God himself, whereas reason gives knowledge of God 'from below', by way of mundane objects. Cognition of the natural order is not the culminating-point of human knowledge – there is a realm which transcends the natural order and its truths of reason, the realm of the supernatural, which is the realm of divinity. Cognition of the supernatural realm cannot be attained from this world by the mere exercise of our natural cognitive powers, but only through divine revelation and faith in the content of this revelation. The truths of revelation that are assented to by faith cannot be derived from the natural order; they are revealed to us by God, and we assent to them with the conviction of faith, not because we grasp them with our natural cognitive powers, but because God has elected to reveal them to us.[32] 'Revealed' and 'natural' theology therefore have different starting-points, though they are concerned with the same reality, that is, the reality of God. From this Aquinas proceeds to argue that the method of the two is also different:

> in the teaching of philosophy [i.e. 'natural theology'] which considers creatures in themselves and leads us from them to knowledge of God, the first consideration is about creatures; the last, of God. But in the teaching of faith, which considers creatures only in their relation to God, the consideration of God comes first, that of creatures afterwards. And thus the doctrine of faith is more perfect, as being more like the knowledge possessed by God, who, in knowing Himself, immediately knows other things.[33]

From this passage it is apparent that Aquinas grants primacy to 'revealed' over 'natural' theology. 'Natural theology' trades on the assumption that God is an 'existent', that is, an object to be apprehended by men and women as thinking subjects, and hence *potentially* reduces the transcendence of God to an 'immanent' transcendence. 'Revealed theology', on the other hand, does not relativize the reality of God to human reality, and so preserves the possibility of affirming the absolute transcendence of God. Our attempt to eschew a purely cosmological approach, by grounding Aquinas's implicit analogy theory in his ontology of creation, accords with the primacy of 'revealed' over 'natural' theology – it purports to view God's creative activity from the perspective of deity (or God as 'subject'), and not from a mundane perspective (or God as 'object'). So, in effect, our account of the implicit analogy theory is an obversion of the explicit theory traditionally ascribed to Aquinas: that theory starts from the world, ours starts from God. There are, then, two analogy theories (or more precisely, two foundations for an analogy theory) which can be derived from Aquinas's theological system. This leaves us with the task of specifying the relation that these two theories have to each other in regard to the distinction between 'natural' and 'revealed' theology. We shall do this by way of determining which of the two theories constitutes the more adequate theo-logic.[34]

Aquinas maintains that since revelation yields knowledge of the inner life of God, the final attainment of this knowledge must await the beatific vision (*visio beatifica*) in the afterlife. It follows from this that the articles of faith, which are established by deriving them from the content of God's mind, will be *eschatologically verified*: their truth, unlike that of the propositions of 'natural theology', cannot be inferred here and now from the reality of the world. When we attain to the beatific vision, that event will verify or falsify the articles of faith, and to this extent these articles only stand provisionally: they cannot be established by our natural cognitive powers in this life.[35] Where does this leave the theo-logic entailed by our 'ontological' analogy theory, with its grounding in Aquinas's doctrine of creation? This doctrine of creation, with its central assertion that there is an 'isomorphism' of being between God and his creatures, makes the implicit 'ontological' analogy theory a fully-fledged *analogia entis* – our being is anchored in the being of God via the *imago Dei* of the creation.[36] The explicit analogy theory, with its dependence on a cosmological interpretation of the God–creature relation, is not really an *analogia entis*, because it does not aspire to speak from the perspective of the (inner) life or being of God, even from a necessarily eschatological perspective. It cannot be an analogy of being, because it does not come up against the being or reality of God, but only testifies to the reality of *human* thinking about the being of God.[37] Now since the final revelation of the precise nature of this *analogia entis* must await the consummation of history, to this extent it is also an *analogia fidei*: we have to accept it, in this life at any rate, as an article of faith. This conclusion has the somewhat novel consequence of confirming Barth's basic insight concerning analogy, for in terms of the reality of the world the analogy of faith must of necessity prevail over the analogy of being. Barth's analogy of faith has an essential eschatological dimension that is only inchoate in Aquinas's notion of the beatific vision in the afterlife. To make this dimension explicit in the version of the analogy theory we have outlined, we have to resort to two items in Aquinas's system: (i) his ontology of creation; and (ii) his conception of 'revealed theology'. By incorporating these two items in the implicit analogy theory, we can see that Aquinas too has an *analogia fidei*, and, moreover, one that is cast in a thoroughly eschatological mode. But the grounding of this *analogia fidei* is, and indeed has to be, the *analogia entis* – the locus of the *analogia fidei* is the being of God, from which he reveals himself to, and through, his creation. For God's *promise* that he will reveal himself at the consummation of history is grounded in the *imago Dei* manifested in his creation. The *imago Dei* in the creation betokens the fulfilment of this divine promise; it intimates to us, in the decisive form of the incarnation, that this promise has been made, and it gives us, through the cross and resurrection of Jesus Christ, an anticipatory insight into the mode of its potential fulfilment. Through his image God has bound himself to fellowship with human beings (Anderson, *Historical Transcendence*, p. 137). Barth, perhaps, did not attach sufficient importance to the *imago*

Dei: its articulation in terms of a theology of creation seemed to deny his assertion of the fundamental priority of revelation over creation. For Barth such an *imago Dei* possessed too many connotations of 'natural theology', and he was led to undervalue it.[38] However, by acknowledging the rightful importance of the *imago Dei* in our analogy theory, we can avoid this baneful tendency of Barth's. So, to put it schematically, Barth provides the eschatological dimension essential to a proper understanding of the (Thomist) *analogia entis*, while Aquinas's 'ontological' analogy theory furnishes the requisite ontological foundations for the (Barthian) *analogia fidei*. Or to put it even more briefly: analogy from the divine perspective is analogy of being, analogy from the human perspective is analogy of faith, and the two are complementary because the human creature has his or her being, through God's act of creation, in the being of God (the *imago Dei*).[39]

IV Conclusion

This leaves us with our final question, namely, why does Aquinas merely hint at the version of the analogy theory we have sought to expound on his behalf? The answer, I think, lies in his account of the nature of faith, and particularly in his assertion that grace does not supplant nature, but perfects it (*ST*, i. i. 8). This principle leads him to view faith as a gift of God's grace, while being at the same time an extension of our natural cognitive powers. To quote Terence Penelhum:

> For [Aquinas] faith is essentially a matter of assenting to propositions which, though they cannot be arrived at by reason alone, it is nevertheless reasonable to assent to because certain others can be known to be true by reason alone.... While faith is not tentative acceptance, but whole-hearted acceptance, of revealed truths, it is not irrational, since someone who has learned the truths of natural theology ... can then reasonably give voluntary assent to the truths of revelation.... The assent which the faithful freely give to the truths revealed to them is shown to be rational assent because grounds for expecting God to have revealed them can be found in natural theology....[40]

Aquinas's account of the nature of faith can be seen to have two key features. Firstly, it is propositional, in that faith is essentially a matter of assenting to certain *truths*.[41] Secondly, the assent given by the faithful to these truths is grounded in the activity of the reasoning intellect. The first feature makes for a somewhat deracinated analogy of being: if God's revelation is of certain propositional truths, then it cannot constitute any revelation of *himself*, that is, a revelation of God's *being*. And since the analogy theory we have propounded is founded on the principle that divine revelation is precisely God's revelation of himself, it follows that this account of faith will have difficulty in accommodating the analogy theory we have extracted from Aquinas's theological system. The second feature, by according primacy to the reasoning intellect in grasping the contents of divine revelation, effectively subordinates 'revealed' to 'natural' theology when it comes to giving a theological account of divine revelation. To put it crudely: Aquinas seems to think that we would all be 'natural theologians' but for certain limitations of the intellect. 'Revealed theology' is preeminent only when theology is viewed from the standpoint of God himself, but it must surrender this status when theology is approached from the human perspective. The upshot of this is to make anthropology the essential framework within which *all* theological activity is conducted. By contrast, our analogy theory is rooted in a Barthian framework which subordinates anthropology to revelation: this is the only way in which theological speech can express the reality of God. A viable theo-logic has to take revelation, and not anthropology, as its starting-point. This is our only reason for preferring our rendition of the analogy theory to the explicit theory of the cosmological approach. It also explains why Aquinas could not himself develop the 'ontological' analogy theory we have found to be implicit in his doctrine of creation. The fundamental issue here is, I think, irresolvable: it comes down, ultimately, to one's own 'pre-theological' perception of what it means to be historically-constrained human beings and to stand in relation to God.[42] To see theology in these terms is to predispose oneself to regarding revelation as the starting-point of theological activity. This in no way implies that anthropology is irrelevant or that it is trivial: it is only to say that anthropology is important precisely because of the relation in which human beings stand to God, and it is this relation which is mediated by God's decisive act of revelation. An analogy theory which aspires to be a *theo*-logic must take cognizance of this act, by attempting to speak it. If God is spoken of, his reality *is* expressed in the language of the world. God can be spoken of because he first speaks in his act of revelation. Therefore the reality of God can be expressed in an analogy theory which acknowledges the primacy of revelation.[43]

2

The Trinity and philosophical reflection: a study of David Brown's The Divine Trinity

I 'Proving God's existence'

The first part of David Brown's *The Divine Trinity*[1] is devoted to a vigorous apologetic undertaken on behalf of a God who 'intervenes'. Brown is convinced that, given the appropriate 'interventionist' assumptions, 'religious experience' can provide genuine knowledge about the existence and character of God. This conviction prompts Brown to formulate an alleged 'proof' of God's existence, which is worth reproducing in full, since it provides an accurate insight not only into Brown's understanding of 'religious experience', but also places into sharper focus the epistemology which lies at the heart of his argument in this book:

(1) Religious experience is a distinct type of experience.
(2) Whenever a type of experience occurs with which one is not personally acquainted, then the only rational course is to accept claims made on the basis of this experience, unless sufficient grounds can be adduced for doubting the coherence or intelligibility of such claims.
(3) Therefore, if cognitive claims are made on the basis of religious experience, the only rational course is to accept these claims – with the same proviso.
(4) But all those who have these experiences sincerely claim that they give knowledge of the divine.
(5) Therefore, the only rational course is to accept the existence of the divine – again, with the same proviso.
(6) But the proviso in (2) is met – there are no such sufficient grounds.
(7) Therefore, the divine exists. (p. 35)

It is perhaps worth noting at the outset that *all* such arguments from religious experience, even though they may be logically valid and cogent, are nevertheless *pragmatically futile* as putative proofs of God's existence. It is not difficult to see why. For if the experiences that are the copingstone of an argument of this kind are to be 'veridical' or 'genuine' – as indeed they are required to be by virtue of the fact that the proponents of such arguments are concerned essentially with the question of *proof* – then the experiences that are the subject of such arguments must *already* possess the property of being experiences 'of' their purported object. In the present case, accordingly, the object of religious experience – God – must already 'exist' if there are to be 'genuine' visionary experiences of which he is the (real) object. But the assertion that God exists is precisely the conclusion of the argument from religious experience. To get this argument 'off the ground', its exponent has therefore to assume the very thing that his argument purports to establish! Hence the peculiar futility that attaches to using it as a 'proof' of God's 'existence'.[2]

The historically-minded philosophical theologian will probably not be slow to recognize the Cartesian–Lockean roots of this full-blooded 'foundationalist' argument. It is appropriately to be described as 'foundationalist' inasmuch as (a) a variety of characteristically religious 'experiences' are said to constitute the *fons et origo* of certain cognitive claims ('the laying of the foundations'); (b) the coherence or intelligibility of these cognitive claims is then said to depend on the ability of the claims under consideration to survive a potential process of doubt ('the testing of the foundations'); and (c) the potentially assailing doubt having been repulsed, the cognitively secure conclusion is then able to emerge triumphant ('the certifying of the foundations'). The suggestion throughout seems to be that certain 'raw' experiences form a kind of kernel which is enveloped or overlaid by an interpretive husk, a husk that can subsequently be peeled off in order to facilitate the epistemologist's task (which, in this context, is to scrutinize and to secure cognitive claims) by enabling her to subject this 'raw' kernel to a really good 'look'.[3]

The crucial step in this argument is (2), and this is precisely the point at which the argument becomes problematic as a result of Brown's apparent failure to reckon with what the semiologist would refer to, somewhat cumbrously, as the inescapable 'linguisticality' of experience. In (2) the person engaged in the interlocution of a type of religious experience with which she is not personally acquainted is enjoined by Brown to 'accept claims made on the basis of this experience, unless sufficient grounds can be adduced for doubting the coherence or intelligibility of such claims'. This injunction overlooks a vital feature of the interlocution of any *discourse* generated by a non-familiar experience, namely, the requirement, imposed on the would-be interlocutor, to ascertain how her linguistic and other *practices* accord with (or differ from) those of the subject of the non-familiar experience. For it is possible to determine the *meaning* of this subject's claim to have certain (non-familiar) experience only by locating this claim in the context of behaviour (both possible and actual). It would be beyond the scope of this study to undertake an elaborate discussion of this point – we cannot do better than to attend to Wittgenstein's profound meditations on this subject in *The Philosophical Investigations*, meditations grouped round the following well-known remarks:

> What gives us *so much as the idea* that living beings, things, can feel?
>   And can one say of the stone that it has a soul and *that* is what has the pain? What has a soul, or pain, to do with a stone?
>   Only of what behaves like a human being can one say that it has pains.
>   For one has to say it of a body, or if you like of a soul which some body *has*. [#283]
>   . . . only of a living human being and what resembles (behaves like) a living being can one say: it has sensations; it sees; is blind; hears; is deaf; is conscious or unconscious. [#281]
> The human body is the best picture of the human soul. [p. 178]
> If a lion could talk, we would not understand him. [p. 223][4]

In addition, the *truth* of the claims in question can only be established by placing them in the context of claims which the interlocutor should herself be prepared to make. For what the interlocutor is willing to count as an intelligible pattern of behaviour is, directly or indirectly, a function of what she believes to be true.[5]

If these observations are correct, then the argument from religious experience must be deemed to have begged the vital question of radical interpretation. For if we can understand the other person only if we are prepared in principle to accept that veracity preponderates in his or her beliefs and utterances, that in some sense we both happen to inhabit the same 'world', then the theologian or philosopher must address herself to certain prior questions as a precondition of evaluating an argument for its 'coherence' or truth-status. Questions, *practical* questions, such as 'What is at stake if I am to become an inhabitant of the world projected by the experience I am interpreting?', or 'What practices must be assumed if the claims advanced by the experient in question are to be accommodated with the claims that I myself am prepared to make?' must be addressed as a *precondition* of any logical or epistemological evaluation. For all I know, Brown's argument, after undergoing some necessary elucidation, might still turn out to be a probative argument for the 'existence' of God. (Here I allow to pass the thorny question whether it is at all possible for there to be incontrovertible 'proofs' of this kind.) But as things stand it is simply not possible to tell. And it may be that once the above hermeneutical questions have been addressed, it will appear obvious to us, *qua* interpreters of religious 'experience', that the matter of proving the 'existence' of God on the basis of such experience will not be so terribly important – far more pressing will be the question whether I am willing, or have it in myself, to inhabit the world that has been opened-up by the experience(s) I happen to be interlocuting. In this area, as Bernard Lonergan has noted, *conversion* must precede the conviction supplied by logical proof; and once this priority is recognized, there will be (according to Lonergan)

> a transition from ... abstract logic ... to the concreteness of method. On the former view what is basic is proof. On the latter view what is basic is conversion. Proof appeals to an abstraction named right reason. Conversion transforms the concrete individual to make him capable of grasping not merely conclusions but principles as well.[6]

Brown's deity, however, is not just an experientially available 'object'. That is, for Brown God is not only a datum of religious experience; he is also the One who brings about 'the unveiling of truth ... through his intervention in some aspect of the world' (p. 54), even to the point of intervening 'to suggest thoughts' (p. 73), and '[vouchsafing] very specific experiences ...' (p. 4). This divinity, who is characterized by the author of *The Divine Trinity* with a pertinacious univocality, turns out to be three 'entities' endowed with 'three distinct centres of consciousness, each with its own distinctive mental content' (p. 289). In addition to having 'different mental histories' (p. 287), the three persons also have separate powers (p. 293), and are 'more like a family than an individual' (p. 251).

This divine family accomplishes a decisive 'intervention' at the incarnation. The event of incarnation took place when one of the three divine persons surrendered his divine powers, and 'became' Jesus of Nazareth, '[leaving] the other two persons in full charge, as it were, of running the universe, for so long as the Incarnate one remains bereft of his powers' (p. 251). While on earth, the Incarnate one has certain *human* experiences, which are subsequently recorded in the gospels. These records ('the evidence') show that the experiences of the Nazarene are 'not just of an internal divine power but of an external relation, i.e. to his Father', and so they can serve as the basis for distinguishing between the First and the Second Persons in the immanent Trinity (p. 275).

The separate identity of the Holy Spirit, over against the persons of the Father and of the Son, is then established by adverting to the relevant New Testament accounts (again, 'the evidence') which indicate that in the experience of the first Christians the Father and the Son came across as 'object', whereas the Spirit was experienced as 'subject', from which it can justifiably be inferred that it is 'more appropriate to speak of the experiences as springing from two different persons, rather than merely two aspects, of the deity' (p. 204). Once the doctrines of incarnation and Trinity have been 'evidenced' in this way, it is possible to proceed to demonstrate that they are 'coherent'. This Brown sets out to do in the final part of his book.

Its author's predilection for describing in detail the inner life of the Godhead shows *The Divine Trinity* to be a robustly old-fashioned, pre-Kantian kind of book. *The Divine Trinity* is pre-Kantian in the sense that its author propounds a theory of divine causality which, throughout, employs the concept of 'cause' *descriptively* – thereby violating Kant's stricture that the principle of causality can be schematized only if its application is confined to the world of appearances.[7] One way, and it might even be the only way, to nullify the effect of Kant's stricture would be to cast judgements about divine causality into an analogical mode; an analogical use of 'cause', since it is in principle irreducible to a univocal construal, would not need to posit a perceptible transfer of qualities from cause to effect, as demanded by the causal process *in strictu sensu*.[8] Brown's tendency to place a univocal construction on statements which purport to refer to the mysterious reality of God consolidates this reader's impression that he is perhaps not sufficiently attentive to the irreducibly 'linguistic' or 'grammatical' features of discourse *in divinis*. To be attentive here is to have an awareness of the implications, for theological reflection on the divinity, of the truth (a truth whose provenance is 'logical' or 'grammatical', and not 'theological') that the 'logical space' which can properly be said to circumscribe divinity is to be delimited only by judgements with an analogical semantic structure; and this precisely because, as Aquinas perceived, 'no ratio can be found between finite and infinite'.[9]

Brown's seeming reluctance to broach the subject of an adequate 'grammar' of God, a 'grammar' of indirection that is necessarily austere because it cannot be anything other than an *introductio in mysterium*, deprives him of the syntactic and (especially) the semantic resources needed to express the 'being' of God in terms of meanings that would simultaneously be destabilized and transcended in the very act of utterance. The outcome is that any 'correspondence' of human discourse to the reality of God *must* become, for Brown, a possibility that can only be seen as a capacity of an irreducibly human-centred language. It cannot (for all his advocacy of an 'interventionist' deity) be a 'correspondence' that issues from the Word that God speaks. By making inevitable the identification of theological speech with the speech of a privileged self-constituting human consciousness, a speech in which humanity is the 'subject' and God the 'predicate', this predilection for univocality assuredly undermines the possibility of formulating a viable *theo-logic*. Indeed, as Eberhard Jüngel has shown with percipient clarity, the person who chooses this particular theological route will find herself propelled along the royal road that leads from the self-securing Cartesian *cogito* to the atheism of Feuerbach.[10]

Brown's religious epistemology is of course avowedly 'realist' and 'objectivist' in its intention. Nevertheless, I believe that his reluctance to deal with the 'grammatical' implications of the logical truth that there is no 'ratio' or 'order' between the Creator and creaturely beings forecloses the real likelihood of there being a human speech which is theologically appropriate because it 'corresponds' to the divine mystery. For this 'correspondence' can be obtained only if this mystery is spoken without abolishing (or obscuring or traducing) the logically instituted, and hence 'grammatically' represented, incommensurability between the divine and the human orders. So when Brown propounds his model of revelation as a divine–human 'dialogue', and talks in terms of 'understanding' God (pp. 72ff), it could be that he has failed to realize that since God is essentially such that he is not like any determinate spatio-temporal object, to entertain the very notion of 'understanding' him is already to have succumbed to a most profound *misunderstanding* of who God is.[11]

II A Barthian excursus

It is true of course that there is a real sense in which faith could be said to involve the believer's orientation to God as an 'object', precisely because in faith the believer's subjectivity is opened up to, and grounded in, a transforming 'objectivity'. But God is, nevertheless, not one 'object' among objects. Here the philosophical theologian who reflects on these matters might be able to learn something from Karl Barth. For while Barth is prepared to grant that God is 'object', he stresses at the same time that God is unique in that he alone remains 'indissolubly subject' in the very act in which he shows himself to be 'object'. God is 'object' only because in his freedom he deigns to reveal himself (and in so doing to become 'object' for humankind). The possibility of revelation, and *a fortiori* the possibility of human speech about God, is thus to be grounded in the very being of God, and not in any capacity of human reason or human language. Unlike Brown, however, who seems to countenance the identification of God's being with the content of revelation (p. 70), Barth – who like Brown seeks to ground the possibility of revelation in God's being, but who simultaneously repudiates the *finitum capax infiniti* wholeheartedly upheld by Brown – finds it necessary to introduce a distinction between God's primary and secondary objectivity.

Primary objectivity is God as he is 'object' to himself in the immanent Trinity (*Deus in se*); secondary objectivity is the objectivity that God reveals to humankind (*Deus revelatus*). The reliability of revelation is safeguarded because God's secondary objectivity (i.e. his revelation) is his self-manifestation; a manifestation of the primary objectivity which is the ground of his revealed or secondary objectivity. This distinction therefore enables Barth to maintain that God is encountered in revelation as he really is, while at the same time leaving Barth to insist that revelation cannot be immediately equated with God's primary objectivity. God as subject remains sovereign over his self-manifestation, so that in the very act of revealing himself he remains 'hidden': God reveals himself ('reliably' in his secondary objectivity) precisely as the one who is hidden (in his primary objectivity). All knowledge of God is necessarily an *indirect* knowledge, in that God is known through the creaturely reality he has elected as the vehicle of his revelation, that is, the humanity of Jesus of Nazareth. Jesus Christ, who as God incarnate is the secondary objectivity of God, thereby provides indirect access to God's primary objectivity. This element of indirection is reinforced, for theological reflection, by the fact that God is known in Jesus Christ only through the medium of biblical narrative. But precisely because God's being in Jesus Christ is narrated in scripture, we can come to know God (as 'object'). Theological speech is therefore possible, for God has acted, and hence can be known, in Christ. This responsible theological speech, however, will have to take the form of an *analogia Christi*.[12]

III 'Divine nature' and 'human nature'

Brown's apparent disinclination to engage with the profound issues that theologians and philosophers seek to address in the course of adverting to a doctrine of analogy is complemented by his evident supposition that there is a readily identifiable and fully determinate content to be attached to such terms as 'divine nature', 'human nature', 'divine power', an 'interventionist deity', and so on. He makes no concession to the possibility that human beings might be fundamentally mysterious even to themselves, and that consequently there can be no readily available certitudes concerning the putative signification of the term 'human nature' (let alone that of the term 'divine nature'). Two points are in order here.

The first is that, in a properly-constituted *theo*-logic, the signification of terms such as 'divine power', 'divine love', 'divine wisdom', 'divine creativity', and so forth, will be articulated in terms of a christological semantics, which will therefore provide a *material*, as opposed to a merely formal or syntactic, specification of such terms. In such a semantics, the theologian is behoved to construe such terms with specific reference to the person and deeds of Jesus Christ. Thus, the meaning of 'divine power' is to be appropriately specified in terms of the deeds of the powerless and crucified Jesus of Nazareth, 'divine love' in terms of the unvanquishable love that the Crucified showed for others, and so on. Theological speech, properly so-called, is (again) necessarily an *analogia Christi*. This criticism, however, should not be pressed too far: Brown's espousal of a kenotic christology certainly makes it possible for him to accommodate the principle of an *analogia Christi* within the bare bones of his theological framework. Indeed, it could even be argued that such an *analogia* is implicitly rooted in any version of the kenotic doctrine.

Far more problematic is Brown's tendency to use the terms 'divine nature' and 'human nature' to designate two kinds of *stuff*; kinds of stuff that, moreover, are capable of doing things and having experiences. *The Divine Trinity* is replete with locutions of the following kind: 'the type of intimacy experienced by [Christ's] human nature' (p. 121); 'the promptings of the divine nature' and 'the workings of [Christ's] divine nature' (p. 174); 'the activity of [Christ's] own divine nature' (p. 175); 'a unique flow of experience from the human nature to the divine' (p. 264); 'the divine nature's consciousness' (p. 265); and 'the commitment of the divine nature' (p. 266). These uses of 'nature' are somewhat at odds with the recognized canons of categorical grammar. In such a grammar, the term 'nature' is essentially a heuristic notion, in that to ascertain the nature of something, call it x, is to *ask* the question 'what sort of thing is x?'; and to *answer* this question is to assign x to its appropriate category, for example, 'humanness', 'divineness', 'dogness', and so on. To speak of a *nature* as if it were a 'thing' is to invite us to believe that 'dogness' can be conscious of a plate of 'Pedigree Chum', that unique experiences can flow from the *category* (i.e. the *grammatical* item) 'humanness' to the *category* (i.e. the *grammatical* item) 'divineness', and so forth.[13]

IV 'Incarnation'

Brown's seeming failure to acknowledge the heuristic nature of the philosophical and theological concepts employed by the Fathers of the early church has drastic implications for his understanding of the doctrines of incarnation and trinity. Brown considers in detail two 'models' of the incarnation, the Chalcedonian (or 'two-natures') model and the so-called Kenotic (or 'one-nature') model. He believes both models to be coherent and compatible with the historical 'evidence', but favours the kenotic account because 'it would enable God to experience directly the human situation in a way that is not possible on the [two-natures model]' (p. 271). Each model is set up as a set of propositions, propositions which make affirmations about the inner being or essence of God the Father and of Jesus Christ. Hardly any importance is attached to the historical situation in which the christological dogmas associated with the Councils of Nicaea and Chalcedon were *developed* before receiving their final and definitive conciliar formulation, and so, inevitably, no real awareness can be shown of the intellectual and cultural context in which these dogmas came to be formulated. As a result, what should be a decisive perception has come to be obscured, viz., that these dogmas were the product of systematic reflection on a plethora of pre-systematic symbols, images, titles and predicates applied to God (the Father) and Jesus Christ. The Fathers learned from the Hellenic philosophers the technique of operating on propositions, of formulating propositions that ranged over other propositions.[14] In this way, the patristic Fathers were able to provide a systematic, meta-linguistic (and hence 'grammatical' or 'logical') analysis of the less systematic, because more basic and immediate, affirmations to be found in scripture and in the earlier tradition. Their propositions are thus to be seen not as ontological affirmations about the being of God (the Father) and of Jesus Christ, but as a second-order discourse containing regulative principles for the *modus loquendi theologicus*. St Athanasius, for example, does not gloss the concept of consubstantiality as a coming together of two bits of stuff (which is how Brown evidently construes the Chalcedonian definition); but as a *rule: eadem de Filio quae de Patre dicuntur excepto Patris Nomine* ('whatever is said of the Father is said of the Son, except that the Son is not the Father').[15] The principal architect of the christological dogma formulated at Nicaea therefore understood the *homoousion* not as a union between two entities, but as a rule of theological speech, which stipulates that the Father and the Son occupy the same 'logical space', so that whatever propositions are true of the Father are also true of the Son, even though the Father is the Father and not the Son and the Son is the Son and not the Father.

V 'Trinity'

Brown discusses the two 'models' of the Trinity – the 'Unity Model', which he associates with St Augustine (and which starts with the unicity of the Godhead as given), and the 'Plurality Model' of the Cappadocian Fathers (which takes the threefoldness of the divinity as given). Each model is seen as a set of propositions which have a direct ontological reference. In examining these models for their 'coherence', Brown finds the Unity Model to be 'bristle with difficulties', in contrast to the 'proven coherence' of its Cappadocian counterpart (p. 301). Another reason for favouring the Cappadocian model is that the 'evidence' supplied by the New Testament accounts shows that 'the distinction of the Persons is a more basic datum than their ultimate identity' (p. 287). As is the case with his treatment of the kenotic and Chalcedonian models of the incarnation, Brown sets the Augustinian and Cappadocian models against each other in starkly antithetical terms. Similarly, very little attention (if any) is paid to the historical context in which Augustine and the Cappadocians formulated their trinitarian dogmas, and in consequence the essentially heuristic nature of their formulations is again occluded. This reluctance to consider the ongoing context of doctrinal formulation makes it difficult for Brown to attach any real significance to Augustine's typically Western fear of the threat posed by the recidivist Arianism of the Anomoeist school; an anxiety which accounts, at least in part, for his reluctance to introduce the personalist categories that were *seemingly* employed with greater readiness by the Cappadocian Fathers.[16] Equally, no appreciation is accorded to the distrust of Sabellianism which made the *prima facie* espousal of personalist categories much more congenial to Eastern trinitarians keen to obviate the possibility of a resurgence of modalism.[17]

Within these developing contexts, the various trinitarian concepts were deployed heuristically, as dogmatic formulation advanced, with many side-steps and detours, into the unknown. Clarity was sometimes achieved (as it undoubtedly was when the Cappadocians were able to achieve a principled separation of *ousia* from *hypostasis*); but clarity, with its accompanying philosophical desiderata, coherence and logical rigour, were very much ideals to be reached for, rather than imposed willy nilly in contexts that were thought to be inappropriate. Hence, if two irreconcilable propositions each had something to warrant their acceptance, then both were likely to be retained as possible facets of some yet to be secured truth. There was an acknowledgement of mystery, of the intractable qualities of the faith-affirmed reality that was being grappled with, as well as an appreciation of the ultimate and unceasing poverty of the conceptual resources that were available to theologians for the task. Little of this seems to be faced up to by Brown, who deals very briskly indeed with the alleged shortcomings of the Cappadocians and (especially) Augustine. In his eyes, their respective positions, although containing many valuable insights, are nevertheless beset by an unavoidable logical or 'conceptual' primitiveness or crudity that must be extirpated 'in the light of our knowledge today' (p. 274). This zest for 'modelling' and 'conceptual' elucidation prompts Brown to reify, and thus to absolutize, a (mere) difference of emphasis between the Cappadocians and Augustine. The upshot is that we are left with an unbridgeable dichotomy between Eastern and Western trinitarianism. Now it cannot be gainsaid that there are times when such historically-instituted theological dichotomies just have to be accepted by the contemporary theologian: our theological forebears, whether by design or inadvertence, shaped the theological agenda in *this* way rather than *that*, thereby constraining the present-day theological practitioner to operate with certain irreducible 'givens'. This, however, is simply not the case where any possible dichotomy between Eastern and Western trinitarianism is concerned. It would certainly be foolish to attempt to overturn Brown's argument by trying to homogenize the trinitarian theologies of the Eastern and Western churches. But it must be acknowledged that tradition has given us *two* possible approaches to the mystery of the Trinity, both of which are perfectly orthodox, but which reflect undeniably different attitudes to the mystery. The Cappadocian Fathers began from the plurality of persons established by the immanent begetting, and proceeded to the assertion that the three genuinely distinct persons subsist within the community of a single nature. By contrast, Augustine (and later St Thomas Aquinas) began from the simplicity of the divine nature and went on from there to the affirmation that this one divine nature subsists in three really distinct persons. The upshot, in Irénée Chevalier's words, is that 'these two points of view still come to the same conclusion, namely that the three divine hypostases are distinguished by their properties and the latter are distinguished by differences in origin, which are oppositions of relationship within an essential identity. "Between the three, everything is identical, apart from the relationship of origin".'[18]

Brown believes that the 'plurality' model of the Trinity is required (a) because the kenotic model of the incarnation could not be upheld otherwise, and (b) because the New Testament 'evidence' supports the idea of there being three separate divine persons. The Cappadocian doctrine is favoured by him purely and simply on the alleged ground that it accords more fully, in principle (if not in substance), with the perspective on the Trinity that he takes to be demanded by (a) and (b) (p. 287). Brown's intention is thus to align the 'Cappadocian' position with the modern concept of a person (i.e. the individual as a separate centre of self-consciousness), and so to produce the notion of the Trinity as a divine triad of separate subjectivities. The outcome can only be regarded as a cryptic tritheism, despite Brown's disclaimer to the contrary.

The Cappadocians' apparent reluctance to say how the hypostases might be identified apart from their external mode of operation, and Augustine's use of *persona* or *substantia* as mere conventions of speech, are simply not the result of their lack of philosophical acumen and (or) their misfortune in not having the requisite ('modern') conceptual resources (which, *in nuce*, is Brown's view of the matter). Rather, their doctrines represent a stubbornly persistent attempt to achieve a theological reconceptualization of God's revelation of his three-fold self, a reconceptualization that would, if successful, combine the identity with the distinction of the divine persons, and in so doing bypass the twin dangers of subordinationism (or tritheism) and modalism. Most basic textbooks of patristic theology will provide ample textual evidence for this view: the *Tomus ad Antiochenos* contains an account of Athanasius asking those who believed in one hypostasis whether they were prepared to endorse Sabellianism, and those who believed in three hypostases whether they were tritheists; Gregory of Nazianzen insisted that in the Triad the Monad is adored, just as the Triad is adored in the Monad (*or*. 25, 17); Basil affirmed that the distinction of hypostases in no way undermines the oneness of the divine nature (*ep*. 38, 4), and so on. We are even told by Gregory of Nazianzen that Basil was, in his preaching, circumspect in his advocacy of the deity of the Holy Spirit, for he believed it 'better to use some reserve in the truth, . . . rather than by the openness of the proclamation to risk its destruction' (*ep*. 58). The terms and concepts employed by these theologians were used heuristically, in myriad contexts, and hence with divergent significations, and thus often with considerable ambiguity. These terms were not used purely descriptively, and certainly not with straightforward ontological reference. Their users were profoundly aware of the inescapable brokenness of theological speech; and, indeed, all the Greek Fathers and Augustine pointedly abstained from describing the mode of generation enjoyed by the Word and the Spirit.[19]

The mystery of the Trinity was brought to articulation in a theological context that took scripture and the preceding tradition as its point of departure, but which was also shaped by the liturgy, the sacraments, the preaching of the good news, the catechizing of those awaiting baptism, the *practice* of prayer, and the felt need for repentance and conversion. This mystery was thus given expression in a theological speech that was rooted from the very outset in a wide range of faith-bounded activities and forms of life. And, within this circle of faith, the undertaking of trinitarian reflection was governed by the universally perceived need to do justice to the utter transcendence of God and yet at the same time to mitigate the scandal of this transcendence. Trinitarian dogma was thus intended to orchestrate, to regulate, this perception.[20]

VI Historical truth

It may be that the full implications of the historical 'situatedness' of trinitarian reflection escape Brown because he has, in his *method*, already committed himself to what he calls a 'presumption in favour of some progress in understanding' (pp. xiii and 75); a 'presumption' which, in the context of the Christian revelation, involves acceptance of the principle that revelation has a 'developmental character' (p. xiv). Armed with the presumption that revelation has a 'developmental character', he is able to establish what he takes to be an essential distinction between 'historical original' and 'theological' truth. This distinction is used by Brown to underpin three theses which lie at the heart of his arguments concerning the incarnation (chapter 3), the separate personality of the Holy Spirit (chapter 4), and the Trinity (chapter 7). The theses in question are:

(1) Although Jesus was not conscious of his own divinity, and although the writers of the synoptic gospels did not ascribe to him the status of a divine being ('historical original truth'), it is nevertheless the case that the truth-claim 'Jesus is divine', as upheld by, among others, the Fourth Evangelist and the Fathers at Nicaea, is capable of being fully legitimated ('theological truth').

(2) Although Paul did not distinguish sharply between Christ and the person of the Holy Spirit ('historical original truth'), it is nonetheless possible to espouse the principle, assented to by, *inter alia*, the Cappadocian Fathers, that the Son and the Spirit are separate divine persons ('theological truth').

(3) Although there is nothing in the New Testament that corresponds to what would later emerge as a full-blown doctrine of the Trinity ('historical original truth'), it is still the case that such a doctrine can be shown to be 'conceptually' consonant with, and 'evidenced' by, the New Testament narratives concerning the Father, Son and Holy Spirit ('theological truth').

Brown argues that the distinction between 'historical original' and 'theological' truth is indispensable because 'all historians try to get back ... to what ... actually happened or was said', and in consequence are inclined to make the illicit inference 'that this is all that can or need be said on the matter' (pp. 103–4). Brown explicates this distinction via a discussion of a number of cases in which he purports to show that the failure to employ it has an outcome that is manifestly counter-intuitive. No real attempt is made to characterize the *modus operandi* of the historian, and here it must be said that it is somewhat questionable whether the historian can properly be said to conceive of her task in the way described, or prescribed, by Brown. The following considerations, which can here be outlined only very sketchily, suggest that the historian's task is perhaps not quite as Brown portrays it:

(i) Truistically, only certain sayings or happenings are properly to be designated as 'historical'. For example, since time immemorial millions have crossed the English Channel, but not all these crossings are considered to be historical events. Hence, if a particular historian were content merely to establish that a certain individual (Julius Caesar) crossed a certain channel (the English Channel) at a certain time (55 BC), in the conviction that 'this is all that can or need be said about the matter', she would totally beg the crucial, *because historical-event constituting*, question: (but) what makes *this* particular crossing of the English Channel by Caesar an event of historical import, and not, say, the crossing I made in 1972 when I went to Germany to visit some old school-friends? It would be quite beyond the scope of this essay to attempt to say in detail what exactly it is that makes one event, but not another, 'historical'. Suffice it to say that historical events are what they are by virtue of being reconstructed within a larger narrative pattern, that is, an organizing framework consisting of a particular configuration (of events) which gives significance to the event being designated as 'historical'. And since it is always possible to place the same event in more than one such framework, it follows (*pace* Brown) that the very process of such discursive reconstruction will inevitably take the historian beyond 'what actually happened or was said'.[21]

(ii) The discursive articulation of an event within a narrative framework – i.e. the historical process *par excellence* – will invariably involve relating putatively historical events to other, later events. For example, volume one of the *Monumenta Germaniae Historia*, series *Scriptores*, contains the *Annals of St Gall*, a compilation of events that occurred in Gaul during the eighth, ninth and tenth centuries AD. The entry for 725 reads 'Saracens came for the first time', which clearly suggests that this event was recorded after the Saracens had come at least a *second time*, and that, consequently, the advent of the Saracens was being represented, *qua* historically-*significant* event, in terms of categories under which it could not have been 'observed'. It follows from this (*pace* Brown) that the historical import of an event of this kind will simply not be captured by an account which did no more than 'say what happened'.[22]

(iii) 'History repeats action in the figure of the memorable' (Paul

Ricoeur). Since the events that concern the historian are usually located beyond the fairly recent past, access to them is secured, not directly, but indirectly, through *memory*. But remembering is, typically, an act of will, with a goal or purpose or object; it is not a generalized activity, but is always a remembering of *something*. Besides, that which is remembered is always remembered in *a particular way*, a way that is determined, at least in part, by the attitudes and values of the individual or group whose memory it is. Historical knowledge is thus inextricably bound up with a hermeneutics of human memory, and this (*pace* Brown) will again take the historian beyond 'what actually happened or was said'.[23]

(iv) Brown implies that getting at 'what actually happened or was said' is the only possible way of undertaking the task of historical thinking. This is debatable. The works of historians have quite different formal characteristics, and they show that historians use their conceptualities in such divergent ways that the same sets of data can be explained in fundamentally different, and even incompatible, ways. To quote Hayden White:

> the work of one historian may be diachronic or processionary in nature (stressing the fact of change and transformation in the historical process), while that of another may be synchronic and static in form (stressing the fact of structural continuity). Again, where one historian may take it as his task to reinvoke ... the 'spirit' of a past age, another may take it as his task to penetrate behind the events in order to disclose the 'laws' or 'principles' of which a particular age's 'spirit' is only a manifestation.... Or ... some historians conceive their work primarily as a contribution to the illumination of current social problems ..., while others are inclined to suppress such presentist concerns and to try to determine the extent to which a given period of the past differs from their own....[24]

(v) The understanding of the historian's task which Brown urges us to adopt hinges on the assumption that it is actually possible for the historian to achieve a theoretical restitution, a kind of mimesis, of the past. Brown's belief that it is at all possible for the historian to harbour this ambition suggests that he might have overlooked a very important principle, one which hermeneutical philosophers usually elucidate under the rubric of the 'historicity of understanding'. According to the bare bones of this principle, the historian's understanding of the past is itself bound to the historical conditions that prevail *in her own epoch*, which effectively precludes the possibility that the historian can view her work as something akin to a second creation, a reduplication and restoration of the original. In the words of Gadamer (who is of course responsible for the most significant and detailed formulation of this thesis): 'The reconstruction of the original circumstances, like all restoration, is a pointless undertaking in view of the historicity of our being. What is reconstructed, a life brought back from the lost past, is not the original. In its continuance in an estranged state it acquires only a secondary, cultural existence.'[25]

For all these reasons, then, Brown's distinction between 'historical original' and 'theological' truth must be seen to be somewhat problematic. Indeed, if the proponent of the thesis of 'the historicity of understanding' is right, then it is hard to see how there can be such a thing as 'historical original truth' (at least, in the sense implied by Brown). Fundamental to his characterization of 'historical original truth' is an 'historical atomism', an 'atomism' so-called because it treats events as self-standing, self-constituting and logically and cognitively discrete happenings. This 'historical atomism', however, is only an extension of the quite explicit 'cognitional positivism' that pervades *The Divine Trinity*.

VII 'Cognitional positivism'

In this 'cognitional positivism', the world of immediacy, the sum of what can be seen, heard, touched, tasted and smelt, comes to each human subject as a flux of sense experience. According to Brown, however, this 'content' is never 'neat' (p. 85); it has to be processed into some kind of order through the imposition of a conceptual structure ('the form'). Brown allows that this conceptual structure is shaped by one or more traditions. The same experiential 'content' can be expressed (on p. 84 Brown uses the term 'expanded') in terms of more than one 'form'. The task of the hermeneutical philosopher, on this thoroughly empiricist account, is to alert the theologian to 'past revelatory texts which in the light of the later experiential history of the community might be ... likely ... to become redundant' (p. 86). In effect, these potentially 'redundant' texts are ones that ('in the light of ... later experiential history') have come to be seen to be afflicted by a certain cognitive inadequacy. It is the hermeneutical philosopher's task, therefore, to point the philosophical theologian in the direction of 'forms' that are less cognitively inadequate. It should be clear from this admittedly brief account that Brown is thoroughly wedded to the epistemological metaphor of 'foundation', inasmuch as he conceives of theology as a 'translation' of its 'perfect source' or 'foundation', to wit, religious experience. (The responsibility of the hermeneutical philosopher is of course to help a little with the business of getting the 'translation' right.) Brown's preeminent concern throughout *The Divine Trinity* is with the 'veridicality' or 'provability' of arguments derived in one way or another from 'religious experience'; and it is for this very reason that his philosophical *practice* cannot (despite his approbatory remarks concerning Gadamer) be reconciled with that of a practitioner of a true hermeneutics. For the 'evidentiality' of propositions and the 'provability' of arguments, in Brown's philosophical procedure, rest irremovably on the presupposition that our understanding of reality and ourselves consists of *representations* or basic observational terms, so that the 'evidentiality' of a proposition, call it P, can be said to be determined by the degree to which 'reality' furnishes evidence for the particular representation (of a language-independent object) expressed by P; and the 'provability' of an argument A can then be said to require (at least): (a) the demonstrable coherence of the propositions that comprise A; and (b) the 'evidencing' of these propositions in the way just specified. On this model, the isolated human subject is the largely passive recipient of sensory data from a language- and mind-independent external reality, 'prior' data which are then processed into 'representations' of the objective states of affairs in question, so that adequacy of cognition can be specified in terms of a direct correlation between these privileged representations, on the one hand, and 'objective' states of affairs in the 'independent' world, on the other.[26] But is it straightforwardly possible to assess representations in terms of their successful 'adequation' or 'approximation' to a concept-independent 'reality'? What if the hermeneutical philosopher is not mistaken when she says that all understanding is governed by a certain 'pre-structure', which operates in such a way that what appears from 'real' states of affairs is precisely what the traditions and subjective elements embedded in this as yet unnoticed 'pre-structure' will bring to awareness? This 'pre-structure' or prior background of implicit (or explicit) assumptions cannot, in principle, be included among the specific presuppositions of the theory or hypothesis being scrutinized by the epistemologist. All knowledge, even the very attempt to unravel the operative communally-instituted background of our 'prejudices', is thus always already configured by a set of prior assumptions; assumptions which, since they are pre-reflectively taken for granted, necessarily elude thematization within *that* particular intellectual 'horizon'. The 'foundationalist' urge, the hermeneutical philosopher would say, founders on the rock of such unthematizable and untranscendable pre-reflective assumptions. Or conversely, the 'foundationalist' urge presages the death of any true hermeneutical endeavour: where Brown is interested in *arguments* (which can then be tested for their 'coherence'), the hermeneutical philosopher will be interested in *texts* and *textuality* (or narratives and narrativity); where Brown takes perceptually-based *beliefs* (which can then be examined for their 'evidentiality') to be the primary focus of his investigation, the hermeneutical philosopher will prefer to scrutinize the totality of cultural *practices*, the *forms of life* or the *socio-historical* configurations which make historically situated reflection possible.[27]

VIII 'Resurrection'

Brown's perceptually-based epistemology finds its most intractable manifestation in his discussion of the resurrection. The emphasis throughout this discussion is on the 'objectivity of the disciples' visionary experience' (p. 133). Brown tries to establish this 'objectivity' by excluding alternative explanations of the disciples' experiences, namely, 'the unreliability of the witnesses, the presence of obvious psychological pressures, the complete cultural determination of the interpretation put on the experience, and so on' (p. 134). As one would expect, he does this by resorting to the notion of an 'interventionist' deity. After showing that this resort makes it 'reasonable' to believe in the 'objectivity' of the disciples' visionary experiences, he proceeds immediately to consider the question 'whether there are grounds for endorsing the disciples' implicit judgement that at least from the Resurrection onwards the Risen Christ must be treated as a divine being' (p. 153). There may conceivably be a perfectly acceptable philosophical justification for proceeding in this way. But, its philosophical merits notwithstanding, this approach may be said by some to do violence to the resurrection kerygma.

Many commentators on the resurrection accounts of Luke and John have noted that these accounts place a quite significant stress on the *otherness* of the risen Jesus. Thus, in the Emmaus episode the two disciples perceive the true identity of Jesus only in the moment of his disappearance (Luke 24:31); Mary Magdalene mistakes Jesus for a gardener (John 20:14f); and the seven disciples fishing in the sea of Tiberias fail to recognize the stranger who beckons to them (John 21:4ff). The risen Christ, it would seem, eludes the preceptual–recognitional capacities of even those who had been his very closest associates. Responsible attention to the resurrection kerygma will require the interpreter of these texts to grant a certain priority to this recurrent theme of the unrecognizability of the risen Jesus (as this theme was first formulated and interpreted in the community of faith itself). (The 'cognitional positivist' cannot of course accommodate this theme without abandoning the very *raison d'être* of this 'positivism'.) The interpreter will thus note that, in the case of the Emmaus episode, the two disciples are given a new understanding of the biblical witness concerning the life, death and resurrection of the Risen One (Luke 24:13–32). She will also be amenable to Bultmann's suggestion that when the risen Jesus addresses Mary Magdalene by her own name, he thereby confirms Mary's identity through this very encounter with the risen Lord.[28] She will also be aware that in the christophany by the sea of Tiberias, the appearance of the risen Christ is followed by the commissioning of Peter (John 21:15–17) and the prophecy of his martyrdom (v. 18). The experiences recounted in these narratives, then, are experiences of an initial dislocation, incongruity, bewilderment and speechlessness ('none of the disciples dared ask him . . .'); followed by a renewed perception of self and reality, by conversion and a new constituting of the self.[29]

A properly 'patient' understanding of these originary narratives will therefore show them to possess hardly any trace of the urge to describe and to verify ('a testifying *that*'); instead, they indicate how the disciples are summoned, through an encounter with the barely imaginable Risen Lord, to participate in what they have seen ('a testifying *to*').[30] To believe, as Brown does, that these narratives provide '*grounds* for endorsing the disciples' implicit *judgement* that . . . the Risen Christ must be treated as a divine being' is perhaps to occlude what is really being 'revealed' in these narratives.[31] Indeed, it could very well be that in treating the dense and enigmatic figural representations and associations of the christophanic narratives as a reservoir of foundational 'percepts', one is almost certainly missing the originary point of these texts.

IX Conclusion

The Divine Trinity contains a number of very good things. It is written with an exemplary lucidity. The argument is wide-ranging, refreshingly ambitious, and always rigorous. No logical short-cuts are taken. It is one of the few books of philosophical theology in the Anglo-Saxon tradition to take seriously the findings of New Testament scholarship. Few, if any, philosophers belonging to this tradition would be able to match Brown's theological learning in writing on what is essentially a dogmatic concept. *The Divine Trinity* purports to be a work of philosophy. In many ways it is. In *some* ways it even deserves to be regarded as a first-rate piece of philosophical theology. But Brown's pervasive reluctance to incorporate the absolutely fundamental principle that there is no 'ratio' between finite and infinite into his 'theology', and his besetting 'cognitional positivism', both mean that there is a real sense in which *The Divine Trinity* cannot even begin effectively to articulate the very profound and complex problems and paradoxes that our theological ancestors sought to confront (in their varied and circumspect ways) when they reflected on the ineffable Trinity.[32]

3

'Is it true what they say about "theological realism"?'

I Some prolegomena

A central and recurring issue in the philosophy of religion (in its 'Anglo-American' manifestation at any rate) has been that of the proper form for a theory of meaning for theological (or 'religious') sentences or utterances. Around the time of the renowned symposium 'Theology and Falsification', and for a relatively brief period afterwards, discussions of this issue focused on the various 'verificationist' and 'falsificationist' frameworks for understanding language.[1] Many leading philosophers of religion and theologians took with great seriousness the challenge issued by Antony Flew in his contribution to this symposium – viz. that the 'believer' does not use language assertorially in the religious context because she cannot specify what conceivable states of affairs would *disconfirm* (either in fact or in principle) what she says. As Basil Mitchell points out, Flew is in effect forcing a dilemma on the 'believer': *either* (a) theological languages are 'meaningless' because their sentences cannot be shown to be false; or (b) they are 'meaningful' but their sentences are in fact falsified.[2] In dealing with Flew's dilemma, philosophers and theologians tended to adopt one or the other of two strategies.

1. There is a strategy which consists in the espousal of one of the several varieties of '*non-cognitivism*'. Thus it has been proposed that religious utterances be regarded as '*bliks*' (R. M. Hare); as expressions of 'behaviour policies' (R. B. Braithwaite); as 'stories' (Paul van Buren); as 'symbols' (Paul Tillich); and, more recently, as expressions of 'internalized spiritual principles' (Don Cupitt).[3]

2. Another strategy takes the direction of '*cognitivism*', but argues (*pace* Flew) that 'theism' is not in fact falsified. Thus, for

example, Mitchell himself argues that the 'theist' can and does 'indicate the sort of thing that would count against his assertions, e.g. the occurrence of evil'; and John Hick argues that while it is in principle not possible to *falsify* 'theism', it is nevertheless possible to think of it as being 'eschatologically *verified*'.[4]

It was soon perceived, however, that theological speech fulfils a wide variety of functions, not all of which make it susceptible to the kind of factual disconfirmation (or confirmation) proposed by Flew and other 'falsificationists' (or 'verificationists'). This much was acknowledged, albeit somewhat obliquely, by I. M. Crombie in his response to Flew, but a similar position is taken up in a more developed way by William Alston, who holds that the dilemma posed by Flew for the 'theist' takes religious language out of the framework within which the 'believer' properly deploys it, without supplying a new framework for understanding such language; and by Gareth Matthews, who maintains that Flew's dilemma does not take cognizance of 'theological nonnaturalism' (a position represented by, say, Karl Barth) which does not make any 'empirical' claims. A similar perspective on the nature and status of theological speech is held by D. Z. Phillips.[5]

This very brief sketch of the developments that have taken place since the 'Theology and Falsification' symposium was published in 1951 indicates fairly clearly that philosophers of religion have generally tended to follow the fashions inaugurated by their colleagues in the philosophy of language. Thus, if theory X has come to be favoured by a prevailing consensus of opinion among philosophers of language as the most likely candidate for a 'proper' theory of what it is for the sentences of a language to be 'meaningful', etc., then it is invariably the case that theory X will sooner or later be taken up by philosophers of religion and shown to be *the* theory which (allegedly) gives us the requisite criteria for determining the meaning of specifically theological or religious utterances. These utterances are effectively subsumed under theory X. Ayer, Carnap, Popper, Wittgenstein, Waismann, J. L. Austin and John Searle can thus be seen to have paved the way for the 'Theology and Falsification' symposiasts, Braithwaite, John Hick, van Buren, Donald Evans, D. Z. Phillips, and many others. In recent years, however, the consensus of opinion among philosophers of language has tended to be critical of the above-mentioned theories of meaning. These theories are deemed to be broken-backed, because they are based on the notion of 'analysis', and 'analysis' (it is alleged) is hardly the successful form for a theory of meaning.

'Analysis', these critics aver, has been thoroughly discredited because it is inherently unsystematic, too informal and somewhat arbitrary, and also because even when it is successful (which is open to question) 'analysis' can only account for the meaning of a *fragment* of natural language – if a language contains a potentially infinite number of sentences, then a piecemeal analysis of the various *individual* sentences of that language will not get us very far; what we need, instead, is a theory of meaning whose principles can cover this potentially infinite number of sentences, i.e. we are looking for a theory whose principles can be applied recursively. In short: what we need is a coherent *general* theory of syntax and semantics. If we want such a general theory we simply have to move beyond (but not necessarily ignore) the various unsystematic attempts at analysing *individual* sentences or particular speech-acts of a language, and we also have to acknowledge that issues like verificationism and falsification, important though they may be, are nonetheless only of secondary significance – we have to obtain the general theory of meaning; then only can we proceed to consider the question of 'analysing' particular segments of a language. The philosopher of religion who is looking for a viable theory of meaning for theological languages has no alternative but to move in the direction of a general theory of formal semantics (for the purposes of this essay the question of syntax is not so important). This is the thrust of the following remarks made by John Searle:

> Without any coherent general theory of syntax and semantics on which to base particular linguistic analyses, the philosopher who looks to the so-called use of expressions has no way of distinguishing features of utterances which are due to particular words from features which are due to other factors. . . . [6]

Philosophers of language these days are generally agreed that formal or 'truth-conditional' semantics, when coupled with a 'realist' conception of truth, is our best bet for an adequate theory of meaning for *all* the sentences of a natural language. It is necessary, therefore, for us to see what such a theory would look like when it is made to operate in the context of theological discourse.

II 'Truth-conditional' semantics and theological languages

According to this general theory based on a 'truth-conditional' semantics, the meaning of the sentences of a language is to be specified in just this way: by stating the truth-conditions of the sentences of the language in question. Frege is first credited with the idea of giving the meaning of a sentence by stating the conditions under which it is true.[7] Alfred Tarski proposed a theory of truth which entails, for each sentence of a formalized language whose logical form is the standard logic of quantification, a theorem specifying a necessary and sufficient condition for the sentence to be true.[8] Donald Davidson has urged that Tarski's truth-theory be extended to natural languages to provide us with an empirically-constructed theory of meaning for the sentences of natural languages.[9] The upshot of Davidson's proposal is that a Tarskian theory of *truth* becomes a central component in a Fregean theory of *meaning* for natural language.[10]

Adapting 'truth-conditional' semantics for the purposes of this essay, we can begin by taking the language capable of expressing religious convictions as an object-language, called L. The philosopher of religion (*qua* philosopher of language) then has the task of delineating, and explaining in the meta-language which is her own language, both a *formal theory* and a wider-ranging *informal theory* of L-sentences, including L-sentences concerning what one thinks 'godness' denominates, and what sort of life it is that the religious person must lead, and so forth. If this informal theory is too wide-ranging to reflect truly the diversity and variety of religious convictions, it may be necessary to relativize the sentences of L to a specific population *Pop* of L's users. By relativizing the sentences of L to a particular population *Pop* of L's users, and by accepting that theological languages can be relativized to several such languages, we are enabled to account for the 'elasticity' of theological speech.

Providing a theory of such L-sentences will involve the following:

Firstly, the theologian (*qua* philosopher of language), before she can deal with the more specifically 'religious' aspects of the sentences of L, has to be able to say what each of the sentences of the object-language 'means'. To do this, she needs a *formal* procedure for dividing L-sentences into their primitive semantic components, and a semantical postulate for each primitive component which describes its particular contribution to assertion-conditions. (This procedure will of course have nothing to do with theological or religious ideas or beliefs – it belongs to a purely formal theory presupposed by any and all forms of 'meaningful' discourse.) Having acquired her formal semantic procedure, the theologian (*qua* philosopher of language) is now in a position to say that given any *L*-sentence *s*, *s* can be joined to an assertion-condition expressed in the meta-language by a theorem of the form:

   s is assertible if, and only if, *p*.

The wider-ranging informal theory of *L*-sentences must presuppose that this is the least that could be done for each sentence of *L*. For it is just these assertion-conditions which specify the 'meanings' of the utterances the theologian is interested in: without an adequate understanding of what the sentences of *L* '*mean*', she cannot proceed to deal with the more intrinsically 'religious' features possessed by the wider-ranging informal theory of *L*. (For our purposes the informal theory of *L* will be a characteristic theological discourse of the Christian community, conducted in English.)

As I have already said (in note 10), in choosing to speak of the assertion-conditions of the sentences of *L*, as opposed to their truth-conditions, we have deliberately left open the question whether the assertibility of a theological statement can be 'objective' in the way we standardly expect truth to be. We shall leave undecided for the time being the precise relationship of truth and assertibility. For, as David Wiggins points out, the relationship of truth and assertibility can take more than one form:

(i)   it may be that truth is a special case of assertibility (as happens for a large class of utterances in empirical or scientific theories).

(ii) it may be that assertibility can fall short of truth (as is likely to be the case where theological languages are concerned).

(iii) it may be that truth implies assertibility (as it would do in a theory which glosses truth as simply a version of warranted assertibility).

(iv) more radically, it may be that there is just assertibility and no such thing as 'truth'.[11]

Our answer to the question whether assertibility can diverge from truth will depend on the informal theory (of theological speech) which we can construct upon the formal theory of *L*; and it is not possible for us to give an answer to this question until we have determined what constraints have to operate on the assertibility theory of *L*. I would venture to say that the question whether the truth of theological sentences can diverge from their assertibility is crucial for anyone who is interested in a whole nest of problems connected with the meaning of theological discourse. Thus, for example, it is easy to see that Flew and his fellow critics fault 'theists' precisely because they use a form of language which effectively *requires* (theological) assertibility to fall short of truth.

To determine what constraints have to operate on the assertibility theory of L, we have first to advert to Tarski's 'Convention T' so that we can supply the meta-language with a materially adequate specification of the predicate 'is assertible'. Using 'Convention T', we can say that the meta-language has a materially adequate definition of the assertibility-predicate just in case it has as consequences all sentences which are generated by the theorem 's is assertible, if and only if, p', by substituting for 's' a designation of any sentence of L and substituting for 'p' the expression which is the translation or the interpretation of this sentence in the meta-language.

Before we can understand how the theologian can proceed to construct her informal theory on these foundations, we need to be more forthcoming about the way in which the theory of assertibility operates. For as things stand, the sentence, say, '"*God is infinite love*" is assertible if, and only if, God is infinite love' is simply a tautology: it tells us nothing about how 'God is infinite love' is *used* or *understood* by religious persons or communities of faith; it tells us nothing, in short, about its *assertibility*. The theory of assertibility, in other words, requires supplementation – at the moment we have done nothing more than to say *what it means to say* that something is assertible, and this does not really *show* what 'God is infinite love' means, or how religious people or communities use this expression, or how, if necessary, it can be 'verified' or 'falsified' (if indeed it *can* be 'verified' or 'falsified'), or what epistemological or metaphysical commitments are made by the users of this expression. The assertibility-predicate, which expresses an assertion-condition, is thus just a device for 'semantic ascent', that is, for raising assertions from the object-language to the meta-language. The assertibility-predicate, it seems, is little more than a tool for facilitating *translation* between levels of discourse; it does not, on its own, resolve any questions about *meaning*. It is imperative, therefore, that we augment the theory of assertibility. To do this we have to address ourselves to the question: what conditions must obtain in order that we be justified in asserting a sentence s of L? Thus, if the sentence 'God is infinite love' is a sentence of L, the theologian (*qua* philosopher of language) then has the task of stating, in the meta-language, the conditions which must obtain in order for this sentence to be assertible.

So far it has been claimed that the proper form for a theory of meaning (and *ipso facto* a theory of the meaning of theological utterances) is one which sets out the truth-conditions of the language in question. However, in trying to ascertain, by adverting to Tarski's 'Convention T', just how it is that the truth-conditions of a sentence can be spelled-out, we have found that there are good *prima facie* reasons for not allowing the notions of truth and assertibility to merge into each other. With this proviso in mind, and using 'Convention T', we found a materially adequate definition of the assertibility-predicate to be provided by a theorem of the form '*s* is assertible if, and only if, *p*'. Using this theorem, however, does not seem to serve us in good stead: our theorem tells us nothing about how sentences are *used* or *understood*. It is therefore necessary for us to supplement our assertibility theory, by focusing our attention on the conditions that must obtain in order for a sentence to be assertible.

The philosopher of language can supplement our assertibility theory in the way we have suggested by adopting a framework provided by David Wiggins's characterization of 'regular truth'. The goal is to discover what constraints have to be imposed on the assertibility-predicate as it features in the informal theory of *L* (where this informal theory = a theological language of the Christian community), by first determining the extent to which these constraints diverge (if at all) from those which govern the truth-predicate in a theory of 'regular truth'. Or to put it in plain language: we are attempting to find out whether, and in what sense, theological sentences can be said to be '*true*'. And our paradigm of what constitutes 'truth' is supplied by Wiggins's characterization of 'regular truth'. It is perhaps worth saying in passing that this procedure of ours effectively rules out a 'non-cognitivist' understanding of theological utterances.

Wiggins defines 'regular truth' as 'that species of assertibility which is determined by ... the truisms of regular truth' ('Truth', p. 375). According to Wiggins, these 'truisms' are:

(1) the compatibility of every regular truth with every other regular truth.

(2) the answerability of regular truth to evidenced argument which will under favourable circumstances converge upon agreement.

(3) the independence of regular truth both from our own will and from our limited capacities to recognize the presence or the absence of the property (of regular truth) in a sentence.

(4) that every regular truth is true in virtue of something (this is suggested by coupling (2) and (3)).

(5) every sentence which is a regular truth (or falsehood) possesses (or does not possess) the regular truth in a completely determinate way.[12]

Using this characterization of regular truth we are now able to say what properties a sentence must possess in order to be a regular truth – quite simply, for a sentence to be a regular truth (or falsehood) it must possess all of 'truisms' (1) to (5) of regular truth. If a sentence (or utterance) lacked even one of 'truisms' (1) to (5), then regular truth and assertibility would not coincide where that sentence is concerned.

Where religious utterances are concerned, if assertibility falls *totally* short of regular truth (or falsehood), then no 'theological' predicate can hope to correspond to any 'real' property in the world. In other words: any theory of assertibility for theological languages which does not possess any of the 'truisms' of regular truth is necessarily a theory which construes theological speech in a 'non-cognitivist' way. 'Non-regularly' true or false 'theological' predicates would not be *'factually'* true or false. This of course is precisely what we expect when we expressed our intention to bind our assertibility theory for theological languages to a paradigm of regular truth. For regular truth, in a 'religious' context, commits us to an *'objective'* (i.e. 'factually' significant) 'theory' of trinity, incarnation, resurrection, etc., and this is precisely what the 'non-cognitivist' is not able to countenance.

A 'theological realism', explicated in terms of the above 'truth-conditional' semantics, would therefore take the form of a theory which, at the very least, specified that the central affirmations of the Christian faith are such that it is possible for them to be regular truths (as these are characterized by the 'truisms' (1) to (5)). This is what the theory demands, though whether or not the central tenets of the Christian faith are indeed capable of meeting this demand is something that cannot be determined *a priori*: to determine this we have to conduct an empirical investigation of the truth-claims made by those speech-communities which adhere to the Christian faith and way of life. Once this investigation is embarked upon, however, the philosopher of religion is in a position to claim that she has at her disposal a theoretical 'package' which amounts to a kind of 'theological (or religious) realism'. This, it seems to me, is the best case that can be made for a fully-articulated and comprehensive 'theological realism'. For what we have here is a 'semantic', as opposed to a (merely) 'metaphysical', realism.

A 'metaphysical realism' is one which holds that the truth of an utterance is not reducible in principle to any property that is exclusively and entirely *mind-dependent*. A 'semantic realism' would go quite a bit further than this, for it is one which commits itself, in one form or another, to the thesis that the truth-conditions of an utterance are such that they stand in certain pragmatic relations to a determinate 'reality'.[13] 'Theological realism' is of course currently in vogue – and deservedly so – in many theological circles.[14] Such a 'realism', however, must take the form of a theory which approximates, even if only in intention, to the one we have just outlined. Otherwise it would be a mere 'metaphysical realism', and it is hard to see how such a 'realism' is even remotely interesting as a theory *about* language. 'Metaphysical realism' is wholly salutary but implacably innocuous – any putatively 'realist' account of religious or theological language which aspires to be 'interesting' must surely aim to say a bit more than a (mere) 'metaphysical realism' does.[15] Here, of course, the exponent of a 'semantic realism' has an undoubted advantage: hers, after all, is a theory which, by invoking the correspondence theory of truth, at least ventures what she presumes to be a sustainable account of the connection between language and 'reality' (i.e. an account which, hopefully, is like the one we have just provided for the language *L*).

III On moving beyond 'semantic realism'

Until the last couple of years or so I shared the conviction that the skeleton of 'metaphysical realism' can best be enfleshed by resorting to the kind of correspondence theory of truth which underlies our 'truth-conditional' semantics for the language *L* (i.e. a 'semantic realism'). My version of this theory was perhaps not quite so full-blooded as the one espoused by Brian Hebblethwaite in his contribution to the MacKinnon *Festschrift*, but it was pretty robust nonetheless.[16] However, while I now accept that the correspondence theory can be allowed a strategic place insofar as it serves legitimately to express the irreducible intentionality of human speech, this theory – when accepted as the mainstay of 'semantic realism' – is nonetheless cripplingly limited by a failure on the part of its proponents to attend to the nature and role of *the signifying consciousness* in 'reality-depiction' (to borrow a term used by Janet Soskice). This overlooking of the signifying consciousness has two radical consequences. Firstly, it means that those who espouse the correspondence theory cannot accommodate the suggestion, made by Roland Barthes, that objects can be located in two semiological systems, only one (the lesser one) of which is concerned with modes of representation.[17] Secondly, the concentration on the role of the object in representation demanded by this 'realism' inevitably fosters an occlusion of the role of the subject in the act of signification, and, concomitantly, of the reading community in the act of interpretation. With regard to the former stricture, those who are disposed to accept the correspondence theory tend to see themselves as engaged in the relatively straightforward quest of a naked and unmediated 'referentiality'. Their concern is exclusively with what Roland Barthes calls 'the formal system of the first significations' or 'the language object', and in the process they forget that objects can also be located in a greater semiological system, namely, that of the so-called mythical system.[18] Thus (and this is Barthes's well-known example), when I am confronted by a *Paris-Match* front cover which shows a young Negro soldier saluting the tricolour, the language object would render the meaning of this picture as *a black soldier is giving the French salute.* However, in the historicized and historicizing mythical system, this language object *sign* becomes a meta-language *signification* which notifies me 'that France is a great Empire, that all her sons, without any colour discrimination, faithfully serve under her flag, and that there is no better answer to the detractors of an alleged colonialism than the zeal shown by this Negro in serving his so-called oppressors'.[19] We may need Gertrude Stein to remind us that a flag is a flag is a flag. But the flag on the *Paris-Match* cover is no longer 'just' a flag; it is a flag adapted to a certain pattern of consumption, it is replete with a whole range of racial and geopolitical images. 'Reality' (or, more specifically, its 'meaning') is thus a function of social usage, of a certain imaginative geography. Far from being an inert 'given', one that is immediately 'representable', 'reality' is *produced* by a mythical system which is constituted and sustained by forces that have an irreducible, though often covert, social and political configuration.[20] Secondly, the pursuit of a stark 'referentiality' valorizes the place and the status of the object in signification, and thus leads ineluctably to an attenuation of the subject. The loss of the subject, however, necessarily presages the loss of the object, and thus subverts the whole dynamic of signification.[21] Signification requires the dialectical tension between subject and object to be maintained, and it is doubtful whether proponents of the correspondence theory of truth have at their disposal the theoretical resources needed to hold this dialectic in place – theirs *is* a semantics; and semantics, unlike semiotics, does not in principle allow the (socially-instituted) subject a fundamental role in the appropriation of meaning. Equally, semantics is not in a position to recognize the constituting role of the reading community – which, in a theological context, is the church – in the 'project' of interpreting its originary texts. (It is important to stress the social institution of the subject, for, as Cornelius Castoriadis reminds us, the subject appropriates meaning on the basis of a preexisting, shared universe of discourse.)[22]

It is perhaps significant, and certainly no coincidence, that those theologians who are least reticent in professing their allegiance to 'theological realism' are invariably those who are (seemingly) most indifferent to any invitation to historicize the operation of realistic representation. This historicizing operation, however, is most necessary. For, as many delineations of 'realism' indicate, the historic function of 'realism' has been to undermine and dismantle, and thus to secularize, an antecedent tradition of ritual or sacred narrative paradigms.[23] 'Realism', in its literary manifestation, is a product of the bourgeois cultural revolution, a revolution which overthrew modes of perception, understanding and expression generated by other, now superseded forms of production. The new world of market capitalism was one defined by the principle of market equivalence, a newly quantifiable space, the new metronomic rhythms of chronological time, the production by the commodity system of unprecedented quantities of fungible objects. This cultural revolution generated new discourses, and 'realism' was precisely the new narrative discourse which would be the 'realistic' articulation and reflection of this new social and economic order.[24] A radical historicism of the kind proposed by Fredric Jameson would therefore bracket or dissolve the truth-claims of this 'high realism' by revoking the canonical status it accords to the process of 'representation'. At the same time, though, this historicism would insist on bracketing the currently fashionable post-structuralist denial or displacement of the 'referent', a denial undertaken in the name of an unlimited semiosis, an infinite regress of deferrals, which allows the 'real' to be vanquished by the erasable 'trace'.[25] As Fredric Jameson indicates, in its strategic erasure of the 'referent' in the 'pleasures' of a seamless textuality, post-structuralism overlooks the significance of 'the reality of the *appearance*', an appearance which, while it is necessarily textualized, nonetheless betokens the 'givenness' of a historical absent cause or *subtext* (to use Jameson's term).[26] It is 'the reality of the appearance' – theologically contextualized of course – which serves as the cornerstone of the negative 'ontology' of revelation that will now be the primary subject of this paper. This negative 'ontology' will distance itself from a problematic (because 'foundationalist') 'theological high realism', while resisting the flight into symbolization so insistently commended by, e.g. Don Cupitt in his recent writings.

IV Towards a negative 'ontology of revelation'

The (negative) 'ontology' of revelation I have just alluded to would furnish a 'realism' which, perhaps surprisingly, does not propose to regard God as a signification of 'the real' or as a symbol of some 'thing'. (I leave aside for the moment the likely 'high realist' objection that this proposed use of the term 'realism' can only be unhelpfully perverse.) This 'ontology of revelation' would be one that confutes (even if only somewhat tangentially) most existing 'theological realisms' by pressing home, albeit in modified form, the thrust of Wittgenstein's characteristically 'anti-foundationalist' remark that '[we] predicate of the thing what lies in the method of representing it'.[27] Changing Wittgenstein's remark slightly, and giving it an explicitly theological application, we can say, in the manner of St Thomas Aquinas and Bernard Lonergan, that the theologian 'characterizes' God not by giving divinity 'predicates', but by attending to the method(s) that we use in 'representing divinity'.[28] Pursuing Aquinas's proposal that speech about God is inescapably heuristic, we can say that that which 'divinity' or 'godness' denominates and communicates is precisely what makes these terms (or their cognates) into *religious* symbols. Here theologians can profit from attending to the negative 'ontology' of (social) signification developed by Cornelius Castoriadis.[29] In Castoriadis's account, 'God' is to be seen as a

> central *signification*, one that organizes signifiers and signifieds into a system, [one that] upholds their intersecting unity, and [allows] their extension, multiplication, and modification. And this signification, which corresponds to neither something perceived (real) nor something thought (rational), is an imaginary signification.[30]

The theologian who follows Castoriadis in defining divinity as an 'imaginary signification' will almost inevitably be confronted with the question, posed in all probability by theological 'high realists' and 'deconstructionists' alike, of how this divine 'imaginary significa-tion' is to be perceived or 'experienced'. What difference would God make, they might ask, if 'he' did not in any way impinge upon our experience? In addressing this question, we can take our cue from Aquinas's principle that 'one cannot demonstrate anything of [God] except by means of his effects' (*Summa Theologiae*, 1.3.5), and from his deployment of the Five Ways to show how creaturely speech about God is really possible.[31] The 'reality' of God can be brought to speech because of the 'reality of the appearance' (of God); the theological thematization of the 'reality of the (divine) appearance' being, for the Christian, necessarily constrained by the controlling metaphor of 'incarnation', and, more 'materially', by the life, death and resurrection of Jesus of Nazareth. In other words: the irreducibly Christian theological articulation of the 'reality of the appearance' must take the form of an *analogia Christi*.[32] But the possibility of speech about God does not in any way imply that God is an 'object' or 'referent' of whom we can make 'predications'. God cannot be represented because divinity constitutes a condition of ('religious' or 'theological') representabi-lity, and so cannot (in Castoriadis's words)

> exist in the form of representations that one could, with the aid of analysis, put one's finger on. One cannot speak here of 'images', however vague and indefinite the meaning one gives this term. God may be, for each believer, an 'image' – or even a 'precise' represen-tation – but as an imaginary signification, God is not the 'sum' of these images, their 'average', or what they have 'in common'. God is their condition of possibility; he allows these images to be images 'of God'.[33]

It therefore makes no sense to ask of a truly ultimate or primary 'imaginary signification' whether it *denotes* anything. As Castoria-dis indicates, such 'significations' are what they are by virtue of having a *connotation* which is compatible with any and all *deno-tations*.[34] God, on this view, cannot be spoken of in terms of a relation (or set of relations) to a 'referent'; rather, it is more appropriate to say that *what makes 'referentiality' possible* in 'religious' or specifically Christian discourse is precisely the imagin-ary signification *God*. So for the Christian faith the central significa-tion *God* – which is 'meta-referential' – defines, and indeed constitutes, what is 'real'. 'God' belongs to an indeterminate, unformed and unlimited linguistic totality, a reservoir of 'tropic' potential, out of whose moments the 'real' emerges. This tran-scendent linguistic totality – a *magma* in Castoriadis's parlance – is the fundamental source of representations for a proper *theo-logic*, and is thus the pre-condition of an adequate and appropriate characterization of divinity.[35]

It is quite clear that in comparison to the kind of 'realism' which takes the form of a straightforward 'painting' of reality, the position I have just outlined is fundamentally unrealistic. The notion that God is an imaginary signification subverts any attempt to characterize divinity in terms of the modes of speech habitually employed by exponents of the kind of 'copy-theory realism' I am indirectly criticizing, viz., the discourse of *curiositas*. For if God is an imaginary signification, if 'divinity' is a pressure registered *in*, and not 'before' or 'apart from' textualization, then there is just no divine 'object' to be curious 'about'. But to then be conscious of the constitutional 'unreality' of all theological speech, that is, to know this speech as *essentially* language, while at the same time attending to a 'content' or 'real appearance' that is the life, death and resurrection of Jesus of Nazareth (a generative 'material content' whose deepest modalities are alien to, and interruptive of, the structures of human language), is to explore in the most profound way the 'unreal reality' of true theological speech. A language in which denotation prevails over, or exhausts, connotation, is a language that is incapable of sustaining all that is meant by 'otherness'. This language, because it is effectively a discourse of closure, cannot become a source of hope. By contrast, a language that has a surplus of connotation, or more specifically, which has a 'space' in it which permits the acknowledgement of the imaginary significations that are the source of this surplus, is a radically creative language, one that is capable of remaining a ceaselessly interrogative and demystifying discourse. It can confound the idolatrous and wish-fulfilling religious imagination because it necessarily involves the textualization, but *not* the 'representation', of what Jameson calls 'the unanswerable resistance of the Real'.[36] *As language*, and also by the norms of the commodity world of late capitalism, this language will be deemed to be 'unreal'. But precisely because this language locates signification in the interstices between what is and what could be, and because it insists on the re-creation of this distance (in the way that a discourse of pure 'referentiality' does not), it is a language that is capable of sustaining the insight that, where the things of God and creatures are concerned, the truth *is* the truth because it has not been determined once and for all. What we have been seeking, in other words, is a theological language which can 'house' narratives possessing some (but certainly not all) of the features associated by Jameson with a kind of 'realism' he calls 'magic realism'.[37]

V A 'defamiliarizing' narrative 'realism' which supports a 'pedagogy of discipleship'

According to Jameson, what 'magic realism' engages with is 'certainly History, but then in that case history with holes, perforated history, which includes gaps not immediately visible to us. . . . ' (p. 303). 'Classical' or 'high realism', I have been arguing, cannot engage with such a radically 'perforated history' (or *any* history for that matter), because it fails to reckon seriously with the weight of the contingent historical and social configurations which underpin language – this 'realism' is therefore fundamentally incapable of supplying the appropriate narrative resources, the 'tropic' surplus, needed for the project of a disruptive reading of history (such a reading being the only one capable in principle of heeding Walter Benjamin's injunction that we should 'brush history against the grain', in order to 'make the continuum of history explode').[38] A dislocative reading of history would involve the articulation of a 'counter-history', one which lies beneath the surface of the historical continuum sanctioned and ruthlessly kept in place by the prevailing unredeemed order. This reading may call for a form of narrative attention, and in some cases even a *pro tem* narrative suspension, which effectively discards the categories and principles of classical 'realistic' representation, with the aim of alerting us to what Jameson so vividly describes as

> the shock of *entry* into narrative, which so often resembles the body's tentative immersion in an unfamiliar element, with all the subliminal anxieties of such submersion: the half-articulated fear of what the surface of the liquid conceals; a sense of our vulnerability along with the archaic horror of impure contact with the unclean; the anticipation of fatigue also, of the intellectual effort about to be demanded in the slow apprenticeship of unknown characters and their elaborate situations, as though, beneath the surface excitement of adventure promised, there persisted some deep ambivalence at the dawning sacrifice of the self to the narrative text.[39]

For the Christian, the 'reality of the appearance' (i.e. the pivot of the version of 'theological realism' proposed in this paper) coincides with the events involving the crucified and resurrected rabbi from Nazareth, events narratively rendered in the gospel accounts. The Christian is thus the person who inhabits a narrative 'space'

circumscribed by the gospel texts.[40] The phenomenology of one's
entry-point or 'baptism' into a constituting narrative, sketched by
Jameson in the above passage, is also one that applies in general to
the Christian's entry into this gospel-shaped narrative 'space' – to
sacrifice oneself to these narrative texts, with their controlling
metaphor of 'incarnation', is (at least) to consent to be interrogated
by them in such a way that we learn, slowly, laboriously and
sometimes painfully, to live the way of Jesus. The church, it could
be said, is the historical community where this interrogation takes
place; it is the body which conducts a pedagogy of discipleship that
aims to 'defamiliarize' or 'decompose' all that the Christian takes to
constitute 'reality' (and in so doing to free him or her for the life of
discipleship). These narratives, and the effect of 'defamiliarization'
which they promote, are thus a condition of the existence of what
amounts to a Christ-informed 'counter-history' – the only 'real'
history for those who aspire to be disciples of the man from
Nazareth. Christian faith conceives the inauguration and the main-
tenance of this 'counter-history' in terms of the imaginary signification *God* – by virtue of the historical presence ('the reality of the
appearance') of the Second Person of the Trinity, Christians
profess God to be that which allows the very possibility of this
'counter-history' to be enunciated. This 'presence' is not to be
construed epistemologically, but only syntactically. This opaque or
dark divine 'presence' eludes epistemology not because it resists
intelligibility, like an obstacle, but precisely because it lies beyond
it: it is a hidden 'presence' by virtue of an excess or surplus, and not
a deficiency, of meaning. If there is to be epistemology in theology
it must recapitulate syntax. 'Referentiality' has no place in this
syntax, because 'referentiality' gives the illusion of knowledge
where no knowledge is possible.[41]

Is it true what they say about 'theological realism'? Well, not
quite. Not, that is, if 'theological realists' are content to talk about
'realism' in terms of a (mere) 'metaphysical realism'. And, equally,
not if they purport to be 'semantic realists' by virtue of adopting
one of the many versions of the correspondence theory of truth and
by leaning on the crutch of 'referentiality'. The 'real' is socially
instituted, and so is the language in which it is given expression, and
this means that a non-trivial and historically significant 'realism' can
be found only in the sphere of semiology and a critical theory of
society. And once we move into this domain, we find that the
syntax of 'God' is the syntax of the overflow of tropes.[42]

4

The impassibility of God and the problem of evil

According to a certain strand in the orthodox Christian tradition, God's impassibility is an implication of the divine immutability. For if God cannot change then he cannot 'experience' pain or sorrow. This fundamental principle was appropriated from Plato, who maintained that a being who is perfect can experience neither sadness, pain, nor sorrow. Some modern Christian philosophers and theologians, however, concede that this is perhaps the most questionable aspect of certain forms of orthodox Christian theism.[1]

The following 'facts' are alleged to imply the impassibility of deity:

(1) God, it is said, has no direct experience of sorrow and pain. Whatever experience he has of them is the result of his 'imaginative response' to the sufferings of his creatures. Nothing in God can cause him to feel pain, for the following reasons. God cannot feel *physical* pain because he is incorporeal; he cannot experience *fear* because he is omnipotent; he cannot know the pain of loneliness because he is wholly self-sufficient; and he cannot experience the pain of *guilt* because he is morally perfect. Neither can he know any *mental* pain, if he lives up to Nelson Pike's description of an atemporal being:

> A timeless being could not deliberate, anticipate, or remember. It could not speak or write a letter, nor could it produce sounds or written words on a piece of paper. It could not smile, grimace or weep. Further a timeless being could not respond ... to needs, overtures, delights or antagonisms of human beings.[2]

(2a) God is also said to be impassible because any 'suffering' experienced by him on account of his love for creaturely beings is immediately transfigured by the joy that is necessarily within his uncreated Godhead. This process of 'transfiguration', moreover, is

57

said by some orthodox theists to be a mystery which is beyond human understanding.[3]

(2b) Certain analogies drawn from human experience are alleged to elucidate this 'transfiguration'. Thus it is said that a priest can rejoice in his efforts to bring salvation to sinners even though he loathes sin, a doctor can heal her patients even if she loathes disease. In both these cases 'joy' is said to transfigure the loathing (of the evil) into something positive and good.

It has to be emphasized that none of (1), (2a) and (2b) are, in any proper sense, arguments. They are alleged to be 'facts' by their proponents and, as such, should be accessible to the scrutiny of human experience. And here it has to be acknowledged that (1), (2a) and (2b) cannot survive this scrutiny in any plausible sense. Let us take the case of (1). Here God is said to have an 'imaginative response' to the sufferings of his creatures. Such a response, however, does not seem possible where a timeless being is concerned, as Pike's passage bears out. For the notion that God can only 'experience' the sufferings indirectly is incompatible with the fundamental Christian assertion that God is love. All real responding must involve sympathetic relationship; otherwise we would be justified, like Dostoevsky's Ivan Karamazov, in 'handing back our tickets' (to heaven) to this deity. God, in the role of passive onlooker, was *absent* in Auschwitz or Cambodia. The very principle of the incarnation – that God became *human* – presupposes that God can 'experience' suffering. To quote Jürgen Moltmann:

> In the metaphysical concept of God from ancient cosmology and the modern psychological concept of God, the being of the Godhead . . . as the zone of the impossibility of death, stands in juxtaposition to human being as the zone of the necessity of death. If this concept of God is applied to Christ's death on the cross, the cross *must* be 'evacuated' of deity, for by definition God cannot suffer and die. He is pure causality. But Christian theology must think of God's being in suffering and dying and finally in the death of Jesus, if it is not to surrender itself and lose its identity. Suffering, dying and similar negations simply cannot be predicated of that which is conceived of as pure causality and the unconditioned mover. The God who was the subject of suffering could not be truly God. . . . With the Christian message of the cross of Christ something new and strange has entered the metaphysical world. For this faith must understand the deity of God from the event of the suffering and death of the Son of God and thus bring about a fundamental change in the orders of being of metaphysical thought. . . . It must think of the suffering of Christ as the power of God and the death of Christ as God's potentiality.[4]

On Moltmann's view, then, the concept of God as an impassible being 'evacuates' the cross (and, *ipso facto*, the incarnation) of deity. God could not have been in Christ and not 'experienced' – directly – some of the latter's anguish and suffering. Perfection, in particular moral perfection, does not seem to require the absence of the pain of guilt or the absence of the knowledge of evil. On the contrary, we are assured by writers on the psychology of morals that true goodness is the ability to retain one's moral integrity in the face of evil. Thus, to quote one such writer, Rollo May:

> Innocence that cannot include the daimonic becomes evil.... [Potentialities] for evil increase in proportion to our capacity for good. The good we seek is an increased sensitivity, a sharpened awareness, a heightened consciousness of good and evil.[5]

Or again:

> Trying to be good all the time will not make one into an ethical giant but into a prig. We should grow, rather, toward greater sensitivity to *both* evil and good. The moral life is a dialectic between good and evil. (p. 238)

Or yet again:

> life is a mixture between good and evil; ... there is no such thing as *pure* good; and ... if evil weren't there as a potentiality, the good would not be either. Life consists of achieving good not apart from evil but *in spite of it*. (p. 258. May's italics)

God, then, if he is to avoid being a divine prig, must at least possess an inherent capacity for the *direct* experience of evil, and what is more, he must be deemed to exercise this capacity. The orthodox theist, it seems, confuses goodness with innocence (or more precisely with what May calls '*pseudo-innocence*').[6] Goodness is compatible with knowledge of evil and the pain of guilt, though it cannot be identified with pseudo-innocence. Likewise, self-sufficiency does not imply the absence of the pain of loneliness; for, surely, the self-sufficient person is one who can remain self-sufficient *in spite of* her loneliness? Also omnipotence does not guarantee the absence of (the pain of) fear – I can have full control over a situation and still feel fear about some aspect of it. For example, while God's omnipotence enables him to do everything that it is (logically) possible for him to do, it is still possible that God might fear what it is *not possible* for him to do (for instance, his inability to alter the past). It is clear, therefore, that every statement made in (1) is open to counter-examples.

In (2a) the 'suffering' endured by God is said to be 'transfigured' by the joy that necessarily inheres in the Godhead. The gist of this statement conflicts with the import of (1). For in (1) God is said to be *uninvolved* with evil and suffering, whereas in (2a) he is said to *endure* it: he endures it in order to transform it. But surely one cannot endure something without experiencing what it is that one endures, in which case to endure something is incompatible with being uninvolved in that (endurance-producing) state of affairs. (1) and (2a) therefore conflict with each other.

The problems we have been discussing so far can be summed up in terms of the following dilemma. Either, God, if he *loves* us, must participate in our destinies; or, he is *perfect*, in which case this participation (so it is alleged) cannot be real. What this dilemma does is to drive a wedge between the divine attributes of *love* and the attribute of *perfection* (conceived in terms of this strand of Christian metaphysical theology). Is it necessary for this dilemma ever to have arisen? Surely it has arisen only because theologians in this tradition construe the attribute of perfection in a way that makes it incompatible with the idea that God is a loving being? Having saddled themselves with this dilemma, the theologians in this tradition have no alternative but to adduce fairly implausible solutions as a means of getting round it. One such solution is contained in (2a), which asserts that the sufferings of the world are 'transfigured' by the joy of God, and that this process of trans-figuration is somehow mysterious and beyond human comprehen-sion. Critics of this theological tradition argue that this solution trivializes God and makes him unworthy of our worship: to feel 'joy' at the suffering of another being is quite definitely not a mark of superiority, let alone moral excellence.[7] For, as we have indi-cated, to love somebody is to be involved in the destiny of that person; it requires that a commensurability exist between our emotions and their emotions. To quote a theologian from an alternative tradition:

> The unsurpassable could not be without love – for even we ourselves would surpass a loveless being. To love is to rejoice with the joys and sorrow with the sorrow of others. Thus it is to be influenced by those who are loved.[8]

The theologians in this tradition, it is charged, make God into a stone by so conceiving him. However, some of these theologians have made strenuous attempts to come to terms with this problem in a way that purports (a) to retain their conception of deity, and (b) to show, nevertheless, that this deity cannot be regarded as a stone or a sadist. These attempts find expression in a *theodicy*. Thus, it is argued that God is profoundly aware of human suffering, but this awareness lies in the larger context of a total history which is leading to our eternal joy. In this case, the crux of the objection we have been considering – namely, that God's love must be construed on the same basis as human love – will have to be rejected as being too anthropomorphic. A theodicy would free us from the temptation to say that the only answer to the 'problem' of evil is to conceive of divine love as an analogical extrapolation of human love, i.e. that God identifies with our suffering and pain in the way that human beings identify with the suffering and pain of those they love.[9] A theodicy as we have just outlined it can be called an *Eschatological Theodicy*. Such a theodicy depends on the following assumptions:

1 It presupposes the possibility of post-mortem existence.
2 It presupposes the possibility of a consummation of the course of history.
3 It presupposes the possibility that God can, and will, guarantee the outcome of this course of history.

I want now to examine (3). For this Eschatological Theodicy to work, God will have to guarantee that eternal joy will be the final outcome of the course of history; hence, if history terminates in catastrophe, then God will not have guaranteed the outcome specified by this theodicy. However, and herein lies the rub, if joy will be the *inevitable* outcome of history, what point can there be in human suffering? No doubt it will take a detailed argument to establish this point; even so it raises an issue that is likely to subvert the Eschatological Theodicy. This issue – which surrounds the *point* or the *purpose* we can ascribe to suffering – is not shirked by the proponents of this theodicy. Thus, it is argued that this suffering constitutes the *means* by which eternal joy is ultimately attained. Or, more briefly, suffering is the *sine qua non* of attaining such joy. This condition, however, is morally dubious, in that it implies that anybody who dies without suffering is not entitled to receive this eternal joy. To circumvent this objection the theodicist maintains that 'soul-making' continues after death; so that, in effect, somebody who misses his chance of suffering in this life gets another opportunity to do so in the Celestial City.[10] But this really is no way out of the problem, because it merely dodges the issue. For exactly the same question that we asked about the point of suffering on earth can be asked about suffering in the Celestial City: the theodicist does not answer this objection simply by saying that the suffering takes place at another time and in another place. Pointless suffering can exist even in the Celestial City. Moreover, it could be argued against the theodicist that the degree of suffering that exists anywhere (i.e. the Celestial City included) is too great to justify whatever ultimate joy there is at the end of history. Thus Dorothee Soelle says, 'the God who causes suffering is not to be justified even by lifting the suffering later. No heaven can rectify Auschwitz.'[11] The sort of suffering that cannot be so justified usually goes under the name 'dysteleological suffering', or as Simone Weil preferred to call it, '*affliction*'.[12] Of this type of suffering John Hick says:

> Such suffering remains unjust and inexplicable, haphazard and cruelly excessive. The mystery of dysteleological suffering is a real mystery.... It challenges Christian faith with its utterly baffling, alien, destructive meaninglessness. And yet at the same time, detached theological reflection can note that this very irrationality and this lack of ethical meaning contribute to the character of the world as a place in which true human goodness can occur and in which loving sympathy and compassionate self-sacrifice can take place.[13]

I want to argue now (i) that dysteleological suffering or affliction cannot be justified by a 'soul-making' theodicy, and (ii) that accordingly God's redemptive promise of eternal joy would not constitute an appropriate response to affliction.

(i) There seems to be no alternative to the view that suffering is the outcome of human freedom, coupled with the limitations of knowledge and power that stem from our creaturely finitude. It is this state of affairs that makes tragedy possible. According to this view suffering, or more precisely the existence of suffering, is not a complete mystery: it is a mystery only because its existence is so difficult to reconcile with the existence of an omnipotent, omniscient and morally perfect being. That is to say, suffering becomes mysterious only when we ask the question:

(A) How can suffering exist *when* a morally perfect, omnipotent and omniscient being exists?

According to this view, we harbour the notion that such a being cannot ultimately be responsible for the existence of suffering. It is this notion which results in the need to see suffering as dysteleological. The sense of mystery is more difficult to sustain if we ask the following question instead of (A):

(B) How can suffering exist *when* free, morally imperfect beings exist?

Unlike (A), (B) provides us with the framework for the acceptable teleological answer: suffering exists because human beings are
finite beings. Accordingly, theodicy only becomes relevant in the
context of a question like (A); when we pose the question in terms
of (B) the problem resolves itself, and theodicy becomes superfluous.[14] This proposition, if accepted, will of course discredit the
'soul-making' theodicy. Nevertheless, this proposition is not altogether acceptable. First, although it might give us a teleologically
acceptable explanation of the existence of suffering, it in no way
accounts for its *pervasiveness* or *arbitrariness*. For it is these
features which make suffering (certain forms of it, at any rate) so
awful. Here we have to agree with Hick's view that affliction is
ultimately mysterious. However, if it is mysterious, then *no* theodicy can give it a rationale. On these terms any attempt to give
suffering a rationale in terms of the notion of human freedom also
represents a form of theodicy: such attempts, as made by Teilhard
de Chardin and process theologians, constitute an 'inverted' theodicy. The adherents of the 'inverted' and eschatological theodicies
are playing the same game inasmuch as both are seeking to provide
a rationale for the existence of suffering, albeit from a different
perspective.[15] But how satisfactory are all these attempts to provide
such a rationale? I want now to argue that they are not satisfactory
because the only possible theodicy is one that holds for God as well.
There seems no alternative to the modified-Lutheran position of
Moltmann and Soelle, that is, that the only possible theodicy is one
that makes God a suffering God. Or to put it more strongly, the
only credible theodicy for Auschwitz is one that makes God an
inmate of the place, one that acknowledges the possibility that he
too hung on the gallows. Anything else, Moltmann and Soelle
argue, will be unacceptable. Adherents of the 'inverted' theodicy,
which attempts to give a rationale for the existence of suffering by
using the notion of freedom, may wish to argue that the profound
insight of the position of Moltmann and Soelle can be reconciled
with their own point of view. Unfortunately, such an argument is
untenable for the following reasons. First, if we align this insight
with the 'inverted' theodicy, we will have to accept that God gave
his creatures freedom *in the knowledge* that some of them will use
this freedom to make him suffer, and ultimately, to kill him. And
this is a very strange notion indeed. The only way out of this
difficulty is to argue that although we are free beings, freedom is
not something God can create. (This view we shall argue for later.)
Second, this insight can only be brought to fruition in the context of

a theology of the cross, and a trinitarian theology at that.[16] And it is questionable whether a trinitarian theology can be worked out in the framework of an 'inverted' theodicy. So for these two reasons we have to doubt whether the insight of Moltmann and Soelle can be reconciled *theologically* with the 'inverted' theodicy. The 'inverted' theodicy is unacceptable for another reason. We have argued so far that while the 'inverted' theodicy gives a teleologically acceptable account of the *existence* of suffering, it does not account for the pervasiveness or arbitrariness of suffering. God, if we do not accept the traditional conception of his impassibility, is neither a stone nor a sadist: this much is consonant with the 'inverted' theodicy. But if God is neither a stone nor a sadist, *how* does he exist in the midst of creaturely suffering? To this question this theodicy gives no real answer. To answer this question we have to accommodate the notion of a God who is a fellow-sufferer in the midst of our suffering, but this notion can only be validated in the context of a *theologia crucis*, and this the 'inverted' theodicy cannot undertake to do.

Let us summarize our argument so far. We have argued that affliction cannot be accounted for in terms of a 'soul-making' theodicy, and although we accept that there is an element of plausibility in the 'inverted' theodicy's basic contention that suffering is the outcome of human freedom, we cannot accept this theodicy without substantial reservations. For it neither accounts for the pervasiveness nor the arbitrariness of suffering nor does it tell us what it is that God does in the midst of our suffering. The only acceptable view-point here is one which acknowledges the possibility that God can, and does, suffer along with his creation, and on this matter the 'inverted' theodicy is only slightly less unilluminating than its 'soul-making' counterpart.

(ii) I want to argue now that God's redemptive promise of eternal joy cannot be conceived as offering an appropriate response to affliction. This much can be established from the acceptable element in the 'inverted' theodicy. For when suffering is conceived as the outcome of human freedom and finitude, it cannot be regarded as part of a divine scheme of things which inevitably results in eternal joy. That is to say, if God gives his creatures freedom, then God must, in so doing, allow his creatures to reject the outcome of the divine scheme of things. Hence if we were free we could, in effect, say to God that we would rather be rid of our present suffering; although this would involve giving up the eternal joy promised us as a reward for the 'soul-making' qualities we

cultivated in the face of such suffering. This is what Ivan Karamazov did when he 'handed back his ticket'. Freedom, then, poses a
threat to the 'soul-making' theodicy: we can, to put it strongly,
refuse to be the masochistic accomplices of this sadistic God.
Consequently, the proponents of the Eschatological Theodicy have
a vested interest in denying that we possess the freedom to reject
God's eschatological designs on his creation. At the same time,
however, they are mindful of the problems that are likely to be
caused by a real denial of this freedom: we can then attribute the
existence of evil to God, for it cannot now be said that evil exists
because we misuse our freedom. So it seems that freedom must be
an integral part of any theodicy worthy of its name.[17] We have here,
then, two strands of argument that have to be reconciled. On the
one hand, we have the assertion that human beings, *qua* personal
beings, are essentially free. On the other hand, we have the
possibility that human beings, if they are really free, can use this
freedom to become *protest* atheists, i.e., free to reject, *with
justification*, the divine eschatological scheme of things. In other
words, they can, like Ivan Karamazov, 'hand back their tickets' to
God. How does the theodicist get round this problem? The
standard theodicist manoeuvre at this stage is to argue that God
'created' this freedom of finite creaturely beings, so that they are
endowed 'with a degree of genuine freedom and independence
over against their maker'.[18] That is, humankind has a cognitive
freedom in relation to God, which makes it possible.

> to speak of God as endowing His creatures with a genuine though
> limited autonomy. We could think of Him as forming men through
> the long evolutionary process and leaving them to respond or fail to
> respond to Himself in uncompelled faith.[19]

Therefore:

> In creating finite persons to love and be loved by Him, God must
> endow them with a certain relative autonomy over against
> Himself. . . . In other words, the reality and presence of God must not
> be borne in upon men in the coercive way in which their natural
> environment forces itself upon their creation. (p. 317)

But then if God *endows* us with a freedom that involves an
'epistemic distance' from him, how are we going to become
acquainted with his redemptive promise of eternal joy? The answer
is that

> this divine economy makes it possible for man, thus reaching self-
> consciousness at an epistemic distance from God, freely to accept

God's gracious invitation and to come to Him in uncompelled faith
and love. ... Man can be truly *for* God only if he is morally
independent of Him, and he can be thus independent only by being
first *against* Him! And because sin consists in self-centred alienation
from God, only God can save us from it, thereby making us free for
Himself. (p. 323)

In a nutshell: God *bestows* freedom upon his creatures, so that they
can freely accept his redemptive promise ('gracious invitation') of
eternal joy. This, it could be said, is rather like bestowing upon a
bird the freedom of its cage while promising it eternal joy in an
avian post-mortem existence. For Hick's view simply does not
enable us to answer the following questions: Even if we grant that
God bestows freedom upon us, why does he have to bestow it on us
in *this* (suffering) world?[20] If we really are free and autonomous,
why should we not be against God *all the time*, especially since he is
the Maker of an afflicted world? Is it not something of a misnomer
to say that freedom, real freedom, is something that can be
bestowed? For if God *brings it about* that we are 'free', then is this
not another way of saying that he *determines* that we are free? The
view that a created freedom is a form of predetermination has been
advanced, in his characteristically pungent way, by Nicholas Berdyaev, who says:

Man is not free if he is merely a manifestation of God, a part of Deity;
he is not free if he has been endowed with freedom by God the
Creator, but has nothing divine in himself.[21]

On Berdyaev's view, to say that God creates beings who have
freedom of choice with regard to, say, *A*, *B* and *C*, is to say that he
predetermines the choices of these beings by *limiting* their choices
to *A*, *B* and *C*. In what he calls 'the moral source of atheism' (or
what we have called 'protest atheism'), Berdyaev outlines the
pitfalls of this conception of God-bestowed freedom:

It is precisely the traditional theology that leads good men, inspired
by moral motives, to atheism. The ordinary theological conception of
freedom in no way saves the Creator from responsibility for pain and
evil. Freedom itself is created by God and penetrable to Him down to
its very depths. In his omniscience, ascribed to Him by positive
theology, God foresaw from all eternity the fatal consequences of
freedom with which he endowed man. He foresaw the evil and
suffering of the world which has been called into being by His will and
is wholly in His power; He foresaw everything, down to the perdition
and torment of many. And yet He consented to create man and the
world under these terrible conditions. This is the profound source of

moral atheism. In expecting an answer to His call from man whom He endowed with freedom, God is expecting an answer from Himself. He knows the answer beforehand and is only playing with Himself. When in difficulties, positive theology falls back upon mystery and finds refuge in negative theology. But the mystery has already been over-rationalized. The logical conclusion is that God has from all eternity predetermined some to eternal salvation and others to eternal damnation.[22]

What can we say about Berdyaev's argument? First, the idea that humankind is not free unless it has something of the divine in itself is a profound idea: it implies that God must incarnate himself in humankind, or in the context of the problem of suffering, that God must become a fellow-sufferer, one who, because he himself is a victim, is on the side of the victims and not that of the executioners.[23] Second, the last sentence of the passage just quoted requires the proponent of the Eschatological Theodicy to be a universalist, i.e. to say that *all beings are saved in the end*. If not she will have the extremely difficult task of saying *why* it is that 'God has from all eternity predetermined some to eternal salvation and others to eternal damnation.' And the eschatologist can avoid the charge of arbitrariness only by saying that all are saved or that *all* are damned. However, this raises for her the following question: why have *some* beings got to suffer more than others when *all* beings will ultimately experience eternal joy? By what token can the members of the *SS* and their victims both partake of the same eternal joy? It is not being suggested here that we should adopt a retributive eschatology, since I agree with Professor Hick that the universalist position is the only ultimately tenable one. But the fact remains that the discrepant degrees of suffering endured by different people militate against the Eschatological Theodicy. The eschatologist does not appear to have a satisfactory explanation for these discrepancies, except for what Berdyaev calls the appeal to over-rationalized mystery. 'No heaven', as Soelle says, 'can rectify Auschwitz.' It is on these grounds that the Eschatological Theodicy is suspect: suffering cannot be accounted for in terms of God's eschatological designs; tragedy is, in this sense, 'beyond good and evil'.[24] Our conclusions on the theodicy-question, therefore, are:

(A) That affliction or dysteleological suffering cannot be accounted for in terms of God's eschatological designs for his creation, as the proponents of the Eschatological Theodicy maintain. Neither can it be accounted for in terms of human freedom and finitude, as the 'inverted' theodicies hold. For, as Berdyaev has argued, freedom is not something that can be created by God. God himself is constrained by this freedom; according to Christianity, he himself became a victim of this (human) freedom in the person of his Son. God, if he is to make a morally (or theologically) adequate response to affliction, must indwell himself in the world on behalf of its victims. In a word, theodicy resolves itself into theophany.

(B) That all theodicies, even putatively non-rational ones like John Hick's, arise from an attempt to account for the phenomenon of suffering in teleological terms. This is true even of 'inverted' theodicies. An 'inverted' theodicy which appeals to the notion of human freedom might be better able to account for the existence of suffering, but it cannot account for the *pervasiveness* or *arbitrariness* of suffering. The only thing which can conceivably do so is a theology of the cross. 'For God has nothing to do with . . . suffering – aside from being on the side of the wronged'.[25] And the God who is on the side of the wronged is a suffering God, a fellow-victim of those who are wronged, he is 'the great companion – the fellow-sufferer who understands' (A. N. Whitehead). Whitehead's seminal insight can become theologically relevant only if it is augmented by a *theologia crucis*. Given such a *theologia* we can dispense with the need to say that God takes cognizance of human suffering by guaranteeing that history will have a particular outcome; he does not, so to speak, have to dangle any eschatological carrots before the eyes of the afflicted. God cannot transform affliction in this way; he can only (freely) offer to partake in the lot of the afflicted. The crux of our critique of the classical theodicies, therefore, is this theology of the cross, which we must now consider, albeit briefly and schematically.

(C) We have seen how the proponents of the Eschatological Theodicy appeal to mystery when it comes to accounting for the incidence of human suffering. It seems true to say that the incidence of suffering cannot be given an intelligible explanation, and that ultimately we have to resort to a mysticism of suffering in lieu of such an explanation.[26] But do we have to look to such a mysticism when it comes to giving an answer to the question: where is God, or what does God do, when human beings suffer? In considering this question both Soelle and Moltmann consider a story told by Elie Wiesel in his book *Night*:

> The *SS* hung two Jewish men and a boy before the assembled inhabitants of the camp. The men died quickly but the death struggle of the boy lasted half an hour. 'Where is God? Where is he?' a man behind me asked. As the boy, after a long time, was still in agony on

the rope, I heard the man cry again, 'Where is God now?' And I heard a voice within me answer, 'Here he is – he is hanging here on this gallows.'[27]

The world to this man, then, is *etsi deus non daretur*, 'as if there were no God'. God (if he exists) is to this man a *hidden* God. The real test for a theodicy – perhaps the *only* test – is: how can we answer that man? We obviously cannot answer him by telling him about how Auschwitz is a 'vale of soul-making'; neither can we give him an answer by telling him that man is a free being, and given that he is a finite creature as well, is likely to torment his fellow human beings. Leaving aside the question of the *moral* appropriateness of these answers, it seems to me that the only *intellectually* appropriate answer we can give to this man is the one given by Wiesel, viz., 'Here he is – he is hanging here on this gallows.' For to speak here of a God who made souls or who endowed his creatures with freedom, but who was not suffering at that time, would be to speak of a sadistic or stone-like God. And this God would be 'the moral source of atheism' (Berdyaev). Or to put it in very prosaic terms, that God would not be a religiously available deity. The only God that that man could have *experienced* at the time of these executions was a God who indwelled himself in Auschwitz, and who therefore did not forsake its inmates; any other deity would have been supremely irrelevant. Or as Moltmann puts it, he would have been a demon and not a God. This being so, we can only conclude that the Gods of the 'soul-making' and the 'inverted' theodicies are religiously unavailable deities – only the God of a suffering theophany would be religiously available to the victims of evil.

Let us now turn to (2b) which, it may be remembered, asserts that analogies from human experience can be adduced as parallels to the way in which divine joy transforms evil into something good. Two analogies were cited, namely, the case of a priest and a doctor who *rejoiced in their efforts* to save and cure respectively. This argument is vitiated by a logical confusion. What the priest and the doctor rejoice in are *their* efforts. But surely their efforts and the feelings of the people they heal are not the same. Thus, my sorrows are, in the sense of an elementary truism, *my (own)* sorrows and nobody else's. Admittedly, my sorrows might be easier to bear up with if somebody else shares my sorrow, in the sense of commiserating with me, etc. But that person still cannot share the *having* of my sorrow. So the having of my sorrow is quite distinct from the joy that somebody else derives from my sharing it with him. This being so, God's joy and my sorrow are not the same; and the significance of the one cannot be replaced by the significance of the other. The above analogies must therefore be regarded as failures. Besides, even if God transforms the suffering of the world by whatever joy he 'experiences', it will still be the case that his joy is dependent on our sufferings for its object. God needs our sufferings in order to transform them into his joy. Even if this is not a morally unaccept-able portrayal of God, it still shows that he is *dependent on us* for the object of his transforming joy. We are, therefore, in a *real* sense the objects of divine experience. And yet, St Anselm argues that when God feels compassionate, it is we who experience his com-passion, and not God himself:

> Therefore, thou art both compassionate, because thou dost save the wretched, and spare those who sin against thee; and not compassio-nate, because thou art affected by no sympathy for wretchedness.[28]

God, according to Anselm's argument, has compassion for human wretches, but does not himself experience this compassion. But, surely, if he does not experience compassion in this case, then he cannot experience the joy which stems from the transforming use of his compassion. Joy, on this view, is the *outcome* of God's use of his compassion, and, quite simply, if he cannot experience one how can he experience the other? This argument is fundamentally misconceived, to say the least. The source of this misconception is fairly clear: it lies in the neo-Platonic doctrine that if God is a Perfect Being then he cannot respond to imperfect beings like human wretches. For if he did, then the plenitude of his being would be diminished by the non-being of these wretches. Impassi-bility is therefore required by the perfection and omnipotence of deity.[29] At an intuitive level, this view is not very plausible. For the more powerful one is, or the more being one has, the more responsive one is. (Paul Tillich once made this point in a sermon by saying, 'A life process is the more powerful, the more non-being it can include in its self-affirmation.') Thus, a stone is less responsive than an amoeba; an amoeba is less responsive than a dog; and a dog is less responsive than a human being. Furthermore, the more responsive one is, the more plausible one becomes. Passibility is the corollary of responsiveness, for we cannot respond to someone without relating to that person, and we cannot relate to that person without being affected by her. A God who loves his creation must be a God who is affected by its travails. To sum up our argument with regard to (2b):

(i) The notion that human suffering is transformed by God's joy is an incoherent notion.

(ii) Even if this transformation can take place, it still appears to be the case that God's joy is dependent on human suffering for its object. God cannot therefore escape being in relation to his creatures, which is another way of saying that he is a passible being.

How do we tie-in the principle that God is a passible being with the theodicy-problem? We argued earlier that if God is to be regarded as a religiously available deity then we must move the theodicy-problem into the realm of theophany, i.e. a *suffering* theophany, which in a Christian context means a *theologia crucis*. There are three points that we must bear in mind when we take the step, advocated by Soelle, of resolving the theodicy-problem in terms of the theology of the cross. First, it may be questioned whether in resolving the theodicy-problem by means of a theology of the cross we are actually presenting a *theodicy*, that is, a doctrine which purports to reconcile God's omnipotence and goodness with the existence of evil and suffering. How can we retain God's omnipotence on the basis of a *theologia crucis*? The answer we have proposed presupposes a form of divine *kenosis*: it is implicit in our position that God limits his omnipotence when he identifies with suffering humanity in and through his incarnation in Jesus Christ. There are, of course, substantial objections to the *kenosis* doctrine; nevertheless, I believe, with Donald MacKinnon and Ray S. Anderson, that this doctrine is not fundamentally incoherent and that it can be made to work.[30] So our position is, in effect, a non-theodicy, but it seems to me that this non-theodicy (i.e., a suffering theophany) is the only truly Christian response to the 'problem' of evil. Second, a theodicy *may* aid the self-understanding of those who suffer. But no theodicy, even one which takes the form of a suffering theophany, can offer the sufferer a palliative or premature consolation. For the person enduring his Gethsemane must, like Jesus, assent to his suffering by draining his cup to the full, then only will 'the cup of suffering become the cup of strengthening'.[31] No theodicy can tell a person how to endure suffering. Every afflicted person, it seems, hangs on a cross that is peculiarly her own. No theodicy can circumvent this 'brute' fact of suffering. Third, and this is an implicit criticism of the Moltmann–Soelle strategy, it is not enough to say that we can resolve the theodicy-problem by conceiving of God as a suffering God who identifies with the victims of suffering to the point of death. It is not enough to suggest that God, in identifying with the victims of

Auschwitz, himself becomes a powerless victim of the place. For the Christian message, in addition to showing us that God himself, in the person of his Son, was a helpless victim on the cross, also assures us of the *victory* of goodness over evil, of life over death. In the Christian faith, the cross is inextricably bound up with the resurrection. Or in theological terms: theodicy must always be viewed from the perspective of soteriology. However, we cannot comfort the victims of suffering with a theodicy, even when it is 'sugared' with a soteriology. Evil, in its root and essence, is a mystery. How God grapples with and overcomes it is a mystery too – it is one that we, as theologians, must ponder over in the grasp of his infinite love. We have the assurance of the victory of this love, but we cannot use this assurance (nor the fact that evil is a mystery) either as an excuse for indifference or to provide easy consolation for the victims of suffering. If we do, we may become like the friends of Job, whose all too rational, and plausible, explanations of his plight only added to his torment.[32]

5
Theodicy?

Theodicy, in its classical form, requires the adherent of a theistic faith to reconcile the existence of an omnipotent, omniscient and morally perfect God with the existence of evil. The so-called problem of evil has a venerable ancestry, extending beyond the Christian era, and was apparently first formulated by Epicurus (341–270 BC) in the form of a dilemma which perhaps receives its most succinct formulation in the words of David Hume:

> Is he willing to prevent evil, but not able? then he is impotent. Is he able, but not willing? then he is malevolent. Is he both able and willing? whence then is evil?[1]

A long strand in the history of theology, stemming from St Augustine via St Thomas Aquinas and the Reformers to Schleiermacher and modern times, has addressed itself to the task of reconciling God's omnipotence, omniscience and benevolence with the existence of evil.[2] And yet, despite the efforts of these and other theologians, the thought persists in many quarters that theodicy is perhaps one of the least satisfactory areas of the theological enterprise. Confronted with the seemingly innumerable 'solutions' to the problem of evil that have been advanced over the centuries, one cannot help thinking that Kant's complaint about metaphysics is probably just as applicable to theodicy:

> [it] has rather to be regarded as a battle-ground quite peculiarly suited for those who desire to exercise themselves in mock combats, and in which no participant has ever yet succeeded in gaining so much as an inch of territory, not at least in such manner as to secure him its permanent possession.[3]

Why is it that so many claims to have solved (or resolved) the theodicy-problem appear to be unwarrantedly optimistic? Why is it that so many theodicies possess not even a veneer of plausibility?

There are, in my view, three main reasons why attempts to formulate a viable theodicy are so fraught with the likelihood of failure.

The first reason is broadly historical. It may be that we live in an epoch in which it is no longer possible to address ourselves legitimately to the problem of evil: that is, it may be that ours is an epoch in which historical conditions no longer allow us to view evil as a 'problem' that can be 'answered' by an essentially *intellectual* undertaking like a theodicy. Thus it could be argued that theodicy 'gets off the ground' only if it is granted the supposition that it is possible to see what goes on in the universe in terms of a larger, divine order – for without this supposition (that is, of God as the supreme architect of the universe) it makes no sense to seek a justification of God vis-à-vis the fact of evil. And (the historical argument proceeds) the epoch in which we live is precisely one in which this presupposition is no longer sustainable. If this argument holds, then the theodicist is someone whose sense of 'the historicity of understanding' is non-existent or at best defective: he sets out to solve a problem which presupposes an intellectual horizon that is no longer available to individuals like us who live in a secular or desacrilized age. Let me attempt to develop this somewhat schematic argument.

An important watershed for theodicy is represented by the Enlightenment. The revolution in physics and cosmology brought about by Galileo and Newton, leading as it did to the break-up of the so-called 'mediaeval synthesis', posed several intellectual problems which simply could not have arisen for the theologians of the mediaeval world. One of the more formidable of these problems was concerned with the existence of evil. Newton had succeeded in showing that the world was a self-contained mechanical system, capable of being represented mathematically by the concepts of motion, matter and space and time. The problem for the person who accepted Newtonian mechanics was this: if the nature of the world was represented by this mechanistic system, was so precisely ordered, so aesthetically proportioned, then why was there evil in the world? The problem of evil still existed, but given this mechanistic system with its ultimately deistic and even atheistic implications, it was difficult to reconcile the existence of evil with the workings of divine providence. This, of course, was only one aspect of a more general problem posed for philosophy and theology by the *Aufklärer* – namely, how are *morality* and *religious faith* to be accommodated in a world governed by the laws of a rigidly mechanistic, and ultimately godless, system? The primary intellectual figures of the Enlightenment and post-Enlightenment – Newton, Descartes, Leibniz, Spinoza, and later, Hume, Kant and Hegel – were not of course moral nihilists or out-and-out atheists; nevertheless they were confronted, or perceived themselves as being confronted, by a problem (that of accommodating morality and religious faith in a mechanistic, desacrilized universe) which simply could not have posed itself to their intellectual forebears, the thinkers of 'the mediaeval synthesis'.[4] The need, therefore, was for a new form of theodicy which would enable us to circumvent the problem of reconciling the existence of evil with the existence of an increasingly 'absent' God. As Ernest Becker, in his characteristically trenchant way, puts it:

> Something entirely different had to be done to explain evil in the world, a theodicy without divine intervention. The new theodicy had to be a natural one, a 'secular' one. . . . Evil had to be explained as existing in the world apart from God's intention or justification.[5]

How was this to be achieved? Becker continues:

> The only way to achieve this new explanation was gradually to shift the burden from reliance on God's will to the belief in man's understanding and powers. This was a shift that was to occupy the whole Enlightenment, and it was not accomplished easily. In fact . . . the separate . . . traditions each had their own kind of ingenuity, and fashioned quite different notions of 'secular' theodicy, or 'anthropodicy'.[6]

The thinkers of the Enlightenment and their successors, having eschewed the principle of cosmic order (and thus the notion of a divine Cosmic Orderer), had in this way shifted the burden of the problem of evil from God to man himself. The intellectual thrust of the Enlightenment was, as Becker notes, to 'secularize' this 'problem', to transform theodicy (properly so-called) into 'anthropodicy'. This process of 'secularization' was continued as the spirit of the Enlightenment progressively permeated the other natural sciences before proceeding to affect the social and human sciences, with the ultimate consequence that, as Becker says,

> By the time of Hiroshima . . . not only . . . was theodicy long since dead, but the burning problem of good and evil was removed from most people's lives. At best, overcoming evil was a 'job to be done' –

someone else's job; it was not a way of life to heed. And how could it
be otherwise? – the world was so matter-of-fact.... The great
prophet of the outcome, of the bureaucratization of good and evil,
was Max Weber.[7]

The Enlightenment, as our brief discussion indicates, poses a
daunting intellectual agenda for the theodicist. After the
Enlightenment, the very possibility of doing theodicy is thrown into
question. And yet so many discussions of the problem of evil
proceed as though the Enlightenment had never taken place.
Theodicists approach the problem of evil as though this problem
were not in itself a problem, as though theodicy were not in itself
faced by a 'crisis of legitimacy'. It seems to me that the theodicist
can hope to do her subject justice only if she takes seriously the
possibility that doing theodicy may in fact presuppose an intellectual horizon which no longer exists. It is conceivable that the
historical conditions brought about by the Enlightenment have
created a hermeneutical 'gap' – between an intellectual horizon
which did acknowledge the principle of cosmic order and one which
does not – that is potentially fatal for (strictly so-called) theodicy.
    If this is true, then the theodicist is an anachronism, a creature
who could have existed happily in the University of Paris in the
thirteenth century, but who has no place in a modern world which
finds it difficult to make sense of the notion of a divine Cosmic
Orderer. In a world where the voice of God is no longer to be
heard, the theodicist's words can strike no resonance: she shares the
fate of her God, and she too can no longer be heard. The theodicist,
then, overlooks the question of the hermeneutical 'gaps' created by
Enlightenment and post-Enlightenment thought at her own peril: if
she does not come to terms with these 'gaps', she could face
extinction.[8]
    Another reason why attempts to formulate a viable theodicy are
apt to end in disappointment can be found in the abstract conception of evil used by the theodicist. The use of an abstract, deperso-
nalized conception of evil is the unavoidable concomitant of
regarding theodicy as an undertaking with exclusively theoretical
implications. It seems to be in the very nature of theodicy to have
implications that are purely theoretical. To quote Alvin Plantinga,
one of the foremost of contemporary theodicists:

> Neither a Free Will Defense nor a Free Will Theodicy is designed to
> be of much help to one suffering from ... a storm in the soul....
> Neither is it to be thought of first of all as a means of pastoral
> counseling. Probably neither will enable someone to find peace with

himself and with God in the face of the evil the world contains. But then, of course, neither is intended for that purpose.[9]

I want now to argue that it is difficult to justify the view that theodicy is a purely theoretical undertaking. To see it in this light is already to possess the perspective on good and evil which Max Weber found to be characteristic of modern times: namely, an essentially bureaucratic view of the nature of good and evil.[10] If this is in fact the case, then to regard theodicy as a purely intellectual exercise is to provide – albeit unwittingly – a tacit sanction for the evil that exists on our appalling planet. Crucial to our argument is the principle that *all* philosophical and theological reflection, no matter how 'theoretical' such reflection may be, inevitably mediates a certain social and political praxis. All profoundly significant intellectual visions have a purchase on reality. They thus have the capacity to determine the way(s) in which a certain segment of reality is either to be transformed or else maintained in its existing form. The philosopher and the theologian do not theorize *in vacuo*: it is their responsibility, therefore, continually to ask themselves what particular praxis it is that their work mediates. For it is only by such self-scrutiny that they can avoid irresponsible theological speech, and guard themselves 'from indulging in the "easy speeches that comfort cruel men" '.[11] What social and political praxis could possibly be mediated by an approach to the problem of evil which favours a totally abstract conception of evil? Evil (moral evil, that is) owes its existence to the deeds of human beings; evil is manifested *in concreto* in the deeds of humans; it exists at a certain place and a certain time; and it 'needs' its human victims and their torturers and executioners. The most terrible visions are conjured up by names like the Warsaw ghetto, Auschwitz, Cambodia, the Gulag Archipelago, the refugee camps in Beirut, and so forth. The evil perpetrated in these places was not abstract. On the contrary, it was of such a palpable magnitude that some writers, Sartre, for example, have been moved to assert that such evil is irredeemable.[12] The theodicist who formulates a doctrine designed to overlook the radical particularity of human evil is, by implication, mediating a social and political praxis which averts its gaze from all the cruelties that exist in the world. The theodicist, we are suggesting, cannot remain serene in a heartless world. If she does, her words will be dissipated in the ether of abstract moralizing, and she will become like the persons described by Joseph Conrad in his great short story 'An Outpost of Progress', who talk with indignation and enthusiasm;... talk about oppression, cruelty, crime, devotion, self-sacrifice, virtue, and ... know nothing real beyond the words. Nobody knows what suffering or sacrifice mean – except perhaps the victims.[13]

Theodicy, then, has to engage with the sheer particularity, the radical contingency, of human evil. The theodicist cannot, of course, guarantee that her doctrine will have any significance for the victims of extreme suffering. But if, as Conrad says, only the victims can understand what suffering and sacrifice mean, then theodicy must necessarily be articulated from the standpoint of the victims themselves. Otherwise, theodicy will succumb inevitably to what Paul Ricoeur calls 'the bad faith of theodicy': 'it does not triumph over real evil but only over its esthetic phantom'.[14] A theodicy is not worth heeding if it does not allow the screams of our society to be heard.

The third reason why theodicy seems so precarious an undertaking, so incommensurable with the magnitude of the evil and suffering that exist in the world, stems from the fact that theodicy, by its very nature, involves the application of the principles of *reason* to a problem which is essentially such that it defies the application of all rational principles. Evil and suffering in their innermost depths are fundamentally mysterious, they confound the human mind. And yet the goal of theodicy is, somehow, to render them comprehensible, explicable. The cornerstone of theodicy is the attempt to provide a *teleology* of evil and suffering, to slot evil and suffering into a scheme of things consonant with the workings of divine providence. The theodicist, in a sense, takes on the role of Job's comforters. She seeks to render the intractable tractable. Confronted by a wordless abyss, she trusts in the efficacy of words. No wonder the theodicist is accused by Ricoeur of triumphing over an 'esthetic phantom'. However, before attempting to evaluate this accusation a little more fully, it is necessary to consider in greater detail what it is that the theodicist proposes (in principle) to achieve. This is necessary, for it could be argued against us that we have been able to raise these three objections to theodicy only because we have radically misconceived the nature of the theodicist's task. Thus, it might be said against these three objections that they seem convincing only because we have tried to get the theodicist to perform a task[15] which by its very nature is one that she cannot hope to accomplish successfully.

Our argument, as it has been developed so far, is (admittedly) not very clear on what we expect the theodicist to accomplish – our position appears to have conflated various theoretical and practical aspects of the problem (or perhaps more appropriately, the *problems*) of evil which had best be kept separate.

In its *theoretical* aspect theodicy appears to be concerned with two primary questions:

i)   Can *moral evil* in itself be rendered intelligible?
ii) Is *'theism'* intelligible in the face of the fact of moral evil?[16]

In addition, there is a *practical* aspect to theodicy which can be expressed in terms of the following questions:

iii) What does *God* do to overcome the evil and suffering that exist in his creation?
iv) What do *we* (*qua* creatures of God) do to overcome evil and suffering?[17]

There appear to be two strands of thought in modern theology concerning the relation between theodicy's theoretical and its practical aspects. On the one hand writers like Alvin Plantinga and John Hick believe that the basic problem for theodicy lies in what we have termed its theoretical aspect.[18] On the other hand, theologians like Jürgen Moltmann and Dorothee Soelle argue that a morally acceptable deity would be justified in creating a world which contained so much evil and suffering only if he were prepared to share the burden of pain and suffering with his creatures. To quote Moltmann:

> With the Christian message of the Cross of Christ, something new and strange has entered the metaphysical world. For this faith must understand the deity of God from the event of the suffering and death of the Son of God and thus bring about a fundamental change in the orders of being of metaphysical thought.... It must think of the suffering of Christ as God's potentiality.... God suffered in the suffering of Jesus, God died on the cross of Christ, says Christian faith.... [19]

The theologian who endorses Moltmann's point of view will want to say that, from the perspective of soteriology, the practical aspect of the theodicy question takes precedence over its theoretical counterpart. This, of course, is the view that we have been seeking to sponsor in this essay.

According to the person who looks at the problem of evil from the standpoint of soteriology, the question of the coherence of 'theism' in the face of the fact of evil is an important, but nevertheless *secondary*, question: we can justify our belief in a benevolent God who creates a universe with so much pain and anguish in it only if we acknowledge, or allow, the possibility that this God is a God who is, in A. N. Whitehead's famous phrase, 'the great companion – the fellow-sufferer, who understands'. We shall amplify this claim in the next section of this essay. However, before proceeding to do this (that is, showing that there can be no justifiable purely theoretical 'answer' to the problem of evil), we need to clarify the relationship that exists between the four primary questions that constitute the theoretical and the practical aspects of the theodicy problem.

Where (i) and (ii) are concerned, it seems safe to say that the question of the coherence or intelligibility of 'theism' in the face of the fact of moral evil is more important, from the standpoint of theodicy, than the question whether moral evil can in itself be rendered intelligible. There are two reasons for saying this.

a) Question (i) has nothing specifically to do with God – a mere metaphysical curiosity is enough to raise the question of the intelligibility of moral evil *per se*, and so no specifically theological issues are posed by it. Thus, question (i) could arise just as much for the 'anthropodicist' as it could for the *theo*dicist.

b) The person who is convinced by theodicy will in all probability believe that to explain why God allows moral evil to exist in itself constitutes a way of rendering moral evil less unintelligible. In other words, there is a sense in which the answer to question (i) is 'contained' in the answer to question (ii). In which case, the crux of the theodicy-problem (for those who believe that the issues it raises are primarily theoretical) will be question (ii), namely, whether 'theism' is coherent vis-à-vis the fact of moral evil.

Similarly, where questions (iii) and (iv) are concerned, it seems reasonable to say that, for the Christian theodicist, primacy must be accorded to the question 'What does God do to overcome evil?' rather than to the question 'What do we (*qua* creatures of God) do to overcome evil?' For it is a central tenet of the Christian faith that the creature is enabled to overcome evil only by the sovereign grace and power of God. Therefore, for the Christian, if (supposing) God himself does nothing to overcome evil, then the question, 'What can creatures do to overcome evil?' can easily be answered: creatures, without God, can do virtually nothing to free themselves from the power of evil.

The discussion just concluded indicates that the primary questions for theodicy, in both its theoretical and its practical aspects, are (ii) and (iii), namely, whether the fact of evil renders 'theism' incoherent (the theoretical question) and whether God acts decisively in order to deliver human beings from the power of evil (the practical question). We are now in a position to see whether it can justifiably be argued that the practical question (iii) must be accorded priority over the theoretical question (ii).

II

It is important to be clear at the outset exactly what area of the theodicy-problem we shall be concerned with when we advocate that the 'answer' to the problem of evil is to be sought by adverting to the concept of a God who does not disengage from the evil that afflicts his creation and who 'shares' the sufferings of his creatures. The theodicist, we have already seen, has the task of reconciling the omnipotence, omniscience and benevolence of God with the existence of evil. In claiming that the theodicist can accomplish this task most adequately by resorting to the notion of a God who suffers with his creation, we are of course concerned solely with demonstrating that such a God is a benevolent deity; our argument leaves untouched the relation between divine omnipotence and omniscience and the fact of moral evil.[20]

The problem of evil, we have indicated, does not arise *in vacuo*. It is invariably a problem for a certain individual at a certain place and a certain time. So the question arises: for whom is the problem of evil a 'problem'? What sort of person is it who finds the fact of evil so difficult to reconcile with the existence of an almighty and benevolent God? Quite obviously, the problem of evil (in its classical form) is not a problem for the atheist, nor is it a problem for someone who believes in a finite God or a malevolent deity. Nor is it a problem for the person who denies that evil has any 'reality' – evil would not, for example, be a problem for the person who believes that good and evil are simply states of mind, purely subjective phenomena, lacking any objective basis in 'reality'.[21]

The theodicy-problem, then, can only arise for the person who believes (or once believed) in the perfect goodness and infinite power of God and who believes in the 'reality' of evil. In what follows we shall discuss the case of Ivan Karamazov in Dostoyevsky's novel *The Brothers Karamazov*. Ivan Karamazov is just such a person who believes, or who had hitherto believed, in the omnipotence and the love of God and who is tormented by the

terrible realities of the evil that surrounds him.[22] Of this God and
the world he has created Ivan says:

> I accept God plainly and simply.... I accept his divine wisdom and his
> purpose.... I believe in the underlying order and meaning of life. I
> believe in the eternal harmony into which we are all supposed to
> merge one day.

(pp. 274–5)

However, almost immediately he tells his brother Alyosha:

> I refuse to accept this world of God's.... Please understand, it is not
> God that I do not accept, but the world he has created. I do not accept
> God's world and I refuse to accept it.

(p. 275)

Ivan then proceeds to explain why he cannot accept this world of
God's. He mentions a number of cases of extreme and gratuitous
cruelty, in particular, the report of an army general who fed an
eight-year-old boy to his hounds because the boy had slightly
injured his favourite dog with a stone. Ivan says:

> Listen: if all have to suffer so as to buy eternal harmony by their
> suffering, what have the children to do with it – tell me, please? It is
> entirely incomprehensible why they, too, should have to suffer and
> why they should have to buy harmony by their sufferings. Why should
> they, too, be used as dung for someone's future harmony?

(p. 285)

Ivan then concludes:

> I don't want harmony ... too high a price has been placed on
> harmony. We cannot afford to pay so much for admission. And
> therefore I hasten to return my ticket of admission.... It is not God
> that I do not accept, Alyosha. I merely most respectfully return him
> the ticket.

(p. 287)

The 'atheism' of Ivan Karamazov has been described as a 'protest'
atheism, a moral rebellion. As Stewart Sutherland points out in an
illuminating discussion of *The Brothers Karamazov*,[23] it is somewhat misleading to locate the atheism of Ivan in the context of
religious epistemology. As the above quotations indicate, his
atheism has nothing whatever to do with 'believing' (or 'disbeliev-
ing') certain propositions relating to the existence of God. Rather,
the problem for Ivan is above all a moral problem: he rejects God
not because he finds it impossible to believe that there is a God – on

the contrary, he clearly believes there is such a being – but because he finds it morally repugnant that God should (seem to) expect such a terrible price to be paid for the final bliss and harmony that he will bestow on humankind at the consummation of history. It is clear that for Ivan the question of the coherence of theism in the face of the fact of evil is not at issue ('I accept God plainly and simply. . . . I accept his divine wisdom and purpose. . . . I believe in the underlying order and meaning of life'). What exactly it is that is at issue for Ivan is something we have to ascertain, by determining whether the resources of classical theodicy can be used to answer him.[24]

It should be clear that it is something of a misnomer to speak of theodicy in this generic sense. We have done so up to now, for reasons of convenience, but it should not be overlooked that there are several different, even incompatible, approaches to the problem of evil, and that it is therefore more accurate to regard theodicy as a rubric for all these diverse undertakings.[25] Consequently, I shall restrict my argument to the 'soul-making' theodicy developed by John Hick in his *Evil and the God of Love*: few theodicies can rival Hick's for clarity and comprehensiveness, and his espousal of the Irenaean (as opposed to the Augustinian) approach to theodicy seems more in accord with the belief (which lies at the heart of the Christian faith) that God is love.[26] In *Evil and the God of Love* Hick says:

> If man's pain and sin are revealed in the final reckoning, at the end of human time, as having . . . played a part in the fulfilment of [God's purpose for His creatures], then in the ultimate perspective they have contributed to good.
>
> (p. 375)

This position entails that

> pain and suffering are a necessary feature of a world that is to be the scene of a process of soul-making . . . even the haphazard and unjust distribution and the often destructive and dysteleological effects of suffering have a positive significance.
>
> (p. 389)

According to Hick, *all* forms of suffering are ultimately constructive because they somehow advance God's purposes in creating the world. We live in a providential world where souls can grow, despite their sufferings, into a true and lasting relationship with their Creator.

Is this 'soul-making' theodicy likely to change the outlook of a 'protest' atheist like Ivan Karamazov? Will Ivan be persuaded to view the sufferings of humankind from the larger eschatological perspective of a total history which is leading to our eternal joy? The answer, I believe, is: No. For Ivan already believes that the world is a providential place, he accepts the whole Christian eschatological scheme of things which affirms that we will share the divine bliss at the consummation of human history. What Ivan cannot accept is the price, in terms of innocent human suffering, that has to be paid in order that men and women may come to enjoy what he calls 'eternal harmony'. God has a providential relationship with his creation, yes, but this divine providence is just too costly. Ivan, it seems, has steeled himself (in the end his spiritual turmoil drives him insane) to the point where he decides that he must decline to be the masochistic accomplice of this God – according to him we ought not to allow ourselves to be loved by such a God.[27] The 'soul-making' theodicist holds that human suffering constitutes the means by which eternal joy is ultimately attained: suffering is a *conditio sine qua non* of attaining such joy. This the 'protest' atheist cannot accept: she questions the moral propriety of a process which submits innocent children to so much pain and anguish in order that they may enjoy 'eternal harmony'. For Ivan, there is no possible moral justification for the belief that the sufferings of the innocent can be redeemed or expiated, either in this life or in a post-mortem existence. The impasse between Ivan and the 'soul-making' theodicist can be illustrated by comparing the following passages from *Evil and the God of Love* and *The Brothers Karamazov* respectively:

> If there is any eventual resolution of the interplay between good and evil, any decisive bringing of good out of evil, it must lie beyond this world and beyond the enigma of death. Therefore we cannot hope to state a Christian theodicy without taking seriously the doctrine of a life beyond the grave.... The Christian claim is that the ultimate life of man – after what further scenes of 'soul-making' we do not know – lies in that Kingdom of God which is depicted in the teaching of Jesus as a state of exultant and blissful happiness.... And Christian theodicy must point forward to that final blessedness, and claim that this infinite future good will render worthwhile all the pain and travail and wickedness that has occurred on the way to it.

(pp. 375–6)

However, it is this very idea of an eschatological resolution of humankind's earthly travails which Ivan Karamazov rejects so vehemently:

I understand, of course, what a cataclysm of the universe it will be when everything in heaven and on earth blends in one hymn of praise and everything that lives and has lived cries aloud: 'Thou art just, O Lord, for thy ways are revealed!' Then, indeed, the mother will embrace the torturer who had her child torn to pieces by his dogs, and all three will cry aloud: 'Thou art just, O Lord!'. . . . But there's the rub: for it is this that I cannot accept. . . . I make haste to arm myself against it, and that is why I renounce higher harmony altogether. It is not worth one little tear of that tortured little girl who beat herself on the breast and prayed to her 'dear, kind Lord' in the stinking privy with her unexpiated tears! They must be expiated, for otherwise there can be no harmony. I don't want it, out of the love I bear to mankind.

(pp. 286–7)

Ivan Karamazov, then, rejects the root-principle of the 'soul-making' theodicy, the principle that there can and will be a post-mortem transfiguration of all the sufferings that afflict human-kind in this life.[28]

It seems obvious from this brief delineation of the moral atheist's position that the point at issue for him or her is not really the theoretical question of the coherence or intelligibility of 'theism' in a world where much pointless suffering exists. This raises the following question: in what direction must we look for an approach to the problem of evil which is capable of avoiding the strictures of the moral atheist?

III

Both Jürgen Moltmann and Dorothee Soelle discuss the following passage from Elie Wiesel's book *Night*:

The *SS* hung two Jewish men and a boy before the assembled inhabitants of the camp. The men died quickly but the death struggle of the boy lasted half an hour. 'Where is God? Where is he?' a man behind me asked. As the boy, after a long time, was still in agony on the rope, I heard the man cry again, 'Where is God now?' And I heard a voice within me answer, 'Here he is – he is hanging here on this gallows.'[29]

Let us grant the imagination the possibility that Ivan Karamazov was acquainted with this story of Elie Wiesel's. How is Ivan likely to respond to this story? Is it plausible to envisage him 'handing back his ticket' to a God who is himself hanging on the gallows – a God who identifies with the sufferings of his creatures to the point of death? *Prima facie*, it would seem that it is less likely that Ivan would 'hand back his ticket' to a God who is himself hanging from the gallows, or who is himself torn to pieces by a pack of hounds. But before we can take up this theme and examine it further, let us dwell a little longer on Wiesel's story.

The world to this agonized Jew, who cried out in despair, is *etsi deus non daretur*, 'as if there were no God'. The only (religious) 'experience' available to this man is the experience of the absence of God – God (if he exists) is to this man a hidden God. For the man who has to endure the experience of godforsakenness, the theoretical aspect of the theodicy problem can be of no real significance: the intellectual problem of theodicy will be so much 'metaphysical chatter'.[30] A purely 'theoretical' justification of God would be totally superfluous to the needs of the man whose experience is an experience of godforsakenness. The real test for theodicy – and in a profound sense, the only test – is: how can we answer that Jew? As we have indicated, we cannot really answer him by telling him about how Auschwitz is a 'vale of soul-making'; neither can we resort to a 'free-will defence' and tell him that humans are free beings, finite and fallible creatures, who are therefore disposed to subject their fellow creatures to the most excruciating of deaths. It seems to me that the only religiously appropriate answer that can be given to this Jew is the one given by Wiesel: 'Here he is – he is hanging here on this gallows.' The only religiously available deity in situations of extreme affliction is a God who can share the sufferings of his tormented creatures, a God who is 'the great companion – the fellow sufferer, who understands'. Any other God can only be the moral source of atheism. The only God who could have been experienced by that Jew at the time of the executions described by Wiesel is a God who indwelled himself in Auschwitz, and who therefore did not forsake its inhabitants – any other deity would have been supremely irrelevant. Only a suffering God can help (Dietrich Bonhoeffer).[31] The only theodicy that can make itself available to the inmates of the 'kingdoms of death' on this earth is one that resolves itself into a theophany, in this particular instance, a suffering theophany. The question that is of crucial import to the sufferer of extreme pain and anguish is not 'Is theism unintelligible because I am in torment?' but 'Is this God a God of salvation – is this God a God who can help?' Given the extremities of suffering to be found in the dark places of this earth it is quite likely that the latter question – if it is asked – will be answered in the negative by the victims of extreme suffering. Nevertheless, it is this question which will lie at the forefront of the intellectual horizon of the person who is afflicted, not the question of the intelligibility of 'theism'.

An approach to the problem of evil from the standpoint of the victims of evil will therefore lead us to soteriology, or more precisely (given the framework of the Christian mythos), into the Christian doctrine of the atonement. As the great and much neglected Scots theologian, P. T. Forsyth, put it, 'the only possible theodicy is an adequate atonement'.[32] Again:

> The final theodicy is in no discovered system, no revealed plan, but in an effected redemption. It is not in the grasp of ideas, nor in the adjustment of events, but in the destruction of guilt and the taking away of the sin of the world.[33]

From within 'the circle of faith', there is for the Christian the basis of an 'answer' to the problem of evil. It is, however, the practical, utterly concrete answer constituted by the life, death and resurrection of Jesus Christ:

> It is not really an answer to a riddle but a victory in battle. . . . We do not see the answer; we trust the Answerer, and measure by Him. We do not gain the victory; we are united with the Victor.[34]

An 'answer' to the problem of evil by means of the theology of the cross (which is what Forsyth's proposal amounts to) will of course create its own problems, since it is, necessarily, an answer that is circumscribed by an 'incarnational' faith. Such an answer will make sense only to the person who is not prepared to dismiss as patently absurd the idea of a God who 'incarnates' himself in the midst of human suffering.[35] But (as we have argued) theodicy must incorporate the principle of a redemptive incarnation if it has anything to say to the moral atheists of this world. The only other alternative is silence.[36]

In the foregoing sections we have outlined a basis for treating the problem of evil which resorts to the language of atonement. Our proposals have taken the form of a number of largely unqualified propositions. It may be that our approach is insufficiently dialectical. It may be that we have not given enough emphasis to the elements of paradox and mystery, notions which must lie at the heart of any theodicy that purports to be taken seriously. As a result, we may have appeared to overlook some of the more intractable features of the problem of evil. Theodicy is inherently flawed: it requires us to be articulate in the face of the unspeakable. Theodicy, it seems, will always be at variance with the profound truth that the problem of evil will cease to be a problem only when evil and suffering no longer exist on this earth. Until then, the theodicist's implicit belief that words can express the reality of the unspeakable can only serve to trivialize the pain and suffering of this world.[37] So why do we persist with the enterprise of theodicy?

IV

'I must discover what God has concealed from me.' It is these words of Nicholas Berdyaev which provide a *raison d'être* for theodicy (as indeed they do for any form of theological reflection).[38] And if Berdyaev's dictum is augmented by the principle that human beings can discover what God has concealed from them only if God first elects to reveal himself to human beings, then it follows that theodicy is, in an important sense, an extension of the theology of revelation. Theodicy is done so that the theologian can find out what God reveals to humankind about the pain and suffering that exist in his creation.[39]

It is important to note, however, that this revelation (if it is genuine) is only secondarily, and not primarily, an impartation of knowledge, a 'gnosis'; primarily, it can only be God's action to bring salvation to humankind through the life, death and resurrection of Jesus Christ. The focus of this 'answer' to the problem of evil, therefore, is God's revelation of himself on the cross of Christ. The self-revelation of God on the cross of Christ is the self-justification of God, 'in which judgement and damnation are taken up by God himself, so that man may live'.[40] In the face of this divine self-justification on the cross of Christ the attempt by *humans* to justify God vis-à-vis the fact of evil (which is what theodicy essentially is) becomes superfluous. The believer who takes the atonement seriously has no real need for theodicy.[41]

Theodicy waits on God's revelation of himself in the event of the cross of Christ. This is the only approach to the problem of evil that can do justice to the spiritual predicament of the Ivan Karamazovs of this world. Of course for the person in a different situation and with a correspondingly different intellectual horizon (say, the professor motivated by apologetic considerations who, in the tranquillity of his study, seeks to present a theoretical justification of God in the face of the fact of evil and suffering), the primary question may well be the issue of the intelligibility of 'theism'.[42] The truth of the matter is that how we 'theologize', and what doctrines we formulate in the course of theologizing, depends crucially on what we identify the important theological problems or issues or questions as being. This truth applies to all forms of intellectual inquiry. Alan Garfinkel has called this the 'interest-relativity' of explanation, and argues that a 'why-question' (in the context of our discussion, the question 'Why does God allow evil to exist?' will serve as a good example) always presupposes a 'space' of relevant alternatives. Garfinkel makes this point by referring to the famous (or perhaps one should say infamous) American bank robber William Sutton who is supposed to have been asked the question 'Why do you rob banks?' by a clergyman anxious to reform him. Sutton's reply was: 'That's where the money is.' Garfinkel argues that two conceivable 'spaces' surround the question asked by the clergyman: (i) the 'space' which surrounds the clergyman's *own* asking of the question, whereby the question really means: 'Why do you rob at all?'; (ii) the 'space' which surrounds the question to which Sutton's question would have been the appropriate answer; that is, a question like 'Why do you rob banks as opposed to, say, jewellers' shops?'[43]

Applied to theodicy, Garfinkel's argument reminds us that the explanations provided by a theodicy are always 'interest-relative', and that we must therefore ask ourselves the question, 'What "space" is being presupposed by our asking of the questions that come under the rubric of theodicy?' We have sought to argue, of course, that the 'space' presupposed by these questions must always be the 'space' which puts as paramount the plight of the victims of evil. This position, which locates the problem of evil in the 'space' occupied by its victims, has certain important consequences for theodicy.

First, it means that the problem of evil cannot be dealt with from a cosmic perspective. As Donald MacKinnon rightly points out, to do this is 'totally to misunderstand both the difficulty and the consolation of its [the Christian faith's] treatment'.[44] Rather, the believer should eschew the cosmic perspective and give up the thought that by adopting such a perspective we can provide an intellectual 'answer' that will be adequate to the needs of those who are the victims of evil. Quite simply: for those who experience godforsakenness there can be no 'answer' except the stammeringly uttered truth that God himself keeps company with those who are oppressed, excluded and finally eliminated. For these sufferers, the utterance of this truth, no matter how deeply felt it is by those who utter it, can only be half a consolation.

Theodicy, as we have conceived it, is perhaps best regarded as a form of second-order theological discourse facilitating a first-order praxis. The 'answer' to the problem lies in a praxis, involving the very being of God, intending to overcome the cruelty and perversion that exist in the midst of our lives. It does not lie in the acquisition of a cosmic perspective which enables us to justify God – the God who shares our sufferings is a God who justifies himself, and the God who disengages himself from our afflictions cannot be justified, either by human beings or himself – the God who is a mere onlooker when confronted with gratuitous suffering is a demon and not a God.[45]

Second, while the decision to view the problem of evil from the perspective of those whose sufferings lead them to the experience of godforsakenness has prompted us to adopt a *theologia crucis* as the way to deal with this problem, it nevertheless remains the case that we cannot understand the action of God which lies at the heart of this theology of the cross in straightforward way. If we do, then we will have an understanding of the power of God which may eventually be confounded by the unfolding of events.[46] It is necessary for us to remember that we cannot truly understand God's salvific deeds on our behalf by using our fragmented and flawed powers; if we do this, then we run the risk of being stupefied by the grim equivocality of human experience. Theodicy, in the final analysis, has to be silence qualified by the stammering utterance of broken words. It cannot be otherwise for the believer; for him or her, the only possible 'answer' to the problem of evil is the being of flesh and bone who plumbed the depths of our malevolence and indifference on the cross at Golgotha. And while evil and suffering continue to ruin the lives of countless persons, the fate of this crucified being will represent a question rather than an 'answer': a question that is directed at my heartlessness in a world where God never ceases to endure the agony that is inflicted on his creatures.[47]

6

Tragedy and the soul's conquest of evil

In an interesting and important essay titled 'The Soul's Conquest of Evil',[1] Professor W. W. Bartley III argues that it is virtually impossible for a person to subdue his or her own evil will. Bartley claims that it is a *conditio sine qua non* of the human conquest of evil that a person possesses self-knowledge, but he is pessimistic about the human capacity to gain the self-knowledge needed to triumph over an evil will. Bartley quotes with approval the words of C. G. Jung:

> The individual who wishes to have an answer to the problem of evil, as it is posed today, has need, first and foremost, of self-knowledge, that is, the utmost possible knowledge of his own wholeness. He must know relentlessly how much good he can do, and what crimes he is capable of, and must beware of regarding the one as real and the other as illusion. Both are elements within his nature, and both are bound to come to light in him, should he wish – as he ought – to live without self-deception or self-delusion.[2]

It is Bartley's contention that the search for self-knowledge is a costly and perilous venture, undertaken successfully by only a few exceptional individuals. *Prima facie*, what Bartley and Jung say seems to be not without plausibility; most of us find it hard to be good precisely because we fail to acquire that clarity of vision which is so important if we are to struggle successfully to be moral beings. Nevertheless, Bartley's position cannot be accepted without substantial reservations, and in this essay I propose to examine his position more closely, and to show why I am inclined to reject his arguments.

It is, as we have already noted, an implication of Bartley's position that only a few exceptionally gifted individuals are capable of acting in a truly moral way. For which person, unless she be blessed in some extraordinary fashion, can honestly claim to live without self-deception or self-delusion? A person with the spiritual resources of a Jung *may* be able to live a life that is graced in this way; but such resources do not seem to be at the disposal of most ordinary human beings. Consequently, it would appear that it is not possible, on Bartley's account, for there to be such a person as the virtuous peasant, i.e. a human being who is virtuous without needing, or being able to reflect deeply on the mainsprings of her selfhood. And yet we know, as a simple fact of history, that the peasant can be virtuous – Franz Jägerstatter (to mention just one noteworthy example), who was beheaded by the Nazis in 1943 as an 'enemy of the state' for repeatedly refusing to serve in what he declared to be an 'unjust war', was an Austrian peasant.[3] Bartley, one cannot help thinking, is attaching too much importance to self-knowledge when he claims that it is the *sine qua non* of acting morally: complete self-knowledge is virtually impossible to attain, and besides, even if one can achieve it, it does not seem necessary for us to possess it in order to be virtuous. What Iris Murdoch has to say on the subject of self-knowledge in connection with morality is quite relevant to our argument:

> 'Self-knowledge', in the sense of a minute understanding of one's own machinery, seems to me, except at a fairly simply level, usually a delusion. A sense of such self-knowledge may of course be induced in analysis for therapeutic reasons, but the 'cure' does not prove the alleged knowledge genuine. Self is as hard to see justly as other things, and when clear vision has been achieved, self is a correspondingly smaller and less interesting object.[4]

My second reservation over Bartley's position is that although self-knowledge may arguably be a necessary condition for the soul's conquest of evil, it is more importantly sometimes a *sufficient* condition for the individual's conquest *by* the forces of evil. This is exactly what happens in certain forms of tragic experience. Typically, the tragic individual is a man or woman who, after a long and arduous struggle, manages to acquire a measure of self-knowledge, to live (perhaps!) without self-deception or self-delusion, but who then finds himself or herself the victim of a crushing external design which threatens the substance of his or her being.[5] The Oedipus story, in many ways the paradigm of tragic experience, is about just such a person. Oedipus confidently pursues self-knowledge, but when he achieves it, he finds that it is more than he can bear. The truth that it reveals about his world and his place in it cannot be endured, and so he blinds himself; he refuses to go on looking at what he cannot bear to perceive. An individual like Oedipus may now be more able to reckon fully the cost of her own past actions, and of the burdens unthinkingly cast upon her by the actions of kith and kin; she may now have a clearer vision of her purpose in life; but she may still find that life is intolerable – her greater insight into the forces of life that bear down upon her may afflict her all the more with a sense of life's futility and waste. The articulators of tragic experience – the great dramatists and novelists – show us that sometimes self-knowledge can come too late, or be acquired at too great a price, so that the tragic individual, far from being enabled to overcome evil, finds herself more than ever before the powerless victim of arbitrary forces that will destroy any moral advances she may have made. The tragic individual, despite her greater self-awareness and more highly developed moral consciousness, may find herself so constrained by these forces that she becomes affected by what Jeannette King calls the characteristic 'inability of the tragically aware individual to give form and expression to his consciousness in significant action'.[6]

All this is very plausible, but it may nevertheless be argued against us that the argument based on the fact of tragic experience is not really relevant – Oedipus, like everyone else, is a creature of his time and culture, in this case the product of an ancient Greek consciousness. However, this argument goes on to say, the 'hermeneutical gap' between this ancient Greek consciousness and our modern consciousness is simply too great to enable us to conceive what it is really like to be an Oedipus, i.e. a tragic protagonist. The tragedy of Oedipus is possible only because the ancient Greeks had a certain conception of heroism, of how a tragic individual should conduct himself or herself, and this conception is simply not *experientially* available to the person of today. (For this reason some writers, notably George Steiner, have argued that tragedy is 'dead'.) I do not propose to deal with the substance of this objection – that would take up too much time, and, moreover, it is not within the scope of this essay to deal with the problem of 'hermeneutical gaps' between cultures nor to decide whether tragedy is still an experientially significant art form. Instead we can bypass this objection by adverting to the fact that modern literature provides numerous examples of *modern* individuals who are tragically destroyed even though they have got to know themselves and have grown into moral maturity. The novels of Thomas Hardy, for instance, show us how sometimes the tragic protagonist, having at last acquired a costly self-knowledge, can destroy himself or herself and others in the very process of attempting to redeem the past.

Such tragic individuals may attempt, in perfectly good faith, and with a full consciousness of their motives, to repair the damage of their past actions, and be totally ruined in the process. Acts of atonement and expiation seem, in Hardy's tragic novels, to be utterly futile and insignificant in an apparently indifferent universe. In such a universe it appears, paradoxically, that the individuals who survive are just those persons who appear on the surface to be least equipped to cope with tragic realities. Knowledge, whether of self or others, is no guarantee of happiness or fulfilment or even salvation, as Clym Yeobright, the ill-fated would-be school teacher in Hardy's *The Return of the Native*, ruefully acknowledges: 'I, who was going to teach people the higher secrets of happiness, did not know how to keep out of that gross misery which the most untaught are wise enough to avoid.'[7] Clym's wife Eustacia dies, along with her illicit lover, Wildeve. Clym survives, he has gained a little in wisdom and humility, but his existence is so poisoned by his tragedy that he longs for death to release him from his suffering. Similarly, in *Tess of the d'Urbervilles*, Tess, as a result of the isolation and suffering which accompanied her seduction by Alec, slowly loses her self-delusions, and grows into a hard-won maturity. Her final tragedy is that this maturity is unavailing: her quest for a less troubled future which would enable her to surmount her past leads her to the slowly dawning certitude that her future is inextricably bound up with the past she is trying to overcome. She is driven to kill Alec, in the hope that this deed will expiate her past. As Jeannette King correctly remarks, 'it is a kind of suicide, aligning her with all the great tragic heroines prepared to die to save or avenge their honour.'[8] Tess's courage, resilience and self-awareness *cannot* prevail over her tragic predicament, and she is finally overwhelmed by what can only be regarded, artistically, as a modality of Fate. The tragic irony is that Tess would probably have survived if she had acquiesced in her fate instead of making a courageous but ultimately futile attempt to come to terms with it.

The thrust of the argument that we have been developing is not really diametrically opposed to Bartley's position – his claim that self-knowledge is a *necessary* condition of the soul's conquest of evil, and our contention that self-knowledge, in certain forms of tragic experience, is a *sufficient* condition of the soul's conquest *by* evil, do not really contradict each other: they would do so only if Bartley claimed that self-knowledge is a sufficient condition of the soul's conquest of evil, and this of course he does not do. If anything, the literary examples on which our argument is based effectively reinforce Bartley's pessimistic conclusion that the conquest of evil is an almost impossibly difficult undertaking. But there is an important difference between our respective positions. For Bartley, the difficulty in overcoming evil resides essentially in the sheer *psychological* complexity of the business of knowing ourselves:

> We can neither *act* morally nor evaluate with much competence the actions of other persons without an extraordinarily deep knowledge of ourselves and our surroundings. Without such deep understanding we discriminate only in the clumsiest way between good and bad consequence or between good and bad intention. An important reason for this is that we are much at the mercy of our projections – that is, in the psychological sense, those interior states which we impose on the external world in the course of interpreting it.[9]

Again, it seems difficult to disagree with what Bartley says in this passage. However, as we see it, the conquest of evil is difficult not only because we can at best only hope to be partly successful in the onerous task of getting to know ourselves, but also because the very possession of this obviously valuable self-knowledge can be instrumental in bringing about a human being's downfall, as tragic experience indicates. As we have noted, it is perhaps a paradox of tragic experience that disaster invariably bypasses the less self-aware individual, and that it is precisely the person with the greater insight into herself (and others) who tends to be the most afflicted: it is the person who plumbs the depths of herself who often finds herself engaging with a reality that can somehow reduce her to mute incomprehension. She may have gained some knowledge of herself, but life for her still remains 'that mysterious arrangement of merciless logic for a futile purpose. The most you can hope from it is some knowledge of yourself – that comes too late – a crop of inextinguishable regrets.'[10] Let us attempt now to see how it is that self-knowledge can be instrumental in bringing disaster upon the tragically aware individual. Conrad depicts this aspect of tragic experience with a deep understanding of the mainsprings of human character. If we follow the various insights to be gained from his novels, we may arrive at something approximating to the following viewpoint. The tragically aware person may find herself, often very reluctantly, brought up against the 'finality' of the several facets of her own character (the tragic personage invariably having a complex personality) and the character of other persons; indeed, she may have to endure the 'finality' of the external world. Perceiving this 'finality' – a sometimes fatal perception – can lead to

action or the failure to act in a crucial situation, and it is the
resultant action or failure to act which is instrumental in bringing
about the tragic individual's downfall. The individual who is less
self-aware, for this very reason rarely engages with the 'finality' of
persons and events: her disengagement from the 'finality' of the
things of life diminishes her capacity for tragic experience. We may
fail to engage with this 'finality' for many reasons: lack of awareness
(Bartley's reason); a certain rigidity of character; ill-health; moral
laziness; fear, etc., and Conrad is right when he perceives that it is
our drawing back from this 'finality' of things and persons which
'prevents so many heroisms and so many crimes'.[11] Bartley is
correct in saying that the acquisition of self-knowledge is an
arduous undertaking, but he seems to overlook the fact that having
embarked on this undertaking, and having gained some insight into
herself, the self-aware individual who seeks to conquer her evil will
is now, perhaps more than ever before, at the mercy of those tragic
forces which could destroy her life. There is a crucial sense in
which, *pace* Bartley, the individual's task of overcoming the evil in
her soul only begins *after* she has engaged with the elements of
'finality' both in herself and in the external world. Self-knowledge,
as the articulators of tragic experience point out, is often a merely
preparatory stage in an undertaking which reveals its truly difficult
nature only when the tragic individual has been brought to an
awareness of herself and of her surroundings which enables her to
appreciate what is happening or going to happen to her. This is
perhaps the reason why artistic representations of tragic experience
sometimes depict the blinding of the tragic protagonist: she cannot
bear to see any more of what her self-knowledge has revealed to
her. Thus Oedipus puts his eyes out when he perceives the true
nature of his relationship to his dead wife, and Clym Yeobright
suffers from failing eyesight at the end of *The Return of the Native*.
Of course the tragic victim's refusal to continue to look on the
realities revealed by her self-knowledge is always a refusal that is
laden with ambiguities, and we cannot therefore expect an absolutely compelling reason (or set of reasons) for the tragic protagonist's repudiation of her unbearable self-knowledge. Nevertheless,
the tragic individual's rejection of this self-knowledge suggests that
self-awareness cannot by itself lead to salvation: how can it, when
as a result of gaining this self-knowledge, she is now brought face to
face with a reality that will drive her inexorably towards her
destruction? The tragic heroine or victim (or heroine-as-victim) is
enabled to 'see' because of her self-knowledge; yes, but what she

perceives is – her self-destruction. Thus it is one of the terrible ironies of Sophocles' play that Oedipus gains his self-knowledge in order that the prophecy of Teiresias – 'He that came seeing, blind shall he go' – may be fulfilled. Oedipus, like Tess, struggles towards a moral and spiritual maturity, but the self-knowledge he gains so constrains him (as it does Tess) that his self-blinding becomes for him (as her murder of Alec does Tess) a final act of freedom, an almost despairing assertion of the tragic individual's ability to act in the face of the paralyzing external design which threatens to overwhelm her (or him). Such acts are intended to impose a last vestige of coherence on what, for the tragic individual, is in danger of becoming an irretrievably futile and senseless life. It is some-times easy for the onlooker to be mistaken about the 'inner logic' of the apparently senseless acts that occur in the denouement of tragic events – we tend to think that these events have somehow unhinged the mind of the tragic individual, and that such seemingly pointless and often excessively violent deeds are committed 'while the balance of *X's* mind has been disturbed' (to mention the standard legal formula that is used in such cases). There are doubtless a great many cases where the tragic individual's mind is unhinged by her experiences, but it may be that some such apparently senseless acts are meant, by some tortured and involuted logic, to render coher-ent a life that seems condemned to be futile and meaningless. (If anything, such apparently senseless acts are committed by the tragic individual with the somewhat paradoxical intention of restor-ing or *retaining* her balance of mind.) The intentionality for such apparently senseless acts is supplied by the individual's life *as a whole*, and not by the feeling of remorse or regret for *particular* baneful actions done in the past – tragic individuals usually regret not so much their hurtful actions in the past, but the fact that they have ever been born. They regret the sheer 'facticity' of their lives (to use a notion of Heidegger's). For the tragic personage the very fact of life itself is her sin, and it follows, therefore, that death is the only appropriate end for the tragic heroine – only death can be the expiation of her sin. If our arguments are correct, Bartley (it would seem) has been a little too simplistic in his understanding of the connection between self-knowledge and the soul's conquest of evil: he seems to overlook the tragic dimension of human experience, which indicates that self-knowledge, far from enabling the tragic protagonist to master her evil will, is often the very instrument of her downfall. The tragic personage is destroyed because she is *already* in possession of an unbearable self-awareness, and not

because she cannot acquire the self-knowledge that is needed for
the soul's conquest of evil. Bartley's position founders on the fact of
tragedy. That his position founders on the fact of tragedy is perhaps
indicative of a deeper weakness in Bartley's conception of morality.
This brings me to my third reservation concerning Bartley's position. A great deal of what follows is speculation, because Bartley
does not provide a fully developed theory of morality in his writings
on the subject.

The fact that Bartley is prepared to attach so much importance to
the possession of self-knowledge (as the *sine qua non* of being
virtuous or acting rightly) suggests (though it does not entail) that
he understands morality as involving, primarily, the making of
decisions and the moral assessment of the intentions and actions of
others. Morality, understood in this way, is a sort of decision-
procedure, which becomes the possession of the man or woman
with self-knowledge (who can perhaps be likened to the scientist
with the biggest and best computer who is thereby able to 'know'
things that other less fortunate scientists cannot 'know'). This
conception of morality is somewhat naive – there are no plausible
grounds for believing that there is any kind of decision-procedure
which the self-aware individual possesses, and which will enable
her to work out, in any given situation, what she should do or what
appraisals she should make. In morality there are no 'magical
formulae', and if the 'magician' happens to be a decent human
being, virtue can never be one of her arts. The universe is a morally
complex, even 'untidy' place: moral dilemmas, perplexities and
predicaments are not uncommon. A person needs more, much
more, than self-knowledge if she is to thread her way through such
a universe. Any theory of morality which acknowledges that evil
manifests itself *in concreto* in the acts of human beings will seek to
come to terms with the radical contingency and the particularity of
human evil. Self-knowledge may (and in most cases it probably
will) be an asset to the moral agent, but then it may not. It all
depends on the 'reality' which confronts the moral agent. This is
not an argument in favour of moral relativism; it only betokens an
austerely 'realist' conception of morality (which we shall sketch
shortly).

I have already indicated that the only conception of morality
which is adequate to the 'fact' of tragedy is an austerely 'realist'
theory. A 'realist' conception of moral judgement will hold that
such judgements are descriptive and assertorial, so that they
involve claims that can be regarded as, and *known* to be, true or

false. Moral judgements are 'factually cognitive', and changes in values are accompanied by changes in *'factual'* appreciation; it follows from this that a moral judgement and its negation are incompatible – they cannot both be true. In short, the truth of a moral judgement is determined by the extra-linguistic, mind-independent 'reality' which we call the 'real' world. However, because the recognitional capacities of finite beings are correspondingly limited, there can be moral truths which we do not recognize for what they are – viz., the (moral) truth. Hence, when a person undergoes *metanoia*, repents, experiences a moral or spiritual conversion, she comes to perceive a truth that hitherto she had failed to recognize. In a complex and morally 'untidy' universe it is possible for our recognitional capacities to be overwhelmed by the sheer complexity of the moral universe. This is precisely what happens in tragic experience – the tragic personage, for all her moral and spiritual maturity, can be destroyed by an external design supplied by this universe. Action, particularly moral action, in such a complex universe is always fraught with ambiguity and the possibility of failure – the moral individual is a finite being who is trying to grapple, in ways which exceed her unaided practical capacities, with a recalcitrant world. There is more to the world than the finite being can accommodate: the human being and the world are not entirely suited; we live and act in a world that we have not created (as Heidegger points out).[12] This theory of 'moral realism' is, in effect, a much abbreviated 'secular' restatement of the doctrine of original sin. For if the human being and the world are not entirely reciprocally suited, and if moral failure can be said to arise from this fundamental discrepancy between us and our world, then there is a sense in which evil (moral failure) *preexists* the deeds of evil men and women. Bartley is right to be pessimistic about the soul's inability to conquer evil. But he is wrong in thinking that this inability stems from our failure to know ourselves – a person can know herself and still be destroyed, she can know herself and there can nevertheless be *more* evil (albeit a tragic evil) in the world. Bartley cannot accommodate the fact of tragic evil because his position is essentially 'Pelagian' – this is evident from the following passage in which Bartley briefly describes the sort of person who is to be accounted virtuous (on the basis of the conception of morality which he sponsors):

> [The] Cambridge and Bloomsbury Group . . . were preoccupied with the development of the interior life at the same time that they were able to deal shrewdly with the outer world. . . . They were capable of

enormous evil, and – knowing it – did considerable good.... Yet perhaps the self-conquest that at least a few of them attained – and which some weaker men mistook for weakness – lay in the kindness and gentleness of which they were capable, that which one finds perhaps best expressed in the novels of Forster.[13]

The good sort of 'man', then, is the Bloomsbury man, the virtuous man as portrayed in the novels of E. M. Forster. I do not wish to deny that there were good men and women in the Bloomsbury group, nor do I wish to quarrel with Forster's portrayal of the good 'man' in his novels. I am more inclined to the view that the members of the Bloomsbury group were neither very good nor very bad: they occupied a privileged position in their society, and this afforded them the money and the leisure needed to cultivate a certain style of life which was neither terribly good nor terribly evil. In general the members of this group believed in the perfectibility of the human individual (but not necessarily that of the human race); they had no sense of 'original sin'. Their way of life, their profoundest moral convictions, were probably never really put to the test: G. E. Moore and Bertrand Russell, for example, seemed never to have a sense of the 'moral schism' that runs through the universe; the profound moral anguish that afflicted their Cambridge colleague Wittgenstein was totally alien to them. I am not claiming that a feeling of *Angst* is essential if we are to have genuine moral convictions (this would be patently absurd); rather, my contention is that our moral convictions must always be accompanied by the realization that evil has an intractably tragic quality, a quality which makes the good person only a 'poor sort of good person'. Thus Wittgenstein seemed to possess this moral poverty, but not Russell and Moore. I am inclined to think that they lacked moral poverty because they had an essentially simplistic conception of moral virtue: Moore, for example, believed that there are only *two* questions with which ethics should legitimately be concerned, namely, 'Has it (i.e. the ethical 'object') intrinsic value?' and 'Is it a means to the best possible?'.[14] But what things possess 'intrinsic value'? Moore's answer, which must seem extraordinarily quaint to a society marked by the realities of Auschwitz and Hiroshima, is: 'By far the most valuable things, which we know or can imagine, are certain states of consciousness which may roughly be described as the pleasures of human intercourse and the enjoyment of beautiful objects.'[15] It would be fatuous to assert that *all* the members of the Bloomsbury group were as naive as Moore (Keynes, for instance, was more worldly-wise), but we cannot ignore the fact that Moore's *Principia Ethica* (and *ipso facto* the morality of the Bloomsbury group) has been bypassed by the 'real' world – after Auschwitz our moral consciences do not easily permit us to discern 'intrinsic value' in pleasant conversation and in the contemplation of beautiful things. And yet Bartley enjoins us to regard the members of the Bloomsbury group as the exemplars of the soul's conquest of evil; theirs is the example we should follow!

I have argued that a radically different conception of the nature of human evil is needed before we can account for the fact of tragic evil. The soul *cannot* conquer tragic evil. On the contrary, tragedy is often responsible for the soul's conquest by evil. The soul cannot conquer tragic evil because tragic evil (and very likely all the more intractable forms of evil as well) preexists human evil. This evil preexists the individual's (evil) deeds because she lives and acts in a world that she has not created. For the person who is both a moral 'realist' and a 'theist' the final implication of this argument is obvious: if such evil is to be overcome, it can only be overcome by the creator of the world. Bartley, then is right to be pessimistic about our ability to overcome our evil wills. But if my arguments are correct, he is right for the wrong reasons.[16]

7

Atonement and moral apocalypticism: William Styron's Sophie's Choice

I Introductory

In this essay I shall be discussing William Styron's depiction of a theologically significant incident in his novel *Sophie's Choice* (London: Corgi Books, 1979). Since our discussion will approach the novel from a theological as opposed to a purely 'literary' standpoint, it behoves us to begin by specifying the theological context of the argument we hope to develop in this essay. This essay is concerned with that area of theological reflection which traditionally goes under the rubric of the doctrine of the atonement. More specifically: we shall argue that Styron's narration of the episode which gives his book its title provides a basis for a criticism of all purely 'subjective' interpretations of the atonement. The adherent of a purely 'subjective' conception of the atonement emphasizes the manner in which the believer makes the work of Christ her own – the saving significance of Christ's work is reckoned by the 'subjectivist' to lie in the ways in which individuals *appropriate* that work. That is to say, Christ's saving work takes the form of a 'subjective' process; it is, in the words of Donald Baillie (a notable modern proponent of the 'subjective' conception), a 'reconciling of us to God through a persuasion in our hearts that is ... a realizing of his eternal love'.[1]

'Subjective' understandings of the atonement have come to prevail in recent years. This is mainly because 'objective' conceptions are invariably bound up with 'incarnational' christologies, and 'incarnational' christologies no longer totally dominate the theological consensus. Instead, so-called 'functional' christologies tend increasingly to be in vogue, and since an 'objective' understanding of the atonement accords better with a fully 'incarnational' (or 'ontological') christology, there has been a recognizable drift away from 'objective' conceptions of the atonement.[2] My purpose in this essay, however, will be to show, via an examination of this aspect of Styron's novel, that those theologians who seek to eschew an 'objective' interpretation of the atonement in favour of a 'subjective' one only succeed in entering a whole minefield of problems: 'subjective' conceptions are so inherently problematic that our only real hope for an adequate Christian soteriology seems to lie in the direction of an 'objective' doctrine of the atonement. I am well aware that all this has been put rather too tidily, and it should be emphasized that I am trying to capture a 'drift' or 'tone', rather than to engage in substantive theological formulation.

II The case of Dr von Niemand and the Christian understanding of sin

Styron's novel, *Sophie's Choice*, contains an account of a man who sought to reconcile himself to God – by bringing himself to commit a most evil deed. Sophie Zawistowska, the 'heroine' of the novel, was arrested in Poland during the Second World War, and has been deported to Auschwitz, along with her children Jan and Eva. Arriving at Auschwitz railway station they are faced with the dreaded 'selection' procedure, some to be consigned immediately to the gas chambers, others to slavery. The 'selection' is conducted by an *SS* doctor, Jemand von Niemand:

> '*Du bist eine Polack*', said the doctor. '*Bist du auch eine Kommunisten?*'.... [instead] of keeping her mouth shut she said, '*Ich bin Polnisch! In Krakow geboren!*' Then she blurted helplessly, 'I'm not Jewish! Or my children – they're not Jewish either'. And added, 'They are racially pure. They speak German.' Finally she announced, 'I'm a Christian. I'm a devout Catholic.'
> ... she heard Dr von Niemand say, 'So you're not a Communist. You're a believer.' '*Ja, mein Hauptmann.* I believe in Christ'.... 'So you believe in Christ the Redeemer?', the doctor said. ... 'did he not say, "Suffer the little children to come unto me"?' He turned back to her, with the twitchy methodicalness of a drunk.
> Sophie ... was about to attempt a reply when the doctor said, 'You may keep one of your children.'
> '*Bitte!*' said Sophie.
> 'You may keep one of your children', he repeated. 'The other one will have to go. Which one will you keep?'
> ... Her thought processes dwindled, ceased. Then she felt her legs crumple. 'I can't choose! I can't choose!' She began to scream...
> The doctor was aware of unwanted attention. 'Shut up!' he

ordered. 'Hurry now and choose. Choose, god dammit, or I'll send them both over there. Quick!'

'Don't make me choose', she heard herself plead in a whisper, 'I can't choose.'

'Send them both over there, then', the doctor said to the aide, '*nach links*'.

'Mama!' She heard Eva's . . . cry at the instant that she thrust the child away from her and rose from the concrete with a clumsy stumbling motion. 'Take the baby!' she called out, 'Take my little girl!'

At this point the aide – with a careful gentleness that Sophie would try without success to forget – tugged at Eva's hand and led her away into the waiting legion of the damned. She would forever retain a dim impression that the child had continued to look, beseeching.

(pp. 641–3)

This, then, is Sophie's 'choice'. Words are totally inadequate to the task of representing to us the truth of the unspeakable darkness and shame of von Niemand's deed. The nature of this deed is such that it begs us to affirm the hard words of Professor Ulrich Simon (whose father perished in Auschwitz): 'I do not myself believe that there can be forgiveness for Auschwitz. . . . Not only the monstrosity, but also the impersonal "nothingness" of the evil render this remission immoral and impossible.'[3] Any attempt rationally to comprehend the enormity of what went on in Auschwitz is bound to be futile – as George Steiner points out, the world of the extermination camps is a world that is 'extraterritorial to reason'.[4] The opacity to reason which characterizes the deeds of those who ran these camps precludes the possibility of making a straightforward moral evaluation of individuals like Dr von Niemand. The great merit of Styron's book is that he does not attempt a moral appraisal of von Niemand: Styron seems implicitly to be aware that we do not possess a vocabulary that is capable of plumbing the depths of such barbarism. Instead, Styron provides a penetrating analysis of the motives that Dr von Niemand may have had for forcing this gruesome choice on Sophie:

> And what, in the private misery of his heart, I think he most intensely lusted to do was to inflict upon Sophie, or someone like her – some tender and perishable Christian – a totally unpardonable sin. It is precisely because he had yearned with such pain to commit this terrible sin that I believe that the doctor was exceptional, perhaps unique, among his fellow automata: if he was not a good man, *he still retained a potential capacity for goodness, as well as evil, and his strivings were essentially religious.*

(pp. 643–3. Italics added)

Later Sophie found out from one of the other inmates of the camp, who knew the doctor from her youth in Berlin, that Dr von Niemand was 'a steadfast churchgoer and that he had always planned to enter the ministry. A mercenary father forced him into medicine' (p. 644). Styron then goes on to say: 'I have always assumed that when he encountered Sophie, Dr von Niemand was undergoing the crisis of his life: cracking apart like bamboo, disintegrating at the very moment that he was reaching out for spiritual salvation' (p. 646). The doctor's crisis had been precipi- tated by the nature of the terrible work he had to do in the 'selections'. He 'began to drink, to acquire sloppy eating habits, even to miss God. *Wo, wo ist der lebende Gott?* Where is the God of my fathers?' (*ibid.*). The doctor found the answer on the day he encountered Sophie and her children:

> the revelation made him radiant with hope. It had to do with the matter of sin, or rather, it had to do with the absence of sin, and his own realization that the absence of sin and the absence of God were inseparably intertwined. No sin! He had suffered boredom and anxiety, even revulsion, but no sense of sin from the bestial crimes he had been party to, nor had he felt that in sending thousands of the wretched innocent to oblivion he had transgressed against divine law. All of his depravity had been enacted in a vacuum of sin and business-like godlessness, while his soul thirsted for beatitude.
>
> (*ibid.*)

Dr von Niemand, then, had to find a way of restoring his faith in God. To do this he found that it was necessary to ' ... affirm his capacity for evil, by committing the most intolerable sin that he was able to conceive.... Goodness could come later. But first a great sin. One whose glory lay in its subtle magnanimity – a choice' (pp. 646–7).

Styron's novel is a remarkable study in the psychology of morals. The perceptive and remarkable characterization of Dr von Niemand, showing as it does a man who has to regain his sense of being a sinner as a precondition of *experiencing* a reconciliation with God, has important implications not only for the doctrine of the atonement, but also for the Christian understanding of sin. It has long been normative in the Christian tradition to characterize sin in terms of our refusal to accept a divine 'bestowal' of grace or as a rupture in the relationship between God and human beings that is of our own doing. Thus, in a notable contemporary treatise on sin, it is asserted that:

> Grace is proffered in some way to each man, since God wishes all men
> to be saved. At any rate, each man is assumed in the order of grace
> and destined to a supernatural end. That is why, in our world, sin
> always possesses a supernatural character; even when, on account of
> its content, sin might be called natural, it remains supernatural,
> inasmuch as *it is a negative answer to a supernatural bestowal of grace.*[5]

Without seeking to impugn his claim that sin has a 'supernatural'
dimension, we have (I think) no alternative but to regard as too
simplistic Schoonenberg's understanding of sin as 'a negative
answer to a supernatural bestowal of grace'. In the case of Jemand
von Niemand we have (*pace* Schoonenberg) a person who sins not
so much because he gives 'a negative answer to a supernatural
bestowal of grace', but because he believes that the very *experience*
of such a negative answer is a necessary prerequisite of being
redeemed by God. The SS doctor craves God's proffer of grace, but
at the same time he believes that he can justify the receipt of this
grace only if he first descends to the depths of human sinfulness.
Schoonenberg's characterization of sin, it seems, overlooks the
possibility that someone like von Niemand might actually regard
sin as the essential precondition of the bestowal of divine grace. A
penetrating literary treatment of human wrong-doing like *Sophie's
Choice* serves as a reminder to philosophers and theologians that
we have to acknowledge the heterogeneity of human motivation if
we are to formulate an adequate conception of sin and sinfulness.

The theologian writing on the subject of sin and human evil
cannot really afford to ignore the writings of the great dramatists
and novelists – the works of a Sophocles or a Dostoyevsky may be
able to teach us more about this subject than many a scholarly
treatise. If the theologian fails to do justice to the complexity and
particularity of human motivation, then his or her characterization
of sin and human sinfulness will fail to show us the truth of what we
are, both as we are in ourselves, and as we are in relation to others
and to God.

Sophie's Choice, however, is more than just a reminder to
theologians that it is possible for the 'experience' of sin and the
hope for the 'experience' of salvation to go together very
closely; close enough, in the case of Dr von Niemand, for them
to be inextricably bound up with each other. For Styron's depiction of von Niemand's horrific quest for atonement is of crucial
significance for our interpretation of the salvation wrought by
God in and through the life, death and resurrection of Jesus
Christ.

III 'Moral apocalypticism' and atonement

A purely 'subjective' conception of the atonement can never be really adequate to the *awfulness* of the evil perpetrated by the von Niemands of this world. The tormentor of Sophie Zawistowska is a man who, in a way that is all too human, seeks the *experience* of redemption by first expending his capacity for evil. As long as we subscribe to a merely 'subjective' doctrine of the atonement, i.e. a conception which lays stress on *the individual's personally distinctive way of appropriating the work of Christ,* then we will have to concede the possibility that some individuals will appropriate this saving work in perverse and even cruel ways. Such individuals may do the most terrible things simply in order to undergo some form of catharsis, or inner purgation, which (they hope) will free them once and for all for the experience of forgiveness. They seek the moral apocalypse that will cleanse their souls.

Our task in this essay will be to ask what, from a theological standpoint, can be said about this moral apocalypticism, which leads its exponents to believe that human beings can attain their salvation precisely by succumbing to the depraved impulses which lurk in the depths of their souls. Our answer to this question will not take the form of an attempt to articulate a sustained perception: this is not possible, because we possess no more than a few glimpses, from several different angles, of the belief and practice of the moral apocalypticist. Rather, the force of our argument will be cumulative, in that it is hoped that each succeeding vision will contribute to an overall conception of the 'essence' of moral apocalypticism.

Firstly, the moral apocalypticist conceives of salvation in essentially *individual* terms: he is concerned, above all, with the conquest of evil in his own soul. In so doing, he goes against one of the fundamental tenets of the gospel message, namely, that our salvation consists in the creation of a universal community of saints, that deliverance from the power of evil can only be achieved in solidarity with our fellow human beings. To quote from the following summary of evidence in the New Testament, provided by Edward Schillebeeckx in the second volume of his magisterial work on christology:

> at the heart of the New Testament lies the recognition that we are redeemed for brotherly love. . . . [To] quote three passages: 'We have passed from death to life because we love the brethren' (1 John 3:14); 'that we should believe in his son Jesus Christ and love one another' (1

John 3:23); 'he who says he abides in him ought to walk in the same way in which he walked' (1 John 2:6). Redemption is freedom for self-surrender in love for fellowmen; that is abiding in God.... [L]ove of one's neighbour is the public manifestation of the state of being redeemed.[6]

Von Niemand, whose understanding of the saving work of Christ implicitly relegates the saving work of Christ to an essentially private sphere, is unable to appreciate that love for our fellowmen and fellowwomen is the inescapable concomitant of Christian salvation. Lacking this appreciation, he imposes a tragic choice on Sophie in the vain hope that this tragedy will somehow give him the key to his own salvation. What he fails to see is that Sophie's tragedy is *his* tragedy; that in failing to acknowledge the humanity of his innocent victims he abrogates his own humanity; that in dealing out death to them he is signalling the death of his own capacity to love. He is blind to the truth, which lies at the heart of the Christian faith, that the death of our own capacity to love is death *simpliciter*.[7] If von Niemand had instead realized that Christ's saving work frees us to love our own brothers and sisters, he would not have been inclined to seek his salvation in a cataclysmic experience produced by a wilful descent into the mire of human viciousness and savagery.

Secondly, the moral apocalypticist seems to assume (even if only unconsciously) that he must undergo experiences of a certain type as a precondition of being delivered from evil. He believes – implicitly or explicitly – that he needs to have *experiences* of a specific kind in order to undergo the salvific process. He thinks that he must subject himself to these experiences as part of a cathartic process associated with the possession of salvation. The crux of the moral apocalypticist's position is that he believes that salvation is something to be grasped, it is something that can be possessed *if only* he can find 'the precious metal that lies in the dirt'. Salvation, in the moral apocalypticist's view, is essentially something that can be striven for, something that human beings can quest for in the way that they look for gold or oil. This grasping after salvation is a consequence of a deeper failure on the part of the moral apocalypticist: namely, his refusal or his inability to commit the future into the hands of God. He fails to recognize that it is the prerogative of God, and God alone, to determine our way to salvation. Instead, the moral apocalypticist tries to usurp this divine prerogative by forcing a crisis – in a place and at a time of his *own* choosing – in which the issue of salvation can be totally and finally resolved. In this respect he is like Marlowe's Doctor Faustus, who seeks 'to practise more than heavenly power permits'.[8] The moral apocalypticist is not unqualifiedly Faustian, however: Faustus forms a pact with the Devil in order that he might become like God, whereas the moral apocalypticist has no real desire to become like God – on the contrary, he casts his lot with the Devil in the hope that God will fight the Devil for possession of his soul. But Dr von Niemand is nonetheless like Faustus in that he is 'a man who tried to do what only God can do, a man who refused to leave to God what ought to be left to him'.[9] The Faustian character, according to D. Z. Phillips, lacks the religious virtue of patience. He cannot wait on God. He fails to perceive that God's way for us may not coincide with the way that we choose for ourselves. The von Niemands of this world are impatient to the point of wanting the question of salvation to be resolved in an instant, of wanting to bypass the ordinary but still arduous routes that an individual might have to traverse in order to meet his or her salvation. In his impatience the moral apocalypticist tries to make salvation a matter of policy or strategy. Why does the moral apocalypticist lack the religious virtue of patience? The most likely answer here, it seems, is that he fails to commit his future into the hands of God because he cannot accept that deliverance from the power of evil is a free and undeserved gift from God. Moral apocalypticism is contrary to the central tenets of the Christian faith, in that Christianity sees faith as a gratuitous gift from God, and not as something that a human being can mechanically attain for himself by having experiences of a certain sort. As Ernst Käsemann vividly puts it, for Christians: 'faith is a door to salvation history which has not been pushed open by them but wonderfully open to them'.[10] A human being does not have to expend the capacity for sin within himself before he can be redeemed. The view that sin is a capacity that has to be expended before salvation can be attained rests on the mistaken assumption that sin is something quantifiable, something which can be spent. It overlooks the truth, fundamental to soteriology, that though sin manifests itself in exterior actions, it is essentially a *power*, a power which can only be overcome through the sovereign grace of God. Some men and women *may* have to experience the devastating forces within themselves before they are brought to the point of acknowledging their need for deliverance, but then others may not. There is no sanction, either in the gospel message or the ecclesiastical tradition, for the absolute prescription: 'to be saved, first plunge yourself into the abyss of sin'.

Thirdly, and this point is bound up with the notion of sin as an expendable capacity, the moral apocalypticist appears to have a legalistic conception of God's way of dealing with the world. Thus, for example, Dr von Niemand believes that he must transgress against divine law prior to experiencing the need for divine forgiveness. 'Only the sick need a physician', he seems to say, 'let me transgress so that I may need the divine physician.' The 'essence' of this position is that the sinner has first to plunge into the morass before God will deign to extricate him or her. At this juncture the moral apocalypticist may wish to advert to certain strands of Pauline theology as a way of securing the theological foundations of his apocalypticism. In particular, he may draw our attention to the following verse from Paul's *Epistle to the Romans*: 'Law came in to increase the trespass; but where sin increased, grace abounded all the more' (5:20). W. G. Kümmel has given this verse the following explication:

> [The] law is also counted among those powers which hold man in the world and try to hinder his turning to God. . . . Paul dares not only to describe this state of affairs . . . but to trace it to God's will, because he can understand all events ultimately as arising from God's saving intention and as in harmony with his plan of salvation. . . . Thus, in accordance with God's will, it is only by means of the law that man actually becomes a transgressor and thus guilty, 'that every mouth may be stopped and the whole world guilty before God' (Romans 3:19). But therewith also is created the pre-condition for the intervention of divine grace: 'where sin abounded, grace was more abundant. . . .'
>
> (Romans 5:20)[11]

According to Paul, therefore, it is part of God's plan of salvation to have more transgression in order that there can be more grace. But, and herein lies the rub, is it not possible to say that exactly the same 'Pauline' principle can be discerned in von Niemand's decision to transgress so that he might become the recipient of God's mercy and forgiveness? It would not of course be possible for von Niemand (or anybody else, for that matter) to advance this as some sort of theological justification for his cruel deed. But is it not somehow still the case that the von Niemands of this world lend substance to Paul's affirmation that 'where sin increased, grace abounded all the more'? Simply attempting to answer this question will involve us in the complexities of Pauline exegesis, in problems surrounding the legalistic and juridical conceptual framework used by Paul to articulate his soteriology, and perhaps even in the question of theodicy. I have talked about von Niemand's deed in the context of Paul's affirmation in Romans 5:20 simply to bring to mind the haunting possibility that, perhaps unbeknownst even to himself, even Dr von Niemand, the thwarted would-be minister of Christ, may in fact have clung to a view of salvation that possessed a somewhat 'Pauline' resonance.

But we need not entertain this possibility for too long. For if we did impute to von Niemand a notion of divine salvation that was roughly consonant with Paul's, then we (and Dr von Niemand – if he did in fact possess this notion) would have failed to grasp an essential feature of Paul's conception of God's salvific 'plan' for humankind, namely, the *eschatological* perspective from which Paul talks of this 'plan'. As Rudolf Bultmann makes clear, Paul articulates his soteriology from the standpoint of ' . . . the decisive eschatological event in which the time of salvation, the acceptable time (2 Cor 6:1) has dawned. . . . '[12] And precisely because (for Paul) this eschatological event has dawned, Bultmann continues, 'grace may be spoken of [by Paul] as a personified power which works against the power of sin and takes over its lost command: "but where sin increased, grace abounded all the more, so that, as sin (had) reigned in death, grace also might reign through righteousness to eternal life through Jesus Christ our Lord" (Romans 5:20f)'.[13] In *Sophie's Choice* Styron shows von Niemand to have in mind, even if only unconsciously, some sort of divine salvific plan. The plan which von Niemand entertains is, however, totally lacking in any kind of eschatological perspective, and cannot therefore be likened to Paul's salvation-scheme. For if von Niemand's salvation-scheme had possessed a properly 'Pauline' eschatological perspective, then the *SS* doctor would surely have realized that the time of salvation has indeed dawned in the life, teaching and fate of Jesus of Nazareth, and that he would not therefore need to embark on his quest for a moral apocalypse.

There is another reason why we should not impute to the moral apocalypticist a salvation-scheme that accords with Paul's own understanding of God's 'plan' for human salvation. In Paul's scheme of things, it is *God* who 'uses' evil to make real the love of Christ, whereas in Styron's story it is a *man* (i.e. von Niemand) who, in a vain attempt to bring the love of Christ into his own life, so uses evil. Consequently, any endeavour to ground the moral apocalypticist's salvation-scheme in Paul's soteriology is bound to end in failure – someone like von Niemand may be able to cobble together fragmentary insights from Paul, but the guiding principle of the apostle's soteriology (viz. that God, and God alone, is the architect of our salvation is totally absent from the moral apocalypticist's understanding of the mystery of divine salvation. This, however, is only to be expected: the moral apocalypticist, we have argued, is an implicitly Faustian character, and thus he will not let God be God. In a moment I shall return to the moral apocalypticist's failure to incorporate an eschatological perspective in his reflection on God's saving act on the cross. For the time being I want to make the point that the moral apocalypticist's belief that he can acquire his 'entitlement' to divine forgiveness is against the essential spirit of the Christian faith. According to this faith, the vicious circle of disordered passion and self-deception (i.e. sin) cannot be broken in this legalistic way – divine grace is not manifested in legal conditions, rather it introduces human creatures into an altogether new order, an order of love, where legal conditions do not obtain. This of course is an essentially Pauline view, and it is reflected in the following passage from John Oman's classic work, *Grace and Personality*:

> We are justified because by faith we enter the world of a gracious God, out of which the old hard legal argument, with the old hard boundaries of our personality and self-regarding claim of rights, have disappeared, a world which is the household of our Father where order and power and ultimate reality are of love and not of law.
>
> In that world atonement ... is a new world with new and healing moral conditions, where legal ideas of meeting God's judgement fall away from us.[14]

The tragedy of Sophie and her innocent child is that in Auschwitz they met a man with just such 'legal ideas of meeting God's judgement'.

Fourthly, and this a point to which we have already made some reference, the moral apocalypticist has a view of divine reality and salvation that lacks an eschatological dimension. Thus, in *Sophie's Choice*, we are told that von Niemand's realization that 'the absence of sin and the absence of God were inescapably intertwined' came to him as a 'revelation that made him radiant with hope'.[15] The *SS* doctor, it seems, had arrived at the conclusion that he was in a position to *understand* divine mercy and salvation. But what he had discovered was nothing more than a form of 'knowledge', a gnosis – albeit a 'knowledge' sufficient to enable him to try to force the hand of God by tormenting Sophie. In theological terms, what the moral apocalypticist does is to displace the mysterious God who is to come for the God who is; he allows *knowledge* of the God who is to supplant *hope* in the God who is to come. Hope, or what Paul Ricoeur calls the 'passion for the possible', is open to the radically new, and the person who has this hope will not succumb to the moral apocalypticist's essentially manipulative outlook on salvation history. Such an outlook, which seeks to force salvation history to a culminating-point in the here-and-now, is alien to the individual possessed of real hope: the man or woman who has this hope will be able to trust in the future of God without averting his or her gaze from the reality of the present. The moral apocalypticist is perhaps someone who needs to make a sustained study of Christ's temptation in the desert. In the climax of Christ's ordeal in the wilderness he is challenged by Satan to hurl himself from the pinnacle of the temple – in the words of Donald MacKinnon, Christ is asked 'to put the question of his status to the test, to yield to a fundamental impatience, the end either total victory or nothingness'.[16] Christ was able to resist the lure of this primal impatience because he had yielded his destiny to the God of the future. The patience that issues in the enunciation of the words, 'Thy will be done', is a costly patience; and the cost may not be restricted to the forfeiture of victory – it may even involve the surrender of one's own life (as indeed was the case with Christ). From such patience is born real hope, the radical hope which is often a 'hope against hope' and which enables us stammeringly to affirm that evil will not have the last word in human history because God has given us the victory in and through his Son Jesus Christ. The sad truth of the matter, of course, is that von Niemand is in a position where it is simply not possible to have hope – the very nature of his job as one of Hitler's 'angels of death' precludes the possibility of having such hope. It was one of the profound ironies of concentration camp life, an irony attested to over and over again in the remarkable accounts provided by the survivors of these camps, that invariably the only people with hope in places like Auschwitz were the inmates: the administrators and guards, finding themselves in circumstances where their most depraved instincts could be given untrammelled expression, led loveless lives in which hope simply could not function as a significant category of experience. Hope is a modality of love, and where there is no love there can be no hope. And where there is no hope there can be no faith in the God of the future; and where there is no faith in the God of the future there can be no surrendering of our own future into the hands of God, no trust in the mystery of God. This is perhaps why von Niemand snatched so desperately at the chance to engineer his own salvation. His faith – for he *is* a religious man – lacks an eschatological dimension, and hence resides in the 'already' of the God who is instead of the 'not yet' of the God who is to come. Without an understanding of the God of the future, the God of the Resurrection, the God who brings about the death of death, the reality of the present becomes the only available horizon for human thought and action. And since the reality of the present, as experienced in a place like Auschwitz, is a reality characterized by death and dominated by the power of evil, the human attempt to secure one's salvation within the horizon of the present is doomed to failure – salvation will come only when the God of the future transforms the reality of the present by defeating death and depriving evil of its power. Without the God of the future there can be no genuinely Christian transformation of 'the terror of history' (to use a phrase of Mircea Eliade's). Only this God, by virtue of the deed accomplished on the cross of Christ, can bring about our *irreversible* deliverance from the power of evil.[17]

Fifthly, because the moral apocalypticist lacks an eschatological faith, he cannot possess a faith beyond all assurance and protection. The *SS* doctor is in the classic position of all failed believers – he cannot understand the silence of God. In the face of God's continuing silence, von Niemand can only lament: 'Where is the God of my fathers?' (p. 646). He finds the sense of abandonment generated by the absence of God too much to endure, and the harrowing choice he forces on Sophie is a manifestation of this inability to live without the reassuring and consoling presence of the God of his fathers. Von Niemand hears the scream in the night, the intermittent buzz and sizzle of the electrified fence in the distance as yet another broken victim casts herself against it in search of oblivion; he sees and smells the smoke that rises from the chimneys of the crematoria: all these speak to him with the most shattering eloquence, but God, the God of his fathers, is silent. In Auschwitz the natural and the divine economy are being over-turned, and the religious man, von Niemand, is a despairing participant in the process. Von Niemand comes to share the rueful insight reflected in these words of Goethe's Faust:

> I come at last to recognize my measure,
> And know the sterile desert in my breast.[18]

Confronted by the external hell of camp life and the internal hell of 'the sterile desert' in his breast, von Niemand finds that he cannot wait on God. In his impatience, he chooses the easier legalistic alternative of committing a ghastly crime so that God will *speak* in judgement against him, and in the hope that out of this judgement will flow the waters of grace. The mystery of God is reduced by him to the moralizing role of judge; for von Niemand there is no God of Job, no God who speaks 'out of the whirlwind'. Instead of turning hope (real hope) to this God, the God who is heard through the categories of the concealed, the unexplained and the arbitrary, he tries to wrest a *guarantee* from this consoling, moralizing deity. There are remarkable affinities (but also a crucial difference) between the story of Job and the story of von Niemand. Where Job is concerned, God and Satan strike a wager which involves the use of suffering as a means of putting Job's faith to the test. The story's perspective is thoroughly theocentric. By contrast, the perspective in the story of von Niemand is essentially anthropocentric – in effect, von Niemand makes a wager with Satan to use (Sophie's) suffering as a means of putting the God of salvation to the test. Job begins by thinking that he knows the ways of the God of his fathers, but gradually his experience of undeserved suffering compels him to tread the path of unknowing. He arrives at a faith that is beyond all purely personal concerns. Von Niemand, on the other hand, begins by experiencing the silence of God, and thus his starting-point is really the end-point of Job's pilgrimage. The *SS* doctor cannot endure this silence, and so he craves a gnosis which will show him at once the ways of the God of his fathers. He seeks to make a transition from a state of unknowing to a state in which he can be justified, consoled and comforted. In seeking the faith of his fathers he loses the opportunity of acquiring a genuine faith and of undergoing a true *metanoia*. While Job spurns the consoling platitudes of his 'comforters', and learns to love God's creation as it is, von Niemand is unable to achieve anything more than a loveless attempt at justification. The God von Niemand seeks is an idol. What he does to Sophie is not only a crime against humanity; it is also a blasphemy against the true God. Both Job and von Niemand long for certainty. Job learnes to live with the unknowable God who comes in the shape of a whirlwind. Von Niemand, unable to trust in the God of the future, never manages to overcome his nostalgic longing for a protecting father figure.

IV Conclusion

For all these reasons I believe that we have to conclude that the principal features of the moral apocalypticist's position are deeply at variance with the central affirmations of the Christian faith. This is so because the moral apocalypticist, in so far as he is a man of faith, and to the extent that he subscribes to a doctrine of the atonement, is committed to a purely 'subjective' conception of the atonement – he longs for a new insight, a reordering of his passions, which he construes as the overcoming of the evil that resides in his evil will. That is to say, he looks for a personal 'experience' which vouchsafes to him the bestowal of divine salvation. He will not let God be God; he wants God to be the author of our salvation, yes, but at the same time he wants the book of salvation to be written according to a plot that is really of our own devising.

The upshot of this is that only an 'objective' understanding of the atonement can do justice to the fundamental truth of the Christian faith that the grace of God which liberates humankind from the power of sin is a free and sovereign grace. As a result of God's saving deed on the cross of Christ, humanity or creation (the latter being of course the more 'inclusive' notion') is *irreversibly* delivered from the power of evil.[19] There is, therefore, no need for the individual to plunge himself or herself into the abyss of sin in the delusionary expectation that by so doing he or she can *deserve* God's forgiveness. The salvation proffered to humankind through Jesus Christ does not depend on our capacity to recognize the way things have been, are and will be.[20] If salvation is 'independent' of our human cognitive mechanisms, then we can only wait on the hidden God who makes salvation possible for us. As St Augustine said so wisely:

> since man cannot rise of his own free will . . . let us hold with steadfast faith the right hand of God stretched out to us from above, even our Lord Jesus Christ. Let us wait for him with certain hope, and long for him with burning charity.[21]

It is precisely this certain hope and burning charity which the moral apocalypticist lacks.

8
Atonement and christology

One of the more important issues raised in the debate connected with *The Myth of God Incarnate* concerns the relation soteriology has to the incarnation. Is the Christian understanding of salvation, as traditionally formulated in the doctrine of the atonement, inextricably bound up with the incarnation? If it is, do we necessarily have to reject the doctrine of the atonement if we think there are adequate grounds for questioning the tenability of the notion of the incarnation? Or can we at least retain the fundamental insights of the atonement by modifying our understanding of the incarnation, perhaps by opting for a 'functional', as opposed to an 'ontological', christology? In any case, the doctrine of the atonement and the christological question cannot be discussed in isolation from each other. Our interest in the relation soteriology has to christology may also be heightened by the fact that in recent years particularly impressive 'functional' christologies have been developed by Geoffrey Lampe and Edward Schillebeeckx.[1] Our preference for one or the other type of christology may be determined, in part, by our basic theological approach. As Stephen Sykes, following J. F. Bethune-Baker, has pointed out, there are two basic approaches, with different starting-points: 'The anthropological approach defines man and his needs and finds in Christ a saviour. . . . The other approach is theological, which starts with God and his sovereign activity. Christology is possible because God has acted. Man is saved because God acted to save him.'[2] Generally speaking (and I must emphasize the fact that we are speaking generally here), theologians who prefer a 'functional' christology tend to adopt the anthropological approach, whereas those who espouse an 'ontological' christology have tended to favour the approach which starts with God.

It should be obvious that in talking of the relation between atonement and christology we are dealing with substantial and complex issues that extend back to the New Testament itself, and which lie at the heart of the Christian faith. To deal thoroughly with even a few of these issues would be beyond the scope of an essay like this. My task in this paper, therefore, is limited to two objectives. First, I want to argue that 'functional' christologies are lacking in one important respect where the Christian understanding of salvation is concerned, namely, that from them we cannot derive a salvation-scheme which accords fully with the affirmation, central to the Christian faith, that in Jesus Christ God acted decisively in history to bring salvation to humankind. Second, I shall outline, without developing fully, a view of christology and atonement which conceives of the incarnation in 'ontological' terms. In attempting this I shall resort to the *imago Dei*, a strategy adopted by Irenaeus. I also hope to show that the theological approach, as defined by Sykes, is a viable starting-point when it comes to explicating the relation between atonement and christology.

I

In his profound essay on the atonement in the *Festschrift* for H. H. Farmer, Donald MacKinnon has argued that an adequate doctrine of the atonement must bring out very clearly 'the dark ambivalence of human action intended somehow to rectify an inherently false situation, and restore perception of its truth'.[3] To achieve this clarity, we need, according to MacKinnon, two things: (i) a phenomenology of moral evil; and (ii) the resources of ontological metaphysics. We need a phenomenology of moral evil because the place of the atoning life and death of Jesus Christ is precisely this ambivalent world of ours, an ambivalence which, as MacKinnon sees it, is the very essence of tragedy. The resources of ontological metaphysics are required because the atonement necessarily involves the idea of incarnation, and we must use these resources to bring out the significance which the incarnation has for the atonement (or so MacKinnon maintains). MacKinnon's claim that the doctrine of the atonement needs a phenomenology of moral evil and the resources of ontological metaphysics is one we hope to bear out later in this chapter. He is also right, from the standpoint of the Christian tradition, in saying that the atonement necessarily involves the incarnation. For the Christian faith, traditionally understood, has affirmed that the atoning life and death of Jesus brings salvation to humankind precisely because in and through this life God has identified with humankind: quite simply, without the incarnation there would be no atonement. Or as MacKinnon puts it, there *can* be salvation without the atonement (and hence the incarnation), but it would be a redemption which could be wrought by a *deus ex machina*, a deity who saves humankind but who does not identify with humanity in the process. However, while MacKinnon's views may accord with the mainstream of the Christian faith, it must be acknowledged that it is just this mainstream, or more precisely, its doctrinal expression, which has come under critical scrutiny in recent years. The theologians in the vanguard of this critical enterprise, who eschew an 'incarnational' christology which accords with the Chalcedonian definition, have argued that the traditional Christian understanding of atonement, which hinges necessarily on the incarnation, must be rejected because of the so-called 'scandal of particularity' which surrounds the incarnation: salvation thus conceived, say these theologians, will *eo ipso* be confined to the adherents of an 'incarnational' faith, and this is deemed to be unacceptable in a world that is characterized by a plurality of faiths.[4] The theologians who adopt this line of argument usually go on to argue that an 'incarnational' christology, explicated via an ontological metaphysics, must therefore be supplanted by a christology which does not ascribe a unique ontological status to Jesus Christ.[5] What these theologians want, therefore, is a salvation-scheme which is not tied to the incarnation understood in ontological terms. In short: these theologians reject the traditional Christian understanding of atonement.[6] It is too easy to label the position of these 'non-incarnational' theologians as 'unitarian' or 'non-Christian', and to let these labels stand proxy for the careful examination of arguments. It is not sufficient, either, to repeat our traditional credal affirmations or to talk of an 'essence' of the Christian faith, and to execrate these theologians because they do not share our conception of such an 'essence' or our fervour for the traditional affirmations of the faith. What we need to do, instead, it seems to me, is to accept the broad outline of their 'non-incarnational' approach to christology, and from this to attempt to derive certain consequences which these theologians may be reluctant to accept. Quite obviously, such an attempt on our part would not in itself constitute a decisive refutation of their point of view; but such a refutation, in my view, is neither possible nor perhaps even desirable. We can proceed in the manner just outlined, by addressing ourselves to the following question: what real alternative is there, where salvation-schemes are concerned, to the traditional Christian scheme which hinges on the incarnation? What we are looking for here is a view of salvation which is non-incarnational, but which can be accommodated, no matter how tenuously, within the doctrinal edifice of the Christian faith. In looking for the beginnings of an answer, we can turn to MacKinnon's conception of the atonement.

According to MacKinnon, the alternative to a view of atonement intrinsically linked to the incarnation is one in which God brings salvation to humankind, but does not identify with humankind in the process. That is, a redemption which can be wrought by a *deus ex machina*. This, perhaps, is to state the matter too strongly: it does not follow that a 'non-incarnational' salvation must necessarily be one which could be wrought by a *deus ex machina*. We cannot, for instance, foist this dichotomy – 'incarnational' salvation or redemption which could be wrought by a *deus ex machina* – onto Lampe, at least not without further argument, because he (for one) would strongly reject a salvation-scheme which involves a *deus ex machina*. Lampe, after all, is concerned only to argue that God's identification with humankind can be understood in a way which does not require the ascription of a unique ontological significance to Jesus Christ: he still wishes to retain the notion of divine identification, albeit construed in an inspirational, as opposed to an ontological, sense. It is because theologians like Lampe (and Hick, at least, where his 'Christology at the Cross Roads' is concerned) still retain the notion of God's identification with humanity that we should hesitate to label them as 'unitarians' or 'non-Christians'. Nevertheless, it may be possible to argue that the salvation-schemes which these theologians propose, based as they are on an explicit rejection of an 'ontological' christology, are generally consonant with a view of redemption which could be wrought by a *deus ex machina*. But this has to be argued for, and not presumed to be a self-evident truth. I want now to formulate such an argument, designed to show: (a) that their salvation-schemes are consonant with a view of redemption which could be wrought by a *deus ex machina*; and (b) that such salvation-schemes are inadequate – not because they reject an 'ontological' christology, but because they fail to come to terms with the depths of human evil and suffering.[7]

As MacKinnon sees it, the atonement brings together our depths of moral evil and the work of Jesus. He wants to argue, of course, that a truly acceptable salvation-scheme is one which seeks to understand God's reconciling work in and through the utmost depths of this moral evil. Such a salvation-scheme would touch 'the deepest contradictions of human life, those contradictions which writers of tragedy have not hesitated to recognize, and to recognize without the distorting consolation of belief in a happy ending'.[8] Precisely such a salvation-scheme, MacKinnon believes, is to be found in the Passion-narratives of the gospels. One of the necessary requirements of a properly-constituted salvation-scheme (and here we include salvation-schemes which belong to *other* religions) is to tell 'the truth of what we are',[9] and in so doing make explicit the moral evil which permeates the very depths of our lives. It is only when this evil has been rendered explicit that we have a basis for undergoing that transformation or *metanoia*, that healing, which constitutes our salvation. A truly acceptable salvation-scheme, then, must contain the theme of divine judgement as well as the one of divine reconciliation – it is in this judgement that we are shown the truth about ourselves, the truth which makes our moral evil explicit. It should be noted that so far we have not included any christological considerations in this delineation of a typical salvation-scheme: the principles involved in our delineation are purely soteriological, though they are grounded in a quite specific view of humanity and its needs, i.e. an anthropology.[10] This approach of ours, which grounds soteriology in an anthropology via a phenomenology of moral evil, is essentially none other than the anthropological approach as defined by Sykes. It is not the approach we shall be adopting later in this chapter, but since it is the one generally used by 'non-incarnational' theologians, we have adopted it as part of our policy of accepting the broad outline of their position as a starting-point for discussion.[11] The next stage in our argument is to show that the typical salvation-scheme which we are in the process of delineating is one which requires a christology formulated in 'ontological', and not 'functional', terms.

A properly-constituted salvation-scheme, we have suggested (following MacKinnon), is one which shows us the truth about ourselves and thus makes explicit our depth of moral evil, which adequately represents 'the conflict that splits human beings in two, compelling them to serve truth and justice, or forbearance and pity, but always forbidding them the very possibility of reconciling these obligations, thereby estranging them from the very substance of themselves'.[12] Why can this 'truth about ourselves' not be adequately represented by a salvation-scheme which incorporates a 'functional' christology? In answering this question we have to resort to a phenomenology of moral evil.

Let us begin by considering the claim that God's work of judging and reconciling human beings to himself is one which requires him to *identify* with his creation through Jesus Christ. The claim, in itself, is hardly controversial: problems start to creep in only when we attempt to spell-out the nature of this divine identification with creation through Christ. However, to avoid any serious problems initially, let us say that even a 'revelation', as opposed to an 'incarnation', of God would constitute an acceptable sense (for the purposes of argument) of this divine identification with creation. Or to say the same thing in christological language: why can a purely human Christ, serving as a supreme revelation of God and his love, not render explicit our depth of moral evil, and in so doing enable us to undergo that *metanoia* which lies at the heart of salvation? We are considering, in other words, the acceptability of the proposition, upheld by 'non-incarnational' theologians, that God could reveal himself to humanity through a purely human Jesus, and in so doing bring about our salvation. This proposition, with its implicitly reductionist overtones, is of course unacceptable to 'incarnational' theologians. As Brian Hebblethwaite expresses it, '. . . reductionism leads to an unrealistic exposition of Christian belief. For the purely human Christ, however, open to the will of God, cannot possibly carry the weight of significance still attributed to him.'[13] It is not unreasonable to assume that when Hebblethwaite talks of 'the weight of significance' attributed to Christ he means to refer, at least in part, to the salvific significance attributed to Christ in traditional Christian salvation-schemes. The charge seems to be that 'non-incarnational' soteriology has to be rejected because it is reductionist, and reductionism in turn has to be rejected because, among other things, it does not do justice to 'the weight of significance' we traditionally assign to Christ. But this alleged 'reductionism' cannot be dismissed so easily; and as an argument against it, Hebblethwaite's charge amounts to a *non sequitur*. For it is precisely this 'weight of significance', articulated in terms of an incarnational christology, which the 'reductionists' are concerned to deny in regard to the person of Jesus Christ. These 'reductionists' say, in effect, that because Christ *is* purely human we cannot possibly attribute to him the 'weight of significance' which the Christian faith has traditionally attributed to him – what they want to do involves, on the contrary, a *scaling-down* of this 'weight of significance'; it is pointless, therefore, to accuse them of giving Christ a status which does not accord with this 'weight of significance', since as far as they are concerned this is the very point that is at issue. Hebblethwaite's charge simply begs the question at the outset – to refute the 'non-incarnational' theologians we cannot, as I have already said, beg any vital christological questions from the start. It may be that in so doing we are already conceding too much valuable ground to the 'reductionists', but this is a risk that we have to take if we are to attempt a satisfactory resolution of the very complex issues that are at stake: no other approach will suffice.[14] So the question remains: why can a purely human Christ, serving even as a supreme revelation of God, not render explicit our depth of moral evil, and in so doing provide a basis for our salvation. The answer, as MacKinnon suggests, lies in a phenomenology of moral evil which thus becomes an essential component of our typical salvation-scheme. It is to this that we must now turn.

The phenomenology of moral evil that we shall now outline is approached from the standpoint of anthropology, and (at this stage) deliberately eschews any christological considerations. It should be emphasized that it is only a sketch of an outline and as such makes certain generalizations concerning humanity which will have to be suitably amplified and qualified in a more detailed account; nevertheless, we can take these generalizations to provide a viable framework for the formulation of such an account.[15]

A characteristic feature of any theological view of humanity is that human beings are undeniably finite beings, in that they have typical experiences 'of limitation, contingency, temptation and internal and external conflict'.[16] We are creatures, and because of these experiences we have an inescapable awareness of 'the precariousness of human identity', an awareness which causes us to be driven by fear and horror, and which expresses itself in the form of hatred, both hatred of self and others, and even of God.[17] However, it seems part of the ineluctably contradictory nature of human life that even in our attempts to overcome, or escape from fear or horror, we cannot avoid evil: the roots of tragedy, and the ensuing hurt and suffering, seem to be implanted in the very foundations of the universe. The noblest intentions do not forestall tragedy, and since we are creatures disposed to act, tragedy manifests itself *in concreto*, its reality is truly inexorable, and its seeming necessity is best expressed in many cases by the modalities of fate. For soteriology, of course, the story of humanity cannot end here, with the tragedy thrust on us as one of fate's exacting necessities. If it did, the salvation intended by God for human beings would be inconceivable. As soteriology sees it, it is precisely because our evil is concretized in our deeds that we are capable of

undergoing that healing which is our salvation. The person who
sees herself as she truly is, i.e. the person to whom the depths of
evil (and suffering) have been rendered explicit, is the person who
can experience sorrow and forgiveness. As Rowan Williams puts
it, 'If we believe we can experience our healing without deepening
our hurt, we have understood nothing of the roots of our faith.'[18]
In other words: before we can undergo this healing we have to
experience our evil, and its accompanying hurt, at its worst. To
quote Sebastian Moore, 'Christianity . . . invites us to experience
our evil as never before, at last unmasked, . . . and in that experience to feel for the first time the love that overpowers evil.'[19] The
salvation of human beings, grounded in the infinite mercy of God,
arises from this confrontation of suffering, sorrow and healing; to
quote Moore again, '. . . evil made totally explicit is resolved in the
forgiveness of God'.[20] God, as faith sees it, resolves our evil in his
forgiveness, by identifying with it. By accepting us at our worst,
God's love brings about our salvation. At this point we have to
conclude our brief, somewhat programmatic, outline of a phenomenology of moral evil, and turn our attention to the christological
question. For it is a central assertion of the Christian faith that it is
in and through Jesus Christ that God identifies with, and overcomes, the evil and suffering inherent in the human condition.
And it is here that the argument between the proponents of 'ontological' and 'functional' christologies begins to crystallize. The
adherents of an 'ontological' christology want to say that this
identification must involve the notion of God's *being* in Jesus,
whereas their opponents want to say that it is sufficient for us to
regard Jesus as an exemplar or mediator of God's redeeming love,
without resorting to the notion of consubstantiality. I want to
argue now that this divine identification with our evil and suffering, in and through Jesus Christ, must be construed in 'ontological'
terms if it is to have a salvific significance. We cannot shirk the
question, even if it means stretching language to the utmost limits,
of how it is that God breaks into the reality of our lives, shows us
the truth of what we are, and thereby heals us. The connection
between interruption and truth is expressed thus by Eberhard
Jüngel:

> . . . of all creatures, man is that being to whom God wishes to draw
> near . . . so near, in fact, that he, God, is closer than anyone to man.
> Thus it is not man who can be closest to himself. It is precisely in his
> desire to be closest to himself in his self-correspondence that man is
> interrupted by God. God wants to draw nearer to man than man is

ever able to be himself. It is just for this that man is created as man in such a way that he can be interrupted, and he is human precisely in that he allows himself to be interrupted. God is man's original interruption. He intervenes. For this reason God is, at the same time, the truth of life. He is this as the one who intervenes.[21]

Jüngel, of course, wants to say that God breaks into our lives by *being* the truth of Jesus Christ, that is, he opts for an 'ontological' definition of God's intervenient identification with human beings. In other words: God's intervenient identification with the evil and suffering of the human race is grounded in the historical particularity of Jesus Christ. In no other way can we confront the ultimate depths of our evil and suffering. According to Jüngel, God interrupts the continuity (a continuity-in-evil) of our lives by allowing our sin and death to interrupt *his* own life in and through the death of Jesus Christ. Now the actions signified by the terms 'intervening', 'interrupting' and 'breaking-into' are the actions of personal beings *par excellence*: they virtually imply direct, tangible agency. To this extent the idea of a God who interrupts is superior, where soteriology is concerned, to even the most profound exemplarism; for we know from our own human experience that sorrow, forgiveness and healing only take place in the actuality of a lived relationship with other beings – we only perceive the full significance of our wrong-doing when we see, palpably, what it is that we have inflicted on others, what devastation we have wrought in their lives. Similarly, God's saving and intervenient identification with humanity has to be explicated by means of an ontological metaphysics if it is to capture this sense of the palpable immediacy of a genuine encounter with other beings. God's saving identification, according to the Christian faith, takes place in the Passion of Jesus Christ, when the *being* of God engaged and interrupted the evil and death of human beings in and through Jesus of Nazareth. To explicate this relation between God and Christ in terms of the notion of mediation not only makes this saving engagement too abstract, but also evacuates it of tension and reality, and thus ultimately trivializes the evil and suffering of human beings. A divine acceptance of humanity which stops short of a divine identification with the very depths of human wrong-doing is a redemption which could be wrought by a *deus ex machina*, and we can now see a little more clearly why MacKinnon has insisted on posing so stark an alternative: either an atonement hinged on the incarnation or a redemption which could be wrought by a *deus ex machina*.[22] The position we have just argued for, then, begs no questions about 'the weight of significance' which the Christian faith ascribes to the person of Jesus – it is worked out entirely within the confines of an anthropologically-grounded phenomenology of moral evil. We have, as far as possible, avoided the temptation to deduce this phenomenology of salvation – for that is what it amounts to – from an antecedently formulated christology. However, at least three important problems remain with the position just outlined. First, it could be argued against us that the decisive emphasis in our phenomenology of moral evil is on the transformation of human moral consciousness, which effectively makes ours a *subjective* conception of the atonement. Thus, it could be said that the deadliest and most horrible evil is often that which seems to be inherent in the very fabric of the universe; it is there, we are almost tempted to say, because the universe is there, and not because of any flaws in our moral consciousness. This evil, seemingly unaccountable in its origins, often violently capricious, threatens the very intactness of our lives, and in the end testifies overwhelmingly to the frailty of our human moral powers.[23] What we need here, if anything, is an *objective* conception of the atonement, and it should now be apparent why MacKinnon has striven so determinedly to reconcile the 'subjective' and 'objective' conceptions. However, as already noted (see note 3), there is a difficulty with this putative reconciliation: if the deepest contradictions in life are non-moral; if as Nicholas Berdyaev maintains, tragedy is 'beyond good and evil'; does this not rob the atonement doctrine of the significance it is meant to have?[24] In attempting to overcome this difficulty, it should be acknowledged at the outset (i) that tragedy in its profoundest sense is often 'non-moral', and (ii) that, as John Cowburn rightly maintains (see note 23), the true nature of evil is ultimately mysterious. This is not to evade problems; it is simply to state what seems to be a 'brute' fact about evil. The appeal to 'brute' facts, nevertheless, can be no more than the preliminary to a proper answer if we are to preserve the significance of the atonement doctrine (which, as MacKinnon points out, is to bring together our depth of moral evil and the work of Christ). Here it seems to me that we can still do this even though the deepest contradictions in life are ultimately 'non-moral'. While there is no gainsaying the truth that the *origins* of tragedy are 'non-moral', it does not follow from this that tragedy is totally and unreservedly outside the compass of human consciousness and activity. For what makes tragedy so horrific, what accounts for its capacity to evoke pity, is precisely the fact that it invades, undermines and ultimately destroys the lives of *human* beings. The transcendent origins of tragedy notwithstanding, its manifestations are ruthlessly immanent: humanity is unavoidably engaged with the *awfulness* of tragedy. It is true, of course, that our salvation in the face of this engagement cannot be wrought solely by means of a transformation of the human moral consciousness (i.e. the atonement cannot be conceived purely 'subjectively'), but it still remains true that our confrontation with the forces that make for tragedy occurs, or must occur, to some extent at least, in the realm of human experience. It is not easy to specify in advance what form this salvific experience must take: a heightened perception, a renewed hope, a more sustained endurance, a greater courage, a deeper fidelity, or more harrowingly, a more profound suffering, a more fearful dereliction. For what the passion of Christ shows us is that we do not necessarily experience salvation *as salvation*. So, while the deepest contradictions in life are ultimately 'non-moral', they still make themselves real in the context of our lives as personal beings; and as long as we are concerned with the question of human salvation, there will be a place for the doctrine of the atonement ('objectively' conceived).[25] The non-moral source of the deepest contradictions of human life does not preclude the formulation of such a doctrine: the only thing that could legitimately do so would be the demonstration of the fundamental untenability of the notion of atonement. This brings us back to the other two objections to our position.

The first objection concerns the so-called 'scandal of particularity' and all that that implies for our typical salvation-scheme. The second problem requires us to provide a more detailed treatment of God's intervenient identification with humanity as he engages with the deepest contradictions of life. We shall approach these problems in the next section.

II

Implicit in the typical salvation-scheme outlined in the previous section is the belief that God saves us through interrupting the continuity of our alienated lives, and thus brings us into a new relationship with him. This belief presupposes the capacity on our parts to enter into a conscious relationship with God, a capacity deemed to have been granted us by God at the creation. The drift of our argument, it would seem, is that the incarnation and the atonement cannot be separated from the creation: God's identification with humanity in the life, death and resurrection of Jesus Christ is the culminating-point of a relationship that has existed since the creation. At the same time, we must agree with George Newlands that '. . . nothing is to be gained from swallowing up the doctrine of creation into christology'.[26] The temptation to assimilate the doctrine of creation into christology must be resisted in the same way as we have refrained from regarding soteriology as a mere derivative of christology. Our starting-point then was a phenomenology of salvation accompanied by a phenomenology of moral evil, both approached from the standpoint of theological anthropology. This is not to suggest, however, that theological anthropology is the starting-point of soteriological and christological reflection: if we inferred our christology from the experience of salvation, having previously construed that experience in terms of a theory of human consciousness, i.e. an anthropology, we should be doing what Schleiermacher did, which is, in effect, to reduce the figure of Christ to a datum of human consciousness. This would run counter to the objectives we have espoused in opting for a view of the atonement which hinges on an 'ontological' christology. We chose, it will be remembered, to take the phenomenology of moral evil and its concomitant phenomenology of salvation as our starting-point simply in order to avoid making 'unwarranted' christological assumptions in our attempt to resolve the conflict between 'ontological' and 'functional' christologies vis-à-vis the atonement. Having argued, without resorting to any christological considerations, for the view that an adequate doctrine of salvation requires God to identify with humanity to the point of *being* in Christ, we can now turn to the doctrine of creation to get a fuller understanding of what is involved in God's identification with humanity in its alienated condition. Our starting-point here, as stated in the beginning of this paper, is the *imago Dei*.[27]

The phrase 'the image of God' has implications which have to be elucidated carefully, especially if we are to avoid lapsing into anthropomorphism. It is perhaps more useful to regard it as 'limit' concept, since it gives us a broad but essential framework for understanding the relation between God and his creation, and thus enables us to conceptualize the inner structure of the concrete relationship of God to the world.[28] If human beings are created in God's image, then an 'isomorphism of being' exists between God and creaturely persons. This 'isomorphism of being' is *personal*, because a God whose essential nature it is to love, to interrupt, to break into our lives, must be a personal being who can *act* in his creation – he cannot be a *deus ex machina*. And inasmuch as we are created by God so that he can 'draw near to us' (Jüngel), i.e., to participate in this relationship with him, we too have a nature that enables us to interrupt the life of God and the lives of our fellow humans. At the same time, this 'isomorphism of (personal) being' which is entailed by the *imago Dei* must be suitably qualified by a *via negativa* – God's being is infinite and unfathomable, and although we can know something of his being because it is manifested in the sphere of his creation, we cannot presume to know it fully. We can know God through his interruptions in the continuity of our lives, but we cannot 'explain' him fully in terms of these interruptions, which is another way of saying that divine transcendence must be preserved.[29]

Through the *imago Dei*, then, we have a means of expressing the principle that God is, to some degree, and in a suitably qualified sense, present in all his creatures. We are, in the sense constituted by the *imago Dei*, the humanity of God, though as yet a flawed humanity. All creaturely beings manifest God to some degree, simply by virtue of being his creatures. At this point an objection presents itself. According to the view just expressed, God is said to be manifested, in a suitably qualified sense, in *all* his creatures, and this must surely raise the question of the purportedly unique status of his manifestation in Jesus Christ. For the Christian faith affirms that God was *uniquely* incarnate in Jesus Christ, which therefore makes it imperative for us to say clearly what the difference is between this unique divine manifestation in Christ and the universal divine manifestation in beings like us. In looking for an answer, we have, I think, to go back to Irenaeus, whose great merit is that he refuses to divorce the incarnation of God in Christ from God's *continuing* work in creation, and that he holds firm to the principle, accepted by us, that the salvation of human beings must be effected in the realm of humanity. As Irenaeus sees it, the uniqueness and decisiveness of God's incarnation in Christ is to be accounted for in soteriological terms – Jesus Christ is the re-creator of a humanity whose relationship with God has been distorted by sin – and this soteriological theme is in turn grounded in a doctrine of creation, or more specifically, re-creation. Irenaeus emphasizes the continuity of God's creative activity, and God's salvific act in Christ is seen by him as part of this continuing re-creation, in which communion is restored between God and humanity as result of the salvific life, death and resurrection of Jesus Christ. Irenaeus does this by means of his doctrine of 'recapitulation',[30] which is an amplification of the

Pauline image of Christ as the new Adam. The governing principle
in this doctrine of recapitulation is the comparison and contrast
between Adam, who fell into disobedience and thereby distorted
his and his descendants relationship to God, and Jesus Christ,
whose unfailing and total obedience reversed the disobedience of
Adam and thus restored us to a proper relationship with God; or as
Irenaeus puts it, 'The Son of God became the Son of Man that man
... might become the Son of God' (v, 6, 1). Jesus Christ, according
to Irenaeus, is thus the 'archetype' of a re-created humanity.
Following Irenaeus, we can account for the uniqueness of God's
incarnation in Christ by adverting to his status as the archetype who
enables us to attain our salvation by conforming our lives to the
pattern established by his. Or in terms of our typical salvation-
scheme: it is by following the pattern established by the life, death
and resurrection of Jesus Christ that we are enabled to transform
our evil and sin into that healing which lies at the heart of
salvation.[31] The uniqueness of Jesus Christ is explained by the
fundamental asymmetry which exists between one whose life
establishes an archetypal pattern and those whose lives have a
pattern that can only aspire to a derivative significance. The
uniqueness of the incarnation is thus to be sought in soteriology and
not christology itself, which again accords with our policy of
avoiding any 'unwarranted' christological assumptions in accounting for the uniqueness of the incarnation. Unfortunately, this
manoeuvre of ours still does not extricate us from the difficulty of
accounting for the uniqueness of the incarnation. For a further
objection can be raised against us, namely, that while our
manoeuvre may suffice to show that a figure whose life has an
archetypal significance must exist in order that God may bring
salvation to humankind, it still does not establish the truth that this
archetypal figure *must* be a Nazarene who lived nearly two thousand years ago, and who was executed on a cross by the Romans. In
other words, the uniqueness of the incarnation which our
manoeuvre purports to establish is merely a uniqueness of 'function', in this case the salvific function of the life, death and
resurrection of Christ. And, the objection proceeds, unless we can
account for the uniqueness of the incarnation in terms of God's
engagement with the concrete existence of Jesus of Nazareth, we
have succeeded only in serving-up a thinly disguised 'functional'
christology. The view of Christ which results from our manoeuvre
does not take us one whit beyond the mere exemplarism we have
striven so hard to discredit. In this objection to our position we
meet the full force of a cluster of problems which have their locus in

the so-called 'scandal of particularity'. We cannot circumvent these problems: if we did the main contentions of this essay would surely be rendered utterly insubstantial. We have, it seems to me, no alternative but to confront these problems directly.

An attractive, somewhat 'Barthian', way of meeting this difficulty would be to actually welcome the 'scandal of particularity', to say that God's becoming incarnate in Jesus Christ is exactly how he 'chose' to reveal himself to humanity. The incarnation is a truth of revelation *simpliciter*. However, without wishing to deny the 'givenness' of God in revelation, I do not think that an appeal to revelation can, in itself, be regarded as an acceptable answer to the problem posed by 'the scandal of particularity'. For revelation, as George Newlands has pointed out,[32] is neither self-interpreting nor self-authenticating, and therefore presupposes an epistemology of revelation, which necessarily proceeds beyond the merely 'given' to a wider complex that includes metaphysics, the philosophy of history, the sociology of knowledge, hermeneutical theory, and so forth. Having ruled out the possibility that revelation can, in itself, extricate us from this problem, we have to look for another justification for saying that God engaged himself uniquely in the particularity of the life of Jesus of Nazareth. Revelation, as centred in the gospels, is part of the answer, certainly, but there must be other strands in any such justification. These strands may include any or all of the following:

(i) the extraordinary impact that Jesus had on the lives of his followers.[33]

(ii) the unique way in which Jesus experienced his relationship to God, in particular, the nearness and familiarity of address evidenced in his 'Abba experience'.[34]

(iii) the continuing Christian experience of God and human life since New Testament times.[35]

It may be that a combination of these strands will, in addition to the appeal to revelation, enable us to accept, legitimately, the sheer particularity of God's engagement in the life of Christ. Nevertheless, I am not certain that this solves our problem: a moment's reflection will reveal two weaknesses in the above proposals. First, it could be argued that while (i)–(iii) above show Jesus to be a remarkable individual who had extraordinary impact on humankind, they do not, *on their own*, entail the ascription of a unique *divine* status to him. Second, the mere fact that we are prepared to accept (i)–(iii) as a putative justification for the uniqueness of God's incarnation in Jesus Christ presupposes the logical coherence of the notion of a being who, while remaining human, was at the same time truly divine. The logical coherence of this notion has to be demonstrated, and not merely taken for granted.

Doubtless these objections have been put to the proponents of 'ontological' christologies before, and strategies have been devised for overcoming them. We cannot discuss all these strategies here, and our discussion will be restricted to one of them, namely, the proposal, made by MacKinnon and Schillebeeckx, that we use the distinction, made in the philosophy of logic, between first- and second-order propositions, to help us understand the way christological statements are supposed to work, and to avoid the charge that 'incarnational' propositions are not logically coherent.[36] Using the distinction between first- and second-order propositions, MacKinnon and Schillebeeckx contend that first-order propositions express 'the simpler, more direct and immediately moving christological affirmations of the Gospel' (MacKinnon), whereas second-order propositions are more abstract and complex christological propositions which range over these basic evangelical affirmations. Or more simply: first-order propositions are about Christ, whereas second-order propositions are about propositions about Christ. Or as Schillebeeckx puts it, the first-order propositions constitute a 'theology of Jesus of Nazareth', whereas second-order propositions constitute christology *per se*. Their proposal has a number of merits. First, as Schillebeeckx never tires of insisting, it has a basis in exegesis because it does seem to be the case that the gospel traditions were in the first place a 'theology of Jesus of Nazareth', out of which grew a more relative christology.[37] Second, the use of this distinction enables us to circumvent a whole minefield of problems expressed in questions concerning the moral perfection, omniscience, passibility, etc., of the divine Christ. It enables us to affirm both the true humanity of Jesus of Nazareth and God's total involvement in his life, death and resurrection. Unfortunately, this proposal of MacKinnon's and Schillebeeckx's has a serious defect which threatens its effectiveness. For by construing the ascription of divinity to Christ on the basis of a *human* understanding of the relation between Christ and the Father, rather than on the basis of the manner (*per se*) of Christ's relation to the Father, we are introducing a disturbing element of subjectivity and abstraction into christology, and this is something which MacKinnon for one has ceaselessly enjoined us to avoid. How can we avoid this element of subjectivity and abstraction? The answer, I think, lies in another area of the philosophy of logic. In a well-known paper criticizing Russell's Theory of Descriptions, P.F. Strawson has argued that the assignation of truth-value to a proposition in certain cases *presupposes* the truth of other propositions. A proposition Q is said to presuppose a proposition P if and only if Q is neither true nor false unless P is true. For example, the truth of the proposition 'Mrs Smith has a son' (P) is a *necessary condition* for the proposition 'Mrs Smith told her son a story' (Q) to be either true or false: in short, the proposition that 'Mrs Smith told her son a story' *presupposes* the proposition 'Mrs Smith has a son'.[38] Using this notion of a *presupposition* I want to argue that it is preferable to construe 'incarnational' propositions not as second-order propositions, but precisely as instances of propositions whose truth has to be presupposed in order that we may assign a truth-value to other more abstract theological propositions. Thus, for example, I would argue that the proposition 'God's identification with the human condition brought human beings salvation' presupposes the proposition 'God became incarnate in Jesus Christ', because it is a necessary condition of determining whether or not humankind is saved that God salvifically identifies with humankind by becoming incarnate in Jesus of Nazareth. To put it starkly: without 'incarnational' propositions we could not even say that it is *false* that God brought salvation to humankind, because the question of salvation cannot arise unless the depth of evil that confronts us is rendered explicit, and this, as our typical salvation-scheme indicates, can only be done by God's direct and personal engagement with the depths of this evil. I would say that every proposition involved in the articulation of this salvation-scheme presupposes the truth of 'incarnational' propositions, where the incarnation is understood in 'ontological' terms, i.e. as the personal presence of God in the life, death and resurrection of Jesus Christ. Our proposal differs from that of MacKinnon and Schillebeeckx in one crucial respect, namely, that whereas their proposal would involve christology being done 'from below', i.e. from the starting-point of our understanding of the relation between Christ and the Father, our proposal involves christology being done 'from above'. I am well aware of Nicholas Lash's cogently argued case for a moratorium on the use of the terms 'above' and 'below' where christology is concerned,[39] but I still find that there is a use for these terms provided we understand that there is a sense in which christology has to be done from both 'above' and 'below'.[40] I am saying, therefore, that if we approach christology from 'above', i.e. from the standpoint of God, we then have to affirm the divinity of Christ as the presupposition of any further christological reflection, a

point rightly made by Pannenberg.[41] We have to approach christology from 'above' for another reason – it is a direct consequence of
the way we have understood the incarnation in relation to soteriology that they are inextricably connected. Admittedly, we formulated our typical salvation-scheme without any initial christological
elements, but we cannot use this as a justification for subordinating
christology to soteriology. The reason for this is that, as Irenaeus
rightly perceives, the incarnation is bound up with the continuing
re-creative work of God in the world. The incarnation has a
soteriological significance for Irenaeus, but this significance is
located within the wider framework of God's continuing work of
creation. The governing principle is the doctrine of creation, and
within it, the *imago Dei*. And since God the Creator is, of course, a
transcendent reality, christology must for this reason be done from
'above'. However, the doing of christology from the perspective of
a transcendent God leads to a problem – of this God, as he
essentially is, we can claim to know hardly anything. This opacity of
the divine nature has led some theologians (Sykes cites the example
of Bethune-Baker) to discount the possibility of a viable approach
which starts with God, and to start with anthropology instead. In so
doing they interpose an anthropology between God's saving
activity in his creation and the incarnation, with the consequence
that they have a preestablished doctrine of what it is that essentially
constitutes human nature, and this anthropologically-saturated
doctrine is then going to leave them with no scope for reconciling
the divinity of Christ with his humanity, simply because his humanity is understood in such a way as to detract from his divinity, and
vice versa. Here I am in agreement with those theologians – Sykes,
Lash and Schillebeeckx among them – who maintain that the
'essence' of human nature is just as opaque as the divine nature,
especially when this 'essence' is defined in abstract and *a priori*
terms.[42] And if it is true that human nature is just as opaque to our
understanding as the divine nature, then we have no real justification for ruling out the theological approach.

What we should do instead is to have a less simplistic conception
of the relation between anthropology and christology. We have
argued that it is necessary to use a phenomenology of moral evil,
grounded in anthropology, to understand the saving significance of
the life, death and resurrection of Jesus Christ. At the same time it
can be seen that our salvation-scheme implies an ortho-praxis: by
conforming our lives to the archetypal pattern established by Christ
we are enabled to achieve that healing which lies at the heart of

salvation. Our true goal in life, according to the Christian faith, is to attain that perfection of humanity which Jesus Christ proffers us. And in attaining to this humanity we are reconciled to God. Or as Sykes neatly puts it, 'Christ reveals the perfection of which humanity is capable.'[43] We attain to our true humanity because God identifies with the utmost depths of evil and suffering in our lives, he interrupts our continuity-in-evil in and through Christ. This is equivalent to saying that the divinization of humankind is accomplished through Christ – through him God comes nearer to us than we are to ourselves, as Jüngel points out. So in the end our reconciliation with God consists in our being both truly human and truly divine. Is this not what the incarnation seeks to convey to us?

9

Revelation, salvation, the uniqueness of Christ and other religions

I

Karl Barth is widely held to be the foremost modern proponent of the principles (i) that Jesus Christ is the decisive, unrepeatable and unsurpassable 'locus' of divine revelation; and (ii) that consequently it is only by following the way of Christ that humankind can possibly hope for its ultimate salvation. These Barthian principles find expression in the following passage of *The Church Dogmatics*:

> Jesus Christ does not fill out and improve all the different attempts of man to think of God and to represent him according to his own standard. But as the self-offering and the self-manifestation of God he replaces and completely outbids these attempts, putting them in the shadows to which they belong. . . . The revelation of God in Jesus Christ maintains that our justification and sanctification, our conversion and salvation, *have been brought about and achieved once and for all in Jesus Christ.* He is the assistance that comes to us. *He alone is the Word of God that is spoken to us.*[1]

A further indication of Barth's uncompromising '*Christocentrism*' is provided by his characterization of revelation:

> Just as a man can have only one father, is born once and dies once, so he can only believe and know one revelation. It is possible to collate and compose a number of religions, not a number of revelations. He who says revelation says – a revelation which is unique, taking place once for all, irrevocable and unrepeatable.[2]

It has been argued, against such a 'Christocentrism', that since it effectively withholds the possibility of salvation from adherents of non-Christian faiths, it is therefore unacceptable in a world that is characterized by a plurality of faiths and theologies.[3]

Few theologians would commit themselves without qualification to a 'Christocentrism' that is as absolute as Barth's (and this despite Barth's manifest willingness not to exempt Christianity from his critique of 'religion'). Various alternatives are proposed by theologians in their attempts to attenuate, and in some cases to repudiate, the implicit triumphalism of a 'Christocentrism' which denies that truth and salvation are to be found in any revelation except that of Christianity.[4] These attempts to attenuate and to repudiate the austere view that salvation is to be found only in and through Jesus Christ take several forms. Some of these are well-known, and we shall give them only a cursory mention.

1. There is Karl Rahner's famous proposal that the devout adherents of other religions be regarded as 'anonymous Christians'.[5] A similar suggestion is made by Hans Küng. Küng holds that non-Christian believers are 'pre-Christian, directed towards Christi.... The men of the world religions are not professing Christians but, by the grace of God, they are called and marked out to be Christians.'[6] These proposals, it is clear, still assert – at least implicitly – the primacy of the Christian faith vis-à-vis the world religions: the formula *extra ecclesiam nulla salus* seems tacitly to be upheld by Rahner and Küng, except that on their view membership of the *ekklesia* is somewhat less restricted. I will not criticize the views of Rahner and Küng in this essay: this has been more than adequately done by other theologians. Thus Jürgen Moltmann (rightly, in my opinion) says of Rahner's notion that it enables

> the whole group comprising all men 'of goodwill' (who are no more closely defined than that) to be pronounced capable of salvation. This certainly opens the frontiers of the visible Church, defined by baptism and membership, and makes them more permeable; but the problem remains unresolved. A milder, opener, perhaps even 'more enlightened' absolutism takes the place of the old rigorous and violent one.[7]

2. There is the strategy, similar in some ways to the one espoused by Rahner and Küng, which while still ascribing supreme significance to the figure of Christ, nevertheless does so without the ecclesiological constraint (i.e. the 'absolutism') which underpins the views of Rahner and Küng. Exponents of this strategy understand the 'finality' and 'decisiveness' of Christ in a way which makes it possible for non-Christians to attain salvation. To quote Schubert Ogden, who takes up this position:

> The claim 'only in Jesus Christ' must be interpreted to mean, not that God acts to redeem only in the history of Jesus and in no other

history, but that the only God who redeems any history – *although he in fact redeems every history* – is the God whose redemptive action is decisively repeated in the word that Jesus speaks and is.[8]

A similar view is expressed by the late John Robinson, who says of Jesus that

> his incarnation or enmanent of God is no temporary theophany restricted to a particular life but is permanent and dynamic, the first fruits of a universal humanization of God.[9]

The person of Christ is understood by Ogden and Robinson in terms of a 'functional', as opposed to an 'ontological' christology – Christ's nature is to be defined by virtue of what God '*does*' in him, rather than what God '*is*' in Jesus. And since the saving work that is accomplished in Jesus is for the redemption of God's creation in its entirety, it follows that the uniqueness of Christ cannot be inter-preted in a way that excludes those who belong to other religions. It is worth noting, though, that the exponents of this strategy still assert the *uniqueness* of Christ – they do not, however, take the uniqueness of Christ to entail an 'exclusivist' view of salvation.

3. There is another strategy which bypasses, or attaches less importance to, the ecclesiological and christological considerations that motivate the positions outlined in (1) and (2) above, by adverting to an alleged common factor (or factors) in all the major religions. This common factor can be located in one or more areas of the different religious traditions: in certain forms of religious experience (usually mystical); in certain spiritual and ethical values which are to be found in religious traditions that are *seemingly* incompatible; the similarity, from a phenomenological standpoint, of worship and ritual in different religions; in a supreme sacred reality which, despite their diverse forms, all religions have as their focus; and so forth. Thus, it is said that

> there is but one God, who is maker and lord of all; that in his infinite fullness and richness he exceeds all our human attempts to grasp him in thought; and that the devout in the various great world religions are in fact worshipping that one God, but through different, overlapping concepts or mental images of him.[10]

What this approach does, it is easy to see, is to isolate a certain *nucleus* within all the religious traditions, and then to regard this nucleus (be it experiential, axiological, or the godhead who is worshipped by men and women of all faiths) as the *invariant* core of all religious traditions, which in turn enables the proponent of this strategy to *relativize* certain features of the world religions that are apparently unique (and which therefore serve to reinforce the boundaries between the different faiths).

4. There is an approach which argues that each religious tradition is fundamentally incomplete, and that consequently each religion needs to conduct a 'dialogue' with other faiths before it can attain to completeness. In the context of such an ongoing dialogue, Christianity must surrender its exclusive claim in relation to the other world religions, and instead seek a less grandiose role among these faiths. One such role is that of being a critical catalyst. To quote Jürgen Moltmann:

> A catalyst causes elements to combine simply through its presence. The simple presence of Christians in environments determined by other religions provokes effects of this kind, provided that Christians live, think and act differently. This can be called the indirect infection of other religions with Christian ideas, values and principles.[11]

There is a variant to this position. Rather than regarding Christianity as a 'catalyst' in the dialogue with other religions (the very idea of according such a role to Christianity seems unavoidably to accord it a special status among the world religions), some theologians prefer to see the different religions as complementary to each other. Thus, for example, it is sometimes said that the uncompromising monotheism of Islam upholds the 'transcendence' of God, while an 'incarnational' faith like Christianity qualifies this otherwise absolute 'transcendence' with the principle of God's *immanent* identification with humanity through his Son Jesus Christ.[12]

5. There is yet another strategy for understanding the relationship between Christianity and other faiths, which combines the position I have just described (under the rubric of position (4)) with a modified 'Barthian' point of view. According to the proponents of this strategy, the various world religions are in dialogue, albeit a dialogue in which Christianity is very much the dominant partner. These theologians hold that while salvation is available to the devout members of *all* religious traditions, and while God reveals himself in *all* faiths, in the non-Christian traditions the truth that God reveals about himself is, unfortunately, admixed with a great deal of falsehood and error. To quote John Baillie, whose views are fairly representative of this position:

> we must not say that in the pagan religions there is no apprehension of God's healing and saving power and no measure of trustful accept-

ance of it. The ardent seeking which is there manifested bears witness
to minds that have already been invaded by the presence of God. . . .
Each one of the pagan religions has some light in it, but it has also
much darkness – and how great is that darkness! There is something in
each that makes for spiritual health, but there is much also that makes
for spiritual disorder and sickness.[13]

Baillie goes on to say:

I have thus no hesitation in reaffirming my conviction that only by
following the Way of Christ is there any hope for the ultimate
salvation of mankind.[14]

Non-Christian faiths, then, contain a measure of divine truth and
saving efficacy, but Christianity is 'superior' to them because it, and
only it, contains God's definitive self-revelation. A similar point of
view is held by the late Cornelius Ernst, who argues that just as
Christianity, at the time of its historical beginnings, decisively
transformed and superseded the religious traditions around it
(Judaism and the pagan religions are the faiths in question), so too
it can today fulfil a similar function in relation to the other world
religions.[15] The views of Baillie and Ernst, it might be said by critics
of a 'Christocentric' approach to the other world religions, fall only
just short of Barth's unrelenting dismissal of any religion that does
not sanction a following of the way of Christ.

In the foregoing I have briefly delineated five main strategies
which have been adopted by those theologians who refuse to
endorse, either fully or in part, the view that divine truth and
salvation reside exclusively in Christianity. Some of these strategies
involve a total rejection of Christian 'triumphalism'; whereas
others still insist on the primacy of Christianity, but do not take this
'superiority' on the part of Christianity to involve the total rejection
of the claims of other faiths. It is not my purpose in this essay to
evaluate the strategies just outlined. However, what I wish to do
instead is to work out the full implications of a dilemma which, I
believe, lies at the heart of the problem posed by 'Christocentrism'
for soteriology. This dilemma is: either 'Christocentrism' is tenable
or it is not. If, on the one hand, 'Christocentrism' is tenable, then
wholehearted acceptance of the truth-claims of Christianity will
necessarily entail the denial of a substantial number of the truth-
claims made by other faiths; if, on the other hand, 'Christocentrism' is untenable, then some of the central affirmations of the
Christian faith (e.g. the doctrine of incarnation) will have to be
discarded or else 'demythologized'.[16]

II

Before we can solve, or resolve (or dissolve), the problem posed by this dilemma of 'Christocentrism', we have first to address ourselves to a crucial question which arises for the advocate of a 'Christocentric' position on the uniqueness of Christ; namely, how do we acquire a theological validation of the affirmation that God acted in a totally unparalleled way in the life, teaching and death of Jesus of Nazareth?

If we seek to answer this question from something approximating to a 'Barthian' standpoint, then the theological validation of 'Christocentrism' will take the form of a theology of the Word of God, that is, a theology which 'begins' from the divine self-*revelation*. Barth maintains that human beings can have knowledge of God only because God first condescends to reveal to humans the truth about himself. As Barth puts it:

> The truth that God is God and our Lord, and the further truth that we could know him as God and Lord, can only come to us through the truth itself. This 'coming to us' of the truth is revelation.... The activity which corresponds to revelation would have to be faith; the recognition of the self-offering and self-manifestation of God. We need to see that in the view of God all our activity is in vain ... that of ourselves we are not in a position to apprehend the truth, to let God be God and our Lord.... We need to be ready and resolved simply to let the truth be told to us, and therefore to be approached by it.... The man to whom the truth has really come will concede that he was not at all ready and resolved to let it speak to him.... For in faith, man's religion as such is shown by revelation to be resistance to it. From the standpoint of revelation religion is clearly seen to be a human attempt to anticipate what God in his revelation wills to do and does do.[17]

That is to say: we cannot, by ourselves, arrive at the truth about God: on our own we are only good enough to be idolators. For Barth, revelation is self-authenticating and self-interpreting – the 'object' of revelation is simply 'there' and has to be accepted as such.[18] But the acceptance of what is 'given' in revelation is an acceptance that is made by *human beings* in faith: because revelation cannot be unmediated theophany, there is an undeniable 'anthropological' dimension to revelation, inasmuch as revelation can be what it is only because its truths are revealed to *human beings*, and because revelation requires the response of faith on the part of the human creature if it is to 'complete' itself. To say this is not necessarily to endorse the 'liberal' view of revelation, so execrated by Barth, which in his eyes makes revelation *immanent* in human religion, thus effectively reducing revelation to a human possession. For to say that revelation has an 'anthropological' component is not necessarily to *limit* or *reduce* revelation to 'anthropology', to 'speak of God simply by speaking of "man" in a loud voice' (which is what Barth accused the liberal theologians of doing).[19]

The dilemma faced by the 'Barthian' conception of divine revelation is this: is the knowledge given in revelation a real knowledge, accessible to ordinary human understanding; or is it some ineffable understanding, perhaps available only to those who are inspired in some extraordinary way? This dilemma lies at the heart of Bonhoeffer's criticism that Barth allows a hiatus to exist between revelation and the reality of the world. For once the neo-orthodox theologian allows that human beings can have 'real' knowledge of that which is 'given' in revelation, that revelation can be accommodated within the canons of ordinary human understanding, then revelation will be drawn inexorably into the sphere of human religion, and will thus run the danger of becoming *immanent* in human religion. On the other hand, if the neo-orthodox theologian seeks to avoid this horn of the dilemma by arguing that revelation transcends human understanding, then she will run the risk of allowing a lacuna to exist between revelation and the world, and of rendering unavoidable the eternal 'non-objectivity' of God.[20] The problem for the theologian who seeks to avoid positing a lacuna between revelation and the world is that once she allows that human beings can have 'real' or 'ordinary' knowledge of that which is 'given' in revelation, then the less likely it is that revelation will be *entirely* self-interpreting and self-authenticating. Indeed, it is difficult to see how a revelation that is capable of accommodating itself to the canons of ordinary human understanding can at the same time be totally self-interpreting and self-authenticating. A revelation susceptible of such an accommodation will presuppose an epistemology of revelation, which necessarily proceeds beyond the merely 'given' to a wider complex that includes metaphysics, the philosophy of history, the sociology of knowledge, hermeneutical theory, and so forth. And this wider complex comes under the rubric of (for Barth – the 'earlier Barth' at any rate) 'natural theology'. It follows from this, *pace* the 'earlier Barth', that 'natural theology' is unavoidable if we are to circumvent a situation in which 'all the truths of revelation confront the whole worldly life of men without meaning'.[21] The upshot of this is that a 'Barthian Christocentrism', resting as it does on a 'positivist' doctrine of revelation, is not entirely securely grounded: it rests on an untenable dualism between the life of the world and the infinite realm from which the Word of God is sent forth.

Does this mean that there can be no place, in any discussion of the relation between Christianity and other faiths, for a theology which takes the irreducible particularity of Christ as its starting-point? Is the way now wide open for those who advocate a 'pluralism' which has no place for the so-called 'scandal of particularity'? These questions will be addressed in the next section.

III

In his essay 'Jesus and the World Religions', John Hick says that acceptance of a religious and theological 'pluralism' means that

> we have to present Jesus and the Christian life in a way compatible with our recognition of the validity of the other great world faiths as being also, at their best, ways of salvation.... The Christian gift to the world is Jesus, the 'largely unknown man of Nazareth' whose impact has nevertheless created such powerful images in men's minds that he is for millions the way, the truth and the life. Within the varying cultures and changing circumstances of history he can still create fresh images and can become man's lord and liberator in yet further ways.[22]

Explicit in this passage of Hick's is the view that the great world faiths are, *inter alia*, ways of *salvation*, and that Jesus of Nazareth can be characterized as 'men's lord and *liberator*'. Jesus is the one who liberates, his is the way (albeit not the only way) to salvation. Soteriology, therefore, has a vital part to play in the theology of world religions. The question now is: what necessary conditions have to be met by a faith that purports to be genuinely salvific and liberating?

Answering this question will require excursions into two important areas of soteriology, namely, a phenomenology of moral evil and a religious anthropology. A phenomenology of moral evil is essential if we are to understand precisely what it is that human beings require saving from; and a religious anthropology is necessary because we cannot answer this question ('What does human salvation consist in?') without answering certain important and relevant questions about the 'nature' of human beings.[23]

A phenomenology of moral evil will be one which renders explicit the depths of human evil. Such a phenomenology is required because it is almost a truism that human salvation is essentially the *overcoming* of evil; the true nature of evil has to be made transparent as a necessary preliminary to the construction of a properly-constituted salvation-scheme. 'The diagnosis has to precede the cure.'

The purpose of a phenomenology of moral evil, and the 'model' of salvation into which it is incorporated, is to tell 'the truth of what we are',[24] and in so doing to make explicit the moral evil which permeates the very depths of our lives. For it is only when this evil has been rendered explicit that we have a basis for undergoing that transformation or *metanoia*, that healing, which constitutes our salvation. The delineation of such a salvation-scheme will not include any initial christological considerations – the inclusion of any christological elements, whether explicit or implicit, will amount to a prior 'weighting' of the salvation-scheme in favour of Christianity, and would lay us open to the charge that our proposed 'model' of salvation is tacitly Christocentric. Our task, then, is to ground soteriology in anthropology via a phenomenology of moral evil.[25]

A characteristic feature of any theological view of human nature (and for our purposes, such a view will also encompass the major non-Christian faiths) is that the human creature is an undeniably finite being, in that he has typical experiences of limitation, contingency, internal and external conflict, and temptation. These typical experiences are so fundamentally constitutive of human nature that it is possible to locate *some* of their origins in the fact that we are a biological species – because the human creature is a member of a biological species he or she is constrained in important ways by heredity, by genetic constitution. We are creatures, and because of these characteristic experiences (which betoken our creaturely status) we have an inescapable awareness of 'the pre-cariousness of human identity', an awareness which causes us to be driven by fear and horror, and which expresses itself in the form of hatred, both hatred of self and of others, and even of God.[26] However, it seems part of the ineluctably contradictory nature of human life, that even in their attempts to overcome, or escape from, the sources of horror, human beings cannot avoid evil: the roots of tragedy, and the ensuing hurt and suffering, seem to be implanted in the very foundations of the universe. The noblest intentions do not forestall tragedy, and since we are creatures disposed to act, tragic evil manifests itself *in concreto*, with an inexorable reality, and its seeming necessity is best expressed in many cases by the modalities of fate. There is a profound sense in which evil can be said to *preexist* the deeds of evil human beings – its sheer intractability demands that we use the category of *preexistence* to explicate this particular quality of evil.

What conception of morality will be adequate to the facts of tragic evil? In my submission, only an austerely '*realist*' conception of morality will do justice to the tragic dimension of human evil. A 'realist' conception of moral judgement will hold that moral judgements are descriptive and assertorial, so that they involve claims that can be regarded as, and *known* to be, true or false. Moral judgements, on this view, are not merely prescriptions, recommendations or imperatives; they are not simply expressions of attitudes; they are not solely expressions of moral 'sentiments'. Moral judgements, according to the 'realist', are factually cognitive, and changes in values are accompanied by changes in *factual* appreciation. It follows from this that a moral judgement and its negation are incompatible – they cannot both be true. In short: the truth of a moral judgement is determined by the extra-linguistic, mind-independent 'reality' which we call the ('real') world. However, because the recognitional capacities of finite beings are correspondingly limited, there can be moral truths which we do not recognize for what they are, viz., the (moral) *truth*. Hence when a person repents, undergoes *metanoia*, experiences a moral or spiritual conversion, he or she comes to perceive a truth that hitherto he or she had failed to recognize. In a complex and morally untidy universe it is possible for our recognitional capacities to be overwhelmed by the sheer complexity of the moral universe. This is precisely what happens in tragic experience – the tragic personage, for all her moral and spiritual maturity, can be destroyed by an external design supplied by this universe.[27] Action, particularly moral action, in such a complex universe is always fraught with ambiguity and the possibility of failure – the moral agent is a finite being who is trying to grapple, in ways that exceed her unaided practical capacities, with a recalcitrant world. There is more to the world than a finite being can accommodate: the human being and the world are not entirely 'suited'; we live and act in a world that we have not created. It is this basic truth – namely, that the human being is a frightened, anxious and guilty creature who is 'thrown' into her cosmos – which makes her the most devastating of all the animals. We wreak havoc and destruction by our perverse (but nonetheless sincere) attempts to make ourselves at home in this universe, to cancel the fundamental discrepancy between ourselves and the world. It is a paradox of the human condition that it is precisely when we seek to lessen our hurt, when we strive to transcend our organismic condition, when we endeavour to deny our 'animality', that we are at our most dangerous – for such seeking, striving and endeavouring invariably take place at the expense of our fellow creatures. This is perhaps a much abbreviated 'secular' restatement of the doctrine of original sin. The root-principle of this doctrine is the assertion that the human individual *cannot* conquer tragic evil. The individual cannot conquer tragic evil because, as we have said, tragic evil (and very likely all the more intractable forms of evil as well) preexists human evil. We cannot conquer evil of such tragic dimensions because we live and act in a world we have not created; the human creature and her world are not entirely reciprocally suited.

For soteriology, of course, the story of the human creature cannot end here, with tragedy thrust on her as one of fate's exacting necessities. If it did end here, the salvation intended by God for his creation would be inconceivable.

As soteriology sees it, it is precisely because human evil is concretized in our deeds that we are capable of undergoing that healing which is our salvation. The person who sees herself as she truly is, i.e. the person to whom the depths of her evil has been rendered explicit, is the person who can experience sorrow and forgiveness. As Rowan Williams puts it: 'If we believe we can experience our healing without deepening our hurt, we have understood nothing of the roots of our faith.'[28] In other words: before we can undergo this healing we have to experience our evil, and its accompanying hurt, at their worst. For it is only in this experience that we encounter for the first time the divine love that overcomes evil. We have to see that the failure of love, i.e., the failure (stemming from our abysmal egotism) to acknowledge the humanity of the other person (and hence our own humanity), really presages the death of the other and the death of our capacity to love. Only when we have *seen* this, will it be possible for us to have our evil resolved in the forgiveness of God. The salvation of human beings arises from this confrontation of suffering, sorrow and healing.

God, as our salvation-scheme sees it, resolves human sin by his forgiveness. The depth and completeness of his forgiveness are indicated by his solidarity with sinful humanity on the cross of Christ. God brings about our salvation by breaking into the sinful reality of our lives, showing us the truth of what we are, and thereby healing us. God's identification with sinful humanity, in which he enables us to confront the brokenness of our lives, *is* our salvation. This conception of God's saving activity is the unavoidable conco-mitant of the moral 'realist' position outlined earlier: *if the sheerly intractable forms of evil are to be overcome, then they can only be overcome by the creator of the world.*

The 'model' we have constructed in the above paragraph gener-ates the 'grammatical' core of an *'incarnational'* specification of salvation. Critics of such an 'incarnational' soteriology may wish to argue that this is not in fact so: all our salvation-scheme entails is the proposition that the *being* of God engages with human evil, and it does not follow from this that God has to *'become human'* in order to save human beings, let alone 'take on' human form in the figure of a rabbi who lived in Palestine two thousand years ago (as Christian orthodoxy affirms).[29] The salvation-scheme just adum-brated, it could be argued by critics of an 'incarnational' soterio-logy, is entirely compatible with the 'non-incarnational' christolo-gies of, say, Maurice Wiles and John Hick. It is arguable whether there is an intrinsic connection between 'non-incarnationalism' in christology and 'exemplarism' in soteriology, but it does seem to be the case that 'exemplarism' is embraced by most theologians who reject 'incarnational' christologies.[30] The crucial question raised by this espousal of 'exemplarism' by 'non-incarnational' theologians is: can an acceptable salvation-scheme be sustained by an 'exemplarist' soteriology? For if a merely 'exemplarist' soterio-logy will suffice, then the way is open to regard Jesus Christ as a purely human figure, which in turn makes possible the claim that non-Christian faiths can also be vehicles for human salvation.[31]

'Exemplarism', as its name implies, holds that Christ is not in any way 'divine', but is instead only the supreme exemplar of all that human beings are capable of becoming. Christ, on this view, is not God 'incarnate', but only a supremely inspired individual; and as such he is not the architect of our salvation, but only the first of the redeemed.

It might be true, of course, that Jesus Christ is a mere human being, a truly virtuous individual; one who differs in degree, but not in kind, from the Mahatma Gandhis and Mother Teresas of this world. This, after all, is the view of many 'reductionist' christolo-gies.[32] Nevertheless, it can justifiably be argued that the salvation-scheme just outlined, which presupposed the notion of a divine irruption into the human order, is one that is not consonant with an 'exemplarist' soteriology.

The problem with 'exemplarism', from the standpoint of our

'model' of salvation, is that it begs the *real* question of redemption. According to the 'exemplarist', salvation consists in conforming our lives to the pattern established by an exemplary figure. But, surely, in order to follow the exemplary figure, we need – salvation! From time immemorial we have been confronted by exemplary figures: Socrates, Gautama, Mohammed, Guru Nanak, Gandhi, and so forth, but the human creature is still what she was before, and her situation has not changed. At the heart of 'exemplarism' lies the belief that salvation is something that the human being can confer on herself. However, as we have argued, the human animal cannot be the author of her own salvation, because human evil has a tragic dimension which arises from the fundamental discrepancy between the human creature and her world – we are 'thrown' into evil because we are 'thrown' into a world that we have not created. The architect of human salvation cannot therefore be a merely exemplary figure.

It could be objected, as indeed the late Geoffrey Lampe has done, that it is simply false to assume that 'exemplarist' soteriologies necessarily present us with a 'beautiful picture' but leave it entirely up to us to respond to the exemplary picture in question. Lampe holds that in addition to presenting us with the exemplary figure of Christ, the God of 'exemplarism' is also powerful and effective, and so bestows on human beings the effective grace needed to respond to the figure of Christ.[33] This is not the right place in which to conduct a detailed examination of Lampe's argument. However, I believe his argument to be flawed in some important respects. Firstly, it is transparently obvious that there are many cases of individuals who have been presented with the exemplary figure of Christ, but who have not, it seems, possessed the effective grace needed to respond adequately to the salvific pattern established by the life and death of Jesus of Nazareth. Does it follow from this that the God who graciously enables (only) *some* individuals to conform to the exemplary pattern of Jesus is, therefore, an arbitrary and capricious deity, one who haphazardly bestows his gracious favours on certain privileged individuals? Secondly, Lampe understands grace as God's 'personal presence within his creatures',[34] which renders problematic the need for an exemplary figure like Christ: for if God is genuinely present within his creatures, then communion has *already* been restored between God and human beings. It would appear, therefore, that we can be redeemed without really having to strive to become Christ-like. This objection can be stated more briefly in the form of the following dilemma. Either divine grace is efficacious or it is not. If it is not efficacious, then human beings have not the means to become Christ-like (and hence to be redeemed); on the other hand, if it is efficacious, then *ipso facto* human beings are saved, and this without having to make a personal response to the pattern established by Jesus. 'Exemplarism' has the unavoidable consequence of diminishing the significance of what God achieves in and through the life and death of Jesus.[35]

'Exemplarist' soteriologies, Lampe's arguments notwithstanding, are hardly plausible. Apart from the problems involved in adverting to the notion of a divine grace which enables us to follow the pattern established by an exemplary individual, 'exemplarism' is unacceptable because it ultimately implies that salvation is something that human beings can confer on themselves (with a measure of divine 'assistance'). It makes salvation depend on the free response of human beings, and in so doing overlooks the fact that no human response, no 'persuasion in our hearts', can hope to overcome the fundamental discrepancy between the human animal and her world which is the source of the more intractable forms of evil.

It is time for us to take stock of our argument. The salvation-scheme just delineated, which eschews any overtly christological elements, nevertheless suggests that a viable soteriology *must* be a discourse which employs the notion of 'incarnation' (as opposed to being one that is merely 'exemplarist'). This point brings us to the nub of the debate between those theologians who adopt a 'Christocentric' (and hence a necessarily 'incarnational') approach to the question of human salvation, and those who reject 'Christocentrism' in the name of religious 'pluralism', and who therefore espouse a 'non-incarnational' (because 'exemplarist') soteriology. If our arguments are correct, then the theologians who adopt an 'incarnational' approach to soteriology have a grave problem on their hands: any faith, if it purports to be genuinely salvific, must (according to our 'model' of salvation) incorporate elements of an 'incarnational' discourse.[36]

But what about the 'Christocentric' approach to soteriology? Does the argument developed in this essay, since it questions the implicit 'exemplarism' of those who reject the 'Christocentric' approach, not lend support to those who maintain that outside Christ (and his church) there can be no salvation? Have we not delineated a salvation-scheme which, despite all our protestations to the contrary, is really such that it cannot but vindicate a

'Christocentric' view of salvation? Our answer to these questions is that the position developed here cannot be used to support *every* aspect of the 'Christocentric' view of divine revelation and salvation. For while the 'model' of salvation outlined above accords with the belief in a divine irruption into the natural order, a divine 'identification' with humankind to bring salvation to human beings, it cannot be used to justify or validate the claim that the *locus* of this divine identification is a Jew who lived in Palestine nearly two thousand years ago. Our salvation-scheme simply does not enable us to come to terms with the so-called 'scandal of particularity' which lies at the heart of 'Christocentrism'. Those who believe that the history of Jesus of Nazareth is also the history of God's unique 'identification' with his creation (in and through Jesus) to bring salvation to humanity can hope to obtain a vindication of this belief only by resorting to the notion of a divine revelation which makes this truth accessible to human beings. Barth, therefore, was right to make revelation the basis of his 'Christocentrism' – indeed he had no other theological alternative. For 'Christocentrism' cannot be vindicated via a soteriology grounded in anthropology, because soteriology (on its own) can only furnish a schema or 'model' that is *broadly* 'incarnational'; it cannot specify '*content*' for this schema that is restricted exclusively to the person of Jesus. In a word: 'Christocentrism' cannot find its proper home in soteriology unless it is grounded in revelation.[37] If the 'Christocentric' theologian cannot, in the last analysis, derive any real support from our salvation-scheme (though this scheme does certainly allow the *possibility* that God brought an 'incarnational' salvation to humankind), how is the religious pluralist to regard our salvation-scheme? This question will be addressed in the next two sections.

IV

The way is always open to the pluralist to question the 'incarnational' soteriology developed in this essay. This 'incarnational' soteriology is at odds with a theology that sets out to be 'pluralistic', inasmuch as it suggests, quite plainly, that an 'incarnational grammar' is integral to 'proper' soteriological speech. Thus, our salvation-scheme would be entirely compatible with the views of those theologians who espouse an attenuated 'Christocentrism' (John Baillie, for example) by saying that Christianity is still the only real way to salvation, because Christianity, of all the world religions, is the one faith that can properly be deemed 'incarnational'. To this claim the pluralist can raise at least two objections.

Firstly, the pluralist can ask any exponent of 'Christocentrism' to state clearly her position on the thorny question of the 'scandal of particularity'. Does the 'Christocentrist' assert that the history of Jesus totally expresses, indeed exhausts, the significance of God's saving 'identification' with humankind, or does she allow the possibility that *other* events and persons can *also* express the significance of this 'identification'? If the 'Christocentrist' chooses the former alternative, then she is open to the charge that the truth of her assertion can be determined solely on the basis of revelation (and what is more, a revelation which – on a 'Barthian' account – is self-authenticating and self-interpreting); on the other hand, if she adopts the latter alternative, then she no longer views the 'incarnation' of Christ as a unique and exclusive event, and so she effectively countenances the possibility that other faiths can also be ways to salvation. 'Christocentrism', it would appear, can only be maintained in its absolute ('Barthian') form. Any attempt to compromise its absoluteness will undermine it – the 'moderate Christocentrist' is the inevitable engineer of her own destruction.[38]

Secondly, the pluralist can object to the claim that Christianity is the only way to salvation (because it is the only properly 'incarnational' faith) by pointing out that Christianity is *not* in fact the only 'incarnational' faith – theistic Hinduism, for example, makes use of the concept of a divine *avatar*, and this opens the way for us (i) to explicate the significance of Christ in terms of the *avatar* concept, and (ii) to say that God could identify with humankind through personages who belong to other faiths (e.g. Krishna in the theistic Hinduism of the *Bhagavad Gita*).

How might the 'moderate Christocentrist', the individual who is likely to subscribe to our salvation-scheme, respond to these two objections? Where the question of the uniqueness and the unrepeatability of the incarnation is concerned, she has to show that our salvation-scheme allows the possibility of this divine 'identification' with humankind to culminate in the history of a single person (viz. Jesus), which makes the history of this person 'qualitatively different' from the histories of all other individuals and religious personages, because the history of Jesus is nothing other than the once-for-all 'inhistorization' of God.[39] In this connexion, however, it has to be said again that our salvation-scheme cannot of itself show that Jesus is, of all human beings, the person in whom God 'chose' to 'incarnate' himself – our salvation-scheme, we have

already said, is no more than a schema for describing the 'identification' of God with human beings; in other words, it uses 'incarnation' as a *concept*, without in any way indicating that Jesus of
Nazareth is (or must be) the *instantiation* of this concept.[40]
However, what our salvation-scheme can accommodate is the
possibility that God's work to overcome evil does reach a climax in
the events concerning Jesus of Nazareth – since evil manifests itself
in concreto in the particular events of history, it makes sense to say
that God's work to conquer evil can (and does in fact) reach a
culmination at a particular point in human history. There is simply
no logical incongruity involved in the idea that God's work of
reconciling human beings to himself comes to a decisive and perfect
expression in the life of Jesus. For this reason I disagree with John
Hick when he says that the ' . . . doctrine of unceasing divine
sympathy and suffering removes this particular need for incarnation'.[41] On the contrary, the incarnation (i.e. God's 'identification'
with humankind to the point where death and suffering become
events in the life of the Godhead) is the perfect manifestation of
this 'unceasing divine sympathy', and what is more, without the
incarnation (which is the *conditio sine qua non* of human redemption, as our salvation-scheme indicates), God's 'unceasing sympathy and suffering' would be in vain – evil would continue to prevail
in the world, despite God's unceasing compassion for all those
afflicted by earthly travails. The doctrine of God as our co-sufferer,
which Hick sponsors, is thoroughly inadequate from the soteriological point of view unless it is augmented by a schema which
provides some understanding of the divine triumph over evil. The
doctrine of God as our fellow-sufferer is certainly relevant to the
question of the *goodness* of God in the face of human suffering, but
it is not of itself of any great *soteriological* import – a finite deity, a
demiurge, could be our co-sufferer, but still not be able to overcome the evil that resides in the human condition and thus to
reconcile human beings to himself. And, as I have already suggested, no canons of logic are breached in asserting that God's
work to defeat the power of evil reaches its completion in the events
surrounding the life of one particular individual. It is entirely
compatible with the position just outlined that God reveals himself
to other human beings, in other times and in other places. Though,
of course, it remains true that these other revelations, while they
'*contribute*' to God's saving work, are not in themselves decisive for
the successful outcome of that divine work.

The second objection that can be raised by the pluralist – viz.

that Christianity is *not* in fact the only 'incarnational' faith (and that consequently it is not the *only* way to salvation) – can be dealt with more easily by our 'moderate Christocentrist'. Obviously, if the concept of 'incarnation' is used in such a way that Jesus of Nazareth becomes of necessity the only instantiation of this concept, then it becomes virtually axiomatic that Christianity is the only truly 'incarnational' faith.[42] However, if we instead viewed the concept of 'incarnation' as a rubric for a divine intervenient 'identification' with humankind in the person of one or more historical individuals, then it becomes conceivable that Christianity is not the only 'incarnational' faith.[43] If there are other 'incarnational' faiths – and theistic Hinduism, with its *avatar* doctrine, seems to be one such faith – then it ought to be possible for us to adopt one of the following alternatives: (1) to account for the significance of Christ in terms of categories belonging to other faiths: and (2) to say that God could 'identify' with humankind through individuals who are adherents of non-Christian faiths. The upshot of adopting (1) and (2) would be that Christianity is no longer to be regarded as the only genuinely salvific faith. What could be said, even if only briefly, about proposals (1) and (2)?

Where proposal (1) is concerned, it would seem that even if we overlooked the fact of the unique status ascribed to Jesus Christ by (orthodox) Christianity, it would still not be possible for us straight-forwardly to interpret the significance of Christ by means of categories that belong to other faiths. Even if this problem were posed in terms of our salvation-scheme, which eschews making any explicit claims about particular religious personages (and so, potentially, should be 'open' to any and all faiths), it is still difficult to see how the concept of a divinely 'incarnate' individual, which is posited by our salvation-scheme, can be integrated into any of the other world religions. The most likely of the world religions to accommodate this salvation-scheme is Hinduism, and in the next section I shall consider the possibility of embedding our salvation-scheme in a soteriological framework supplied by Hinduism.

V

The suggestion that the *same* salvation-scheme can straddle the boundaries of two seemingly incompatible or incommensurable religious traditions is one that is inherently syncretistic, and of the major world religions, Hinduism (especially in its modern neo-Sankaran variant) is perhaps the one that tends most towards syncretism, inasmuch as it holds to the view that all religions, their apparent differences notwithstanding, point to the one truth. ('All rivers flow into the ocean', etc.) And, as has already been mentioned, the Hindu *avatar* doctrine appears to have certain affinities with the Christian doctrine of the incarnation.

However, although the possibility of embedding our salvation-scheme into a framework supplied by a Hindu 'theology' (and thus of bringing about a *rapprochement* between the Hindu *avatar* doctrine and the Christian understanding of 'incarnation') appears initially to be promising, a swarm of problems can be seen to arise as soon as we embark on this undertaking. The following are some of the difficulties created by this attempt to place our salvation-scheme in a theological framework that is Hindu (as opposed to Christian).

1. There are the *methodological* difficulties which surround any attempt to formulate a plausible version of syncretism.[44] One such difficulty concerns the markedly different ways in which Christianity and Hinduism (in its theistic form) understand such important notions as 'God' and 'the presence of God', notions which are vital for any proper understanding of the 'incarnation' of deity. To be acceptable syncretism has to furnish suitable trans-religious definitions of these notions. The problem here, however, is that Christians and Hindus do not talk about God in a completely general way, or *in vacuo*: they talk about the-God-who-is-the-Father-of-our-Lord-Jesus-Christ, whereas Hindus talk about the supreme-*Brahman* (*para Brahman*)-who-can-only-be-spoken-of-in-terms-of-It. Thus, the 'God' referred to in these expressions is a divinity who is *confessed* to be such-and-such, and it is this confessional element that seems to stand in the way of the theologian who wants to provide a trans-religious definition of 'God'. For it is hard to see how the Hindu can confess the 'God' who is the Father of Jesus Christ in quite the same way as the devout Christian, just as it is difficult to see how the Christian can confess '*Brahman*' in quite the same way as the orthodox Hindu. It does not look as if there can be a trans-religious specification of 'God' without distorting the mainsprings of the two religious traditions in question.

2. The concept of 'the presence of God *in* history' is vital to any understanding of divine incarnation, and if we are to embed our salvation-scheme into two seemingly disparate religious traditions (viz. Christianity and Hinduism), we must be certain that we are able to frame a concept of the 'inhistorization' of God that is

appropriately trans-religious. Unfortunately, two important discrepancies between the Hindu and the Christian appreciation of
history stand in the way of such an enterprise. Firstly, there is the
problem that Christianity (like Judaism) has a *'linear'* view of the
historical process, as opposed to the essentially *'cyclical'* view that
prevails in Hinduism: the latter symbolizes the time-process as a
wheel, the former as a road.[45] Secondly, this problem is compoun-
ded by the fact that Christianity and Hinduism make radically
different, even incompatible, valuations of the historical process.
Christianity, primarily because it views the historical process as the
place of the mighty acts of God, accords history and historicity a
significance absent in the Hindu tradition. In Hinduism, by contrast, there is a devaluation or depreciation of the 'reality' of the
historical process: history belongs to the realm of *maya*, of illusion,
and thus has only a provisional and secondary significance. This
fundamental discrepancy in their respective estimations of the
significance of history, means that while it is possible for us to
ground our 'model' of salvation in the Christian religious tradition,
the same possibility does not really exist where Hinduism is
concerned. The 'cyclical' view of history rooted in Hindu thought
means that Hinduism cannot subscribe to the notion of a *single*
divine 'incarnation', which is what our salvation-scheme requires –
the idea that divine *avatars* come into being 'age after age' (which is
what the Hindu principle of repetition maintains) is not consonant
with the idea that God 'incarnate' *decisively* overcomes the power
of evil at a *particular* point in the time-process.[46] It would seem,
therefore, that our salvation-scheme would accord better with the
view of history which underlies the Christian doctrine of the
incarnation, since the Christian understanding of history allows for
the sheer particularity and concreteness of God's 'identification'
with humankind. The Hindu doctrine of *maya* (*mayavada*), which
asserts the 'unreality' of the world, is important from the standpoint
of soteriology because it endorses the view that salvation or
liberation is really salvation *from* the world (of illusion), and not
salvation and sanctification *of* the world (as is the case in Christian
soteriology). The contention that the world is 'unreal' also implies
that the *avatara* cannot in any way be a product of the historical
process or a fulfilment of it. Besides, it makes hardly any sense to
talk of animal incarnation (which is what the *avatar* doctrine assents
to) as if it were the outcome of the historical process. The *avatara*
descends into the world, without really partaking of it – he, she or it
remains divine, and only possesses the vestiges of humanity or

animality. It is hardly surprising, therefore, that those Hindu thinkers who evince an interest in the figure of Christ seem interested only in a docetic Christ. John Robinson discusses this devaluation of historical 'reality' on the part of several Hindu thinkers who show an interest in the figure of Christ, and quotes the following passages which reflect a view of Christ as an essentially docetic figure:

> GANDHI: I have never been interested in a historical Jesus. I should not care if it is proved by someone that the man called Jesus never lived, and that what was narrated in the Gospels was a figment of the writer's imagination. For the Sermon on the Mount would still be true for me.[47]
>
> AUROBINDO: Such controversies as the one that has raged in Europe over the historicity of Christ would seem to the spiritually-minded Indian largely a waste of time; he would concede to it a considerable historical, but hardly any religious importance. If the Christ, God made man, lives within our spiritual being, it would seem to matter little whether or not a son of Man physically lived and suffered and died in Judea.[48]
>
> VIVEKANANDA: Christ was God incarnate; they could not kill him. That which was crucified was only a semblance, a mirage.[49]
>
> RADHAKRISHNAN: Christ is born in the depths of the spirit: we say that he passes through life, dies on the cross and rises again. Those are not so much historical events which occurred once upon a time, as universal processes of spiritual life, which are being continually accomplished in the souls of men.[50]

These passages evince a striking disregard on the part of their writers for the historical Jesus, they suggest an interest in a purely 'yogic' Christ, unconstrained by the characteristic features of a genuine human existence, and untroubled even by crucifixion. Our salvation-scheme, however, requires God to engage with the realities of the human situation, to confront our sin and suffering, and in the process to overcome them. And this engagement, if it is not to be evacuated of tension and reality, has to be one in which it makes sense to talk of the genuine 'enfleshment' of God, as opposed to God merely walking on this planet in human form. The God who possesses the semblance, but not the substance, of humanity, is the God of some docetic mime, and he cannot (according to our salvation-scheme) be the God who saves. Again, it can be seen that our salvation-scheme can be less easily accommodated within the framework of a Hindu, as opposed to a Christian, soteriology.[51]

3. Another reason why it would be difficult to implant our

salvation-scheme into Hindu soteriology is connected with the Hindu understanding of salvation as something which human beings bring about by their own ethical strivings. To quote Santosh Sengupta:

> In the Hindu view, liberation, which has an ethical content, is also ethically conditioned. Liberation is a matter of attainment through moral actions. The strict Hindu position is that liberation does not come as a gift. We know that in the Christian view, liberation is a matter of grace. To whom and when grace comes depends on the divine will itself.[52]

According to our salvation-scheme, redemption is not something that the human creature can bring about by her own unaided efforts. If there is a profound sense in which the evil that exists in the world *preexists* the deeds of human beings, then only the Creator of the world can overcome the evil of the world. Our moral strivings are ultimately powerless in the face of such intractable forms of evil. Or to use the language of 'atonement': only an 'objective', in contradistinction to a merely 'subjective', atonement will suffice. The Hindu view of salvation has closer parallels with a purely 'subjective' conception of the atonement.[53]

For these three reasons, then, it must be concluded that our salvation-scheme is closer to the Christian scheme of things than it is to Hinduism. Therefore, if the significance of Christ is articulated in terms of our salvation-scheme, it follows that the significance of Christ cannot be expressed by resorting to categories that belong to Hinduism, or any other faith which does not uphold a view of divine incarnation that is essentially similar (in outline, at any rate) to the Christian conception.

We must now consider proposal (ii), which holds that if there are 'incarnational' faiths in addition to Christianity, then it might be that God could identify with humanity through personages that belong to other faiths (e.g. Krishna, Rama, the Buddha, etc.). The adoption of this proposal would therefore effectively destroy any basis Christians might have had for ascribing a unique status to the person of Christ. Here it must be admitted that, solely from the standpoint of our salvation-scheme, there is no real reason why, say, Krishna, should not be the individual in and through whom God 'identifies' with humankind, provided of course that Krishna fulfils all the desiderations of our salvation-scheme. But, as has been pointed out, if Krishna is to occupy this role in our salvation-scheme, he cannot really remain an *avatara* – he must in several crucial respects become more 'like' the figure of Christ.

In conclusion, what are the final implications of our argument? If it is accepted that only a faith which can accommodate our salvation-scheme (or a variant of it) is properly entitled to be regarded as a religion of *salvation*, then it follows that *only* an 'incarnational' faith can be salvific (in the strict sense of the term). 'Non-incarnational' faiths may enlighten human beings, they may ease their anguish, they may make them more compassionate, they may make them more moral beings, but in the last resort only an 'incarnational' faith embodies the true way to salvation. Now, inasmuch as Christianity is – historically – the only such faith, the following conclusion seems inescapable: Christianity is, strictly speaking, the only religion of salvation. This argument provides no support for Christian triumphalism. On the contrary, by insisting that, ultimately, we can in no way be the architects of our salvation, it reinforces our finitude, our status as creaturely beings (albeit creatures of God). This truth counsels a more profound humility on our part (humility being defined as the unstinting acceptance of our finitude); it means that even the best person among us, who therefore is the one most 'worthy' of being redeemed, can never be anything more than 'a poor sort of good man' (to use a phrase of Iris Murdoch's). There is no scope here for Christian triumphalism. My main purpose in developing this argument is not to vindicate 'Christocentrism'; it is, rather, to draw attention to something which I fear has been overlooked by the protagonists in the current debate about the relationship between Christianity and the other world religions. The so-called pluralists taking part in this debate have, in the main, sought to advance the cause of 'pluralism' by doing away with a 'high' christology (and the allegedly 'exclusivist' conception of revelation that usually accompanies a 'high' christo- logy). These pluralists prefer, instead, a 'low' christology, and its concomitant 'exemplarist' soteriology. They seem to think that the best way to legitimize 'pluralism' is to use soteriology (and religious anthropology) as a starting-point for christological reflection. In this way (they seem to think) we can make certain 'Christocentrism' does not lurk in our christologies. However, if my arguments are correct, the threat to pluralism is in no way obviated by making anthropology and soteriology the starting-point for christology. For I hope I have been able to show that certain theses very dear to the 'Christocentrist' can be established using just such an anthropologi- cal starting-point.[54]

10

'Many religions and the one true faith': an examination of Lindbeck's chapter 3

I Introductory

Since its publication in 1985 George Lindbeck's *The Nature of Doctrine* has come to be widely regarded as a profound and suggestive treatment of a broad range of issues which lie at the forefront of current debates in theology and religious studies.[1] Its wide reach notwithstanding, the book is two-pronged in respect of its substantive theses. Lindbeck is concerned in the main to do two things. Firstly, he sets out to formulate a 'cultural-linguistic' model of religion. This undertaking is avowedly 'non-theological' (p. 46). Secondly, he wants to develop a meta-theological option, a 'way' of doing systematic or dogmatic theology, which he calls an 'intratextual' theology (pp. 112ff).

The 'cultural-linguistic' or 'regulative' model is, in Lindbeck's eyes, less unsatisfactory than its two principal competitors for the status of a properly-constituted theory of religion. The two rivals in question are 'cognitive-propositionalism' and 'experiential-expressivism' (to use Lindbeck's designations).

Proponents of the 'cognitive-propositionalist' model take religions to be essentially, but not necessarily exclusively, forms of speech and action focused on a mind-independent sacred or divine reality. Religious doctrines are 'cognitive' inasmuch as they embody truth-claims, at least in some part 'about' this reality, which are genuinely informatory.

Proponents of 'experiential-expressivism', by contrast, generally do not view religions as cognitive enterprises. They tend invariably to regard religious doctrines as non-assertorial and non-discursive entities, expressive or evocative of the interior life of the faithful person.

Against these two models of religion – models which he considers
for a variety of reasons to be coherent but nonetheless quite
implausible – Lindbeck promotes a 'cultural-linguistic' explanation
of religion. According to the 'cultural-linguistic' theory, religions
are systems containing both discursive and non-discursive idioms
connecting intentionalities with action; they also provide regulative
structures which guide reflection, feeling and conduct. These
regulative systems will govern the irreducibly *public* discourses of
whole communities (and *ipso facto* the speech of their members),
and not just isolated individuals.

The second prong of Lindbeck's argument hinges on a differentiation of an 'intratextual' from an 'extratextual' theology. The latter
theology is one which locates the 'meaning' of a sacred text either in
realities external to it, so that the text is a figuration of these
realities (this being the 'cognitive-propositionalist' version of extratextualism); or in an experience or set of experiences, so that the
text – *qua* symbol-system – is an appropriate expression of the
experience or experiences in question (this being the 'experiential-
expressivist' version of extratextualism). It is a presumption of
extratextualism that all interpreters – solely by virtue of their
possession of a 'common humanity' or of their being partakers of 'a
common human experience' – have access to the universal and
invariant structures which underpin these realities as they are
're-presented' in religious texts. Equipped with this presupposition,
the extratextualist (as portrayed by Lindbeck) is then able to
espouse a religious hermeneutic which is global in its extension,
i.e. a hermeneutic which discloses to the skilled interpreter a set of
truths of the widest generality, truths adverting to what David
Tracy has called the 'limit-character of common human experience'. A Christian theological hermeneutic is thus to be seen as a
component of this global hermeneutic. Exponents of extratextualism therefore see the 'meanings' contained in religious texts as
'correlatable' in principle with those 'meanings' secured via an
application of the global hermeneutic. Theology functions as an
indispensable translation-scheme for making such correlations. It
thus consists essentially in a method of correlation, and as such
incorporates a 'master code' in terms of which the Christian
'sub-code' *must* be rewritten if it is to be understood and appropriated.

An intratextual approach, by contrast, affirms that the 'meaning'
of a text is inseparable from the particular idiom or discourse which
happens to be constitutive of that particular text. It holds that the

Christian 'code' is *sui generis*: it is the 'master code' (*pace* the extratextualist). As Lindbeck puts it in a passage that bears extended quotation:

> [Intratextual theology] does not make scriptural contents into meta-phors for extrascriptural realities, but the other way around. It does not suggest, as is often said in our day, that believers find their stories in the Bible, but rather that they make the story of the Bible their story. The cross is not to be viewed as a figurative representation of suffering nor the messianic kingdom as symbol for hope in the future; rather, suffering should be cruciform, and hopes for the future messianic. More generally stated, it is the religion instantiated in Scripture which defines being, truth, goodness, and beauty, and the nonscriptural exemplifications of these realities need to be trans-formed into figures (or types or antitypes) of the scriptural ones. Intratextual theology redescribes reality within the scriptural frame-work rather than translating Scripture into extrascriptural categories. It is the text, so to speak, which absorbs the world, rather than the world the text. [The text is] able to absorb the universe. It supplies the interpretive framework within which believers seek to live their lives and understand reality.
>
> (pp. 117–18)

Integral to this intratextualism, therefore, are the related principles that it is the biblical linguistic world which subsumes extrascriptural reality, and that it is this world – the only 'true' world – which is decisive for the shaping of Christian 'identity'.[2]

Lindbeck asserts that intratextualism is 'compatible' with the 'cultural-linguistic' model (cf. p. 114), and he makes it clear that one of his aims is to motivate a 'descriptive' (i.e. a systematic or dogmatic) theology undertaken in a 'cultural-linguistic' mode. The cohesiveness of Lindbeck's programme notwithstanding, the real importance of keeping clearly in mind its two-pronged nature will, I hope, be borne out in the course of this discussion.

II The 'cultural-linguistic' model and the Christian theology of religions

These days the running in discussions of the inter-relationships between the world religions seems very much to be made by those who profess to be exponents of one or the other of the several brands of 'religious pluralism'. Even those who are reluctant to embrace this 'pluralism' somehow find it necessary to define their own positions by referring to the parameters established by advo-cates of 'religious pluralism'. Chapter 3 of *The Nature of Doctrine* indicates quite clearly that Lindbeck is not to be counted amongst these 'pluralist' runners. Neither is he concerned even to engage with them in any kind of oppositional way. They are simply bypassed.

In chapter 3 Lindbeck applies his 'cultural-linguistic'/intratextual approach to religion to a cluster of issues usually posed under the rubric of a theology of religions. His application is particularly noteworthy in at least two respects. Firstly, as mentioned, Lindbeck's account does not in any way endorse, either tacitly or overtly, the irreducibly syncretistic ideology of 'religious pluralism'.[3] Secondly, and this point is related to the previous one, his theory is (not unexpectedly!) entirely devoid of the 'experiential-expressivism' which pervades so many of the above-mentioned theologies and philosophies of 'religious pluralism'. This is because Lindbeck explicitly repudiates the assumption of the underlying unity of religious experience, a highly problematic assumption which he rightly takes to be constitutive of the 'experiential-expressivism' which we can easily discern in the philosophies and theologies of 'religious pluralism' adumbrated by John Hick and Wilfred Cantwell Smith.[4] Lindbeck's 'cultural-linguistic'/intratextual theory of the interrelationships between the religions would thus seem to merit close scrutiny precisely because it makes possible an acknowledgement of the 'facts' of religious diversity without propelling us down the *cul-de-sac* of 'religious pluralism'.

The third chapter of *The Nature of Doctrine*, which deals with the phenomenon of religious and theological diversity, begins with the following declaration of intent:

> It is not the business of a nontheological theory of religion to argue for or against the superiority of any one faith, but it does have the job, if it is to be religiously useful, of allowing the possibility of such a superiority. It must not . . . exclude the claims religions make about themselves, and it must supply some interpretation of what these claims mean.
>
> (p. 46)

Lindbeck selects three 'interreligious problems' – namely, 'unsurpassability, dialogue, and the salvation of "other believers"' – for discussion within the framework of such an approach. This essay will be concerned with the first and the third of these 'problems'.

III 'Unsurpassability'

Lindbeck believes that three specifications of 'unsurpassability' are forthcoming, depending on the particular model of religion that happens to be employed. Each model will have its attendant conception of 'truth', so that the putative unsurpassability of a particular religious tradition will generally be glossed in terms of that which, relative to other such traditions, can be accounted 'true' in it:

(i) Proponents of 'propositionalist' or 'cognitivist' models of religion tend to make comparisons between religions by invoking something approximating to a 'correspondence' theory of truth, and arguing that the superior religion is one which 'makes the most significant veridical truth claims and the fewest false ones' (p. 47). The 'superior' religion is thus one that is free from error – if it were otherwise it could in principle, if not in fact, be surpassed. Lindbeck also states that the 'propositional' model makes it a *conditio sine qua non* of unsurpassability that the purportedly unsurpassable religion 'contain the highest of what Aquinas called *revelabilia* (i.e. religiously significant truths capable of being revealed within the space-time world of human experience)' (p. 49). To fail to possess *revelabilia* to this maximal degree will leave open the possibility of a religion being wholly true (in the sense that its stock of truth-claims contains no items that are false) and yet incompletely true (in the sense that this stock is relatively limited, both in respect of its scope and its possible or actual significance). On a 'propositionalist' account such a religion would of course be 'surpassable'. Many Christians have traditionally maintained that this is exactly how the relationship between their faith and the religion of Israel is to be conceived (p. 49).

(2) Exponents of 'experiential-expressivism' view truth as a function of 'symbolic efficacy'. Religions are compared 'in terms of how effectively they articulate or represent and communicate that inner experience of the divine ... which is held to be common to them all. All religions are by definition capable of functioning truly in this nondiscursive, symbolic sense, but they can vary in their potential or actual degree of truth (i.e. efficacy)' (p. 47). Nevertheless, says Lindbeck, it is hard to see how an 'expressivist' account can attach a 'definite meaning to the notion of "unsurpassably true"' (p. 49). For there is no logical upper limit to the adequacy and effectiveness of a symbol-system. Just as we can grant the (mere) logical possibility of human beings who swim across the Atlantic or jump over the Post Office Tower in London (even though as yet no human being *actually* possesses the physical capacities required for such accomplishments), it is also possible – logically – for there to be a symbol-system which, while it may at present be confined to the bounds of mere conceivability, is nonetheless more adequate and more effective than its counterparts which happen already to

be in existence. Furthermore, it is possible for there to be several otherwise different, and perhaps even incompatible, symbol-systems which possess the same *actual* highest degree of effectiveness and adequacy. For example, the person endeavouring to persuade the attendant in the car-park of an expensive hotel to allow her to park in front of a 'No Parking' sign may find the possession of a 'right' accent to be just as symbolically 'powerful' for this purpose as the possession of a Porsche or Daimler. (I hasten to add that this is my example and not Lindbeck's.) These difficulties notwithstanding, 'expressive' conceptions of truth can still allow a religion to be 'unsurpassable'. However, they can do this only in a weak sense: historical accident determines whether or not the religion in question is in fact 'unsurpassable'. Thus, if this religion happens to have superseded its rivals at the termination of history, it will be deemed not only to have 'surpassed' them, but also to be 'unsurpassable' (p. 50).

(3) Adherents of a 'cultural-linguistic' model will view religions 'primarily as different idioms for construing reality, expressing experience, and ordering life'. In addressing the question of the 'categorical truth' of a religion, they will focus primarily 'on the categories ... in terms of which truth claims are made and expressive symbolisms employed' (pp. 47–8). Categories deemed to be adequate are those 'which can be made to apply to what is taken to be real, and which therefore make possible, though they do not guarantee, propositional, practical and symbolic truth' (p. 48). A religion possessing such categories can then be deemed to be 'categorially true'. Claims to unsurpassable truth made by adverting to the 'cultural-linguistic' model can be much stronger than those made via its 'experiential-expressivist' counterpart, but they may also be, for different reasons, both stronger and weaker than those validated by a 'propositional' account.

In its *stronger* form, the 'cultural-linguistic' or 'categorial' gloss on the claim to unsurpassable truth would assert that there is

> only one religion which has the concepts and categories that enable it to refer to the religious object, i.e., to whatever in fact is more important than everything else in the universe. This religion would then be the only one in which any form of propositional, and conceivably also expressive, religious truth or falsity could be present. Other religions might then be called categorially false, but propositionally and expressively they would be neither true nor false. They would be religiously meaningless just as talk about light and heavy things is meaningless when one lacks the concept 'weight'.

(p. 50)

The *weaker* form of the claim to 'categorial' truth is formulated thus by Lindbeck:

> Categorial truth does not exclude propositional error. Rather, it makes error as well as truth possible. Even if there is only one religion in which reference to God can occur . . . yet it will be open to all sorts of falsehoods in what it affirms of him.

(p. 51)

Lindbeck, as one would expect, is concerned preeminently with a specification of 'unsurpassability' that can be shown to be congruent with the 'cultural-linguistic' model. Nevertheless, he makes it clear that this model's delineation of the claim to unsurpassability *vis-à-vis* religious truth is consonant with a modest and qualified 'propositionalism' – Lindbeck eschews a full-blown 'propositionalism', but does not in the process discard the notion of truth as 'correspondence'.[5] On the contrary, Lindbeck wants to reconcile his 'categorial' account of religious truth with an ingenious hybrid truth-theory which combines the correspondence, coherence and pragmatic theories of truth. He does this by likening a lived religion to 'a single gigantic proposition', which 'may as a whole correspond or not correspond to what a theist calls God's being and will' (p. 51). Hence:

> It [i.e. a religion] is a true proposition to the extent that its objectivities are interiorized and exercised by groups and individuals in such a way as to conform them in some measure in the various dimensions of their existence to the ultimate reality and goodness that lies at the heart of things. It is a false proposition to the extent that this does not happen.

(p. 51)

A 'categorially true and unsurpassable' religion can then be defined as one which 'is capable of being rightly utilized, of guiding thought, passions, and actions in a way that corresponds to ultimate reality, and thus of being ontologically (and "propositionally") true, but is not always and perhaps not even usually so employed' (p. 52). This characterization of 'unsurpassability', however, can be seen to be deeply problematic.

Firstly, given that religions are historical entities, the capacity of a religion to function in a 'categorially true and unsurpassable' way will be crucially affected by historical particularities and socio-economic forces. Thus, given that Christianity was (at least notionally) the religion of the majority of those who administered the Nazi death camps, it would seem to follow from Lindbeck's definition that Christianity is precluded from being a 'categorially true and unsurpassable religion' *when viewed from the standpoint of the inmates* of Dachau, Treblinka, Auschwitz, Sobibor, Bergen-Belsen, Majdanek, Buchenwald, Ravensbruck, Sachsenhausen, Belzec, Mauthausen, etc. For it was only in the all too infrequent deeds of resistance and martyrdom undertaken by, e.g. Kolbe, Delp and Bonhoeffer, that we find manifested a *Christianity* which can properly be said to be 'rightly utilized' in Lindbeck's sense. It is true of course that Lindbeck incorporates a *ceteris paribus* clause ('but is not always and perhaps not even usually so employed') into his definition of 'unsurpassability', but it is hard to see how Christian theologians, or theologians of any other faith for that matter, can repeatedly invoke Lindbeck's caveat without ultimately derogating from the claim that Christianity (or the other faith in question) truly has the capacity to be character-forming and action-guiding 'in a way that corresponds to ultimate reality'. To provide a definition of 'unsurpassability', which seemingly evinces no recognition that Christianity would betray or erode its mainsprings if it were to possess this 'capacity' in a merely 'theoretical' way, is inevitably to sanction a form of Christianity that is prey to illusion and distortion. This is not to suggest that Lindbeck is entirely neglectful of Christianity's irreducibly 'performative' aspect: on the contrary, he insists that Christianity is at its core a faith which accords primacy to practice. But this insistence is compromised by a failure to perceive that to include what amounts to an 'exemption clause' (with respect to the failures of performance on the part of Christians) in his definition of 'unsurpassability' is effectively to leave unchallenged, even if only unintentionally, the 'idealism' that vitiates more than a few contemporary forms of Christian speech and conduct.[6]

Secondly, Lindbeck's espousal of an 'eschatological *fides ex auditu*' approach to the question of the salvation of non-Christians sits uneasily with the suggestion, implicit in his definition of 'unsurpassability', that Christianity can in principle retain its claim to unsurpassability even if, historically, it can be shown that Christians have, as individuals or a generality, failed lamentably in the practice of their faith. In presenting his 'prospective *fides ex auditu*' approach Lindbeck invites his readers to grant that the following proposal is not utterly implausible:

> dying [is] itself [to] be pictured as the point at which every human being is ultimately and expressly confronted by the gospel, by the crucified and risen Lord. It is only then that the final decision is made

for or against Christ; and this is true, not only of unbelievers but also of believers. All previous decisions, whether for faith or against faith, are preliminary. The final die is cast beyond our space and time, beyond empirical observation, beyond all speculation about 'good' or 'bad' deaths, when a person loses his rootage in this world and passes into the inexpressible transcendence that surpasses all words, images, and thoughts. We must trust and hope, although we cannot know, that in this dreadful yet wondrous end and climax of life no one will be lost. And here, even if not before, the offer of redemption is explicit. Thus it is possible to be hopeful and trusting about the ultimate salvation of non-Christians no less than Christians even if one does not think in terms of a primordial, prereflective experience of Christ's grace.[7]

(p. 59)

Central to this unavoidably metaphorical treatment of transcendence and eternity is the assumption that, at death, we 'lose our rootage in this world' and 'proceed' to a location 'beyond our space and time'. Intrinsic to this discourse is what Nicholas Lash has termed the image of the 'two tracks': we picture God's existence as a timeless state in which things do not happen successively, as a non-durational state which runs parallel to the historical process, so that when we die we 'jump the tracks' and continue to exist in this non-temporal divine sphere. The obvious implication is that, in a non-trivial sense, we *first* 'live' and *then* 'die': we 'live' in the one (historical) sphere and 'at the end' we then 'die' into the other (divine) sphere.[8] This picture is highly misleading. It is doubtless true that at death our physical or bodily existence comes to an end. My body, however, is not just some bit of material 'stuff' in spatio-temporal contiguity with other similar bits of 'stuff'. It is not even that bit of 'stuff' which I 'use' instrumentally to interact with other human beings. My body is more than this. My body, to use the terminology of current literary theory, is a 'text' replete with filial and affiliative inscriptions. As Lash puts it: 'My body is . . . the world constituted by the personal, social and economic relationships in which I share. These all form part of me. My language, my family, my city, are parts of my body' (p. 174). Hence, says Lash, at the moment of my death

it is not merely this lump of matter that dies: the whole network of personal family and social communications of which I formed a part, dies a little too. It therefore follows that the process of dying starts much earlier than the moment of terminal death. It is not only at the moment of terminal death that our world, our body, dies. . . . Dying is not something that takes place during our last few weeks or hours. . . .

[It] is true of the whole of our temporal existence that the process of living is *also* the process of dying. They are not *two* processes that succeed one another.

               (p. 175. Lash's emphases)[9]

It is an implication of Lash's understanding of 'eternal life' that (*contra* Lindbeck) the concept of 'risen life' signifies not a separate realm of existence which 'follows on' from existence in the historical realm, but a unitary historical process, 'with its beginning and its end defining and delimiting its particularity, as experienced from the standpoint of God who, in the stillness of unchanging love, creates, sustains and enlivens that process' (Lash, p. 178).

The problem with Lindbeck's account for anyone who is disposed to accept this Lashian understanding of 'eternal life' is that the author of *The Nature of Doctrine* posits a quite definite disjunction between a state of existence in which we have a 'rootage in this world' and one in which this 'rootage' has disappeared. Let us, however, grant Lindbeck his 'subsequence' model so as to be able better to see where it takes us.

If it is acknowledged that our bodily (and hence our 'personal') identities are socially and culturally constituted (and it is certainly possible to make this acknowledgement *without* necessarily having to discard the 'subsequence' theory), then the non-Christian individual who, as Lindbeck sees it, confronts Christ and the gospel at the *eschaton* will certainly not do so as a *tabula rasa*.

He or she will be someone whose body had, in 'this' life, been the bearer of a quite specific set of cultural and social inscriptions. But what if, say, this set of inscriptions is such that it is part of a system of narrative projection which recounts a series of unfortunate and deeply painful encounters with individuals who professed to be followers of Christ and his gospel? What if this person – say, a Jewish victim of the Nazi death camps – were so moved by her experiences of what Christian anti-semites had done to her that she is not able in a Lindbeckian 'after-life' to attach any sense, let alone credence, to the notion of Christianity as a religion which, in his words, is 'capable of being rightly utilized ... in a way that corresponds to ultimate reality'? One assumes that Lindbeck would want to say of this particular individual that her estimation of Christianity, formed as it was in 'this' life, could not therefore be so *absolutely* unchangeable as to prevent her, when she attains to the 'other' life, from 'hearing' the proffer of redemption made by the crucified and risen Jesus. In a 'post-mortem' existence she would be so profoundly healed that her 'this worldly' negative assessment of

Christianity and Christians would not survive her encounter with the risen Lord. In the world to come she would be given grounds for revising her (inevitably provisional) estimation of Christianity and for conceding that the religion of Christians was in principle, even if not *de facto*, unsurpassable in the sense specified by Lindbeck. Or would Lindbeck be willing to concede the above-mentioned possibility that someone could be so damaged in 'this' life that, come the *eschaton*, she would be quite unable to 'hear' Christ's proffer of redemption? In this case, there would be, for this one individual at any rate, no 'prospective *fides ex auditu*' – the barbarism of her notionally Christian tormentors would have rendered her deaf in advance of any such proffer of salvation. To make this admission, however, would be to admit that the *fides ex auditu* is *not* universal in scope – and this would be contrary to Lindbeck's explicitly stated theological intentions. So Lindbeck has very little alternative but to affirm that no 'this worldly' circumstances can ultimately threaten or irretrievably destroy our capacity to 'hear' an eschatological proffer of salvation from the crucified and risen Lord. It would appear that Lindbeck's eschatology harbours what amounts to a latent but nonetheless extremely powerful theodicy! In fairness to him, it must certainly be granted that it is a central affirmation of the Christian faith that, in and through the Spirit, all things are possible for the Father and the Son. No earthly power can thwart God in his proffer of redemption to creaturely beings. There is thus no Christian warrant for retaining any certitudes about who can or can not 'hear' God when the divine word of salvation is spoken. Thus, where our concentration camp victim is concerned, it is hard to see how it could be asserted that she was irremediably precluded from hearing this Word because of what her Christian torturers and murderers had done to her – to say this would not only be a blasphemy, it would also be tantamount to holding that God's sovereign purposes for his creatures are susceptible – in this 'episodic' way – to frustration by human beings. So Lindbeck's account would seem to be intact as long as he allows that in the final reckoning *all* would have had the opportunity to 'hear' this Word, be it in a 'pre-mortem' *or* a 'post-mortem' existence (this of course assumes that his 'subsequence' model has not been discredited on other grounds). To this extent, Lindbeck's position, while it requires an explicit confession of Christ on the part of all who are candidates for salvation, can appropriately be described as an eschatologically-qualified 'universalism'.[10]

But there is another difficulty for the supporter of the 'prospective *fides ex auditu*' approach. The acknowledgement or hope that *all* will ultimately 'hear' God's utterance of salvation in Christ, and *only* in Christ, robs the question of the unsurpassability of Christianity of any real point or urgency. It is not difficult to see why. Given a 'cultural-linguistic' perspective which views religion as something irreducibly communitarian, any attempt to reconcile the *Christus solus* with the salvation of non-Christians will involve the positing of an extension or else a dismantling of the visible boundaries of the Christian community. This enlargement or dissolution is said by the proponent of the *'fides ex auditu'* theory to take place in the world 'to come', as opposed to being in 'this' world (the view of Karl Rahner). In 'the life to come' each and every human being will be confronted by Christ and his gospel. Indeed, Lindbeck is prepared to state that this confrontation – the 'locus' of which is the church – is a necessary condition of *both* salvation *and* damnation. Thus he says of the Bible that

> [it] balances Cyprian's claim that there is no salvation outside the church (*extra ecclesia [sic] nulla salus*) with an at least equally emphatic insistence that the beginning of damnation, of deliberate opposition to God, is possible only within the church, within the people of God: Jesus pronounced his woes (and wept) . . . over the cities of Israel, not those of the Gentiles. On this view there is no damnation – just as there is no salvation – outside the church. One must, in other words, learn the language of faith before one can know enough about its message knowingly to reject it and thus be lost.

(p. 59)[11]

The implications of this position are clear: at the *eschaton* (glossed in terms of the Lindbeckian version of the 'subsequence' theory) all human beings will at least be endowed with the capacity for hearing and accepting the true religion, and so, as required by the 'cultural-linguistic' model, all would have been incorporated into the linguistic community that is the church. All would, willy-nilly, have been 'moulded' by the Christian language, and so all will be 'in' the church, regardless of whether or not they are disposed to reject Christ.[12] Christianity would turn out to be 'the categorially true and unsurpassable' religion, in the sense that it, and it alone, can give us the words with which to 'hear' Christ, and this regardless of whether or not it had been 'rightly utilized' by us in a 'pre-mortem' state. Given this strong assertion of the eschatological unsurpassability of Christianity, the question of its 'categorial adequacy' becomes quite superfluous. For if those who are non-Christians in a 'pre-mortem' existence can be redeemed and damned *only* by 'hearing' the divine proffer of salvation in and through Christ in a post-mortem state, then the question of Christianity's correspondence with 'ultimate reality' (such a correspondence being one of Lindbeck's marks of 'categorial adequacy') is a question that will necessarily be of significance to us only so long as we remain 'this side of the tracks'. Come the *eschaton* only one categorial scheme will be isomorphic with the ultimate reality that is the three-personed God – all who 'jump the tracks' will therefore find themselves proceeding to salvation or damnation in a strictly 'monolingual' condition (at any rate, in respect of the language of faith). So while Lindbeck starts off by furnishing an exposition of the connection which – ostensibly – obtains between 'categorial adequacy' and 'unsurpassability', thereby giving the impression that this connection is designed to shoulder a not insubstantial conceptual and theological burden, his subsequent advocacy of a 'prospective *fides ex auditu*' theory – especially one so tightly harnessed to the *solus Christus* – ensures that in the end this putative connection really has no work to do! The inevitable outcome here is that there can only be one genuine candidate (viz. Christianity) for the status of *the* categorially true, and hence the unsurpassable, religion; and, what is more, the categorial scheme deemed – 'neutrally' or 'objectively' – to be normative and generative of the status of 'unsurpassability' will, *a principio*, bear a suspiciously close resemblance to that set which comprises those categories regulative of Christian speech and action. Christianity (i.e. a particular understanding of it) will, so to speak, deliver the goods in advance of their being ordered by the 'postliberal' theologian.[13] On this 'postliberal' view, the categorial schemes of the non-Christian religions are to be assigned an essentially supplementary, though a not unimportant, role in relation to Christianity. As Lindbeck himself puts it:

> To hold that a particular language is the only one that has the words and concepts that can authentically speak of the ground of being, the goal of history, and true humanity (for Christians believe that they cannot genuinely speak of these apart from telling and retelling the biblical story) is not at all the same as denying that other religions have resources for speaking truths and referring to realities, even highly important truths and realities, of which Christianity as yet knows nothing and by which it could be greatly enriched.

(p. 61)[14]

It is perhaps not too difficult to see why David Tracy finds himself persuaded that Lindbeck is a 'confessionalist' and a 'fideist'.[15] But we are not fated to share Tracy's estimation of Lindbeck's pro-gramme. Any identifiably *Christian* intratextual theology, such as Lindbeck's, will possess an intrinsic tendency to articulate its claims to 'categorial adequacy' (or 'categorial truth') from the perspective of an irreducible 'christomonism'.[16] And this 'christomonistic' perspective ensues immediately in the *solus Christus* and its direct or indirect categorial and doctrinal offshoots. So intratextual theologies like Lindbeck's do not in principle behove their exponents to look to a fundamental theology or a global hermeneu-tic for a specification of 'categorial adequacy'. Tracy is of course renowned for the necessarily complemental, even if not 'foun-dational', role he grants fundamental theology (i.e. as a delimiting philosophical or hermeneutical framework for systematic or dog-matic theological reflection), and his animus against Lindbeck's intratextualism must be seen in the context of the latter's typical refusal to engage in the task of finding and framing such a prolegomenon. Where this refusal is concerned, however, it is hard to see how the intratextualist can be too distressed over being labelled a 'fideist' or a 'confessionalist' simply because he or she abstains from such prolegomenary activity: a recognizably Chris-tian intratextualism will of necessity take God's action in Jesus Christ for us (the *gratia Christi*) as an irremovable starting-point for doctrinal formulation, and will thus accord its concomitant – the *solus Christus* – a powerful regulative status, thereby dispensing with the need for the kind of prolegomenon commissioned by the extratextualist. A Christian intratextualism is a discourse whose proper form is necessarily that of an *analogia Christi*. In this *analogia* and its attendant bundle of sub-discourses the question whether Christianity is unsurpassable ceases to be of primary significance and becomes peripheral. What is central is the articu-lation, the extending, of this *analogia*.[17] The upshot is that, for the intratextualist, any equation of 'unsurpassability' with 'categorial adequacy' is nugatory: for the issue of unsurpassability to be compelling there has to be an antecedent commitment to an 'essentialist' understanding of the particular religions, an under-standing which views religions as discrete 'entities' with transpar-ent, or at least non-opaque, 'essences'. But once this view of religion is discarded (and it is clear that Lindbeck is not prepared to have any truck with this kind of 'essentializing' language), the problem of unsurpassability (as a *theological* problem) disappears as well. The upshot of all this is not too difficult to trace. Once a discourse of religion-constituting 'essences' is spurned, the way is paved for the crucial acknowledgement that all specifications of 'categorial adequacy' are inescapably *intra*-theoretical. This possibility is granted by Lindbeck, since he says that '[u]nlike other perspectives, [the 'cultural-linguistic'] approach proposes no common framework such as that supplied by the propositionalist's concept of truth or the expressivist's concept of experience within which to compare religions' (p. 49). There is then simply no Archimedean (linguistic) point from which we can compare all the different religions. Lindbeck is happy therefore to allow the possibility that religious paradigms are 'incommensurable' (in a sense accordant with T. S. Kuhn's use of the term).[18] Given a full-blown intra-theoretical explication of 'categorial adequacy', the linking of 'unsurpassability' to 'categorial adequacy' (or 'truth') becomes entirely trivial. For the language in which the notion of 'categorial adequacy' has saliency is effectively a meta-language which merely 'quotes' or 'conceptually redescribes' those propositions which constitute an object-language designative of the convictions and practices of the members of the believing community. In showing how 'unsurpassability' can be enunciated in terms of the 'cultural-linguistic' model, Lindbeck has provided a resource which he, *qua* intratextualist, has no real means of deploying. This resource is there to be used – by anyone but the intratextualist.

Taking the possibility of 'incommensurability' seriously, however, has some rather drastic consequences for the 'prospective *fides ex auditu*' theory, and especially for the question of the salvation of 'other believers'.

IV 'Salvation and other faiths'

Like Rahner, Lindbeck is concerned to reconcile the *Christus solus* with the salvation of non-Christians. He cannot of course employ what he takes to be Rahner's 'experiential-expressivist' presuppositional framework when it comes to finding a basis for achieving this reconciliation. The problem for both Rahner and Lindbeck is this: if the *Christus solus* is to prevail and non-Christians are to be saved, then, to state the obvious, non-Christians and Christians must at least be said to have in common this divine bestowal of salvation in Christ. For Rahner (and Lonergan as well, according to Lindbeck), this commonality is already a present reality: non-Christians have made an implicit – whereas Christians have made an explicit – response to the saving grace of Christ. For Lindbeck this supposed commonality, whether it exists in the present or at some future time, is one that is necessarily embodied in the speech-forms, and generated by the forms of life, of specific religious, and hence linguistic, communities (cf. p. 62). But, and herein lies the rub, it is evident that there is at present no such pan-religious linguistic community, in which case the commonality posited by this account must be regarded as something that will exist only at some future time. The salvation of non-Christians is a future salvation, reserved for that time in 'the life to come' when they will 'hear' God's proffer of salvation in and through Christ, and when they will have 'interiorized the language that speaks of Christ' (p. 62).

The problem with this *'fides ex auditu'* explanation is that it does not sit well with the thesis, commended in this essay, that the languages of the different religious traditions are incommensurable, especially when this thesis is made to operate in a context like ours which jettisons Lindbeck's 'subsequence' theory of the relation between time and eternity. Lindbeck has two options open to him at this point. First, he can assume that this incommensurability no longer obtains when non-Christians move into a 'post-mortem' existence, that when it comes to 'interiorizing the language that speaks of Christ' in this existence, non-Christians find themselves speaking the 'same' language that Christians have spoken in response to the divine self-revelation in Christ. Second, he can maintain that though all will eventually use a language that 'speaks of Christ', it in no way follows from this that, come the *eschaton*, there will have to be just *one* such linguistic paradigm. It is perfectly conceivable that there could, in a projected 'after-life', be several paradigms which speak of Christ, some or all of which are in theory incommensurable. Kuhn, after all, is concerned to stress that the proponents of competing paradigms are not free to 'invent' the world that is conceptualized in terms of their respective paradigms:

> the proponents of competing paradigms practice their trades in different worlds. . . . Practicing in different worlds, the two groups of proponents . . . see different things when they look from the same point in the same direction. Again, this is not to say they can see anything they please. Both are looking at the world, and what they look at has not changed.[19]

Assuming Lindbeck's commitment to the 'subsequence' theory, Kuhn's disavowal of a veritable ontological anarchism renders more palatable to the intratextual theologian a conceivable eschatological situation in which several languages can be 'about' Christ, although no one vocabulary dominates such christological discourse, and even if there is no common background theory which all 'post-mortem' christological idioms share. I am suggesting, in other words, that what Richard Rorty calls 'abnormal discourse' can not implausibly be said to prevail in this hypothetical eschatological state: it is possible for that exotic creature – the theological disciple of Richard Rorty – to hope for a truly postmodern heaven![20] However, it is hard to come to a straightforward conclusion on the question whether, for Lindbeck, there are grounds for hoping that there will be just one paradigm for 'interiorizing the language about Christ' on the 'other side of the tracks'. He does not really address this question (and, one might add, with good reason). But if one attends to the rhetorical strategies deployed in *The Nature of Doctrine*; if one recognizes that while Lindbeck's treatment of 'textuality' is meant to be 'postliberal', it nonetheless falls well short of being truly 'postmodern'; if, in scrutinizing Lindbeck's substantive theses, one looks not only at what is actually said, but follows Roland Barthes's advice and attends just as much to what is left unsaid; then it will be fairly safe to conclude that Lindbeck would be more comfortable with the affirmation that the discourse which prevails on the 'other side of the tracks' is very much what Rorty would call 'normal discourse'.[21] The problem with choosing the option of 'normal discourse' in this context is that Lindbeck will be obliged to address the obvious objection that he must then posit a quite radical disjunction between a 'pre-mortem' situation where 'abnormal discourse' is very much the norm, and a 'post-mortem' existence where it is replaced by its 'normal' counterpart. A host of difficulties surround this option.

How, in this 'post-mortem' state, will someone who had in 'this life' been, say, a Hindu, be able to 'interiorize the language about Christ'? Are we justified in hoping that there will be only one such 'post-mortem' language? If there is, which one will it be? Will our Hindu speak 'about Christ' in the idiom of John Paul II or Oral Roberts? Or will she speak in the accents of St Augustine or Jonathan Edwards? Or will there be just one language, albeit an entirely new and pure language, an *Ursprache*, which all, Oral Roberts and our Hindu alike, will speak? What are we hoping *for* when we are persuaded to think along the lines prescribed by the 'prospective *fides ex auditu*' theory? We cannot even begin to contemplate what the appropriate answers to these questions would be like, and this should be sufficient indication that we have this difficulty because we cease to be faithful to the Judaeo-Christian *Bilderverbot* when we start to think about the 'after-life' in such positive terms. Lindbeck, to be fair, confines himself to talking about a possible state of affairs which can be the suitable object of our hope. This is a prepossessingly modest undertaking. Nevertheless, it may be that in inviting us to contemplate even this much he has already, and inadvertently, invited us to traverse territory which is not really ours to explore. It is perhaps for this very reason that we must eschew talk of life 'after' death and discard the 'two tracks' image when talking about the resurrected life.

The foregoing discussion of the 'after-life' serves only to reinforce the view I have already sought to argue for, namely, that the 'subsequence' theory of the relation between time and eternity is too flawed to be given the task of underpinning the 'prospective *fides ex auditu*' theory (and that, consequently, this theory must itself be jettisoned). Earlier, I confessed to being in broad agreement with a number of theologians – Barth, Jüngel, Rahner and Nicholas Lash amongst them – who sought to understand the notion of a 'resurrection from the dead' without adverting to the presupposition of a 'life *after* death'.[22] If 'eternal life' is understood in this way, that is, as our participation in God's timeless glory, a participation the 'locus' of which is a single historical process, then our participation in that glory begins when the relationship between God and creatures begins, i.e. at the creation. At the creation God 'makes room' within the mystery of the divinity for the order of finite things. The creation enables us to see ourselves as terminating a relation of radical dependence on that from which we have our being.[23] If the creation is the inauguration of the world's relatedness to the mystery of God, then this relatedness, and hence our participation in that mystery, receives its decisive 'utterance' in the 'taking flesh' of God's Son. This relatedness can only be brought to speech by human beings because in that human speech it is God who 'speaks', and God 'speaks' in the mystery of the 'taking flesh' of his Word. This divine self-donation on the cross of Christ is thus the possibility of our participation.[24] Theologically, then, there can be no lacuna between 'creation' and 'incarnation' (and hence 'salvation').[25] All, therefore, are *created* in the condition of being participants in God's glory. The assertion that all are so created is entirely consonant with the affirmation, central to the Christian faith, that this participation receives its decisive expression in the 'enfleshment' of the Second Person of the Trinity. Needless to say, while *all* may be created in the condition of being participants in the timeless divine glory, it is undeniably the case that not everyone speaks an explicitly christological language which grounds its very possibility in that event of 'enfleshment'. At this level, therefore, our various religious languages are incommensurable, and they are incommensurable *ab origine*. All human beings are thus created in the condition of being participants in God's timeless glory even though their religious languages are constitutively incommensurable, an incommensurability which obtains even as human creatures participate in that glory. It does not follow from this, necessarily, that all are saved at the culmination of the historical process, though this possibility is not immediately ruled out by this account. But what is excluded, from the standpoint of the Christian faith, is the possibility of narrating the story of this single world history apart from the history of Jesus of Nazareth. My alternative account is therefore resolutely intratextual, and, moreover, it has a soteriological core which is irreducibly 'christomonist'. But it is not committed to making it a condition of salvation that the saved be in a position to 'interiorize the language about Christ' in a 'post-mortem' existence (Lindbeck's option), and neither does it imply that all have a pre-reflective and unthematized experience of Christ (Rahner's option).[26]

On this alternative account, it has to be acknowledged from the outset that we have no real way of knowing what is *'going on' in our language* when we endeavour to say either that 'all' are saved or that only 'some' are saved. Implicit in Lindbeck's 'prospective *fides ex auditu*' theory is the suggestion that each person's history of redemption (or damnation) terminates at death, that my history of redemption ends when my history ends. The danger in this suggestion is that it encourages Christians to think that the history of Jesus Christ too ended with his death (though it is allowed that he went on to have some kind of supra-historical existence in his Father's domain), so that all that needs to be done, now that he has ceased to have an earthly life, is for Christians to register his life, death and resurrection as an unsurpassable 'achievement'. This belief, however, betokens a certain indifference to the fact, hard to contest, that human histories, after the death of Jesus, have continued to be histories of pain, anguish and mass immiseration – the histories of an unredeemed human race. While it may be difficult to controvert the belief that, for Christians, the mission, death and resurrection of Jesus constitute an unsurpassable 'achievement', the danger nevertheless remains that Christians, in acknowledging this truth about the one who is the author of our redemption, may be too easily tempted to substitute a *theory* of reconciliation for its enactment. The necessity to give the Christian hope a concrete historical embodiment can become less urgent for the Christian who believes that the 'project' of a redeemed human-ity – which is God's 'project' – comes to an end (at any rate, 'for me') at my death. And what is more, at my death I need no longer even register the achievement of Jesus – it is rendered palpable to me. At my death I 'go' to meet my Maker, and thus I am effectively withdrawn from any participation in the 'project' of a redeemed humanity: what is absolutely decisive for my salvation is *this* climactic encounter with the Father and the Risen Christ in the 'after-life'.[27] But if it is granted that the history of Jesus does not end, and will not end, until the histories of human redemption have received their full and complete enactment, then we are free to dispense with the assumption – crucial to the 'eschatological *fides ex auditu*' theory – that what is vital for human salvation is the *individual* confrontation which each human being will have with the gospel and the crucified and risen Lord 'after' his or her death. The highly individualistic soteriology on which Lindbeck's '*ex auditu*' theory is premised lends tacit support to a kind of ideology which can be combated only if it is acknowledged that since the history of Jesus will end only when the history of redemption has concluded, the attainment of my own salvation is contingent upon the full enactment of that redemption which in principle has already been accomplished on the cross of Christ. Until that time the questions whether all or only some are saved, whether Christians only are saved, whether *I* am saved, etc., are questions which are not patient of the kind of 'answer' demanded by Lindbeck's '*ex auditu*' theory.

V Conclusion

If it is a besetting fault of theologians that they invariably promise more than they can deliver, then George Lindbeck is certainly free of this fault: at least, where his 'eschatological *fides ex auditu*' theory is concerned, he (rightly) promises little, but he ends up by delivering too much. He is concerned, admittedly, only to paint a picture of a possible state of affairs. Nevertheless he ends up by providing too 'rich' a picture of what is possible 'after' death. If what I have said in this essay is even remotely tenable, then it has to be said that we can safeguard what Lindbeck wants to retain – viz. the 'cultural-linguistic' model of religion, intratextualism, the *solus Christus*, the acknowledgement that the possibility of salvation is not withheld from those who happen to be non-Christians in 'this life' – without having to resort to so problematic a set of notions as those which constitute the back-bone of the 'prospective *fides ex auditu*' theory. We may quarrel with his choice of vehicle, but in furnishing us with the rudiments of a theology of religions which eschews the currently fashionable ideology of 'religious pluralism', Lindbeck has certainly pointed us in what seems to be a not unpromising direction. But to proceed in that direction it is necessary for us to be more resolutely 'postmodern', that is, to take as our starting-point the principles that religious discourses are incommensurable to a point where the notion of 'unsurpassability' cannot be explicated in terms of a notion like 'categorial adequacy', and that, moreover, the grammar of 'unsurpassability' is problematic in so far as it requires us to sponsor the 'essentialization' of religions and their discourses. It may also be necessary to strip-off the identifiably generally 'Protestant' (and more specifically Lutheran) overlayer which girdles some of Lindbeck's substantive theses. (It in no way follows from this that we then have to become more explicitly 'Catholic'.) The perhaps surprising outcome of all this is that we may then find ourselves being able to retain everything that is important for the integrity of Christian conceptual self-description. And that is clearly no bad thing for a Christian intratextual theology of religions.[28]

11

Contemptus mundi *and the disenchantment of the world: Bonhoeffer's 'discipline of the secret' and Adorno's 'strategy of hibernation'*

It is widely acknowledged that the history of Western society is characterized above all by the rise and spread of a socio-economic rationalization and its concomitant ideological manifestation, cultural rationalism. In theological circles, it has become something of a commonplace to affirm that the contemporary theological agenda is shaped decisively by this 'rationalistic' post-Renaissance and post-Enlightenment intellectual setting.[1] In the same theological circles, it is also widely believed that of the significant theologians of this century, none tried harder or more rigorously than Dietrich Bonhoeffer to face up to the implications, for theology, of the 'disenchantment' of the world associated with the rise and growth of social rationalization and cultural rationalism. It is hard to gainsay that Bonhoeffer's greatness as a theologian lies in the freshness and intellectual vigour he brought to the task of understanding what would be involved, theologically, in facing the central tenets of the Christian faith up to a world that is (allegedly) 'religionless'. My purpose in this essay is five-fold. Firstly, to use some of Max Weber's ideas to chart the course of the world's progressive 'disenchantment'. Secondly, to evaluate Bonhoeffer's proposals for a properly-constituted theological response to the essentially 'this-worldly' intellectual horizon brought about by the 'disenchantment' of the world. Thirdly, to argue that Bonhoeffer's proposals, which centre on this notion of the 'discipline of the secret' (*Arkandisziplin*), are rendered problematic by a dialectic inherent in the processes of social rationalization. Fourthly, to show that the only remotely plausible way of overcoming or circumventing this dialectic is via a 'strategy of hibernation' of the kind advocated by T. W. Adorno, the pioneering member of the so-called Frankfurt School of Critical Theory. Fifthly, to draw attention to a surprising theological implication of espousing this 'strategy of hibernation', namely, that we are behoved to accept Karl Barth's, as opposed to Bonhoeffer's, view of the connection between saving revelation and saved creation (this connection is no more than a form of words where Barth is concerned: he is of course famous for positing a *disjunction* between revelation and the created realm).

I Some socio-historical prolegomena

Ascetic practices, which have existed in the life of the church from New Testament times, acquired an institutional form with the rise of the monastic movement in the fourth century. In that century Constantine's decision to legalize the Christian religion ended the era of persecution, and Christians were no longer compelled to live as members of an outcast eschatological community. After the Edict of Milan (313), Christianity – which had hitherto been marginalized by the prevailing social and political order – came to enjoy official patronage and subvention. Martyrdom ceased, Christians were able to occupy positions of power and privilege, and the church took on the function of supplying a religious legitimation for existing forms of secular authority. The church and the world were in a position to accommodate each other. As it became increasingly difficult for the primitive apostolic tradition to innervate the religious life of the growing numbers of half-converted pagans, conviction and fervour were dissolved by a *Zeitgeist* which preferred to compromise with, and uphold, the secular realm. This imperial assimilation of Christianity, which culminated in 389 with Theodosius's decree that Christianity was henceforth to be the official religion of the empire, induced a retreat into the desert by individuals who wanted to live a wilderness faith uncorrupted by the debased and nominal Christianity of the Roman state. In Bonhoeffer's words, these individuals spurned the 'cheap grace' of the secularized church of the *imperium* in favour of a 'costly grace' faithful to the spirit of the apostolic tradition:

> As Christianity spread, and the Church became more secularized, . . . realization of the costliness of grace gradually faded. The world was christianized, and grace became its common property. It was to be had at low cost. . . . It is highly significant that the Church was astute enough to find room for the monastic movement. . . . Here on the outer fringe of the Church was a place where the older vision was kept

alive. Here men remembered that grace costs . . . . This monasticism
became a living protest against the secularization of Christianity and
the cheapening of grace.[2]

The theological rationale for this *contemptus mundi* is supplied by
the principle that salvation is not to be found within the world – as
far as the ascetic is concerned, the world is a *massa perditionis*, a
repository of sin, which must be renounced and contemned. The
monk forsook the world because it was impossible for him to
pursue the 'imitation of Christ', and thus to live in a state of grace,
in the profane realm – only in the wilderness could the ascetic hope
to proceed from the *status naturae* to the *status gratiae*.

Max Weber is the great theoretician of the socio-historical
foundations of the rise and development of Christian asceticism.
Weber believed monasticism to possess an essentially rational
character, and argued accordingly that the rule of St Benedict, as
well as the constitutions which governed the Cluniac Benedictine,
the Cistercian and the Jesuit orders, represent a systematic attempt
to avoid a haphazard otherworldliness and purely gratuitous forms
of austerity. The founders of Christian monasticism may have been
motivated by a *contemptus mundi*, but the principles of monastic
living were designed to

> subject man to the supremacy of a purposeful will, to bring his actions
> under constant self-control with a careful consideration of their
> ethical consequences. Thus it trained the monk, objectively, as a
> worker in the service of the Kingdom of God, and thereby further,
> subjectively, assured the salvation of his soul. . . . [The] end of the
> *exercitia* of St Ignatius and of the rational monastic virtues every-
> where, . . . was to be able to lead an alert, intelligent life: the most
> urgent task the destruction of spontaneous, impulsive engagement,
> the most important means was to bring order into the conduct of its
> adherents.[3]

The monks of antiquity and the Middle Ages fled the world in order
to practise an 'otherworldly asceticism' (*ausserweltliche Askese*).
But with the radical 'disenchantment of the world' (*Entzauberung
der Welt*), a process which Weber regarded as the inescapable
concomitant of the purposive rationalization of religion and
culture, this 'otherworldly asceticism' came to be replaced by an
'innerworldly asceticism' (*innerweltliche Askese*) which required
the individual to be involved in the world, even if only to live in
opposition to the institutions of the progressively rationalized
world.[4] Whereas the 'otherworldly asceticism' had not really
affected the character of daily life in the everyday world, its

'innerworldly' counterpart left the salvation-seeking individual with no alternative but to seek his or her salvation in the everyday world.[5] In the 'disenchanted' world, the project of the individual's life was no longer an *opus supererogationis*; instead the individual had to live 'within' the world and come to terms with its institutions (albeit for the sake of the world beyond). In this way, the inexorable 'disenchantment' of the world transformed Christian asceticism, so that this asceticism now 'strode into the market-place of life, slammed the door of the monastery behind it, and undertook to penetrate just that daily routine of life with its methodicalness, to fashion it into a life in the world, but neither of nor for this world'.[6] So, as Weber saw it, the Christian ascetic, especially in the time subsequent to the Reformation, came to be constrained by a new imperative: change the world, because you have to work for your salvation within it. The ascetic's *contemptus mundi* thus ceased to be defined in exclusively transcendental or supernatural terms; this 'contempt', as a result of the world's progressive disenchantment, was rendered compatible with the pursuit of the ascetic's calling in an ever-widening and increasingly significant secular sphere. The history of rationalization transported asceticism from its original place in the desert, where asceticism had an essentially charismatic manifestation, to the fateful prison of the 'disenchanted' world, where patterns of asceticism are significantly affected (and altered) by the routinization of charisma. The 'this-worldly' ascetic, it would seem, continued to practise a *contemptus mundi* while eschewing the traditional *fuga mundi* of the 'other-worldly' ascetic.[7]

II 'This-worldliness' and Bonhoeffer's 'discipline of the secret'

The notion of a world dominated by an instrumental rationality constitutes the horizon of Bonhoeffer's thinking in the last few years of his life. Bonhoeffer accepts Weber's suggestion that the 'disenchantment' of the world was a direct consequence of the Reformation:

> [it] is the original message of the Reformation that there is no holiness of man either in the sacred or in the profane as such, but only that which comes through the merciful and sin-forgiving word of God. . . . The Reformer's biblical faith had radically removed God from the world. The ground was thereby prepared for the efflorescence of the rational and empirical sciences, and while the natural scientists of the seventeenth and eighteenth centuries were still believing Christians,

when faith in God was lost all that remained was a rationalized and mechanized world.[8]

The possibility that God is radically removed from the world creates an immediate and severe problem for any fully 'incarnational' theology, which will of course demand the affirmation of God's 'real' relation to the world in and through Jesus Christ. How can God have a 'real' relation to the world if it is given over to utter profaneness? Bonhoeffer addressed himself to this theological problem throughout his career, but it is his reflections on this issue in the final period of his life that have of course become the focus of so much attention and controversy.

In his attempt to come to terms with the question of God's relation to a fundamentally 'religionless' world, Bonhoeffer introduced the notion of the 'discipline of the secret' (*Arkandisziplin*). The idea of such a 'discipline', first mooted by Bonhoeffer in his Finkenwalde lectures in the 1930s, is treated in the seminal lecture of 30 April 1944. In this letter Bonhoeffer reflects on the likely implications, for both ecclesiology and christology, of a 'religionless' Christianity:

> In what way are we 'religionless-secular' Christians, in what way are we the ἐϰ-ϰλησια, those who are called forth, not regarding ourselves from a religious point of view as specially favoured, but rather as belonging to the whole world? In that case Christ is no longer an object of religion, but something quite different, really the Lord of the world. But what does that mean? .... Does the secret discipline, or alternatively the difference ... between the penultimate and ultimate, take on a new importance here?[9]

The next time the notion of the 'discipline of the secret' is mentioned is in the letter of 5 May 1944, and this time Bonhoeffer uses it in the context of a criticism of Barth's 'positivism of revelation':

> Barth was the first theologian to begin the criticism of religion, and that remains his really great merit, but he puts in its place a positivist doctrine of revelation which says, in effect, 'Like it or lump it': virgin birth, Trinity, or anything else; each is an equally significant and necessary part of the whole, which must be swallowed as a whole or not at all. That isn't biblical. There are degrees of knowledge and degrees of significance; that means that a secret discipline must be restored whereby the *mysteries* of the Christian faith are safeguarded against profanation.[10]

In these brief and somewhat gnomic remarks Bonhoeffer seems to be saying that it is necessary to distance the central affirmations of the Christian faith in a 'religionless' world – this world will almost certainly view these affirmations from a 'reductionist' standpoint, and thus inevitably 'profane' them. It is interesting to observe that Bonhoeffer discusses the danger of 'profanation' in connection with the theology of Barth, and not that of Bultmann, who was thought by his conservative theological critics to have gone 'too far' in his attempt to purge the New Testament of its 'mythological' concepts. Bonhoeffer, in effect, suggests that Bultmann's programme of 'demythologization' ensures that there is nothing left that can be profaned![11] With Barth, however, the danger of profanation is real: by proffering the mysteries of the faith to the 'world come of age' for its unqualified assent, Barth's 'positivism' misses or traduces the real import of the biblical message, which is that God and the community of faith are for the world, i.e. for the '*religionless*' world. But if God and the community of faith are for the 'religionless' world, it must then follow that the dogmatic affirmations which articulate this divine and human being-for-the-world will have to be related to the secular world. However, it is just this need to *relate* the mysteries of the faith to secular life which revelational 'positivism' refuses to acknowledge, and so it ends up by foisting faith's fundamental affirmations on a 'religionless' world that will inevitably dissolve their truth. A 'discipline of the secret' is therefore needed, so that:

(1) the integrity of the mysteries will be protected.

(2) the independence of the secular world (whose growing autonomy the church has traditionally feared as a threat to its own self-preservation) will be respected.

There is an easily discernible tension between these two requirements. Requirement (1), with its emphasis on guaranteeing the integrity of the faith, seems to counsel the community of faith to be detached from a world so deeply immersed in profaneness. Requirement (2), with its stress on the need to respond positively to a world that has come to relinquish the 'religious *a priori*' that many Christians would regard as intrinsic to the existence of the church, seems to counsel some sort of accommodation with the secular world. This apparent tension in Bonhoeffer's theology of God's solidarity with the 'religionless' world is thought by some of his interpreters to ensue in an unavoidable dialectic between the 'discipline of the secret' and worldly life. To quote Ronald Gregor Smith:

> These two elements ... the worldliness of God and the secret discipline, come together in a powerful dialectic in Bonhoeffer's

thought.... [This] is the necessary dialectic. You are both for the
world, with all the strength of the given situation, and against it;
against it not as intellectual rationalization of inaction and absolute
denial of the world, but against it in the depth of this existential
dialectic. The Christian cannot be indifferent to this world which God
made and loves. Yet how can he be other than against it in its evil and
sin and hopelessness? Both positions are necessary, and both at the
same time, and without reserve.[12]

Bonhoeffer, it seems, needs to postulate a dialectical relation
between the 'worldliness' of God and the 'discipline of the secret' in
order to avoid setting-up an 'either-or' between the community of
faith (i.e. the community that practises the 'discipline of the secret')
and the 'religionless' world. However, a little reflection will show
that Bonhoeffer's attempt to neutralize the hiatus between the
community of faith and the 'religionless' world is not successful.
The problem with this dialectic arises from two assumptions which
are embedded in the foundations of Bonhoeffer's theology,
namely: (i) that Christ is the concrete revelation of God; and (ii)
that Christ *exists* (for the community) *as the community* established
between believers.[13]

Together, these two assumptions entail that Christ can be *found*
concretely only in the believing community, and that God's self-
revelation is thus concretized only in *this* community, that is, the
community which practises the 'discipline of the secret'. But in this
case, God's self-revelation is *not* extended to the world at large, the
profane world; and Bonhoeffer is therefore susceptible to the very
objection he levelled against Barth when he charged him with being
a 'positivist' of revelation – viz., that Barth propounds a view of
revelation which posits a lacuna between divine revelation and the
'reality' of the world 'come of age'.[14] It is therefore simply not
sufficient (*pace* Gregor Smith and Phillips) to say that Bonhoeffer's
theology of God's solidarity with the world requires an 'existential
dialectic' between worldly life and the practice of the 'discipline of
the secret'. For the invocation of this 'existential dialectic' will be
fraught with unacceptable consequences as long as Bonhoeffer and
his interpreters fail to provide a specification of divine revelation
which allows for the *out-reach*, into the profane world, of God's
self-revelation in Jesus Christ. Only then will Bonhoeffer's theology of a contemporary interpretation of the Gospel not be jeopard-
ized by a hiatus between the community of faith and the 'religionless' world. Ray Anderson believes that the gap between the
community of faith and the 'religionless' world implicit in Bonhoef-

fer's theology arises from Bonhoeffer's somewhat Hegelian conception of Christ as the fundamental structure of the world. To
quote Anderson: 'If one knows the reality of Christ through an
ontic relation with the world ... then the church has been superseded as the *place* where revelation is concretized' (p. 96). Anderson proposes an alternative way of understanding Bonhoeffer's
conception of the concretizing of divine revelation, a way which
will bypass the threat posed by the hiatus between the community
of faith and the 'religionless' world, and which will therefore not
imply the suspension of the church as the locus of God's self-
revelation in Christ (a danger which lurks in any Hegelian-inspired
christology). Anderson's proposal, which follows the lines of a
similar suggestion advanced by Eberhard Bethge,[15] is that the
problematic of God acting upon human beings in his utter 'worldliness' can be resolved by employing a bi-polar conception of God's
historical transcendence. By the first pole of historical transcendence, the community of faith – the Body of Christ – becomes
the historically concrete manifestation of God's solidarity with the
'religionless' world through its identification with the secular
world. But, and this constitutes the second pole of God's historical
transcendence, the believing community can identify with the
profane world, as a community of *faith*, only if it first possesses a
faith-inspired *identity*, and this identity, in Bonhoeffer's scheme of
things, is formed and sustained by the 'discipline of the secret'. In
Anderson's words:

> [if] the normative character of the relationship is not to *find* Christ
> concretely, but to *be* Christ concretely in the world, the problem is
> resolved and new possibilities open up for our understanding of the
> theology of historical transcendence.... Christ *is* the community
> established between believers.... This is not a reality which stands
> apart from the world and demands a privileged place, but it is part of
> the total logic of historical transcendence which includes the world as
> well.

(pp. 96–7)

The Christian, says Anderson in interpreting Bonhoeffer, com-
pletes the logic of historical transcendence by evacuating all 'secret
places' in which Christ is known in and through the Spirit-infused
believing community, and moves into the profane world to *become*
Christ for the sake of the world. As Anderson puts it: 'the "secret
discipline" must complete itself in worldliness, not by becoming
worldly, nor merely non-religious, but by taking the place of Christ
in the world. It is only in the exposure of oneself to the world in this

suffering way that one can transcend the world in a way in which Christ transcended it' (pp. 97–8).

Anderson's proposal, which is fully consonant with Bonhoeffer's theological intentions, avoids the danger of 'reductionism' by assigning to revelation the all-important function of determining and maintaining the identity of the Christian. At the same time, his proposal enables Bonhoeffer to avoid positing an 'unrelatedness' between the worldly life and revelation by stipulating that the Christian has to confront the secular world in order to *be* Christ in the centre of that world.[16]

The 'discipline of the secret' rescues revelation from a total submersion in life's worldliness, but at the same time the miracle of revelation is not confined to some secret enclave – if it were so restricted God would not be able to exercise his Lordship over the world. A theology which pivots on the notion of a 'secret space' occupied exclusively by the ecclesiastical community cannot really accommodate the themes (a) of God's being-for-humanity in and through the historical Jesus, and (b) of the real being of humankind for each and every one of its members in and through the life of the 'religionless' world. So while revelation is presented to human cognition and experience in the practice of the 'discipline of the secret', its out-reach into worldly life is secured, not at the level of cognition, but at the level of action, by means of an *imitatio* of the powerless and suffering Christ.[17] Jesus Christ, the historic being *pro nobis*, takes the Lordship of his Father into temporality and historical particularity, into the lives of secular men and women. God's action in giving himself to the world in Christ – an action which receives paradigmatic expression in the doctrine of the incarnation – brings God into the profane world, so that as Bonhoeffer says: 'in Christ we are offered the possibility of partaking in the reality of God and in the reality of the world, but not in the one without the other. The reality of God discloses itself only by setting me entirely in the reality of the world, and when I encounter the reality of the world it is always already sustained, accepted and reconciled in the reality of God.'[18] Bonhoeffer's conception of the 'discipline of the secret', when located in the full and proper context of God's out-reach towards the profane world, can therefore be seen as a fascinating and important attempt to rethink the age-old doctrine of *contemptus mundi*, in a way that comes to terms with an intellectual horizon supplied by a world that is (in Weber's terminology) 'disenchanted'. In this 'disenchanted' world, the exponent of *contemptus mundi* can no longer assert the manifest predominance of the realm of grace over the realm of nature; but, equally, the *regnum gratiae* cannot be collapsed 'without remainder' into the *regnum naturae* – if this were to happen the Christian would be bereft of an identity, and the *imitatio* of the suffering Christ would be thwarted:

> So long as Christ and the world are conceived as two opposing and mutually repellent spheres, man will be left in the following dilemma: he abandons reality as a whole, and places himself in one or the other of the two spheres. He seeks Christ without the world, or he seeks the world without Christ. . . .
>   There are not two realities, but one reality, and that is the reality of God, which has become manifest in Christ in the reality of the world. Sharing in Christ we stand at once in the reality of God and the reality of the world.[19]

In a word: the practice of the 'discipline of the secret' represents a somewhat paradoxical Christ-informed contemning of the world for the sake of the 'religionless' (but Christ-formed) world. The irreducibly paradoxical nature of this theological rationale for the pursuit of the 'discipline of the secret' arises, at least in part, from Bonhoeffer's tension-infused endeavour to explicate the essential structure of faith as an adherence to worldly 'reality', before God, in a 'religionless' world whose basic structure is characteristically such that it merits the description *etsi deus non daretur* ('as if there were no God').[20]

  Unfortunately for Bonhoeffer and those theologians who derive inspiration from him (notably Gregor Smith and Ray Anderson), this theology of God's self-identification with the 'disenchanted' world cannot withstand what Jürgen Habermas, with Weber's theories in mind, has called the 'dialectic of rationalization'.[21]

III The 'dialectic of rationalization' and Bonhoeffer's 'discipline of the secret'

Christian asceticism was not the only area of life to be transformed by the historical process of 'disenchantment'. In Weber's view, the process of rationalization was irreversible and irresistible: the growing complexity of society called for more extensive and more sophisticated methods of anticipating and controlling economic and social movements, and in this way promoted the spread of a *purposive rationality* (*Zweckrationalität*), which in time would turn the world into an 'iron cage' (*Gehäuse der Hörigkeit*):

> The capital economy of the present day is an immense cosmos into which the individual is born, and which presents itself to him, at least as an individual, as an unalterable order of things, in which we must live. It forces the individual, in so far as he is involved in the system of market relationships, to conform to capitalistic rules of action. . . . For when asceticism was carried out of the monastic cells into everyday life, . . . it did its part in building the tremendous cosmos of the modern economic order. The order is now bound to the technical and economic conditions of machine production which today determine the lives of all individuals who are born into this mechanism . . . with irresistible force.[22]

Social rationalization thus affected not only the religious institutions of capitalist society, but in time came to penetrate all aspects of collective life. Capitalist society was increasingly administered by hierarchies of experts, trained to carry out narrowly specialist functions, and required to display the 'virtues' of obedience, reliability, efficiency and the capacity to employ one's judgement in an impersonally 'objective' way. In this 'iron cage' freedom itself becomes routinized, and the individual is deprived of his or her autonomy. The overwhelming trend towards bureaucratic rationalization and control allows the individual no escape; to escape the influence of the existing bureaucratic apparatus – 'the living machine' – the individual has to form an organization which will be just as susceptible to the process of bureaucratization.[23] The subjective preferences of the individual cannot be accommodated by the highly-systematized planned procedures generated by the bureaucratic machine, and as a result the individual suffers from self-alienation. In addition to suffering from this loss of freedom (*Freiheitsverlust*), the individual also endures an irreversible loss of meaning (*Sinnverlust*). The desacrilized, mechanized world confronts the modern individual as an infinite sequence of causes and effects, devoid of meaning and value. Threatened by the world-alienation that arises from the world's objective meaninglessness, the human subject has to produce his or her own substantive meaning: 'The fate of an epoch which has eaten of the tree of knowledge is that it must know that we cannot learn the *meaning* of the world from the results of its analysis, be it ever so perfect; it must rather be in a position to create this meaning itself.'[24] So: the burden of creating meaning is thrust on the atomized human subject. But, and *this* is the 'dialectic of social rationalization', this task of meaning-creation has to be undertaken in a social system which extinguishes the very subjectivity of the individual. Bureaucratization eliminates the conditions required for the production of autonomous meaning – the very meaning needed to overcome world-alienation! Confronted by an essentially senseless world, the modern soul becomes 'weary of life' but never 'satiated with life'.[25] There are, according to Weber, only two possible responses to the 'senselessness' of modern life: either a stoical and sober acceptance of things as they are, or else a flight into religion. To quote Weber: 'To the person who cannot bear the fate of the times like a man, one must say: may he rather return silently, without the usual publicity build-up of renegades, but simply and plainly. The arms of the old churches are opened widely and compassionately for him. After all, they do not make it hard for him.'[26] These remarks, made by Weber in his famous lecture 'Science as a Vocation', make it all too clear that he regarded the recourse to faith as a fundamental evasion of the 'dialectic of social rationalization'. Why does the flight into faith not enable the modern individual to overcome the historical impasse associated with this 'dialectic'? The answer, to be found in Weber's essay 'Religious Rejections of the World and Their Directions', is that the way of life made available by faith is '*more alienated* from all structured forms of life ... by confining itself to the specific religious essence'.[27] Religion, in Weber's eyes, only serves to entrench the fateful impasse brought about by the 'disenchantment' of the world.

The 'disenchantment' of the world raises a number of thorny questions for the exponent of the 'discipline of the secret' and the theology of divine solidarity it is intended to motivate. How can one be certain that the 'discipline of the secret' is not irrevocably undermined by (as Weber would see it) the sheer senselessness of the world? Is this 'discipline' not in fact a futile and deluded attempt (made by those who 'cannot bear the fate of the times') to escape ('silently, without the usual publicity build-up of renegades') from the world – an unbearably 'soulless' world? Again, is Bonhoeffer's theology of God's self-identification with the 'religionless' world, whose focal-point is the 'discipline of the secret', not therefore inescapably ideological?[28] Or yet again, how can the practitioners of this 'discipline' hope to retain their *identity* as members of the *corpus Christi* in a world that has effectively extirpated the charismatic basis of this membership? And finally, how can the exponents of the 'discipline of the secret' *identify* in a Spirit-infused manner with the citizens of the profane world, when the structures of domination that prevail in the world threaten to subvert the very possibility of a genuine collective solidarity?

The fragmentary remarks and scattered insights which constitute

the *Letters and Papers from Prison* do not really afford us the
means to resolve or dissolve the difficulties posed by (a Weberian
account of) the world's 'disenchantment'. What Bonhoeffer and his
sympathizers need, urgently, is a *critique* of the 'dialectic of
rationalization', a 'suspicious' hermeneutics of the process of
'disenchantment'. They need to have the theoretical and the
practical resources to become disenchanted with 'disenchantment'.
It may be that Bonhoeffer would have seen the need for such a
critique had he been able to survive the war. But this is a dubious
speculation. For Bonhoeffer really seemed to believe that there is
no need to bring men and women to any sort of realization that
their happiness might be false, their health really a form of
sickness, their vigour a deep-rooted despair. He evidently saw no
need to promote the disenchantment of 'disenchantment'.[29] If
Bonhoeffer's theology needs to be augmented by a critique of the
'disenchanted' world, and if his writings are devoid of a potential
anchorage for a hermeneutics of 'suspicion', it will be necessary to
turn elsewhere for the basis of such a critique.

A critique of the 'disenchanted' world consonant with Weber's
(and Bonhoeffer's) characterization of this world as a realm given
over to profaneness cannot be a critique conducted from a 'theistic'
or 'transcendental' standpoint – such a critique, by presupposing a
paradigm with a 'transcendental' focus, will be strictly incommensurable with the paradigm(s) of the 'disenchanted' world (which of
course have a radically 'immanent' or this-worldly focus). To
deploy the paradigm of a 'transcendental' critique is, *ipso facto*, to
enter a thought-world that cannot – in principle – make any real
sense of the truth-claims of the ('immanent') paradigm(s) of the
profane world.[30]

A critique of the 'disenchanted' world which aspires to success
will have to *represent* the truth of this world as a precondition of
critique, and such a representation will be possible only if this
critique incorporates, as a starting-point for reflection, the 'immanent' paradigm(s) of the profane world. What the critic is seeking,
therefore, is a strategy that will not impose an alien, and therefore
incommensurable, paradigm on the 'reality' that is the intended
objective of critique. Rather, the critic has to proceed *immanently*,
that is, he or she will accept the profane world's prevailing
paradigms, and work *within* the essentially 'immanentist' terms of
these paradigms, but in order to breach them. Or to put it in
somewhat more fashionable terminology, the critic has to become a
practitioner of 'deconstruction'. In Derrida's formulation (made

with reference to the 'deconstruction' of philosophy): 'To "deconstruct" philosophy is thus to work through the structured genealogy of its concepts in the most scrupulous and immanent fashion, but at the same time to determine, from a certain external perspective that it cannot name or describe, what this history may have concealed or excluded, constituting itself as history through this repression in which it has a stake.'[31] If our arguments are correct, Bonhoeffer's 'discipline of the secret', which can be construed as a *contemptus mundi* for the 'disenchanted' world, will need to be reinforced by an immanent critique or 'deconstruction' of this world.

(Overtly, our argument so far has been to the effect that the fully 'disenchanted' world can give *epistemological* sanction only to those critical paradigms that are radically 'immanent'. But ours is no *merely* epistemological argument – it is not being argued here, for instance, that an 'immanent' critique has a greater cognitive adequacy or intuitive plausibility than its transcendental counterpart. Formulating such a purely epistemological argument would require us to uphold one of the several versions of epistemological 'foundationalism', all of which have of course been rendered problematic by the self-same history and cultural forces that have brought about the 'disenchantment' of the world.[32] Our argument, rather, is the essentially *historical* one that a purely 'transcendental' critique will, by its very nature, be such that it cannot be mediated by existing socio-historical conditions. An exclusively 'transcendental' critique will therefore condemn itself to being inescapably ideological, in the sense of promoting a distorted understanding of the 'true' nature of existing social reality.)

IV Adorno's 'strategy of hibernation'

In their *Dialectic of Enlightenment* Max Horkheimer and T. W. Adorno carried out an immanent critique of the 'disenchanted' world. The theme of 'disenchantment' is taken up in the very first paragraph: 'the Enlightenment has always aimed at liberating men from fear and establishing their sovereignty. . . . The programme of the Enlightenment was the disenchantment of the world.'[33] But far from liberating humanity, 'the fully enlightened earth radiates with disaster triumphant', and humankind 'instead of entering into a truly human condition, is sinking into a new kind of barbarism'.[34] In several books and many articles, Adorno sought to comprehend the disturbing and tragic consequences of the 'dialectic of enlightenment'.[35] Enlightenment had professed to improve the condition of men and women by banishing myth and installing reason in its place, and by the conquest of nature. But its strategy was broken-backed: the domination and manipulation of external nature required a domination of the individual's internal nature, that is, our psychic constitution had to be recast so that men and women would be able to forsake the fulfilment of their psychic needs in order to master outer nature: 'The subjective spirit which cancels the animation of nature can master a despiritualized nature only by imitating its rigidity and despiritualizing itself in turn. . . . Everything – even the human individual, not to speak of the animal – is converted into the repeatable, replaceable process. . . .'[36] By the twentieth century, the material preconditions for a free and economically productive society had been created. The creation of such a society had of course been the goal of enlightenment. But the existence of these material preconditions had not resulted in a more humane social order. The very attempt to create a free and more humane society had resulted in one that was oppressive and dehumanizing: the presence of the *material* preconditions for the existence of a liberated society seemed somehow to generate the non-existence of the *subjective* conditions necessary for the realization of such a society. To account for the failure of the project of enlightenment, Adorno advanced the thesis of the reification of the human subject. According to this thesis, the all-pervasive forces of rational administration translate the potentially repressive features of enlightenment into a concrete technocratic praxis. A 'culture industry' is mobilized by dominant social institutions and powerful commercial interests to ensure the 'cretinization of the masses' (*Volksverblödung*), and to produce a helpless conformity (*Anpassung*) guaranteed to perpetuate the subliminal authoritarianism of late capitalist society. Modern society is thus administered to provide a context of unremitting delusion (*Verblendzusammenhang*) in which individuals accept without protest the oppressive 'reality' of their society, which they feel obliged to perpetuate.[37]

    According to Adorno, the relations of production in late capitalist society create a 'socially necessary mirage' which blinds men and women to the real nature of a society which consigns them to be 'cogs to their own machines'.[38] The subjective conditions for the realization of a free and humane social order do not exist because the existing *psychological* constitution of men and women prevents them from imagining the world to be different, to be otherwise than it now appears to be. Human consciousness, instead of revealing to individuals the true nature of the objective social configurations which surround them, had been mutilated by these very configurations. As a result, distorted personal and social relationships, which could have been *changed* by the actions of men and women, were accepted as natural and unchangeable relations between objects. The possibility of an emancipatory praxis is extinguished as the autonomy of the subject (the ego) is eclipsed by the overpowering superiority of the object.[39]

A critique of culture in a 'disenchanted' world will therefore seek to 'demystify' social reality, and thus reveal it to be, not an absolute and immutable nature, but 'second nature', that is, the illusion of something natural which camouflages actual historical conditions, an illusion which is the congealed product of human praxis (and therefore capable of being removed by a countervailing practice). Human beings have only to break the spell of this seemingly objective 'second nature', and in so doing unfetter the potential for liberation which lies in this objectivity, a potential that is 'close enough to touch'.[40] No matter how unbreakable this spell is, it remains what it is – a spell. Hence, those persons who do not fall victim to it may have the chance of surviving long enough to hope for the day when the spell will be broken. But to do this they will have to adopt what Jürgen Habermas has referred to as Adorno's 'strategy of hibernation' (which we might prefer to regard as his radically secularized version of *contemptus mundi*).[41]

The effective critic of culture, Adorno maintains, can engage in potentially liberative criticism only if he or she is sufficiently detached from the domain of social interests. Exclusion from this domain will serve to immunize the critic against the reifying logic of the principle that everything and anything in late bourgeois society is to be experienced as a commodity (e.g. a painting by van Gogh) – a principle that has eaten into the very structures of human consciousness in advanced capitalist society. This commodity principle has become so deep-rooted that even the 'committed' individual is a potential victim of the forces of reification: 'The feigning of a true politics here and now, the freezing of historical relations which nowhere seem ready to melt, oblige the mind to go where it need not degrade itself.'[42] The philosophical underpinnings of this critical enterprise, outlined as early as Adorno's 1931 *Antrittsvorlesung 'Die Aktualität der Philosophie'*,[43] is developed more fully in *Negative Dialektik*, where Adorno addresses himself to the question of the liquidation of the subject by the implacable objectivity of the capitalist order: 'In epistemology the inevitable result is the false conclusion that the object is the subject. Traditional philosophy believes that it knows the unlike by likening it to itself, while in so doing it knows itself only. The idea of a changed philosophy would be to become aware of likeness by defining it as that which is unlike itself.'[44] The truth is thus to be found in all that is estranged, unusual, marginalized and injured by the conformist ideologies of the totally administered society. Freedom can survive in a setting of violence and hopelessness only if it takes the form of negation. The unbroken cohesion of rationalized 'immanence' that is the enemy of hope can be countered only by a 'transcendence', a historical 'transcendence', riveted on the fragmentary, the insignificant, the vanquished and the irrelevant: 'change is present only in the smallest thing. Where the scale is large, death prevails.'[45] In a society where commonsense and reason serve only to reinforce the prevailing universal blindness, every attempt to initiate an emancipatory praxis comes to be regarded as foolishness and insanity. Paradoxically, therefore, it is only the person deemed to be eccentric or even insane who can resist the process of psychic petrification: 'Once it has recognized the ruling universal order and its proportions as sick – and marked in the most literal sense with paranoia, with "pathic projection" – then it can see as healing cells only what appears, by the standards of that order, as itself sick, eccentric, paranoia – indeed, "mad"; and it is true today as in the Middle Ages that only fools tell their masters the truth.'[46] According to Adorno, then, the use of reason to motivate an emancipatory praxis is viewed by institutionalized instrumental reason as a form of madness; just as, conversely, the inability of instrumental reason to sustain and shape patterns of redeemed existence creates a more dangerously insane world. The insanity of instrumental reason must therefore be countered by what one of Adorno's interpreters, Heiner Höfener, has called a 'reasonable insanity'.[47] But this 'reasonable insanity' cannot be systematically pursued: the (insane) technocratically-rational world will not sanction the positive pursuit of a more humane way of living. Moreover, the programmatic implementation of a 'reasonably insane' mode of existence will have to be undertaken with reference to notions like 'justice' and 'truth', the very substance of which has been shrivelled by the reified world: 'An appeal to truth is scarcely the prerogative of a society which dragoons its members to own up the better to hunt them down.'[48] Adorno therefore advocates, as a way of responding (negatively) to the reified world, a strategy of enhancing and exaggerating the merest traces of negativity and idiosyncrasy that manage somehow to resist being integrated into the prevailing mass irrationality: 'there is no longer beauty or consolation except in the gaze falling on horror, withstanding it, and in unalleviated consciousness of negativity holding fast to the possibility of what is better'.[49]

The adoption of an adversarial stance to the reified fabric of social life, focusing as it does on the ruins and detritus of late bourgeois society, is Adorno's radically secularized version of *contemptus mundi*. The secular exponent of *contemptus mundi*, because he or she refuses to become an accomplice of the reifying powers at work in society, is able to confront society's comfortable and comforting (and therefore static) vision of itself with its true nature, which is the unrelenting barbarism of the always-the-same (*das Immergleiche*). By holding up a prism to that which is degraded as seemingly unreal – thereby driving a wedge between society's false image and its true nature – the critic is able to throw a flickering light on the almost vanishing traces of redeemed or reconciled life, traces that the 'disenchanted' world seeks to administer out of existence: 'Truth is inseparable from the illusory belief that from the figures of the unreal one day, in spite of all, real deliverance will come.'[50]

A strategy of self-conscious hermeticism, betokening a 'reasonable insanity', is able to decline late bourgeois society's proffer of false happiness. Only in this way can critique avoid being colonized by the apparatus of mass culture. But a price has to be paid – critique saves the most minute of spaces for the redeemed life by seeming to fall into absurdity.[51]

V Theological implications of Adorno's 'strategy of hibernation'

Adorno's insistence that the human subject – 'which is still for itself, but no longer in itself'[52] – is extinguished by the overwhelming objectivity of the social order has important implications for the practitioner of the 'discipline of the secret'. For if the spontaneity of the subject is crushed by the unrelenting objectivity of social arrangements in market society, then the subject, and *eo ipso* the practitioner of the 'discipline', becomes a wraith-like epiphenomenon of prevailing repressive social configurations. The elimination of a true subjectivity must spell the end of the 'discipline of the secret'. The 'discipline' is clearly intended by Bonhoeffer to be a means to the end of discovering the presence of Christ in the godforsaken world of today, through an identification, on the part

of the practitioner, with the secular world in all its manifold
aspects. The question of locating the presence of Christ in the
'world come of age' is, in turn, part of the wider problematic that
exercised Bonhoeffer throughout his theological career, namely,
the issue of reconciling the reality of God with the reality of the
world.[53] It has been our contention that Bonhoeffer's attempt to
achieve this reconciliation is flawed precisely because he has a
misleading conception of the reality of the world. His mistaken
social-theoretical interpretation of the nature of this 'reality' made
inevitable a flawed *theological* understanding of the way the
reconciliation between the divine and worldly reality was to be
brought about. In his early writings, in particular *Sanctorum
Communio* (1930) and *Akt und Sein* (1931), Bonhoeffer had sought
to bring about a *rapprochement* between divine and worldly reality
by adverting to the concrete structure of the church.[54] However, by
the time he came to write his *Ethik* (1940–4), Bonhoeffer had
ceased to identify the reality of the empirical church with the reality
of God's self-revelation; in this book it is stated explicitly that Jesus
Christ is the revelation of God.[55] At the same time, Bonhoeffer
continued his repudiation of a Barthian theological 'transcendentalism': to take refuge in this 'transcendentalism' would be to
succumb to the Barthian *finitum incapax infiniti*, and thus to
surrender the concreteness of God's self-revelation.[56] So the invocation of the 'discipline of the secret' was very much a mediating
strategy. On the one hand, Bonhoeffer was criticizing the Confess-
ing Church for lapsing into 'conservative restoration' and for
clinging to a problematic 'churchliness'.[57] On the other hand, he
retained the *finitum capax infiniti*, which he saw as the safeguard for
the concreteness of God's self-revelation. The invocation of the
'discipline of the secret' therefore enabled Bonhoeffer to retain
concreteness, but without identifying this concreteness with the
current empirical manifestation of the church. What Bonhoeffer
failed to contend with, however, was the real possibility of the
ideological misappropriation of divine revelation on the part of the
exponents of the 'discipline of the secret' – his ecclesiology lacked a
strategy of 'suspicion'. To possess such a strategy, which would
serve the function of protecting the 'discipline of the secret' from
false consciousness, Bonhoeffer would have needed to endorse the
principle of a *diastasis* between God's Word, which is the word of
reconciliation, and the appropriation of this word by sinful human
beings. What he needed, in other words, was something resembling
the Barthian *finitum incapax infiniti*.

Barth's (to be more precise – the 'early' Barth's) theological 'deconstruction' of the human subject can be said to parallel Adorno's sociological or historico-philosophical 'deconstruction' of the same subject. Barth and Adorno both provide critiques of autonomous human reason, albeit ones motivated by vastly different principles. For Barth, God made flesh redeems because he is not 'identical with the quintessence of human reason, with the "God in ourselves"'.[58] Adorno likewise argues that an object retains its emancipatory potential insofar as it is not subsumable under the canons of human reason: as a consequence of the 'dialectic of enlightenment' this 'reason' has shackled men and women in chains they cannot touch, feel, see or hear. This correspondence between Adorno and Barth is, however, an assonance and not a consonance; to maintain otherwise would be to overlook their diametrically opposed responses to Kant's critique of rational theology. Barth took Kant's abrogation of a speculative metaphysical 'theism' to signal an essential distinction between philosophy (which is incapable of depicting the absolute) and theology (whose proper task was to witness to the absolute, i.e. the Word of God).[59] Adorno would of course have reacted disparagingly to Barth's attempt to press the Kantian critique of metaphysics into the service of theology. He would have been just as critical of Barth's dismissal of an 'immanentist' theology as he was of the Capuchin sermon on the vanity of 'immanence': 'The Capuchin sermon on the vanity of immanence secretly liquidates transcendence as well, for transcendence feeds on nothing but the experience we have in immanence.'[60] Barth's refusal to relate revelation to human subjectivity would be unacceptable to Adorno, who, as befits a Marxist, refused to divorce cognitive structures (be they theological or otherwise) from actual historical conditions.[61] At the same time, however, Adorno's stress on the need to ground transcendence in immanence (thereby preventing the liquidation of transcendence) is not to be taken as an indication that, had he been sympathetic towards theology, he would have favoured Bonhoeffer's, and not Barth's, view of God's relation to the created order. For Adorno's negative dialectics retains a *diastasis* between the world as it is presently constituted and that which presages a redeemed existence. And inasmuch as Bonhoeffer's 'discipline of the secret' is part of his design to overcome Barth's 'transcendentalism', that is, the *diastasis* between the saving revelation and the saved creation, it follows that Bonhoeffer has almost certainly jettisoned the very principle needed to motivate a hermeneutics of 'suspicion', a hermeneutics whose goal will be to call by its true name a world that is oblivious to the screams of its victims. Barth's theology, by contrast, is capable – in principle – of motivating this 'suspicious' hermeneutics. It possesses this capacity because Barth's retention of the *diastasis* between the redeeming and the redeemed realities gives his theology an eschatological orientation that Bonhoeffer's thought appears to lack (or at least fails to emphasize). Joel Whitebook, who describes Adorno as a 'libertarian utopian', has drawn attention to the eschatological core of this particular utopianism: 'If modernity is a self-reinforcing immanent totality, then it cannot be transcended from within. Any transcendence must be an eschatological irruption.'[62]

To understand, theologically, the need for Adorno's 'strategy of hibernation' is to understand the need for a *contemptus mundi* consistent with the principle that 'reality' cannot be transcended from within. And to the extent that this principle accords better with the Barthian *diastasis* than it does with Bonhoeffer's espousal of a 'this-worldly' transcendence, it follows that the theologian who employs Adorno's 'strategy of hibernation' is better advised to uphold the Barthian *diastasis* (or one of its cognate theological formulations), and thus to relinquish Bonhoeffer's strategy of relating the revelation that saves to the world that is saved.[63] To say this, however, is not to suggest that a *rapprochement* between Barth's theology and Adorno's critical theory is really possible or even desirable.

12

'The weight of weakness':
intratextuality and discipleship

All of the language of transcendence is but rhetoric unless there is a visible body of people who are able to escape conformity to the world while continuing to function in the midst of the world.

John Howard Yoder

Unless both the interpreter and the community are real, there is no real world.

Josiah Royce[1]

In his book *The Uses of Scripture in Recent Theology* David Kelsey has rightly observed that the authority which Scripture has for the common life of the Christian community resides in Scripture's being deployed in certain regulative and normative ways; ways which contribute to the creation, sustaining and re-formation of the community's self-identity and the personal identities of those who are gathered within it.[2] The *congregatio fidelium* is what it is precisely because it gains its orientation from Scripture. Christianity, in this sense, is truly to be reckoned 'a religion of the book', a book which 'renders' or 'depicts' a linguistic world that is of decisive significance for Christian reflection and practice.[3] To profess to be a Christian is thus to stand in an undeniable, though as yet unspecified, relation to this all-encompassing biblical linguistic world. Any properly theological discussion of Christian 'discipleship' must therefore involve some consideration of the relation that obtains between specifications of the identity of the Christian community (and the particular identities of its members) and the scriptural linguistic world.[4]

Throughout the centuries countless proposals have of course been advanced for a recognizably Christian, and a properly theological, understanding of the normative relation which obtains between the biblical linguistic world and the identity of the community of believers.[5] One of the more interesting and significant of these proposals, at least for the ecclesiologically-minded theologian, has been the one associated with the 'intratextual' theologies developed by Kelsey, George Lindbeck, Hans Frei, Charles Wood and Ronald Thiemann.[6] My discussion will take the notion of an intratextual theology as its starting-point.

I The intratextual approach to theology

George Lindbeck has characterized the intratextual approach to theology by differentiating it from its 'extratextual' counterpart. An extratextual theology is one which locates the 'meaning' of a sacred text either in realities external to it (so that the text is a figuration of these realities); or in an experience or set of experiences (so that the text, *qua* symbol-system, is an appropriate expression of the experience or experiences in question). In principle all interpreters – solely by virtue of their possession of a 'common humanity' – have access to the universal and invariant structures which underpin these realities or experiences as they are 're-presented' in religious texts. With this general anthropology in place and functioning as a 'master code', the exponent of the extratextual approach (as characterized by Lindbeck) is then able to view the 'religious' hermeneutical enterprise as an undertaking that is global in scope, i.e. as one which discloses to the competent interpreter a set of truths of the widest generality, truths pertaining to what David Tracy has called the 'limit-character of common human experience'. A Christian theological hermeneutic is thus to be seen simply as the regional application of this global hermeneutic. This is precisely the view of Tracy, who is one of the best-known proponents of the so-called extratextual approach:

> [The] limit-character of the 'religious dimension' present to our common human experience is similar in meaning to the limit-character of the religious meaning of the New Testament language. Insofar as this claim can be maintained, the first set of meanings may also be declared appropriate to the Christian tradition and the second set of meanings may also be declared adequate to our common experience.[7]

According to the exponent of the extratextual approach, therefore, the 'meanings' contained in biblical texts are 'correlatable' in principle with those 'meanings' generated by an extratextual reality (this reality being considered to be the 'primary' reality). Theology then has the role of providing an indispensable translation-scheme for making such correlations. It is, so to speak, the repository of a 'master code' – a 'code' in terms of which the Christian 'sub-code' *must* be 'rewritten' if it is gainfully and properly to be understood.

An intratextual approach, by contrast, affirms that the 'meaning' of a text is inseparable from the particular language or discourse which happens to be constitutive of that particular text. It holds that the Christian 'code' is *sui generis*: it is *the* 'master code'. In Lindbeck's words:

> [Intratextual theology] does not make scriptural contents into metaphors for extrascriptural realities, but the other way around. It does not suggest, as is often said in our day, that believers find their stories in the Bible, but rather that they make the story of the Bible their story. The cross is not to be viewed as a figurative representation of suffering nor the messianic kingdom as symbol for hope in the future; rather, suffering should be cruciform, and hopes for the future messianic. More generally stated, it is the religion instantiated in Scripture which defines being, truth, goodness, and beauty, and the nonscriptural exemplifications of these realities need to be transformed into figures (or types or antitypes) of the scriptural ones. Intratextual theology redescribes reality within the scriptural framework rather than translating Scripture into extrascriptural categories. It is the text, so to speak, which absorbs the world, rather than the world the text. [The text is] able to absorb the universe. It supplies the interpretive framework within which believers seek to live their lives and understand reality.
>
> (pp. 117–18)

A similar understanding of the status and function of the believing community's authoritative texts is evinced by Hans Frei in *The Eclipse of Biblical Narrative*:

> [Since] the world truly rendered by combining biblical narratives into one was indeed the one and only real world, it must in principle embrace the experience of any present age and reader. Not only was it possible for him, it was also his duty to fit himself into that world in which he was in any case a member, and he too did so in part . . . by his mode of life. He was to see his disposition, his actions and passions, the shape of his own life as well as that of his era's events as figures of that storied world.[8]

Likewise, Ronald Thiemann argues that

> Scripture ... depicts a real world, temporally structured, which encompasses both the times and stories of the text and those of the reader. Since the world depicted by the Bible is the only real world,

the reader must fit his or her own experience into scripture's cumulative narrative, thus becoming a 'figure' of the text. Christian reality claims (meditation) and the formation of the Christian life (application) follow from and are normed by the explicative shape of biblical narrative.[9]

Integral to intratextual theologies, then, are the related principles that it is the 'scriptural' linguistic world which subsumes 'extrascriptural' reality, and that it is this world – the 'true' world – which is decisive for the shaping of Christian 'identity'. When these principles are fleshed-out into a more comprehensive account by the advocates of the intratextual approach, it soon becomes apparent that their depiction of the biblical linguistic world grants an undeniable primacy to literary considerations. The assertion that this world is *constituted*, and not merely represented or revealed, by a particular ('realistic') narrative is thus seen by our representative intratextualists to involve the acknowledgement that biblical texts possess the following features. Firstly, the 'literal meaning' of these texts is to be emphasized, because it is this 'meaning' which instantiates, more adequately than any other, the common language, the *consensus fidelium*, of the believing community.[10] Secondly, the gospel stories of Jesus, *qua* realistic narratives, contain descriptions of events, sayings, deeds, etc., associated with him, and these descriptions are literal because they can be predicated of Jesus in such a way that they 'render' his identity. These stories are in effect a set of 'intention-action descriptions' (the term is Frei's) which specify the identity of the crucified and risen rabbi from Nazareth (and, by implication, the identity of the One who raised him from the dead).[11] As such, these stories are not to be regarded as historical accounts of Jesus' career and fate; nor are they to be seen as expressions of his significance for existential transformation; and nor are they ascriptions to him of a certain ontological status. The believer, therefore, is not necessarily someone who happens to have certain convictions about the historicity, existential significance or ontological status of Jesus Christ (though the possession of these convictions on the part of the believer is not thereby precluded); rather, the believer is someone who is 'to be conformed to the Jesus Christ depicted in the narrative'.[12] In other words, it is the *conformitas Christi*, and the attendant *imitatio Christi*, explicated in terms of the cumulative narrative that is the New Testament, which defines and safeguards Christian 'faithfulness', and not (necessarily or even primarily) the possession of some 'theory' about the nature and person of Jesus

Christ. The faithful person is the man or woman whose 'identity' – *qua* member of the believing community – can truly be rendered in terms of descriptions congruent, albeit in an appropriately qualified way, with the identifications of God and Jesus Christ ingredient in the cumulative narrative which is Scripture. This much is evident from Frei's assertion that '[the] identity-description that we applied to Jesus in the Gospels must, to a lesser extent and in merely analogous fashion, be applied also to the church as his people'.[13]

Central to the intratextual approach, therefore, is the notion that the identity of the follower of Christ is most appropriately to be specified in terms of identity-descriptions derived – via the *analogia* described by Frei – from that primary pattern of identity-descriptions which communicates the identity of Jesus Christ. At the level of theological (i.e., 'second-order') description, the practical *imitatio Christi* must thus be seen as a recapitulation of the linguistic or textual *analogia Christi* and its counterpart *conformitas Christi*. What the Christian *does*, *qua* follower of Christ, is a derivative of what the narrative *says* about Jesus Christ. The form of the *analogia Christi* and its concomitant *conformitas Christi* (in the sense specified by Frei) is such that it therefore grounds and solicits the *imitatio Christi*. The 'identity' of the one who professes to be a follower of Jesus Christ is, on this view, constituted by the incorporation of this person into the 'Christ-shaped' world that is the cumulative biblical narrative.[14] This is a profoundly suggestive conception, one which remains deeply traditional precisely because of its resolutely 'Christomorphic' specification of the 'identity' of the one who is called to walk the way of the crucified and risen Christ. I want to argue, however, that while the intratextual approach does supply the lineaments of an original and yet traditional account of Scripture's normative function in respect of the 'identity' of the purported follower of Christ, it still needs to undergo some modification before it can be said to provide a wholly satisfactory account of the relation which obtains between the identity of the one who professes to be a follower of Christ and the 'normative' scriptural linguistic world. It will be my contention that the notion of 'intratextuality', at least in the form sponsored by the 'new Yale theology', will have to be recast if such an acceptable account is likely to be forthcoming.[15]

II Animadversions: taking stock of Gary Comstock

The core of the intratextual approach is to be located in its proponents' assertion that the scriptural texts, as 'realistic narratives', are autonomous with regard to the dispositions, attitudes and convictions of the reader. To quote Frei:

> in realistic narratives the depiction coincides with what it is about. The story renders the subject matter, not only by its ordinary and generally accessible language, but by the interaction of character and happening. . . . In [this] interaction they form the story and thereby cumulatively render its subject matter. They render it – and thus the sense of the text – to the reader, no matter how he disposes himself toward the story on a personal level.[16]

Frei's striking contention that the 'sense' or 'meaning' of a text is not linked, except in ways that are trivial, to the reception accorded it by the reader is one that is problematic.[17]

There is, of course, an initial difficulty which faces anyone who is confronted with *any* kind of claim about the 'meaning' of a text, viz., that concerning the highly troublesome notion of 'meaning' itself. For one thing, it is not self-evident that the 'meanings' of texts are indeed their most significant feature (and this apart from any doubts that we may happen to have about the existence of such things as 'meanings'). For another, it may be that interpretation, like explanation, is 'interest-relative', so that the 'meanings' discerned in a text may need to be relativized to the particular 'interests' brought to it by its readers.[18] But these reservations concerning the status of 'meanings' notwithstanding, it is still possible to question the adequacy of Frei's affirmation of the autonomy of the biblical texts.

Where Frei is concerned, the human identity-descriptions which 'identify' Jesus Christ are such that they are accessible, at least in respect of their 'meaning', to Christian and non-Christian alike.[19] Thus, according to Frei, both the Christian and the non-Christian can be said to 'understand' the identity-description 'Jesus from Nazareth is the Saviour who underwent "all these things" and who is truly manifest as Jesus, the risen Christ'.[20] The 'linguistic' or 'narrative' space occupied by the Christian can therefore be characterized in terms of the following 'second-order' proposition: ([According to the gospel story] *Jesus from Nazareth is the Saviour who underwent 'all these things' and who is truly manifest as Jesus, the risen Christ* [and this I *BELIEVE*]); whereas the space occupied by the non-Christian can be expressed in terms of this proposition's counterpart: ([According to the gospel story] *Jesus from Nazareth is the Saviour who underwent 'all these things' and who is truly manifest as Jesus, the risen Christ* [and this I DO *NOT* BELIEVE]). Frei's assertion that the Christian and non-Christian alike are confronted by the same identity-description bespeaking the 'identity' of Jesus Christ may be open to question because he maintains that when reflecting on the 'identity' of Jesus Christ, we 'are forced to consent to the factuality of what we represent to ourselves imaginatively. We must affirm that to think of him is to have him actually present.'[21] Since it is patent that the non-believer is someone who is able – in principle – to 'think' of Jesus Christ without professing himself or herself to be in the Nazarene's actual presence, it would seem to follow (*pace* Frei) that the Christian and the non-Christian do not 'understand' the above identity-description in anything like the same way. On the contrary, it looks as though the non-believer does not even 'understand' the Christian story as such, because he or she cannot make the appropriate and requisite identification of the principal character of this story. This is precisely the criticism levelled at Frei in a recent article by Gary Comstock.[22]

Comstock argues that while Frei does not give an unambiguous answer to the question whether Jesus' identity is vouchsafed only to Christian readers of the gospel story, it is nonetheless clear that he upholds the concurrence of the identity of Jesus in the text with the presence of Christ in the life of the reader. And Comstock takes Frei's positing of this concurrence to be insurmountably problematic. He recounts Frei's understanding of the coincidence of the identity and 'presence' of Jesus Christ in the following terms: 'As the reader sympathetically follows the progressive unfolding of Jesus' identity *in the narrative* she must simultaneously be "affirming" and "adoring" him *in the present*. If not, the reader has missed the story's meaning because she has not identified its major character' (p. 126. Comstock's emphases). Comstock concludes that Frei has thus violated his attested principle of the text's autonomy – 'Frei's actual reading shows that in the case of at least this one realistic narrative, meaning is unintelligible apart from reader response. That is, we cannot say what the meaning of the story is without referring to what is going on with the reader' (p. 126). Comstock, I believe, is right in holding that Frei, despite his declaration to the contrary, has to accept a commitment, at least where the instance of the storied identity of Jesus Christ is concerned, to some kind of notion of 'reader response'. But

Comstock does Frei a disservice by merely alleging that Frei's account of the 'identity' of Jesus is 'ambiguous' on the question whether it is the Christian alone who can properly 'identify' Jesus Christ. Comstock does not proceed to consider a possibility open to Frei or his supporters, namely, that of using this account's internal resources to indicate quite clearly that it in no way assumes that it is the Christian reader only who can 'grasp' the identity of Jesus Christ. Comstock is also less than persuasive in his charge that Frei's affirmation of the 'truth' of the biblical narratives, when put alongside his refusal to provide any extratextual explication or public warrant for this truth-claim, means that 'to put it oversimply, he insists on meaning while sacrificing truth' (p. 139).

It is not too difficult to show, *pace* Comstock, that Frei is not committed, either overtly or implicitly, to the idea that the true 'identity' of Jesus Christ is concealed from all but the Christian reader (whoever this may be). Thus, with regard to the identity-description mentioned in the previous paragraph, it could be affirmed on Frei's behalf that the expression 'Jesus from Nazareth is the Saviour who underwent "all these things" and who is truly manifest as Jesus, the risen Christ' is a description which enables the believer *and* non-believer alike to grasp the 'identity' of the singular individual who is the main character of the gospel story. This, after all, is an extremely modest and simple claim. It may be that Comstock finds it questionable because (and here I am venturing a guess) he apparently thinks it is a claim which *must* be seen in the context of Frei's overall assumption that (in Comstock's words) 'the meaning of the gospel does have an undeniable unicity.... a singular, unified, and transparent meaning' (p. 125).[23] Comstock may be correct in thinking that Frei has shackled himself to the assumption that the gospel has a single and transparent 'meaning'. He may, for all we know, also be correct in thinking that this assumption is palpably untenable. But if my suspicion is justified, Comstock is simply not right in concluding that Frei's claim – viz. that the descriptions which enunciate the 'identity' of Jesus Christ are 'graspable' in principle by the Christian and non-Christian alike – is vitiated by his apparent commitment to an unsatisfactory 'theory' of the gospel's 'meaning'. For this claim has nothing to do with the notion of 'meaning' as such, let alone a particular 'theory' of 'meaning'. It is quite easy to see why.

Frei derives the outlines of his theory of identity-description from P. F. Strawson. Strawson's is essentially a Russellian theory of reference. That is to say, it is a theory which pivots on a dichotomy between 'demonstrative identification' (what Russell called 'know-ledge by acquaintance') and 'descriptive identification' (what Russell termed 'knowledge by description').[24] The motivation for accepting a dichotomy between 'demonstrative' and 'descriptive' identification stems from Russell's conviction that in order to think about an object, the subject must *know*, or be in a position to *know* (this more accurately represents Strawson's position), *which* object it is that he or she is thinking about.[25] Russell's Principle thus requires a knowledge which the late Gareth Evans calls a '*discrimi-nating knowledge*: the subject must have a capacity to distinguish the object of his judgement from all other things'.[26] With regard to the species of identification which Evans calls 'description-based' (and to which the identity-description 'Jesus from Nazareth is the Saviour who underwent "all these things" and who is truly manifest as Jesus, the risen Christ' would belong), it is possible for a subject to have a fully coherent idea of a particular object, *a*, even if there is nothing that would be identified by the idea in question. All that the subject would need to know in making a description-based identifi-cation is what would *make* a particular identity-description true with regard to *a*; it is not necessary for us to impose on this subject the more stringent requirement that she should know that this identity-description is *in fact* true of *a*.[27] If what warrants the subject's use of an identity-description is her *capacity* to know what is in question when she applies this description to *a*, as opposed to her knowing that this description *in fact* depicts *a*, then since the Christian and non-Christian alike are able in principle to know what would make Frei's identity-description true with regard to Jesus from Nazareth, it follows that the non-Christian can have a discriminating conception of the principal character of the gospel story *even* if she happens not to profess that this character is present in her life. Once she has formed this exigent discriminating concep-tion she has 'grasped' the identity of Jesus Christ. In which case, this reader, *qua* non-Christian, can be said to have understood Frei's identity-description *without* simultaneously professing the presence of Christ.

Someone still committed to speaking about such matters in terms of what a text 'means', could say that it is precisely in this sense that the 'meaning' of the biblical texts is intelligible *apart* from the response of the reader: one does not have to accept the Christian story as one's own in order to be able to form the discriminating conceptions sufficient to 'identify' the characters who inhabit the story. Things become very much different once one has accepted this story as one's own. Then, and then only, does a 'grasp' of the 'identity' of the story's main character entail the concomitant profession of Christ's presence. It is this harmless but salutary insight which (arguably) underlies Frei's claim that '[a] formal question, such as "Who is he?" or "What is he like?" is ... a question that will not force an answer that would risk overwhelming either the person or the story'.[28] The Christian story will cease to pose merely 'formal questions' when it becomes the truth for someone, and this will happen only when, in Frei's words, she '[hammers] out a shape of life patterned after its own shape'.[29] For Frei, therefore, it is the enactment of the scriptural narrative on the part of the believer which serves to display its character as truth, and not any 'foundationalist' metaphysical or epistemological theory about the status of Christian truth-claims (i.e. the kind of theory valorized by Comstock). 'Truth', for Frei, belongs just as much, if not more, to the domain of pragmatics than it does to the realm of semantics. This enactment must perforce take place in the public domain, for the discourse through which this enactment takes place is embedded in a shared or collective way of life – in this context, the life of the communion of saints. This much has been advertised by Karl Barth:

> The saints of the New Testament exist only in plurality. Sanctity belongs to them, but only in their common life, not as individuals. In this plurality they are ... identical with the Christian community. . . . The truth is that the holiness of the community, as of its individual constituents, is to be sought in that which happens to these men in common. . . . [30]

This point can also be formulated as part of the more general thesis that language itself is the transindividual product of human social-ity, a thesis formulated thus by Marx and Engels:

> Language is as old as consciousness, language *is* practical conscious-ness that exists also for other men, and for that reason alone it really exists for me personally as well; language, like consciousness, only arises from the need, the necessity, of intercourse with other men. . . . Consciousness is, therefore, from the very beginning a social product, and remains so as long as men exist at all.[31]

The 'consciousness' of the Christian is grounded in an irreducible 'linguisticality'; a 'linguisticality' which, moreover, is constituted *ab initio* as a social product. The particular faithfulness (or otherwise) of the Christian's enactment of this narrative is thus in the public domain right from the start. To profess to act in a way that accords with the central tenets of the Christian faith is *already* to have situated oneself, and irremovably at that, in the public domain. Hence it is not self-evident that Frei's conception of narrative enactment, when understood in the way just specified, involves a 'sacrificing of truth' on his part (as Comstock charges): on the contrary, truth is 'sacrificed' precisely when it is proposed, whether directly or by implication, that the primary affirmations of the Christian faith be considered in isolation from the irreducibly social enactment of the Christian narrative. Comstock's criticism is thus premised, generally, on what amounts to an effective displacement of history, and, specifically, on a failure to perceive that 'truth' for Frei is located preeminently in the sphere of pragmatics. But then Comstock is perhaps not really interested in history or pragmatics. What Comstock wants is a Christianity which lends itself, in main part at least, to systematic description in terms of an overarching and thus canonical epistemological or metaphysical theory. Frei and his Yale confreres of course prefer an approach which gives 'thick descriptions' of the life of faith communities, and so will have no truck with such systematization. In the process, they forswear the kind of 'truth-theory' Comstock seems to want the theologian to embrace, i.e. a 'theory' which, ideally, takes the form of a set of factual or quasi-factual judgements about, say, the resurrection, so that any disagreement between the believer and non-believer over the biblical narrative can in principle be resolved via a 'public conversation' about this narrative's 'truth'. As Frei and his fellow intratextualists would have it, however, the defining and salient feature of a realistic narrative resides not so much in its capacity to generate 'truth-claims', but in its rendering of an agent's 'identity', and through such rendering, to transform human beings. The emphasis in intratextualism is less on what texts 'say', and more on what they are *used* for (in this case, 'shaping' the believer's existence); less on 'theory' and 'foundational' criteria, and more on a skill-based understanding and good practice; less on semantics, and more on pragmatics. As Lindbeck puts it: 'intelligibility comes from skill, not theory, and credibility comes from good performance, not adherence to independently formulated criteria'.[32] Here it is perhaps unfortunate that exponents of intratextualism (with the notable exception of Frei especially in his more recent work) have placed so seemingly preponderant an emphasis on the literary-theoretic considerations which surround their explication of christological identity-descriptions, especially when they go on to say that such identity-descriptions are an intrinsic feature of the biblical narrative. This may or may not be the case, and this claim is something which theologians with an interest in literary theory will doubtless want to ponder deeply. But what tends to be elided in such literary-theoretical discussions is the *theological* necessity to have the 'identity' of the central figure of the gospel stories specified in this particular way. For without a specification of the 'identity' of Jesus Christ, a specification integral to the *analogia Christi* advertised here, there can be no *imitatio Christi*, no *discipleship*. Without the *analogia Christi* (and its concomitant *conformitas Christi*) there can be no church. The critic who is inclined to argue for the sheer dispensability, from the narratological standpoint, of such christological identity-descriptions is therefore in danger of failing to perceive the fundamental *theological* rationale for the deployment of such identity-descriptions. It is this theological, or ecclesiological, desideratum which needs to be brought to the attention of such critics of intratextualism.

Comstock, I have argued, has not vindicated his criticisms of Frei – at least, his strictures have not struck at the heart of Frei's intratextualism. But Comstock is right in his contention that Frei's principle of the autonomy of the text is really untenable. The principle of the text's autonomy, we have seen, is intended by Frei and his fellow intratextualists to safeguard Scripture's status as the ('primary') reality, one definitive of, and supervenient upon, all other realities. What the intratextualists simply fail to see is that the Bible's being the 'primary' reality constitutive of all other realities is something that can be acknowledged *without* any assent being given to the principle of its autonomy as a text. When it comes to specifying the form of a theologically adequate biblical hermeneutics, the theologian is not constrained to make his or her choice from just two alternatives: that the 'meaning' of the biblical texts is to be specified via an interpretation of extrascriptural realities (the 'Chicago School'); or that the 'reality' instantiated by the biblical texts is *sui generis* (the 'Yale School'). There is another possibility: namely, that acceptance of the primacy of the scriptural world can and does go hand-in-hand with acquiescence in the principle that the response of the reader/disciple(?) plays a crucial part in its interpretation. This possibility is one that is perhaps best explored under the rubric of a 'church poetics'.

III Towards an outline of a trinitarian church poetics

It was said above (cf. pp. 206ff) that *any* person with the requisite
minimal discriminating knowledge will be able to use the description 'Jesus from Nazareth is the Saviour who underwent "all these
things" and who is truly manifest as Jesus, the risen Christ' in a way
which appropriately 'identifies' Jesus Christ. Any deployment of
this description which rests on no more than its user's possession of
the needed minimally-discriminating conception will of course
result in a merely formal depiction of the unsubstitutible 'identity'
of the main character of the gospel story: at *this* level, all that the
minimally knowledgeable utterer of this description will be able to
do is to 'pick out' the character in question. For there to be any real
difference between the Christian and the non-Christian there will
have to be the possibility of a much richer understanding of the
terms which enter into this identity-description. We don't reckon
someone a follower of Jesus Christ simply because he or she is able
to *talk* 'informatively' about him! The person who has accepted the
Christian story, in the sense of having (in Frei's words) 'turn[ed]
from *reflection* about Jesus Christ to *proclamation* of him', already
has a quite different christology from that of the non-believer, even
if we confine our understanding of the former's profession of Christ
to that of a merely discursive level.[33] All else being equal, we would
say of the person who has made this transition that he or she is
someone who has a deeper or richer understanding of the terms
that make up one or more descriptions which 'identify' Jesus
Christ. This person's is the more adequate – though not necessarily
the more detailed or theologically informed – specification of this
'identity'.[34] I am suggesting, in other words, that the property of
semantic depth can be ascribed to christological and theological
terms (and *eo ipso* the descriptions comprising these terms), so that
it is possible to begin with a minimal and formal understanding of
the 'meaning' of such a term, and then, through a progressive and
more sustained engagement with the realities of Christian faith and
practice, to deepen our understanding of the terms in question
without our necessarily coming to mean something different by
(say) 'Jesus Christ is Saviour' from what we understood by this
locution at an earlier stage in our christological pilgrimage.[35]
'Progress' in christological reflection is thus a concomitant of
participation in a range of social practices mediated by the Christian semiotic system. Through such participation, the Christian,
among other things, comes to know how to make 'correct judge-

ments' in the doctrinal realm. This intratextual account of the process of Christian convictional formation is Wittgensteinian in its provenance, as Lindbeck indicates:

> just as a language (or 'language game', to use Wittgenstein's phrase) is correlated with a form of life, and just as a culture has both cognitive and behavioural dimensions, so it is also in the case of a religious tradition. Its doctrines, cosmic stories or myths, and ethical directives are integrally related to the rituals it practices, the sentiments or experiences it evokes, the actions it recommends, and the institutional forms it develops.[36]

In the intratextual scheme of things, then, the Christian has 'learned correct judgements' by virtue of having learned a particular way of conducting herself. Her use of doctrinal concepts, as she becomes more competent in her deployment of the Christian semiotic system, is grounded in a congruent growth in her capacity to engage in those practices mediated by this semiotic system. As she is inducted into the life of the community of faith she will add to her repertoire of 'correct judgements' in regard to a certain identity-description (e.g. 'Jesus Christ is Saviour'). With each addition to the repertoire she acquires the theoretical basis for providing a deeper and more profound – i.e. a more 'saintly' – specification of the 'content' of that particular identity-description. Such 'progress' is never inexorable; indeed ultimate failure in this regard is guaranteed for every Christian this side of the *eschaton* – 'perfect' knowledge of the 'content' of the identity-description 'Jesus from Nazareth is the Saviour who underwent "all these things" and who is truly manifest as Jesus, the risen Christ' will be possible only when we share in the inner life of the Godhead, and so the final attainment of such knowledge must await the *visio beatifica*. In an absolute sense, therefore, the Christian cannot plumb the uttermost semantic depths of the identity-descriptions ingredient in the community's articulation of its faith.[37] But failure on the part of the Christian to add to her repertoire of 'correct judgements' is not necessarily destructive: the last specification she gave of this identity-description will suffice, since it will still render explicit 'all that can be found' (by *her* at *that* time) in the concepts which feature in this description. Her failure in this respect notwithstanding, she can still be said to have a grasp of the 'meaning' of this identity-description. She remains a competent participant in the believing community's various rule-governed practices, and by virtue of this participation she continues to possess an 'identity' as a Christian. This is so even though there are *other* such practices which are as yet (and perhaps in the final reckoning will always be) beyond her competence.[38] We therefore possess from the very beginning of our profession of membership of the community a grasp of the 'meaning' of Christian identity-descriptions which is adequate to the task of participating in a 'Christ-shaped' form of life at that particular historical juncture.[39]

Implicit in the foregoing characterization of the notion of 'semantic depth' is the idea that 'knowing how to talk', whether about Jesus Christ or indeed anything else, is something that admits of gradation. The kind of talk we engage in as Christians is a function of our discursive skills, and these can be built-up, consolidated or even lost. These discursive skills in turn are embedded in the shared life of the believing community. This community is what it is because it is a community which inhabits a 'narrative space' circumscribed by the gospel texts.

The above theses are constitutive of the intratextual approach to theology. It has not been my purpose to quarrel with these theses – there is no real need to do this, for, subject to the few modifications and glosses proposed in this essay, they are, I believe, eminently sustainable from a theological point of view. What needs to be done on behalf of intratextualism, however, is a reconstruction of the (problematic) account of 'textuality' which it presupposes.

Intratextualism's firm adherence to the principle of the autonomy of the text conduces to an understanding of the text as a static and homogeneous entity. David Kelsey is the one intratextualist who is perhaps not so vulnerable to this charge – after all, he has said that '[part] of what it means to call a text "Christian scripture" is that it *functions* in certain ways or *does* certain things when used in certain ways in the common life of the church'.[40] Kelsey's functional understanding of Scripture ought, however, to ensue in a theory capable of specifying what it is that a text *does* (as opposed to saying what it *is*). That is to say, his should be a conception of the text which understands the text as a succession of *actions* on the understanding of the reader.[41] It is therefore something of a surprise that this conception is nowhere to be found in *The Uses of Scripture in Recent Theology*. Where Kelsey and his fellow intratextualists are concerned, the text remains an entity, it is not seen as a *process*, as a text-to-be-reconstructed. The intratextual theologians view the text as a repository of achieved 'meaning'. They fail to see that the text is constituted, as text, in the very act of being understood or received by the reader. This is not to say that the text has no 'objective' existence, that it is a mere reflex of the consciousness of the reader. To say this, to collapse the text into the response of the reader, would after all be to subscribe to an understanding of the text which is just as undialectical as that of the intratextualist. What is needed, it would seem, is a truly dialectical understanding of the text, one which takes its 'meaning' to be constituted by the interaction *between* text and reader. Hazardous though it may be, we can make a guess as to why intratextualism fails to avail itself of a truly dialectical conception of the text. Of these possible guesses, the most plausible candidate, in my view, would be the one which had something to say about intratextualism's failure to provide an adequate account of the subjectivity of the reader of the text. Here the proponents of intratextualism show there is a sense in which they are driven by the same theological dynamo which powered the author of the *Church Dogmatics*: Barth's theologically-motivated lack of interest in the *process* of subjectivity is to some extent perpetuated in the formulations of the 'Yale School'. Lindbeck's consistent identification of religion as a *verbum externum* leaves him no alternative but to repudiate 'experiential-expressive' understandings of religion on the grounds that they can 'be easily, though not necessarily, used to legitimate the religious privatism and subjectivism that is fostered by the social pressures of the day'.[42] Lindbeck's insistence that it is the 'objectivities of the religion' which 'come first' prompts him to regard the 'interiorization' of Christian 'identity' as a process in which the believer undergoes a kind of death to her subjectivity. This plunges Lindbeck into an aporia, because the existence of this subjectivity is one of the indispensable enabling conditions of this process of internalization: this subjectivity has to be in place before this 'shaping' process can even begin to occur! The source of this aporia is to be located in the pervasive intratextualist preoccupation with the formation of Christian 'identity', a preoccupation which, ironically, ensues in a new 'foundationalism' consisting this time of a ('foundational') biblical narrative which the intratextualist operates in tandem with a regulative theological 'grammar'.[43] How, if at all possible, is intratextualism to be extricated from this aporia and this inadvertent 'foundationalism'?

We have to begin, not at the point where the narrative is, as it were, already doing its work, but at the earlier point where the subject is about to enter into it, i.e. the point where she is 'baptized' into the Christian semiotic system. At this juncture the human subject is suspended between two narratives, one 'pre-

Christian' and the other 'Christian', poised to undergo what Fredric Jameson has in another context so vividly described as

> the shock of *entry* into narrative, which so often resembles the body's tentative immersion in an unfamiliar element, with all the subliminal anxieties of such submersion: the half-articulated fear of what the surface of the liquid conceals; a sense of our vulnerability along with the archaic horror of impure contact with the unclean; the anticipation of fatigue also, of the intellectual effort about to be demanded in the slow apprenticeship of unknown characters and their elaborate situations, as though, beneath the surface excitement of adventure promised, there persisted some deep ambivalence at the dawning sacrifice of the self to the narrative text.[44]

The church is the community which enables this baptism – 'the dawning sacrifice of the self to the text' – to take place and to be lived through. As the intratextualist would see it, the newly baptized individual has now been inducted into 'the [church's] practice of reading the scriptures in their canonical character, while simultaneously appropriating their concepts to form the fabric of one's own existence'.[45] But this individual, member of the believing community though she may now be, is still a citizen of the world – she is *still* the modern, empty and deracinated subject. Conferring on her a new 'identity', even though that 'identity' may be one that is recognizably 'Christian', may in fact have the undesirable consequence of fixing and stabilizing this still empty subject. To preempt the possibility of the subject's petrification, this newly baptized subject needs to be turned into what Julia Kristeva calls a 'subject-in-process'.[46] The human subject is constituted by language, and so the possibility of turning the subject into a 'work-in-progress' pivots on the possibility of there being a 'new' language marked by a surplus of signification, i.e. a disrupted and creative language which can sustain the church's interrogative and demystifying discourse. The church is the gospel-shaped 'narrative space' where Christians learn to 'sacrifice' themselves, over and over again, to the community's narrative texts, to this 'new' language. This they do by consenting to be interrogated by these texts in such a way that they learn, slowly, laboriously and sometimes painfully, to live the way of Jesus. This interrogation – which is fundamental to the church's 'pedagogy of discipleship' – may, depending on historical circumstances, have the consequence of actually decomposing, as opposed to reinforcing, certain already existing patterns of Christian 'identity'. These alternative 'identities' will be articulated in a language which gives speech to all that is denominated by the category of the 'other'. It will be a language capable of undermining the filiative and affiliative bonds which sustain the unredeemed order.[47] Lindbeck's is a profoundly affiliative theology of, and for, the church; and, *qua* affiliative theology, it does not sit very easily with his interesting suggestion that the church of the future may have to respond to its seemingly inevitable marginalization by embracing a strategy of 'sociological sectarianism'. In Lindbeck's words:

> Religious bodies that wish to maintain highly deviant convictions in an inhospitable environment must, it would seem, develop close-knit groups capable of supplying the psychological 'plausibility structures' ... needed to sustain an alien faith. These groups ... can ... form cells like those of the early Christian movement (or of the more recent international communist one), or develop *ecclesiolae in ecclesia* similar to those of monasticism, early pietism, or some portions of the contemporary charismatic movement.[48]

This 'religious' vision of the church of the diaspora can be contrasted with Julia Kristeva's portrayal of exile as a fundamentally *irreligious* act:

> Exile is already in itself a form of *dissidence*, since it involves uprooting oneself from a family, a country or a language. More importantly, it is an irreligious act that cuts all ties, for religion is nothing more than membership of a real or symbolic community which may or may not be transcendental, but which always constitutes a link, a homology, an understanding. ... For if meaning exists in the state of exile, it nevertheless finds no incarnation, and is ceaselessly produced and destroyed in geographical or discursive formations.[49]

If this view of exile carries even a little conviction, then a church of the diaspora will, if what Kristeva says is acceptable, be the *locus* of new and unpredictable signifying effects. Lindbeck's model of 'sociological sectarianism' cannot therefore accommodate the most radical and profound element in Kristeva's account, viz. her suggestion that the materialities of exile penetrate right into the heart of our discursive practices. Lindbeck's church of the future (or present?) may be immured in a cultural wilderness, but it never appears at any time to have relinquished its stable interpretive position. (In this sense it represents a reversion to, or even a continuation of, the Biblical Theology movement.) It is this (unrelentingly) ahistorical textual stability which is the most troubling feature of the intratextual approach to theology. Does this mean we have to look elsewhere for a more 'hermeneutically' adequate approach? Would we be better advised to turn from New Haven to Chicago? Before I bring this essay to a conclusion by venturing a few tentative remarks in response to these questions, it is important to note briefly some of the implications of the position I have been working towards, namely, that the scriptural texts are not absolutely stable entities existing in isolation from their readers, and that the relation between reader and text is a properly dialectical relationship of the kind described thus by Jonathan Culler: 'The shift back and forth in stories of reading between readers' decisive actions and readers' automatic responses is not a mistake that could be corrected but an essential structural feature of the situation.'[50] This, in outline, is the account of reading I have sought to promote. When it comes to exercising one's capacity to form discriminating conceptions by using an appropriate description to 'identify' a character of the biblical narrative, the reader's response is 'automatic'. However, when it comes to the matter of ascertaining the *semantic depth* of the terms ingredient in that particular identity-description, the reader's 'actions' become decisive because a concept's semantic depth is contingent upon a range of 'praxological' skills acquired by the reader through her participation in the shared practices of the community. Here 'semantic depth' is to be specified in a way which takes pragmatics into account. In this scheme, the reader of the text who participates in the shared life of the community, and who has acquired a number of these skills, has fulfilled one of the requirements of being a follower of Christ. This reader belongs to 'the communion of saints developing itself in time' (to use a phrase of Bonhoeffer's). In this sense, therefore, only the disciple can understand the text. But she is not as yet a fully-fledged member of the *communio sanctorum* (i.e. of that which Bonhoeffer refers to as 'the perfected communion of saints'). A member of the 'perfected communion of saints' will of course possess – among other things – a greater range and depth of 'praxological' skills.[51] If it is accepted that the biblical texts are 'open works' in Umberto Eco's sense, i.e. that they require the reader to be in some sense a '(re)constructor' of the text, then the perfected *communio sanctorum* has a crucial regulative role to play in the process of helping all Christians to acquire the requisite skills for understanding the textual world created by the biblical narrative. The saints are the true interpreters of Scripture.[52]

Finally, the position adumbrated in this essay differs from those of both the 'Yale' and 'Chicago Schools' in one major respect. (This consequently obviates the need to make a choice between them. As will become apparent very shortly, the 'conclusion' that I shall move towards will be extratextual insofar as I take 'meaning' – understood here as a mere *façon de parler* – to reside in the dialectic between master text and reading community, and intratextual, insofar as my position retains the 'Yale School's' insistence on the unnegotiable primacy of the Christian semiotic system. But that semiotic system or master narrative is itself the product of the relation which Christian communities, *qua* historical communities, have to a certain canonical understanding of the text. The canon is determinative for understanding the text, and it is the *communio sanctorum* which mediates the relation that the reader has to the canon by exercising a custodial function with regard to the *discrimen* (the term is Kelsey's) which determines how Scripture is to be construed and used.) The gospel stories concerning the life, death and resurrection of Jesus Christ are 'wholly textual'. But the 'reality' of the Second Person of the Trinity is not exhausted by the 'reality' of Jesus of Nazareth. In this differentiation between the divine Logos and the 'historical' Jesus we are confronted by that which is inherently 'subtextual'. The 'historical' Jesus is 'real', but his is what Fredric Jameson has called 'the reality of the *appearance*', an 'appearance' which is necessarily textualized.[53] By contrast, the divine Logos, insofar as its 'reality' is not exhausted by Jesus of Nazareth, is the Real, that is the essentially unrepresentable and non-narrative 'absent cause', known only through its 'effect', that is, Jesus of Nazareth. The Real, because it is inherently 'subtextual' is able to resist all human formulations and eludes the grasp of all our discourses. The Real – the Second Person of the Trinity – is thus able to be the fathomless source of disruptive significations, significations which 'interrupt' our unredeemed condition, and which are in consequence the source of our true hope. The smallest of these significations can presage our redemption. But for them to presage our redemption they have to be read in the Spirit. For it is only by reading this text – i.e. this concatenation of significations – in the Spirit that the reader comes to be in the *presence* of the Real, that is, the presence of Christ. In such a trinitarian poetics of the church, signification has great weight, but as word, also much weakness – hence it is signification's 'weight of weakness' which redeems. But the Real is brought to figuration in precisely *these* significations, the Real is registered in precisely *this* text. Through this master text the members of the believing community are able, 'asymptotically', to approach the Real.[54] Hence, these ('Christian') significations, this ('Christian') text, are properly to be regarded as the primary reality, the reality which subsumes that reality which is the world of 'common human experience'. But this primary reality is – textual. It is more than text, of course, but to understand what is at stake in saying that it is 'more than text' we have to await the *visio beatifica*, when the profane separation between word and thing will be healed.[55] In the meantime all Christians, as Christians, are constrained to bear the weight of the unredeemed order by being its 'weakness'.[56]

13

'Theistic arguments' and 'rational theism'

The last two decades or so have seen a remarkable resurgence of interest in the ontological, the cosmological and the design arguments for the existence of God.

The ontological argument owes its 'rebirth' to the formulation of a 'second' or modal version of the argument by Norman Malcolm, Charles Hartshorne and Alvin Plantinga.[1] The cosmological argument has been defended in recent years by John J. Shepherd and Germain Grisez.[2] The design, or teleological, argument has been resuscitated by Richard Swinburne and Brian Davies.[3] This renewed interest in the 'theistic arguments' has culminated in Keith Ward's attempt to construct a system of 'rational theism', using the 'theistic arguments' as a foundation, in his 1980 Cadbury Lectures *Rational Theology and the Creativity of God*.[4] In propounding this theological system, Ward operates on the bold and novel principle that *all* the main 'theistic arguments' are valid, and that, moreover, the canons which are implicit in any quest for a rational and coherent conception of 'reality' will serve to establish the truth of the premises of these arguments. In an essay of somewhat limited scope, it will not be possible to examine Ward's theological system in its entirety. Neither will it be possible to scrutinize, in detail, his formulation of *each* of the 'theistic arguments'. However, since Ward himself admits that the ontological argument (primarily by virtue of its peculiar character as a strictly logical or *a priori* argument) is somehow conceptually antecedent to the other 'theistic arguments', it will be in order to restrict our attention to Ward's presentation of the ontological argument: this argument can be said to function as the nerve-point of Ward's theological strategy, and any demonstrable weakness in Ward's formulation of it will inevitably serve to undermine the foundations of his 'theistic' system.[5] But before we can proceed to examine the substance of Ward's rendition of the ontological argument, it will be necessary to comment on two secondary, but nevertheless important, aspects of his approach: (i) his claim that the root-principle of the argument – that any possibly necessary being is actual – is to be found in chapter 3 of St Anselm's *Proslogion*; and (ii) his conception of the relation between the ontological and the cosmological arguments.[6]

I

Although he regards the argument put forward in *Proslogion* 3 as the direct ancestor of the modern ontological argument, Ward's formulation of this argument relies on a number of concepts and principles which owe their provenance exclusively to recent developments in the semantics of modal logic.[7] To maintain with any degree of plausibility that *Proslogion* 3 is the ancestor of the modern or so-called 'modal' version of the ontological argument, it must be possible to translate the modal complex which undergirds the *Proslogion* directly into the language(s) of modern modal logic. This, however, is seemingly impossible, for two reasons:

(a) St Anselm treats modality as part of a general theory of physical dispositions and capacities: necessity, for instance, is equated with constraint (*coactio*) and prevention (*prohibitio*).[8] Any attempt to represent the so-called 'second' version of the ontological argument as a historical exegesis of Anselm's ideas must take due account of his physical interpretation of modality, and this Ward fails to do. Moreover, it is not at all clear how this interpretation, permeated as it is by the neo-Platonic conventional wisdom of Anselm's time, is to be rendered in terms of modern modal semantics. Anselm thought it natural, for instance, to regard celestial entities and 'the eternal principles of things' (i.e. souls) as necessary beings, and shaped his conception of necessity accordingly. So a lot of work outside of modal logic is needed before Ward's implied exegetical claims can acquire any degree of plausibility.[9]

(b) Anselm operated with a theologically saturated conception of necessity. Thus, he suggests that 'God necessarily exists' is equivalent to 'God's existence is due to himself' (*a se*).[10] Anselm also took 'God necessarily exists' to mean 'Nothing has the power to bring it about that God ceases to exist'.[11] However, the latter gloss is favoured in *Proslogion* 5, in which case 'God necessarily exists' does *not* entail 'God exists', as it would in all standard systems of modal logic.[12] Hence a straightforward 'possible worlds' interpretation of Anselm's argument would almost certainly misrepresent its author's intentions, and proponents of the so-called 'second' version of the argument, Ward included, should be more guarded in their attempts to read twentieth-century insights into the *Proslogion*. The modal argument is a child of our logical times, and its proponents are very much revisionists or revolutionaries when stood in relation to Anselm. Ward, as we shall see later, does in fact invoke the concept of aseity when formulating his argument. Now it is possible to formulate a modal ontological argument in terms of God's aseity, provided we combine carefully certain assumptions about the nature (or essence) of God with the standard systems of modal logic. Nevertheless, it is essential, in working out such an argument, that we recognize which of our arguments are due to theology and which to the languages of logical theory. To confuse or conflate the two, as Ward seems to do, is fatal for a satisfactory presentation of the ontological argument.[13]

If these criticisms are accepted, it is hard to see how there can be a real basis, either textual or logical, for maintaining that the insights into modality which provide the foundation for Ward's formulation of the ontological argument are prefigured in St Anselm's *Proslogion*.

II

Ward claims that the ontological argument and the cosmological argument mutually support and reinforce each other:

> the ontological argument depends on the cosmological argument in this way: the latter shows that, given an assumption of intelligibility, there is a self-explanatory being, so that the notion of such a being must be a coherent one. . . .
> . . . by the ontological proof, if God is coherent then he exists; and if God exists, the assumption of intelligibility is justified. Kant was wrong in thinking that the ontological proof did not need the others, and that they could not give support to the idea of God without it.[14]

There are a number of puzzling elements in Ward's conception of the relation between the ontological and the cosmological arguments. Ward's motivation for positing such a relation is clearly stated: the ontological argument is plausible only to the extent that the notion of a Perfect Being can be *demonstrated* to be coherent, and (in Ward's scheme of things) it is precisely the role of the cosmological argument to supply the required demonstration

(p. 32). But, and herein lies the rub, if the cosmological argument is cogent, then it follows that a self-existent being – God – exists. However, if God exists (the very conclusion of the cosmological argument), then why do we need the ontological argument (the conclusion of which is that God exists)? The ontological argument may require the cosmological argument as a vindication of its initial assumption of the coherence of the idea of a Perfect Being, but as soon as the cosmological argument is employed for this purpose it renders the conclusion of the ontological argument redundant. Two arguments can be adduced in support of Ward's decision to work the 'theistic arguments' in harness:

(i) It may be that while each 'theistic argument' is to be regarded as a necessary component in a putative demonstration of God's existence, none of these arguments is sufficient, on its own, to 'prove' that God exists. The arguments must therefore be made to operate conjointly. This strategy is explicitly adopted by Ward. Thus he uses the cosmological argument with the intention of showing that if 'reality' is intelligible, then the idea of God is coherent; he then uses the ontological argument to establish that if the idea of God is coherent, then God exists; and, finally, Ward uses the affirmation of the existence of God (which is yielded by the ontological argument) to support the initial assumption (made by the cosmological argument) that 'reality' is 'intelligible' (p. 33).

(ii) Ward's stated intention is to develop and defend a form of 'rational theism' which, among other things, takes the existence of God to be the ground of 'our demand for the rational intelligibility of the universe' (p. 3, see also p. 29). The 'theistic arguments' are thus the bedrock on which Ward proposes to construct his theological edifice, and his approach to these arguments is (understandably) influenced to a considerable extent by his vision of the final shape of this edifice. In this programme of 'rational theism', the 'theistic arguments' are used to generate three interrelated, but nevertheless distinguishable, characterizations of divinity. The cosmological argument yields the idea of God as 'a uniquely self-determining being' (p. 30); the ontological argument furnishes the idea of God as 'a most perfect conceivable being' (p. 48); and the design argument demonstrates the existence of 'an intrinsically valuable being' (p. 33). If this is a correct interpretation of Ward's theological intentions, then it is easy to see how his attempt to delineate and sustain a certain *conception* or *picture* of God (and, indeed, of all 'reality') can require him to operate the three arguments in tandem.[15]

The problem with Ward's attempt to use the 'theistic proofs' conjointly, it seems to me, is that both (i) and (ii) above are so deeply threatened by the circular nature of Ward's procedure that we may have little alternative but to reject them.

Ward's procedure, as he himself admits, is unavoidably circular – though he insists that 'the circle of theistic argument is not vicious' (p. 33). The task of formulating adequate principles for determining whether or not a particular argument is 'viciously' circular is not an easy one. Even so, it is hard to see how Ward's scheme for deploying the 'theistic arguments' in a mutually reinforcing way can be anything but question-begging and circular in a most 'vicious' – i.e. illegitimate – manner. A cursory examination of Ward's procedure will bear this out, provided of course that it is possible for us to specify more precisely when, and on exactly what grounds, an argument is to be regarded as question-begging and circular. Fortunately, philosophers interested in the logic of explanation and the general theory of evidence have developed principles which enable us to determine when, and for what reasons precisely, an argument can be said to be question-begging and unacceptably circular.

To state matters somewhat truistically: a circular argument is an entirely valid though extremely uninformative argument. If we infer the proposition p from itself, then we have reasoned correctly, but we have not added anything to our store of knowledge. Since Ward uses the 'theistic arguments' to form the basis of an alleged 'proof' of a certain type of 'rational theism', we can supply a semi-formal explication of the notion of proof to his treatment of these arguments. A proof, let us say, is an argument which transmits knowledge.[16] If a person S is to regard an argument as a 'proof' of q for p, the following conditions must be met:

(1) S knows that p.

If it were not the case that S knows that p, there would be no knowledge to transmit. In addition, it must also be accepted that

(2) not-$q \rightarrow$ not-(S believes that p).

For if (2) is not granted, knowledge will not be transmitted by a series of inferential or deductive steps which constitute the argument. It must also be the case that

(3) p entails (or logically implies) q.[17]

It is possible for an argument in support of q to satisfy (1) to (3), and still not be a proof for q, because it begs the question. An argument can be said to beg the question (as a purported proof) when, if S has no knowledge of its conclusion, he would not know (one or more of) the premises. So it is necessary to add the following condition:

(4) not-(S does not know that $q \rightarrow S$ does not know that p).

In brief: a proof must have premises which would not be believed if the conclusion were false (condition 2), but which might be known even if the conclusion were not known (condition 4). Conditions (1) to (4) enable us to say that a proof begs the question for S when: if S did not know that q, he would not know that p. Likewise, we can say that a proof is circular just in case it would beg the question for everyone; when it is the case that for every person S, S would not know that p if he were not able to know that q. Robert Nozick puts this point succinctly when he says:

> Since the aim of a proof is to bring knowledge, the conditions for a proof's being circular or begging the question are stated in terms of knowledge. However, the goal might be to bring or transmit some thing other than knowledge; an argument, for example, aims at producing or transmitting belief or perhaps conviction. We may say that an argument from p to q begs the question for S when: if he weren't to believe q, he wouldn't believe p – and that an argument is circular if it would beg the question for everyone.[18]

There can be little doubt that Ward's use of the ontological and the cosmological arguments is question-begging and circular in the sense just specified. As we have seen, he uses the fundamental principle which underlies the cosmological argument – the assumption of 'intelligibility' – to establish the coherence of the idea of God; he then uses this idea to motivate the ontological argument; and finally he uses the conclusion of the ontological argument – that God exists – to justify the fundamental principle which underlies the cosmological argument, that is, the already invoked assumption of 'intelligibility'.[19]

To pronounce, at this stage, a verdict of circularity on the *modus operandi* of Ward's deployment of the 'theistic arguments' would be a little premature: to justify such a verdict it is necessary to probe more deeply into Ward's assumption that the 'theistic arguments' are the means by which we come to understand the world as 'a rational and meaningful totality' (p. 30). For when such an investigation is carried out, it soon becomes apparent that Ward believes the 'theistic arguments' to be validated precisely by virtue of their enabling us to understand the world in a 'rational' and 'meaningful' way. As Ward makes clear, the existence of God is the presupposition of the application of a certain conceptual scheme which makes possible such an understanding of the world (pp. 25ff). And not just a way of understanding the world, but also a certain way of experiencing it:

> Such metaphysical conjectures [i.e. conjectures involved in formula-
> ting the theistic proofs] do not derive inductively from experience,
> but are related to experience in two ways. First, they are suggested by
> reflection on certain aspects of experience – on causality, for the
> cosmological proofs, and on value, for the ontological argument. This
> suggests, in the one case, the postulate of the completely satisfactory
> causal explanation, and, in the other, the postulate of the most
> valuable or perfect conceivable being. There is no inference in either
> case, but contemplated experience suggests the models of the self-
> explanatory and the perfect, respectively. Then there is a second sort
> of reference to experience when one checks one's postulate against
> what actually occurs, to see if it is adequate.
>
> (pp. 31–2)

There is, then, an 'experiential' dimension to Ward's conception of the 'theistic arguments'. Before we can substantiate the charges of begging the question and circularity, we need to examine Ward's understanding of the way the above-mentioned 'metaphysical conjectures' come to be generated by 'experience'. For if the concept of God furnished by the 'theistic proofs' is a 'model' engendered by an attempt to give 'experience' a rational and intelligible structure, then the (perhaps unavoidable) begging the question and circularity to be found in Ward's delineation of this 'model' need not necessarily be taken to imply that the human mind 'moves' in a similarly question-begging and circular way when it seeks coherence in 'experience'. And since the ontological argument has a 'peculiar importance' (p. 33) in Ward's scheme of things, it is to this argument that we shall direct our attention.

III

Ward presents his version of the ontological argument in three stages. First, he considers the idea of 'a being which, if it is possible, is actual' (p. 26), and argues that since the idea of such a being is not obviously self-contradictory and not vacuous, we are not prevented from using this idea as the starting-point of our argu-ment. Second, Ward proceeds to elucidate the idea of this par-ticular possible necessary being. He begins by identifying this possible necessary being as 'a being which is greater than any other conceivable being' (p. 26). To circumvent the well-known, but also somewhat obscure, objection to the ontological argument that it mistakenly regards 'existence as a predicate', Ward eschews attributing to this possible necessary being the property of *existence*, and instead ascribes to it the property of *being self-existent*. He then says:

> But what is self-existent must be uncaused, and thus it either exists or it is impossible. If it is possible for it to exist, it must do so; for it cannot be brought into being or simply come into being for no reason. And that is to say that the most perfect conceivable being will be a being which cannot be conceived not to exist. If it is possible, it is actual; it is a necessarily existent being. It follows, by the first part of the argument, that the perfect being exists. . . .

(p. 27)

However, in case it is thought that there can be a number of such necessary beings, Ward finds it necessary, in the third stage of his formulation of the ontological argument, to show that 'there can only be one being which is necessary *a se*' (p. 27). This he does by presenting the following *reductio ad absurdum*, based on a principle which is alleged to underlie the first and second of St Thomas Aquinas's 'Five Ways':

> we are asked to conceive of many totally independent beings, which are yet such that, if one exists, all exist (for, if each must exist in every possible world, none can exist without the others). But it is contradictory to say both that *x* is totally self-explanatory, requiring reference to nothing other than itself to account for its existence, and that *x* cannot exist without *y*, which cannot in turn be explained by reference to *x* (since it, too, is self-explanatory). Since *x* and *y* exist in all possible worlds, *x* cannot exist without *y*; therefore *x* cannot completely account for its own existence, which must logically depend on the existence of *y*, which *x* itself does not explain. This is just a spelling-out of what it means to say that a being is wholly self-explanatory – it must not depend on any other being in any way for its existence or nature. It follows that, as matter of logic, there can only be one self-explanatory being.

(p. 14)

To summarize the three strands to Ward's formulation of the ontological argument. First, it is argued that all possible necessary beings actually exist. Second, it is claimed that the most perfect conceivable being is a necessary being, hence it exists. Third, it is argued that any independently existing being must be a self-existent being (p. 28).

Before it can justifiably be maintained that a possible necessary being (i.e. God) actually exists, it is necessary to determine whether or not the concept of such a being is a 'non-defective' concept. For if it can be demonstrated that the idea of such a being is incoherent, then we have no alternative but to conclude, in J. N. Findlay's words, 'that the Divine Existence is either senseless or impossible'.[20] Ward is alert to the force of Findlay's objection, and he attempts to counter it by challenging the two assumptions on which it depends: (a) that there are 'no necessary connections in objective reality'; and (b) 'that there are no non-conventional necessary truths' (p. 39). Even though he repudiates these two assumptions, Ward still subscribes to the fundamental principle which underlies Findlay's position: namely, that if 'God could not fail to exist' is necessarily true, then 'God does not exist' is necessarily false, and vice versa.[21] Now if one asserts that 'God could not fail to exist' is necessarily true, then presumably the notion of existence is taken to be a constituent of the concept signified by 'God'. It follows, therefore, that a denial of God's existence will reflect a failure on the part of the unbeliever to accept a certain, and, according to Ward, proper, understanding of the concept *God*, and that the unbeliever is consequently mistaken not so much on a question of '*truth*', as on a question of '*meaning*' or understanding. Ward and the unbeliever may use a word with the same orthographic form, viz. 'God', but they each mean something totally different by it. In consequence, no real dispute can arise between the unbeliever and Ward on the question of the *truth* of their respective beliefs concerning God's existence. The unbeliever, in assailing an allegedly (logically) necessary truth assented to by Ward, changes the meaning of 'God' in 'God exists', and so only succeeds in changing the subject – the 'God' of the believer is, quite simply, not the 'God' of the unbeliever. 'God exists', however, is not unique in this respect; its fate is shared by any sentence whose truth is supposed to be guaranteed by the stipulation that the negation of the sentence in question is necessarily self-contradictory; denial of 'truth' in such cases will always (and indeed must) bring about a concomitant shift in 'meaning'. Nobody, for instance, can assert that January has 365 days, and still maintain that they correctly understand the meaning of 'January'. The upshot of all this is that Ward's procedure renders the ontological argument *pragmatically futile* as a putative demonstration of God's existence, even if it does not affect its status as a *formally valid* argument: Ward's 'logical theism' ensures that the argument will be acceptable only for someone who already shares his (logical) intuitions concerning 'God', i.e. for someone who has an implicit commitment to the *truth* of 'theism' because of what she takes 'God' to signify, ontological argument or no ontological argument.[22] The ontological arguer who, like Ward, endorses the stipulation that the negation of 'God exists' is a self-contradiction will therefore have to reconcile herself to the ultimate superfluity of her argument.[23] And since Ward's formulation of the first stage of his ontological argument hinges so crucially on this problematic stipulation, I fear that we need to react with caution towards his understanding of God as 'a being which, if it is possible, is actual' (p. 26).

In outlining the second stage of his argument, Ward elucidates the idea of a particular possible necessary being which can appropriately be designated as 'God'. He identifies this being with 'the most perfect conceivable being' and says:

> the most perfect conceivable being will be a being which cannot be conceived not to exist. If it is possible, it is actual; it is a necessarily existent being. It follows . . . that the perfect being exists.
>
> (p. 27)

What Ward seems to be saying here is that since the denial of God's existence is not consistently conceivable, it follows that God exists necessarily. He appears to identify the proposition ' "God exists" is necessarily true' with the proposition ' "God does not exist" is not consistently conceivable'. In other words: he seemingly equates *conceivability* with (logical) *possibility* and *inconceivability* with (logical) *impossibility*. But in so doing, he overlooks the fact that 'conceivability' and 'inconceivability' are typically *epistemological* notions, whereas 'possibility' and 'impossibility' are characteristically *logical* or *metaphysical* notions. And, indeed, as Alvin Plantinga (whose treatment of the ontological argument certainly meets with Ward's approval) himself points out, counter-examples to the equation of 'p is necessary' with 'not-p is not consistently conceivable' are relatively easy to find, like the following true but contingent sentence:

(1) The denial of $10 - 3 = 7$ is not consistently conceivable for me now.

Is the denial of (1) not consistently conceivable for me now? This is a vexed question, and any answer that appears *prima facie* plausible is susceptible to objection at some further point. It is not difficult to see why. If (1) is only contingently true, it could be that:

(2) The denial of $10 - 3 = 7$ is consistently conceivable for me now.

But if I can consistently conceive of $10 - 3 \neq 7$, how could $10 - 3 = 7$ be necessary? And if the proposition 'The most perfect conceivable being exists (necessarily)' is substituted for '$10 - 3 = 7$' in the frame of the above argument, it can be shown that this proposition is not necessarily true, in the same way that doubt can be cast on the necessity of $10 - 3 = 7$ if 'necessity' is glossed in terms of the negation of $10 - 3 = 7$ being not consistently conceivable.

Conversely, it could also be argued that 'p is necessary' could be true, while 'not-p is not consistently conceivable' is neither true nor false, as the example below indicates. We know that mathematicians have not been able to prove (so far) each of Goldbach's Conjecture or Fermat's Last Theorem. Nevertheless, what we do know is that if such proofs are found, then these theorems will be either necessarily true or necessarily false. However, since mathematicians are not able, at present, to furnish us with the requisite proofs, we can infer neither (a) that the truth of these theorems is consistently conceivable, nor (b) that their falsity is not consistently conceivable, and vice versa. Such inferences will be warranted only when the proofs are available for inspection, not otherwise. In which case, from 'p is necessary' Ward's desired inference 'not-p is not consistently conceivable' fails to follow: possibility and impossibility are not logically homomorphous with conceivability and inconceivability.[24] If my arguments are correct, then, it does not follow – as a matter of logical necessity – that God exists because we find his non-existence to be not consistently conceivable. Nothing is to be gained by conflating typically epistemological notions like 'conceivability' with metaphysical notions like 'possibility'. It is precisely this conflation which should deter us from accepting the second stage of Ward's argument. However, damaging though this objection undoubtedly is, it does not really strike at the heart of the point that Ward is endeavouring to make at this stage of his argument. This is the point that since God is a necessary being, he *must* exist if it is *possible* for him to exist (pp. 27, 28 and 33). Or to put it in more cumbersome parlance: because the property *cannot fail to be instantiated* belongs to the divine essence, it follows that there is no possible world in which the concept 'God' is not instantiated. Now, admittedly, if a person accepts that the property *cannot fail to be instantiated* belongs to God's essence, then this person would, on the face of it, appear to contradict herself if she then maintained that God does not exist. But (and this is the thornier and more important question): is a logical contradiction involved in denying that God possesses the property *cannot fail to be instantiated*? That is to say, does a person make a mistake in *logic* when she denies that 'God' has a connotation which requires a denotation? How can the ontological arguer *show* that this person is logically mistaken if she does not ascribe to God the property *cannot fail to be instantiated*? Here the ontological arguer is likely to find herself in some difficulty. From a purely logical point of view there is – in principle – no reason why God should be a Perfect Being who therefore possesses the property *cannot fail to be instantiated*. Even more clearly, it is obvious that no logical fallacy is committed by someone who uses 'God' as the name of a being who, say, exists contingently and is supremely evil. We are not compelled, i.e. logically compelled, to take it as a condition of regarding something as a supremely worshipful being that that being be a perfect, and hence a necessarily existent, being.[25] Doubtless the 'theist' can argue that a merely contingent supremely evil deity would be inferior to even the worst of humans, but even this cannot, on its own, constitute logical grounds for coercing the unbeliever into accepting the understanding of God required by Ward to make the ontological argument work. For, first, it is not self-evidently the case that the sceptic is obliged, logically, to deem worshipful only those beings who are morally better than humans in every respect; and, second, we cannot straightforwardly equate 'being evil' with 'being inferior', because the entire matter depends on the criteria we adopt for applying the latter notion – for example, in a totally evil universe, would a Perfect Being be one that exercises a monopoly over evil, or would it be one least able to exercise such a monopoly? In other words, in such a universe, would a Perfect Being be one that is least able, or one most able, to command that universe, to wield power in that universe? And can one reasonably insist that clear-cut criteria are available for resolving this question?[26]

For these reasons, then, we have to conclude that Ward is mistaken in suggesting that the sceptic makes a logical mistake when she challenges the ontological arguer's principle that God must (in a 'logical' sense of 'must') be regarded as a perfect and necessarily existent being.

The third and final stage of Ward's argument is intended to demonstrate that 'there can be only one being which is necessary *a se*, which does not derive its necessity from something else, and this is the perfect being' (p. 27). It will be recalled that Ward proposes to carry out this demonstration by constructing a *reductio ad absurdum*, using a principle which allegedly underpins the first two of Aquinas' 'Five Ways'.[27] This *reductio* has the following structure: suppose

(1)   Each of x and y is a self-existent cause.

(2)   A self-existent cause will depend upon nothing other than itself for its existence and nature.

We can accept (2) as a truth by definition, and it is a corollary of (2) that

(3)   A self-existent cause will exist in every possible world, since there is no possible world which could cause it not to exist.

From this it follows that

(4) x and y will exist in all possible worlds.

Given (1) to (4), Ward proceeds to infer

(5)   Since x and y exist in all possible worlds, x cannot exist without y, and vice versa.

And from this it can be inferred that

(6) x cannot completely account for its own existence, but must depend on y (which x does not explain).

But (6), in concluding that x cannot account for its own existence, contradicts the specification of a self-existent cause provided by (1) and (2), so that this argument is self-contradictory, and it is indeed absurd to assume that there can be *two* or more self-existent causes. Unfortunately for Ward, this *reductio* cannot be accepted as it stands. Consider (5), which says that since x and y exist in all possible worlds, x cannot exist without y, and vice versa. Now obviously, if x and y exist in all possible worlds, then it follows that there will be no possible world in which x exists, but from which y is missing; and conversely, there will not be a world in which y exists, but from which x is missing. But it need not follow from this that x is therefore the *cause*, or the *explanation*, of y's existence, and vice versa. It is perfectly possible for x and y just to *happen* to exist in all possible worlds, without there being any sort of causal relationship between x and y. Hence it is not too difficult to construct a counter-example to this aspect of Ward's argument. Let us suppose, for the sake of argument, that '$5 + 6 = 11$' is, *qua* mathematical truth, true in all possible worlds. Let us further assume, again for the sake of argument, that a Platonist account of the nature and status of mathematical entities is the correct one.[28] Assuming that '$5 + 6 = 11$' is true in all possible worlds, and also assuming that Platonism (as opposed to conceptualism or nominalism) correctly represents the ontological status of '5' and '6', then since '$5 + 6 = 11$' is true in all possible worlds, the numbers 5 and 6 will, *ex hypothesi*, exist in all possible worlds. And if we substitute '5' and '6' for x and y in Ward's step (5), we shall have to conclude, if Ward's argument is correct, that 5 and 6 cannot 'exist without' each other, that they 'depend on' each other for their existence. But what is it to say that 5 and 6 cannot 'exist without' each other? The use of the expressions 'exist without' and 'depend on' do not appear to be entirely appropriate in this mathematical context, in as much as we do not normally assume that causal relations obtain between mathematical entities. Given the fact that there is something quite inappropriate about saying that causal relations exist between numbers, it is likely that Ward will wish to rebut our criticism by saying that we have travestied his argument by making use of a totally irrelevant counter-example. There is something to this possible line of counter-argument. However, what our counter-example does show, and this is something that Ward would be hard put to deny, is that it cannot be a logical truth *simpliciter* that if x and y exist in all possible worlds then x must 'depend on' y (or vice versa) for its existence, but whether this is in fact the case *depends* on what sort of entity x and y are. Our counter-example shows that it is highly unlikely that x and y, as they feature in Ward's argument, will be natural numbers. Now since Ward formulates his *reductio ad absurdum* in the context of defending the cosmological argument, it is clear that he intends x and y to refer to causes, or perhaps more precisely, to agents capable of causing certain effects. But is it true that if two agents, say x and y, are such that they exist in all possible worlds, then it is *necessarily* the case that x must depend on y (or vice versa)? Before we can even attempt to answer this question, we need to determine whether it is coherent, in the first place, to suppose that there must be agents, like x and y, which are capable of existing in all possible worlds. Consider the following argument. If x is a cause in a possible world W^*, then, truistically, there must be at least one effect, call it y, to be found in W^*, such that x can properly be said to be the cause of y. But suppose there is a totally static world, call it W^*, in which nothing, literally nothing, ever happens. In such a world, clearly, there can never be such a thing as a change, and so, *a fortiori*, there can never be such a thing as the effect y. And if there can never be such a thing as y in W^*, it follows that in W^*, there can be no such thing as x, the alleged cause of y. In W^*, in a word, there can be no such thing as a cause, and hence no such thing as a self-existent cause. But if there is one possible world (W^*) in which neither x nor y exists, it follows, as a matter of logic, that it is not the case that x and y exist in all possible worlds.[29] It follows, further, that we are not logically compelled to accept the principle of a cause that exists in all possible worlds. But we are not yet in a position to claim to have disposed of Ward's *reductio*: it is, after all, still possible for Ward to argue that x is not just any sort of cause, but is rather, something a bit more special, namely, a *self-existent* cause. However, in characterizing x as a self-existent cause, Ward is making an extra-logical claim about the nature of x – there is no basis in logic, or even in a 'non-theistic' metaphysics, for claiming that x is a self-existent cause. It is only when one incorporates certain specifically 'theistic' assumptions about the (causal) relation between a self-existent cause (i.e. God) and the cosmos that one is able to endorse Ward's supposition for a *reductio*. To accept these assumptions, however, is already to subscribe to Ward's view of 'metaphysical theism': one has already committed oneself to a form of 'theism' even before one has begun to construct an argument which purports to demonstrate the existence of God. It is difficult to conceive of anything that could be more question-begging. In which case, we have no alternative but to conclude that Ward is not successful in his elucidation and defence of the third stage of his ontological argument.

IV

We have examined the three stages of Ward's formulation of the ontological argument, and have found his arguments for each of these stages to be defective. Ward's programme of 'rational theism' pivots on the 'theistic proofs', and, ultimately, as he himself acknowledges, it rests on the ontological argument. Since the foundation of Ward's programme is, so to speak, not able even to bear its own weight, it seems highly unlikely that it will be able to support the grand and otherwise splendidly conceived theological superstructure he proposes to construct on it.[30]

Notes

1. Creation, revelation and the analogy theory

1 It must be emphasized at the outset that Aquinas does not present a systematic and comprehensive exposition of the analogy theory in his writings. Rather, his discussions of analogy are scattered in the following texts, *ScG*, I. 32–5; and *ST*, I. 13. 2–6. Most of these texts are reprinted as an appendix in Humphrey Palmer, *Analogy* (London: Macmillan, 1973), pp. 165–76. Aquinas's sometimes confusing insights have been extended into more comprehensive doctrines by his numerous interpreters, with the result that the analogy theory is a Protean creature existing in several different versions. It is impossible, therefore, to specify a definitive Thomist analogy theory, and I shall restrict my discussion to a small selection of analogy theorists whose writings are relevant to the limited objectives of this paper.

2 We shall refer to these two subtheses as (*AL*) and (*AM*) respectively.

3 The full implications of this distinction between the two types of relation will emerge as our discussion proceeds.

4 Aquinas actually formulates four analogy rules, but since only the rules for attribution and proper proportionality feature in his account of the nature of theistic language, we are justified in restricting our attention to these two rules.

5 *ST*, I. 13.2.

6 Logically-minded philosophers have found it easy to demolish this type of formula. See, for instance, G. E. M. Anscombe and P. T. Geach, *Three Philosophers* (Oxford: Blackwell, 1961), p. 123; and James F. Ross, 'Analogy as a Rule of Meaning for Religious Language' in Anthony Kenny, ed., *Aquinas: A Collection of Critical Essays* (London: Macmillan, 1969), pp. 93–138.

7 Thus James Ross's rigorous and ingenious resuscitation of the analogy theory is, I fear, vitiated by the fact that he construes it entirely in terms of (*AL*): he gives us an analogy theory, but not one that can be regarded as a theo-logic. In fairness, it must be said that it is not his intention to propound a theory about statements that apply specifically to God. Cf. Ross, 'Analogy', for his representation of Aquinas's theory.

8 It must be pointed out that Aquinas does not construct the analogy theory with the explicit intention of making it a theory of theistic language. He begins by formulating it as a general theory of the way language refers to things (AL), and only then uses it to resolve the specific question of the cognitive significance of theistic discourse $((AL)$ plus $(AM))$. Even so, his theory must be an amalgam of (AL) and (AM) if it is to be a properly constituted theo-logic.

9 For his proposal, cf. Ross, 'Analogy', p. 134. A lucid presentation of the objections to the Five Ways is to be found in Anthony Kenny, *The Five Ways* (London: Routledge & Kegan Paul, 1969).

10 The very fact that Aquinas uses the 'rational' arguments of the Five Ways to undergird the analogy theory shows that he rejects 'fideism' as a means of getting the theory 'off the ground'. For 'fideism' presupposes that there can be no rational demonstration of the intelligibility and truth of theological statements, and Aquinas, as we have just seen, needs a theory of theological truth on which to hinge his theory of theological *meaning*. Moreover, this truth-theory has to be one which preserves the cognitive significance of the theistic discourse, and 'fideism' cannot give him such a theory. We have no alternative but to reject Ross's proposal.

11 Cf., for instance, E. L. Mascall, *Existence and Analogy* (London: Darton, Longman & Todd, 1966), p. 122.

12 *The Christian Knowledge of God* (London: Athlone Press, 1969), pp. 209–10. When it comes to seeking a clarification of Aquinas's insights, I have chosen to follow analogy theorists who work within the modern tradition of philosophical theology (e.g. Mascall, Owen and Ross), rather than the 'classical' analogy theorists (e.g. Cajetan, Penido and Garrigou-Lagrange), simply because the former group are less rigid in their adherence to the traditional categories of scholastic philosophy. In so doing we run the risk of misinterpretation, but this risk is warranted by the restricted task we set ourselves in this paper.

13 According to this interpretation the Thomistic *analogia entis* would be replaced by an *analogia fidei*. This suggestion has been made by Karl Barth, in his *CD*, I/1, p. 274. Congenial though this suggestion may be to a Barthian, it is not one that the follower of Aquinas can readily accept (*qua* 'natural theologian'). Later I shall argue that the *analogia entis* and the *analogia fidei* presuppose each other and that it is therefore misleading to suggest that the one can be replaced by the other.

14 George Berkeley, *Alciphron, or the Minute Philosopher* (1732), IV. xviii. Quoted in Palmer, *Analogy*, p. 106.

15 The analogy theorist can therefore be likened to someone who drinks alternating doses of two different poisons, each of which is the antidote to the other – to survive she must obtain a very precise balance between the doses of the two poisons. Similar care must be exercised by the analogy theorist as she alternates between the *via affirmativa* and the *via negativa*.

16 To some extent the theory we shall develop is prefigured in *ST*, I. 2. 3, and 6. In these passages we find an ontology of what Aquinas terms

'perfections', existing primordially and preeminently in God, and derivatively in creaturely objects who represent him imperfectly. Even if Aquinas does not make full provision for a theory like ours in his 'natural theology', the opposite is the case in his account of 'revealed theology' (or so we shall argue).

17 Albeit with considerable modification to both Aquinas and Barth, for, as we shall see, our assimilation of an 'ontological' analogical theory to Barth's *analogia fidei* will go through only if we do two things. Firstly, we shall have to use Eberhard Jüngel's thesis that the sphere of God's revelation is his creation, and that the language of the world can speak the truth about God precisely because it is the language of the world created by God. Cf. his *The Doctrine of the Trinity: God's Being is in Becoming*, trans. Horton Harris (Edinburgh: Scottish Academic Press, 1976), p. 10. Secondly, we shall have to rely on the interpretations of Hans Urs von Balthasar in our understanding of Barth's analogy of faith. Cf. his *The Theology of Karl Barth*, trans. John Drury (New York: Holt, Rinehart & Winston, 1972).

18 'God and Analogy', *Sophia*, 8 (1969), 23. A more detailed presentation of this 'incarnation strategy' is to be found in Don Cupitt's Stanton Lectures, *Christ and the Hiddenness of God* (London: Lutterworth Press, 1971), pp. 189–213. The history of this strategy is a venerable one: it can be discerned in St Athanasius's *De Incarnatione Verbi Dei*. Barth too makes use of a christological foundation for his *analogia fidei*, but would almost certainly disapprove of Durrant's programme because for him anthropology must be grounded in christology, and not vice versa, a principle which Durrant would have difficulty in accommodating. For Barth's principle, cf. *CD*, III/2, pp. 84ff. A splendidly clear account of Barth's christological foundation is given by von Balthasar in his *The Theology of Karl Barth*, pp. 100–8.

19 A cleverly defended version of the Sabellian doctrine is to be found in G. W. H. Lampe, *GS*. The main problem with using the Sabellian doctrine to reinforce the 'incarnation strategy' is that it seems to commit us to a questionable 'degree' christology, and an unacceptable christology is just what the exponents of this strategy want to avoid at all costs. So while the Sabellian doctrine may preserve a sense in which the nature of Christ can be adequately expressed in ordinary experience-describing language, it is difficult to see how the 'incarnation strategist' can resort to it.

20 We cannot present these objections here, but a conspectus of them is to be found in J. H. Hick, 'Christology at the Crossroads', *PFT*, pp. 139–66, especially pp. 143–9.

21 On neo-Platonism in Aquinas's thought, see Etienne Gilson, *The Christian Philosophy of St Thomas Aquinas*, trans. L. K. Shook (London: Gollancz, 1957), pp. 48–54; and M. Grabmann, *Thomas Aquinas*, trans. V. Michel (London: Longmans, Green & Co., 1928), chapter 4.

22 It should be noted that it is not straightforwardly obvious that Plato holds the view that universals are ideal examples of themselves.

However, the evidence from his writings is marshalled and carefully examined by Nicholas Wolterstorff, in his *On Universals: An Essay in Ontology* (Chicago: University of Chicago Press, 1970), pp. 264–79, who concludes that Plato subscribes to this view. I am deeply indebted to Wolterstorff for the remainder of my discussion: the Thomist metaphysics of creation proposed here as a foundation for the analogy theory is almost entirely derived from his interpretation of Aquinas (and Augustine, from whom Aquinas borrows much). It should be said, however, that Wolterstorff himself would disapprove of the use to which we put his interpretation, since he argues that this ontology of creation is defective because of its neo-Platonic underpinning. However, since we are not concerned to evaluate Aquinas's ontology of creation as a philosophical theory, but simply to examine its role as a putative cornerstone for his analogy theory, we are justified in overlooking Wolterstorff's strictures. Theological critics of this aspect of Plato's thought might prefer to detach the *imago Dei* strategy completely from its underpinning in Platonic ontology precisely because the latter is vitiated by the controversy over Plato's 'self-predicating assumption'. Their view is plausible, especially since it is not obvious that the *imago Dei* strategy necessarily requires such a Platonic foundation. However, it is not within the scope of this paper to resolve this question (important though it is), even though we can say, with some caution, that it does seem possible in principle to sever the *imago Dei* strategy from this Platonic ontology.

23 For Augustine's Christian neo-Platonism, cf. A. H. Armstrong, 'St Augustine and Christian Platonism' in R. A. Markus, ed., *Augustine: A Collection of Critical Essays* (New York: Doubleday & Co., 1972), pp. 3–37.

24 *De Diversis Quaestionibus*, 83, 46, Migne, *PL*, 40, pp. 30–1, trans. as 'De Ideis' in J. A. Mourant, *Introduction to the Philosophy of St Augustine* (University Park, Pa.: Pennsylvania State University Press, 1964), p. 205.

25 Augustine, 'De Ideis', p. 204.

26 *ST*, I.15.1. See also *De Veritate*, 2.5; and 3.1 and 3.7. For a clear exposition of Aquinas's views, cf. Gilson, *The Christian Philosophy of St Thomas Aquinas*, p. 125.

27 Gilson, *The Christian Philosophy of St Thomas Aquinas*, p. 126. For Aquinas's point, cf. *ST*, I. 15. 2; and *De Veritate*, 3.2.

28 *ST*, I. 44. 3. Cf. also I. 15. 2; and *De Veritate*, 3.2.

29 Jüngel, *God's Being*, p. 33.

30 The argument we have just outlined is derived from the principle, held by both Barth and Bonhoeffer, that 'it is the Word of God which places man into truth, not man's understanding of that Word'. This quotation is from Ray S. Anderson, *HTRG*, p. 80. This difficult book has profound implications for the analogy theory, which it approaches from a generally Barthian perspective. I am deeply indebted to it in my attempt to use Aquinas's doctrine of creation to tease out an analogy theory which reconciles the *analogia entis* and the *analogia fidei* in terms of Aquinas's revealed theology.

31 The notion of human participation in the divine essence, or divinized humanity, seems to be implicit in Aquinas's ontology of creation. This notion is to be found as a central principle in the theologies of the divine illumination of the human soul developed by Nicholas Berdyaev and Vladimir Solovyev. Cf. their respective works, *The Divine and the Human* (London: Geoffrey Bles, 1949), chapter 8; and *Lectures on Godmanhood* (New York: Harmon Printing House, 1944), Lecture 8.

32 For Aquinas faith and revelation are correlative notions: faith is assent to a proposition because one accepts that it is revealed by God. Cf. *ST*, II. I. I; and *ScG*, I. 3. But cf. note 41 for a caveat on an exclusively propositional understanding of Aquinas's account of faith.

33 *ScG*, II. 4. 6.

34 Our case may be slightly overstated at this juncture. The foregoing does not imply that there is an unbridgeable gap between Aquinas's 'natural' and 'revealed' theology. Rather, our purpose is to show that the somewhat rudimentary 'ontological' analogical theory to be extracted from his 'natural theology' needs to be supplemented by ideas derived from his 'revealed theology'.

35 The notion of eschatological verification is used here primarily for convenience. Aquinas of course wants to say something a little different from this – namely, that we shall not grasp the essence of the *content* of the articles of faith until the eschaton. However, verification presupposes knowledge of the content (meaning) of a proposition, because we have to determine the meaning of a statement before we can assign it a truth-value. So in talking of eschatological verification we include Aquinas's notion of the eschatological grasping of the content of the articles of faith.

36 On the *imago Dei* as the constitutive structure of the relation between God and the human creature, cf. Anderson, *HTRG*, pp. 135 and 137.

37 There is another important objection to this cosmological approach. If this approach cannot take us beyond our *thinking* about God, how can we relate the God of cosmology to the God of revelation, the Yahweh of the Old Testament and the Father of the New? Aquinas, for example, has no qualms about equating Yahweh's description of himself as 'I am who I am' (Exodus 3:14) with his own Aristotelian metaphysical definition of God as a being whose essence and existence are identical. This equation can only be accounted for in terms of a theology of revelation, which takes us beyond our mere thinking about God. The reader who thinks that our approach places too much weight on the theology of revelation is referred to note 43 for a brief statement on the role of revelation in our argument.

38 Von Balthasar makes a masterly attempt to correct this undervaluation in his *The Theology of Karl Barth*, pp. 73–150.

39 If we were to expand the scope of our discussion, we would have to stress the importance of locating the *imago Dei* in the *human being*. Aquinas lists as 'perfections' '*ens*', '*vivens*' and '*bonum*' in addition to personal predicates like 'mind', 'will', 'wisdom', etc. '*Ens*' gives us an *analogia entis*, but the really significant predicates in this context are the

personal predicates, whose analogical use in theistic discourse hinges of the human creature being made in the image of God. Such an analogy theory would be a fully-fledged *analogia personae*. It may be possible to relate such an *analogia personae* to the notion of human participation in the divine essence, a notion central to the works of Berdyaev and Solovyev mentioned in note 31 above. I am grateful to an unnamed referee of *The Journal of Theological Studies* for this and other valuable suggestions.

40 Terence Penelhum, *The Problems of Religious Knowledge* (London: Macmillan, 1971), pp. 9–10. The view that Aquinas's conception of faith is exclusively propositional is qualified in note 41 below.

41 In *ST*, II. 2. 31 we find an account of faith which suggests that it is more than just assent to propositions. Nevertheless, it seems fair to say, both on textual grounds and in the interests of the internal consistency of his system, that in the main faith for Aquinas is essentially propositional.

42 To quote Anderson, 'Because theology has to do with a relationship of givenness, in which God confronts us from the outset as subject as well as object, theology is itself a commitment as well as a question.' Cf. *HTRG*, p. xxii.

43 The weight of our argument bears heavily on the principle that the notion of revelation enables us to theologize from the standpoint of God. We need to qualify this principle to avoid suggesting that it is in some way incompatible with Aquinas's treatment of faith and revelation. Aquinas carefully points out that since we shall not grasp the essence of the content of the articles of faith until the eschaton, it follows that even where our ontologies are grounded in an ontology of creation (revelation), we still only know God now in so far as creaturely objects bear the divine image. Hence he insists on making an important distinction, in *ST*, I. 13. 3, between '*id quod significant nomina*' and the '*modus significandi*' of the terms that belong to the language of the world. This being so, we must hold that our principle only requires theology to *start* from the standpoint of God, and not that it be *seen* from that perspective (this is impossible, as Aquinas points out).

2. The Trinity and philosophical reflection: Brown's *The Divine Trinity*

1 (London: Duckworth, 1985). All further references to this work will be cited parenthetically in the text.

2 For an account of the notion of 'pragmatic futility', cf. James F. Ross, *PT*, chapter 1.

3 The suspicion that this is how 'religious experience' is being viewed by Brown is reinforced by a number of statements in which he refers to '*claims* made on the basis of [religious] experience' (p. 35); to 'religious experience and its *interpretation*' (p. 53); to 'the . . . experient's *response* to a particular experience' (p. 70); and to 'revelatory experiences and the . . . truth which might be *deduced* from them' (p. 77). My emphases indicate Brown's proneness to construe 'experience' as a kind of *an sich* from which we deduce 'truths', frame 'interpretations', formulate 'claims', and to which we make 'responses'.

4 All references given in square parentheses are to *The Philosophical Investigations*. For a most brilliant discussion of this aspect of Wittgenstein's philosophy, cf. Stanley Cavell, *CR, passim*.

5 On this point, cf. Richard Rorty, 'The Historiography of Philosophy: Four Genres' in Richard Rorty, J. B. Schneewind and Quentin Skinner, eds., *Philosophy in History* (Cambridge: Cambridge University Press, 1984), p. 55 n. 3. Rorty's position is consonant with the views of W. V. Quine and Donald Davidson. As Quine and Davidson see it, making sense of an unfamiliar discourse (that is, one pertaining to an alien episode or reality) requires the 'radical translator' to seek to maximize agreement concerning what she takes to be obviously true and false. Thus Davidson maintains that grasping the world projected by the object of interpretation requires the interpreter to accept *a priori* that there is no possibility of a comprehensive and deep-rooted disagreement between interpreter and interpreted. To quote him: 'charity is not an option, but a condition of having a workable theory [of radical interpretation].... Until we have successfully established a systematic correlation of sentences held true, there is no mistake to make. Charity is forced on us – whether we like it or not, if we want to understand others, we must count them right in most matters' ('On the Very Idea of a Conceptual Scheme', *Proceedings of the American Philosophical Association*, 47 (1973–4), 19). For Quine's pioneering formulation, cf. *Word and Object* (Cambridge, Mass.: MIT Press, 1960), chapter 2. Radical translation, therefore, is simply the hermeneutical circle designated by another name (as Rorty has rightly noted).

6 Bernard Lonergan, *MIT*, p. 338. The subject of conversion and repentance will surface later in our discussion of Brown's treatment of the resurrection narratives.

7 For Kant's restriction on the schematization of the concept of cause, cf. his *CPR*, p. 511. Cf. also p. 527.

8 Aquinas, who treats the concept of 'cause' analogically, is for this reason justly to be seen as a 'post-Kantian' thinker. For this estimation of Aquinas, cf. David Burrell, *Analogy and Philosophical Language* (New Haven: Yale University Press, 1973), pp. 132–3. It should be said that when it comes to treating divine causality univocally, Brown has a distinguished predecessor in Ian Ramsey, who insisted that 'talk about God's activity must be literal and univocal, straightforwardly reliable'. Cf. his *Models for Divine Activity* (London: SCM Press, 1973), p. 58.

9 For a splendid attempt to work out the implications of Aquinas's perception for the 'grammar' of God, cf. David Burrell, *A*, pp. 55–67. Cf. also the suggestive discussion in Nicholas Lash, 'Ideology, Metaphor and Analogy' in Brian Hebblethwaite and Stewart Sutherland, eds., *PFCT*, pp. 68–94. Brown, while he notes with approval that a thorough permeation of theology by philosophy is evinced in St Thomas's *Summa Theologiae*, would probably not accept Aquinas's unremitting stress on the need for theology to mark the hiatus between the divine and the human orders.

10 Eberhard Jüngel, *God as the Mystery of the World*, trans. D. L. Guder (Edinburgh: T. & T. Clark, 1983), pp. 109ff. Jüngel of course regards the *analogia fidei* as an essential constituent of any projected dismantling of the philosophical foundations of this Cartesian-inspired atheism. Ricoeur too has observed that such a Cartesian 'idealism of consciousness' issues in a Feuerbachian atheism. Cf. his 'Toward a Hermeneutic of the Idea of Revelation' in *Essays on Biblical Interpretation* (London: SPCK, 1981), p. 109. It is also significant that Aquinas's theory of analogy is used by Denys Turner to 'de-centre' the Feuerbachian core in Don Cupitt's recent work. Cf. his 'De-centring Theology', *MT*, 2 (1986), 125–43.

11 Hans von Balthasar has claimed that modern dogmatics gives virtually no place to the theme of God's incomprehensibility. Cf. von Balthasar, 'The Unknown God' in *The Von Balthasar Reader*, ed. M. Kehl and W. Loser (New York: Crossroad, 1982), pp. 181–7. *The Divine Trinity*, one notes, is no exception to this trend of modern dogmatics.

12 For Barth's characterization of the distinction between God's primary and secondary objectivity, cf. his *CD*, II/I, pp. 3–254. It could be argued that Barth's distinction is paralleled by the Thomist separation between the *potentia divina absoluta* and the *potentia divina ordinata*. Indeed, Barth himself endorses St Thomas's distinction on pp. 539ff. On these matters I am indebted to the illuminating discussion in Ronald F. Thiemann, 'Revelation and Imaginative Construction', *JR*, 61 (1981), 242–63. The *analogia Christi* is endorsed in Walter Kasper, *GJC*, p. 158.

13 For this understanding of 'nature', cf. Christopher Stead, *Divine Substance* (Oxford: Clarendon Press, 1977), p. 269. Bernard Lonergan believes that trinitarian thought in the Catholic tradition uses the term 'person', and indeed other theological terms as well, in just such a heuristic manner. Cf. the essay 'Philosophy and Theology' in his *A Second Collection* (London: Darton, Longman & Todd, 1974), p. 200. It cannot be denied that the Greek word *physis* was used by the early church Fathers with a multiplicity of meanings and stresses. Cyril of Alexandria, for example, used this word to denote a concrete 'personality'. But even this particular usage would not accord with Brown's understanding of 'nature' – a *person* has experiences, is conscious, etc., but certainly not a 'personality'. For Cyril's use of *physis*, cf. G. L. Prestige, *Fathers and Heretics* (London: SPCK, 1948), p. 167. Elsewhere Prestige suggests that in relation to the Trinity *physis* implies an identity or similarity of function, and it is certainly nonsensical to imagine that functions can have experiences, etc. Cf. his *God in Patristic Thought* (London: SPCK, 1952), p. 234. I am grateful to Nicholas Lash for drawing my attention to these 'grammatical' considerations.

14 On this cf. Bernard Lonergan, 'The Dehellenization of Dogma' in *A Second Collection*, pp. 22ff; and *The Way to Nicea* (London: Darton, Longman & Todd, 1976), pp. 105–37.

15 Athanasius, *Orat. III c. Arianos*, 4; *MG* 26, 329A. Here I am following Lonergan, *The Way to Nicea*, pp. 90 and 101; *MIT*, pp. 307ff; and 'The

Origins of Christian Realism' in *A Second Collection*, pp. 251ff. For a particularly valuable attempt to extend this regulative view of theological propositions into a general theory of theological discourse, cf. George A. Lindbeck, *TND*.

16 For Augustine's confutation of Arianism, cf. *De trin.* 5, 4; and for his repudiation of the views of Eunomius, cf. *De trin.* 15, 20. At the same time Augustine was explicit in his disavowal of modalism. On this, cf. *De trin.* 5, 9. William J. Hill, Eugene TeSelle and Yves Congar have cited the work of Irénée Chevalier which shows that Augustine was familiar with Athanasius', Basil's and Gregory of Nazianzen's works on the Trinity as well as Epiphanius' *Recapitulation*. Cf. William J. Hill, *The Three-Personed God: The Trinity as a Mystery of Salvation* (Washington: Catholic University of America Press, 1982), pp. 56–7; Eugene TeSelle, *Augustine the Theologian* (New York: Herder & Herder, 1970), pp. 294–5; and Yves Congar, *I Believe in the Holy Spirit: vol. III*, trans. D. Smith (London: Chapman, 1983), pp. 82ff. Cf. also Irénée Chevalier, *Saint Augustin et la pensée grecque: Les relations trinitaires* (Fribourg en Suisse: Collectanea Friburgensia, 1940), pp. 141ff, especially p. 160. Maurice Wiles has also argued against the positing of a dichotomy between the trinitarianism of the Cappadocians and that of Augustine. Cf. the essay 'Reflections on the Origins of the Doctrine of the Trinity' in his *Working Papers in Doctrine* (London: SCM Press, 1976), pp. 11–14. If we accept the arguments of Chevalier, *et al.*, then Brown's attempts to polarize the views of Augustine and the Cappadocians must be open to question. Brown does acknowledge Wiles's argument, but says that any such similarities or differences between the Cappadocians and Augustine are not germane to the problem of finding an adequate basis for distinguishing between the persons of the Trinity (p. 286). Which only raises the question: but what if this supposed 'problem' is not, never has been, and (if my arguments are correct) indeed cannot *in principle* be, a 'problem' for trinitarian reflection? That is to say, there can, in principle, be no 'problem' of distinguishing between the persons of the immanent Trinity once one grants (as did Augustine and the Cappadocians) that there is no 'order' between the divine and the human domains.

17 For the Eastern theologians' abiding mistrust of Sabellianism, cf. Basil of Caesarea, *De spir. sanct.* 59; and *ep.* 126, 184, 210, 214, 235. Cf. also Gregory of Nyssa, *C. Eunom.* 10, 2, 4; and Gregory of Nazianzen, *or* v, 30. The latter states explicitly that his doctrine has the virtue of avoiding both the Sabellian confusion of the hypostases in the divinity and the Arian division of the natures. Basil and the two Gregorys are equally firm in combatting the Arianism of Eunomius. Cf. Basil, *Adv. Eunom.*, *passim*; Gregory of Nyssa, *C. Eunom.*, *passim*; and Gregory of Nazianzen, *or.* v, 41.

18 Chevalier, *Saint Augustin*, pp. 168–9, quoted in Congar, *I Believe*, p. 83. Chevalier cites from Gregory Nazianen, *or.* v, 41.

19 For references to the writings of Basil, the two Gregorys, Cyril of

Alexandria, John Damascene, Athanasius, Didymus and Augustine, cf. Congar, *I Believe*, p. 45 n. 41.

20 This was Aquinas's understanding of the role of the Trinity in theological reflection. Cf. *Summa Theologiae*, I. 32. I. 3; and the discussion in Burrell, *A*, p. 160.

21 Thus Paul Ricoeur rightly says that 'to be historical, an event must be more than a singular occurrence, a unique happening. It receives its definition from its contribution to the development of a plot.' Cf. his 'Narrative Time', *CI*, 7 (1980), 171. Cf. also his *Time and Narrative*, trans. K. McLaughlin and D. Pellauer (Chicago: University of Chicago Press, 1984), pp. 40ff. For other accounts which discuss the importance of such organizing frameworks (or 'plots' or 'configurations'), cf. Louis O. Mink, 'History and Fiction as Modes of Comprehension', *New Literary History*, I (1970), 551; and 'Interpretation and Narrative Understanding', *The Journal of Philosophy*, 69 (1972), 735–7. Cf. also A. C. Danto, *Analytical Philosophy of History* (Cambridge: Cambridge University Press, 1965), p. 140.

22 I owe the example, and the subsequent discussion, of the *Annals of St Gall* to Hayden White, 'The Value of Narrativity in the Representation of Reality', *CI*, 7 (1980), 5–27. Cf. especially p. 12.

23 For Ricoeur's saying, cf. 'Narrative Time', p. 187. Here I have read with profit Hayden White's discussion of Nietzsche, who perhaps first appreciated the importance of memory in the construction of historical narratives, in White's impressive *Metahistory: The Historical Imagination in Nineteenth-Century Europe* (Baltimore: The Johns Hopkins University Press, 1975), pp. 346–56. The primary Nietzschean text is the essay 'The Use and Abuse of History' in *The Birth of Tragedy*. Ricoeur argues from a different context, but stresses the need for the dialectical inter-penetration of hermeneutics and historical inquiry in his 'History and Hermeneutics' in Yirmiahu Yovel, ed., *Philosophy in History and Action* (Dordrecht: D. Reidel, 1978), pp. 3–20.

24 White, *Metahistory*, p. 4. The important point to note, in appraising Brown's characterization of the historian's task, is that several of the modes of historical inquiry mentioned by White in his typology do not actually require the historian to conceive her task in terms of '[getting back] ... to what ... actually happened or was said' in the past.

25 *Truth and Method*, trans. (of 2nd German edn) and ed. Garrett Barden and John Cumming (London: Sheed & Ward, 1975), p. 149. In Gadamer's view, the real task of the interpreter lies in the understanding of the text, and 'to understand [the text] does not mean primarily to reason one's way back into the past, but to have a present involvement with what is said' (p. 353). Also relevant is Ricoeur's insight that 'testimony is not perception itself but the report, that is, the story, the narrative of the event. It consequently transfers things seen to the level of things said.' Cf. 'The Hermeneutics of Testimony', p. 123.

26 Brown therefore upholds some form of what Wilfrid Sellars calls the 'myth of the given'. Cf. Sellars's 'Empiricism in the Philosophy of Mind' in his *Science, Perception and Reality* (London: Routledge & Kegan

Paul, 1963), pp. 127–97. The main thrust of Sellars's argument is that the idea of a concept – or language-independent knowing of sense-data – is insurmountably problematic. Critiques of this Cartesian–Kantian representational model of knowledge are now so much a part of the accepted philosophical wisdom that they can be said to constitute a separate and clearly identifiable genre in Anglo-American philosophy. The leading practitioners are commonly thought to be Richard Rorty, Alasdair MacIntyre, Ian Hacking and Charles Taylor. See their following works: Richard Rorty, *Philosophy and the Mirror of Nature* (Oxford: Blackwell, 1980); Alasdair MacIntyre, 'Epistemological Crises, Dramatic Narrative and the Philosophy of Science', *The Monist*, 60 (1977), 453–72; Ian Hacking, *The Emergence of Probability* (Cambridge: Cambridge University Press, 1975); and Charles Taylor, 'Philosophy and its History' in Rorty, *et al.*, eds., *Philosophy in History*, pp. 17–30. Cf. also the contributions by Hacking, MacIntyre and Rorty in *Philosophy in History*.

27 For evidence of Brown's perceptual model, cf. p. xiii: 'what God does is only of significance if it is *perceived* correctly; . . . [and] the important *perceptions* are not so much those of the [biblical] authors as those whose religious experiences are described within their books'. My emphasis. It is not too difficult, moreover, to discern a link between Brown's adherence to 'the myth of the given' and the 'historical atomism' which pervades his epistemology of history.

28 On this cf. Rudolf Bultmann, *The Gospel of John: A Commentary*, trans. G. R. Beasley-Murray (Oxford: Blackwell, 1971), p. 686.

29 As Rowan Williams states in his profound theological meditation on the enigmatic risen Christ: 'when the risen Jesus appears . . . [the] language given us is that of self-knowledge, penitence, and that of preaching and absolution: it is the language of *confession*. . . .' Cf. his *Resurrection* (London: Darton, Longman & Todd, 1982), pp. 86–7. Also pertinent here is Scott-Holland's claim that 'there is no possible representation of the Man, Jesus, which does not hold in it this impenetrable enigma. . . . He offers Himself to us as an enigma, as beyond and outside our normal nature.' Cf. his *The Philosophy of Faith and the Fourth Gospel* (London: Murray, 1920), pp. 109–10.

30 On the difference between 'testifying to' and 'testifying that', cf. Ricoeur, 'Toward a Hermeneutic of the Idea of Revelation', p. 113.

31 My emphases are intended to underscore the way in which 'foundationalist' assumptions seem to underlie Brown's understanding of the resurrection. At the heart of this 'foundationalism' lies the illusion that knowing consists in 'taking a good look'. For criticism of this illusion, cf. Bernard Lonergan, 'The Subject' in his *A Second Collection*, pp. 76–7. Cf. also 'The Origins of Christian Realism' in the same volume, p. 241.

32 I am grateful to Nicholas Lash for a number of valuable comments and criticisms that have helped to improve this paper.

For Brown's powerful reply to the criticisms formulated in this essay, see his 'Wittgenstein against the "Wittgensteinians": A Reply to Kenneth Surin on *The Divine Trinity*', *MT*, 2 (1986), 257–76.

3. 'Is it true what they say about "theological realism"?'

1 Antony Flew, R. M. Hare, Basil Mitchell and I. M. Crombie, 'Theology and Falsification' in Flew and MacIntyre, eds., *NEPT* pp. 96–108.

2 For Mitchell's point, cf. his 'Introduction' to *The Philosophy of Religion*, ed. Basil Mitchell (Oxford: Oxford University Press, 1971), p. 2.

3 R. M. Hare, 'Theology and Falsification' in *NEPT*, pp. 99–103; R. B. Braithwaite, 'An Empiricist's View of the Nature of Religious Belief', being the ninth Arthur Stanley Eddington Memorial Lecture (Cambridge: Cambridge University Press, 1955); Paul van Buren, *The Secular Meaning of the Gospel* (London: SCM Press, 1963), and 'On Doing Theology' in G. N. A. Vesey, ed., *Talk of God* (London: Macmillan, 1969), pp. 52–71; Paul Tillich, 'Religious Symbols and Our Knowledge of God' in W. L. Rowe and W. J. Wainwright, eds., *Philosophy of Religion* (New York: Harcourt Brace Jovanovich, 1973), pp. 479–88; and Don Cupitt, *Taking Leave of God* (London: SCM Press, 1980), *passim*.

4 Mitchell, 'Introduction', p. 2; and John Hick, 'Theology and Verification', *Theology Today*, 17 (1960), 12–31. Throughout this essay the terms 'theism' and 'theist' will be placed within inverted commas to indicate the irreducibly factitious nature of the seventeenth- and eighteenth-century philosophical 'theism' which many philosophers of religion in the Anglo-American tradition (unquestioningly and mistakenly!) regard as *the* Christian understanding of divinity. For a brief presentation of criticisms of this 'theism', cf. my *TPE*, pp. 3–7. The most important critics of this 'theism' have so far been D. Z. Phillips, Nicholas Lash, Walter Kasper, Theodore W. Jennings and Denys Turner.

5 These critics of Flew are therefore seeking to dismantle his dilemma by arguing that it requires us (implausibly) to conceive of religious language as operating *in vacuo*. Cf. William Alston, 'The Elucidation of Religious Statements' in Rowe and Wainwright, eds., *Philosophy of Religion*, pp. 452–64; and Gareth Matthews, 'Theology and Natural Theology' in the same collection of essays, pp. 428–37. For a representative statement of Phillips's position, cf. his *Faith and Philosophical Inquiry* (London: Routledge & Kegan Paul, 1970).

6 John Searle, 'Assertions and Aberrations' in Bernard Williams and Alan Montefiore, eds., *British Analytical Philosophy* (London: Routledge & Kegan Paul, 1966), p. 54.

7 Gottlob Frege, *The Basic Laws of Arithmetic: Exposition of the System*, trans. and ed. Montgomery Furth (Los Angeles: University of California Press, 1967), pp. 89–90.

8 'The Concept of Truth in Formalized Language' in *Logic, Semantics, Metamathematics*, trans. and ed. J. H. Woodger (Oxford: Clarendon Press, 1956), pp. 152–278; and 'The Semantic Conception of Truth and the Foundations of Semantics', *Philosophy and Phenomenological Research*, 4 (1943–4), 341–75.

9 'Truth and Meaning', *Synthese*, 7 (1967), 304–23; and 'Semantics for Natural Languages' in Gilbert Harman, ed., *On Noam Chomsky: Critical Essays* (New York: Anchor Books, 1974), pp. 242–52. But cf. Susan Haack, 'Is it True What They Say About Tarski?', *Philosophy*, 51 (1976), 323–36, which provides grounds for disputing this particular application of Tarski's truth-definition. (Now that I have mentioned Haack's article the reader will not have to guess where I got my title from.)

10 The interested reader is recommended the following collections of essays for discussions of the central issues posed by the connections between language, reality and human understanding: Gareth Evans and John McDowell, eds., *Truth and Meaning* (Oxford: Oxford University Press, 1976); and Mark Platts, ed., *Reference, Truth and Reality* (London: Routledge & Kegan Paul, 1980). A lucid exposition of 'truth-conditional' semantics and the questions raised by this semantics is to be found in Mark Platts, *Ways of Meaning* (London: Routledge & Kegan Paul, 1979). I am deeply indebted to this exposition for my understanding of formal semantics, as I am also to David Wiggins, 'Truth, Invention, and the Meaning of Life', *Proceedings of the British Academy*, 62 (1976), 331–78. I shall use Wiggins's account (with suitable modifications) in my presentation of a formal semantic theory for theological languages, because his account, by identifying the meaning of a sentence with its assertibility-conditions (instead of its truth-conditions), has the advantage of not deciding *ab initio* whether the assertibility-conditions of the sentences of a language are to coincide with their truth-conditions. The possibility of denying the convergence of truth and assertibility is of course crucially important in theological languages.

11 Truth, on this view, becomes a *façon de parler*, one which we can dispense with. The most notable exponent of this view has been W. V. Quine. Cf. his 'Theory of Reference' in his collection of essays *From a Logical Point of View* (New York: Harper & Row, 1961), pp. 134–8.

12 'Truth', p. 357. In stating the five truisms of regular truth, I have talked about *sentences* being (regularly) true or false, a suggestion that is likely to meet with the disapproval of those who maintain that truth is a property, not of sentences, but of propositions. I cannot enter into this debate here; to do so I would have to enter the minefield which surrounds the question whether there are in fact such entities as propositions. However, to avoid controversy, I see no reason why truth cannot be regarded as a relation between a sentence, a person, and a time. For this idea, cf. Davidson, 'Truth and Meaning', p. 319.

13 For the distinction between 'semantic' and 'metaphysical' realism, cf. Brian Loar, *Mind and Meaning* (Cambridge: Cambridge University Press, 1981), p. 168n. A roughly similar distinction between the two types of 'realism' is made by Michael Devitt when he distinguishes between 'Weak, or Fig-Leaf, Realism' and 'Realism' (*per se*). See his *Realism and Truth* (Oxford: Blackwell, 1984), p. 22. Loar follows the characterization of 'metaphysical realism' provided by Hilary Putnam

in his *Meaning and the Moral Sciences* (London: Routledge & Kegan Paul, 1978), pp. 123–38. Cf. also Putnam's 'Why There Isn't a Ready-Made World', *Synthese*, 51 (1982), 147.

14 I shall not attempt here to distinguish between 'religious realism' and 'theological realism'. For British theologians who embrace 'realism', cf. Janet Martin Soskice, *Metaphor and Religious Language* (Oxford: Clarendon Press, 1985); and Rowan Williams, '"Religious Realism": On Not Quite Agreeing With Don Cupitt', *MT*, 1 (1984), 3–24. It should be noted that Soskice disavows the correspondence theory of truth: on pp. 92–3 she implies that a proper account of the semantics of metaphor necessitates the abandoning of the notion of correspondence. Williams espouses 'realism' in the sense of wanting a theory which guarantees the 'objectivity or intentionality' of religious language, but doubts whether resolving the issue of reference (which, in the context of our discussion, is something that is perhaps best accomplished by embracing 'semantic realism') is *in fact* the sole, or the necessary, way to secure this guarantee. See pp. 18ff. I find myself agreeing with Soskice and Williams on both these scores, but want to push the issue of 'realism' into the territory covered by semiology. Brian Hebblethwaite is perhaps exceptional among 'theological realists' in his championing of a full-blown correspondence theory of truth. See the work cited in note 16 below.

15 It must be said that there is nothing in the accounts of Soskice and Williams which commits them to such an uninformative and trivial 'realism'. My claim that there is a *need* to proceed beyond such a 'metaphysical realism' must not therefore be seen as a criticism of their positions. What I propose – viz. a penetration of 'realism' by semiology – is, if anything, complementary to their formulations.

16 For Hebblethwaite's harnessing of a correspondence theory of truth to a 'realist' account of religious, or more specifically christological, language, cf. '"True" and "False" in Christology' in Hebblethwaite and Stewart Sutherland, eds., *PFCT*, pp. 227–38. The theory I used to espouse – viz. the above formal semantics for language *L* – differs from Hebblethwaite's 'realism' insofar as it permits the possibility that assertibility may diverge from truth in theological utterance. I cannot be dogmatic about this, but it is hard to see how Hebblethwaite's 'realism' can accommodate the principle of such a divergence.

17 But even here, as Annette Lavers points out, Barthes 'came to realize that denotation itself is ideological, like the corresponding concept of "object language"'. Cf. her *Roland Barthes: Structuralism and After* (London: Methuen, 1982), pp. 110–11.

18 Roland Barthes, 'Myth Today' in *M*, pp. 109–59. Barthes, of course, wishes to suggest that myth's structure is the structure of *deceit*.

19 'Myth Today', p. 116.

20 An equivalent way of making the point that 'representation' is tacitly expressive of an unformulated or inchoate politics of culture would be to say that the 'real' is permeated by ideology. For this, cf. John B. Thompson, *Studies in the Theory of Ideology* (Cambridge: Polity Press,

1984), p. 5. Thompson is presenting the view of Cornelius Castoriadis (whom we shall be discussing subsequently) and Claude Lefort. This unreflective appropriation of the correspondence theory of truth by theological 'realists' also overlooks Foucault's reminder that truth is 'produced' through the exercise of power: 'There can be no possible exercise of power without a certain economy of discourses of truth which operates through and on the basis of this association. We are subjected to the production of truth through power and we cannot exercise power except through the production of truth.' Cf. Michel Foucault, *Power/Knowledge: Selected Interviews and Other Writings 1972–1977*, ed. Colin Gordon (New York: Pantheon Books, 1980), p. 93.

21 To quote T. W. Adorno: 'The disproportion between the all-powerful reality and the powerless subject creates a situation where reality becomes unreal because the experience of reality is beyond the grasp of the subject. This surplus of reality is reality's undoing. By slaying the subject, reality itself becomes lifeless.' Cf. Adorno, *Aesthetic Theory*, trans. C. Lenhardt (London: Routledge & Kegan Paul, 1984), p. 45.

22 Discussions with logically-minded philosophers have convinced me that these philosophers generally overlook the role of the signifying consciousness because they are too easily persuaded of the connection to be made between 'semantic realism', the correspondence theory of truth, and the definition of the truth-predicate specified by Alfred Tarski in his famous 'Convention T'. In so doing, they forget that Tarski does *not* present his theory as a correspondence theory. Indeed, Susan Haack has shown that Tarski's definition of truth is perfectly compatible with theories of truth, e.g. the pragmatist, which do not invoke the notion of correspondence. Cf. her 'Is it True What they Say About Tarski?', pp. 323–36. These philosophers are driven to misrepresent Tarksi (and semiology) because of their fear that the failure to accord an absolute primacy to semantics leads inevitably to the denial that language has a 'referential' function. However, as Paul de Man has argued, this fear is groundless: 'In a genuine semiology. . . , the referential function of language is not being denied – far from it; what is in question is its authority as a model for natural or phenomenal cognition.' Cf. his 'The Resistance to Theory', *Yale French Studies*, 63 (1982), 11. The difference between semantics and semiology is neatly put by Fredric Jameson in his *The Prison-House of Language: A Critical Account of Structuralism and Russian Formalism* (Princeton, N.J.: Princeton University Press, 1982), p. 32.

23 Cf., for instance, Roman Jakobson, 'On Realism in Art' in K. Pomorska and L. Matejka, eds., *Readings in Russian Formalist Poetics* (Cambridge, Mass.: MIT Press, 1971), pp. 38–46.

24 For this view of the provenance of 'high realism', and the 'elective affinity' which obtains between it and late capitalism, cf. Fredric Jameson, 'The Realist Floor-Plan' in Marshall Blonsky, ed., *On Signs* (Oxford: Blackwell, 1985), pp. 373–83; and *Marxism and Form: Twentieth-Century Dialectical Theories of Literature* (Princeton, N.J.:

Princeton University Press, 1971), pp. 191–205. An authoritative account of the genesis of market capitalism is to be found in E. P. Thompson, *The Making of the English Working Class* (Harmondsworth: Penguin, 1968).

25 Here I pursue the historicizing strategy recommended by Jameson in 'The Realist Floor-Plan', p. 375. This strategy is brilliantly carried through by Jameson in his *PU*.

For the pivotal formulation of this post-structuralist principle of the 'decentring' of 'presence' (or in the context of our discussion, the 'real'), cf. Jacques Derrida, 'Structure, Sign and Play in the Discourse of the Human Sciences' in his collection of essays *Writing and Difference*, trans. Alan Bass (London: Routledge & Kegan Paul, 1978), pp. 278–93.

26 Cf. *PU*, pp. 81ff. Jameson would not of course endorse the 'ontology' of revelation that I am about to sketch. Nevertheless, he speaks positively of 'the strategic function of theological language' (with specific reference to Walter Benjamin) in *PU*, p. 69.

The hidden affinity between post-structuralism's erasure of the 'referent' and a consumer capitalism which generates a social system based on the principle of simulation is one that needs to be traced. This critique of post-structuralism will base itself on the seminal work done by Jean Baudrillard on this principle. According to Baudrillard, global capitalism is associated above all with a system which frantically produces and circulates on a vast scale identical 'copies' that have no original, so that the late capitalist cosmos comes to be marked by a ceaseless indeterminacy and commutability, a free play of signs, which effectively extinguishes the referential dimension. Cf. his *The Mirror of Production*, trans. Mark Poster (St Louis: Telos Press, 1975); and *For a Critique of the Political Economy of the Sign*, trans. Charles Levin and Arthur Younger (St Louis: Telos Press, 1981). It is not being implied here that Baudrillard is in any sense *himself* a critic of post-structuralism. Baudrillard, after all, welcomes a Derridian transcending of the Saussurean sign and the overturning of the reality-principle. He is thus to be reckoned a 'post-Marxist', although a Marxist with a taste for irony can at least take on board Baudrillard's 'post-Marxist' confirmation of Marx's central point that there is no pure use-value in capitalist society (or in Baudrillard's case, *late* capitalist society).

27 Ludwig Wittgenstein, *PI*, # 104, p. 46.

28 St Thomas Aquinas's point that 'God is not even a prototype within the genus of substance, but the prototype of all being, transcending all genera' (*ST*, 1. 3. 6. 2), for 'God does not belong to the genus of substance' (1. 3. 5. 1), leads to a logico-grammatical understanding of speech about divinity. For helpful discussion, to which I am indebted, cf. David B. Burrell, *A*, pp. 24–6. A similar proposal is to be found in Lonergan's *MIT*, p. 103, when he says that '[in] the measure that we advert to our own questioning and proceed to question it, there arises the question of God'. Cf. also his *Philosophy of God, and Theology* (London: Darton, Longman & Todd, 1973), pp. 52–9.

29 Cornelius Castoriadis, 'The Imaginary Institution of Society' in John Fekete, ed., *The Structural Allegory: Reconstructive Encounters with the New French Thought* (Manchester: University of Manchester Press, 1984), pp. 6–45. This brilliant essay attempts to construct a semiology of the socio-historical and to map the place of 'the radical imagination' in our socially-instituted modes of signification. Castoriadis makes a few, seemingly incidental, remarks about 'God' as an 'imaginary [social] signification'; remarks which I am seeking to give an explicitly 'theological' gloss. The need to augment Aquinas's heuristics of the divine with a semiology (in this particular case that of Castoriadis's) arises as soon as it is perceived that all characterizations of 'the real' are socially encoded or 'produced'. (This thesis of course lies at the heart of the tradition of linguistics associated with Sapir, Whorf, Levi-Strauss and Barthes.) For my understanding of Castoriadis I am indebted to the following: Brian Singer, 'The Later Castoriadis: Institution Under Interrogation', *Canadian Journal of Political and Social Theory*, 4 (1980), 75–101; Dick Howard, *The Marxian Legacy* (London: Macmillan, 1977), pp. 262–301; and John B. Thompson, *Studies in the Theory of Ideology*, pp. 16–41.

30 Castoriadis, p. 23. It should be stressed that Castoriadis uses the term 'imaginary' in a strictly neutral sense to signify a linguistic totality that is capable of generating significations.

31 For this understanding of the role of the Five Ways, cf. Cornelius Ernst, *Multiple Echo*, ed. Fergus Kerr and Timothy Radcliffe (London: Darton, Longman & Todd, 1979), p. 74; and Nicholas Lash, 'Considering the Trinity', *MT*, 2 (1986), 187. There is a remarkable affinity between the viewpoint of Ernst and Lash and Castoriadis's claim that 'one [is] to grasp God as an imaginary signification ... in terms of the shadows (the *Abschattungen*) he projects on the screen of actual social activities. ... God, like something perceptible, is a condition for the possibility of an inexhaustible series of such shadows, even though, in contrast to perceptible objects, he is never there "in person" '. Cf. Castoriadis, p. 25. If we overlook Jameson's explicit identification of the Real with History (*per se*), his delineation of the Real is pertinent to this aspect of our discussion: 'this Real – this absent cause, ... is fundamentally unrepresentable and non-narrative, and detectable only in its effects. ... ' Cf. *PU*, p. 184. As we shall see, in the Christian context, Castoriadis's elaboration of the 'imaginary signification' (and Jameson's thematization of the Real) will have to be transposed into the discourse of an *analogia Christi*. I consider this *analogia Christi* in my 'Some Aspects of the "Grammar" of "Incarnation": Reflections Prompted by the Writings of Donald MacKinnon' in Kenneth Surin, ed., *Christ, Ethics and Tragedy: Essays in honour of Donald MacKinnon* (Cambridge: Cambridge University Press, 1988), chapter 6.

32 The *analogia Christi* is endorsed in Walter Kasper, *The God of Jesus Christ*, trans. M.J. O'Connell (London: SCM Press, 1984), p. 158.

33 Castoriadis, pp. 26–7.

34 Castoriadis, p. 27. Interestingly, the principle, common to Aquinas and Castoriadis, that divinity has no concrete signification, and is thus not to be equated with an 'object', is also endorsed by the Kabbalist tradition. Thus Gershom Scholem has argued that for Kabbalism the name of God 'has no "meaning" in the traditional understanding of the term . . . It has no concrete signification.' Cf. his 'The Name of God and the Linguistic Theory of the Kabbala', *Diogenes* 79 (1972), 59–80, and 80 (1972), 164–94. Quotation taken from *Diogenes*, p. 194. It is important to note, however, that Castoriadis's claim that divinity is not a 'referent' is part of a general thesis concerning the logic of (imaginary) signification, whereas for Aquinas (and the Kabbalists) this claim is of course specific and unique to a '*theo-logic*'.

35 Here I am mindful of Gershom Scholem's echoing of the Kabbalist stress on the divine character of language: 'Speech reaches God because it comes from God.' See his *Major Trends in Jewish Mysticism* (London: Thames & Hudson, 1955), p. 17. A similar stress is of course to be found in the theology of Karl Barth. My essay can thus be seen as an attempt to merge, via an invocation of the notion of (a 'linguistic') 'interruption', Fredric Jameson's category of the historical 'subtext' (which in this discussion is articulated christologically in terms of the *extra Calvinisticum*) with a 'textualization' of Barth's (the 'early Barth's') category of 'incarnation as rupture'.

36 Cf. *PU*, p. 183. It is not being suggested here that the gospel narratives of the life, death and resurrection are anything but 'wholly textual'. But the *extra Calvinisticum*, which is endorsed in this essay, reminds us that the 'reality' of the Second Person of the Trinity is not exhausted by the 'reality' of Jesus of Nazareth, and so here – in the differentiation between the divine Logos and the historical Jesus – we are confronted by that which is inherently 'subtextual', and which therefore is, for Christian faith, precisely 'the unanswerable resistance of the Real'.

37 Cf. his 'On Magic Realism in Film', *CI*, 12 (1986), 301–25.

38 Walter Benjamin, 'Theses on the Philosophy of History' in *Illuminations*, trans. Harry Zohn (London: Fontana/Collins, 1973), p. 259 and p. 263. That these remarks of Benjamin's have an inherent theological thrust is testified to not only by the first of these 'Theses' ('The puppet called "historical materialism" . . . can easily be a match for anyone if it enlists the services of theology, which today, as we know, is wizened and has to be kept out of sight', p. 255), but also by Benjamin in a letter to Max Rychner: 'I have never been able to think and research otherwise than, if I may say so, in a theological sense – namely in accordance with the talmudic theory of 49 levels of meaning of each passage in the Torah.' Cf. Walter Benjamin, *Briefe*, ed. T. W. Adorno and G. Scholem, 2 vols. (Frankfurt: Suhrkamp Verlag, 1966), vol. 2, p. 254; cited in Richard Wolin, *Walter Benjamin: An Aesthetic of Redemption* (New York: Columbia University Press, 1982), p. 248. I have borrowed the notion of a 'counter-history' from David Baile, *Gershom Scholem: Kabbalah and Counter-History* (Cambridge, Mass.: Harvard University Press, 1979). This work contains some fascinating remarks on the

Kabbalistic influences exerted via Scholem on Benjamin's philosophy of history.

39 Jameson, 'On Magic Realism', p. 304. Although he does not acknowledge it in this article, Jameson's characterization of the 'entry into narrative' conforms in outline to the principles of Brecht's theory of the so-called 'estrangement-effect' (*Verfremdungseffekt*). Jameson discusses Brecht's theory in *The Prison-House of Language*, and says: 'For Brecht the primary distinction is ... between the static and the dynamic, between that which is perceived as changeless, eternal, having no history, and that which is perceived as altering in time and as being essentially historical in character. The effect of habituation is to make us believe in the eternity of the present, to strengthen in us the feeling that the things and events among which we live are somehow "natural", which is to say permanent. The purpose of the Brechtian estrangement-effect is therefore a political one ... it is ... to make you aware that the objects and institutions you thought to be natural were really only historical: the result of change, they themselves henceforth become in their turn changeable' (p. 58). In what follows I propose to understand the church as a community, located in a (narrative) 'space' shaped by the gospel narratives, which allows itself to be interrogated by these 'defamiliarizing' narratives.

40 I agree with Stanley Hauerwas when he says that '[the] most important social task [facing Christians] is nothing less than to be a community capable of hearing the story of God we find in the scripture and living in a manner that is faithful to that story'. Cf. his *A Community of Character: Towards a Constructive Christian Social Ethic* (Notre Dame: University of Notre Dame Press, 1981), p. 1.

41 For this understanding of the relation between syntax and knowledge I am much indebted to Barbara Johnson, 'Poetry and Syntax: What the Gypsy Knew' in her *The Critical Difference: Essays in the Contemporary Rhetoric of Reading* (Baltimore: Johns Hopkins University Press, 1985), pp. 67–75. To quote from p. 75: 'Knowledge is nothing other than an effect of syntax, not merely because any affirmation creates an illusion of knowledge, but precisely because syntax is what makes it possible for us to treat as *known* anything that we do not *know* we do not know' (Johnson's emphases). It is the great merit of Ray L. Hart's *Unfinished Man and the Imagination: Towards an Ontology and a Rhetoric of Revelation* (New York: Herder & Herder, 1968) that he was alert to the significance and form of 'theological syntax' nearly two decades before 'post-structuralism' came to the general attention of theologians and philosophers of religion.

42 Earlier and much abbreviated versions of this paper were read to the 'D' Society of the Divinity School, University of Cambridge; the 'Open End' Theological Discussion Group in Birmingham; and 'The Sacred Word' Conference at the University of Lancaster. I am grateful to those present on these occasions for many helpful comments and criticisms. My greatest debt, however, is to Gerard Loughlin, John Milbank and Rowan Williams, with whom I have discussed these

issues in many conversations and items of correspondence in recent years.

4. The impassibility of God and the problem of evil

1 For such a concession see H. P. Owen, *Concepts of Deity* (London: Macmillan, 1971), p. 24. The strand of Christian theism that I am referring to derives mainly from the tradition that allegedly stems from St Thomas Aquinas. An alternative tradition, represented by (among others) Jürgen Moltmann, James H. Cone, Kazoh Kitamori and Geddes MacGregor, is discussed lucidly in Warren McWilliams, 'Divine Suffering in Contemporary Theology', *SJT*, 33 (1980), 35–53. The approach adopted in this paper aligns itself with that of the alternative tradition.

2 *God and Timelessness* (London: Routledge & Kegan Paul, 1970), p. 128.

3 See, for example, Owen, *Concepts of Deity*, pp. 24–5.

4 *CG*, pp. 214–15. Moltmann's book is a profound, but somewhat elusive, attempt to make the theology of the cross the central point of the Christian faith, and to work out the implications of this theology of the cross for the Christian understanding of God. Its great merit is that it does not gloss over the seemingly intractable difficulties posed by the so-called 'problem of evil'. See McWilliams, 'Divine Suffering', pp. 36–9, for a discussion of Moltmann.

5 *Power and Innocence* (London: Souvenir Press, 1974), p. 50 and p. 217.

6 A similar point of view is expressed in Lewis Ford, 'Divine Persuasion and the Triumph of God' in D. Brown, R. E. James and G. Reeves, eds., *Process Philosophy and Christian Thought* (New York: Bobbs-Merrill, 1971), pp. 287–304.

7 Thus A. N. Whitehead charges that if God really were like this, then this conception of God makes him into a tyrant. See his *Religion in the Making* (Cambridge: Cambridge University Press, 1926), pp. 55 and 74–5; and *Adventures of Ideas* (Cambridge: Cambridge University Press, 1933), p. 218. A more polemical critique of this 'theological sadism' is to be found in Dorothee Soelle, *S*, pp. 9–32.

8 Charles Hartshorne, *A Natural Theology for our Time* (La Salle, Illinois: Open Court, 1967), p. 75. A similar argument is used in Moltmann, *CG*, p. 222.

9 This objection to the objection we have been considering was put to me in discussion by John Hick. According to Hick, we are forced into an anthropomorphized conception of God's love as a solution to the 'problem' of evil when we overlook this larger canvas of total history which culminates in eternal joy. Given this larger canvas we can admit that God does not have to love the victims of evil in the way that we human beings do in order to escape the charge that he is a tyrant.

10 This is the view of Hick again expressed in discussion.

11 *S*, p. 149.

12 By this Weil meant a form of suffering that is not *mere* pain and

suffering. See her *Waiting on God* (London: Routledge & Kegan Paul, 1951).

13 *EGL*, pp. 371–2.

14 This in outline is the position on theodicy taken by the proponents of the 'evolutionary optimism', which derives from Teilhard de Chardin's thought. On this 'optimism', cf. John Cowburn, *Shadows and the Dark: The Problems of Suffering and Evil* (London: SCM Press, 1979), chapter 3. It also corresponds roughly to the view of process theists on theodicy. For the view of process theists, cf. the works of Whitehead, Hartshorne and Lewis Ford cited in this chapter.

15 The perspective of the 'inverted' theodicist opens from human freedom, and that of the eschatologist from the unfolding of God's redemptive purpose in total history. An 'inverted' theodicy, as we see it, is one which attempts to give a rationale for the existence of evil and suffering, not merely in terms of the alleged 'soul-making' qualities of the world, but in terms of the notion of creaturely freedom. Essentially, it seeks not so much to justify the ways of God in relation to the world, as to exculpate him by saying that evil and suffering are the consequence of humankind misusing its freedom.

16 For the view that such a trinitarian theology is needed, see Moltmann, *CG*, pp. 255–6.

17 Proponents of the 'free-will defence' give the notion of freedom a very strong underpinning by arguing that 'freedom, including moral freedom, is an essential element in what we know as personal as distinct from non-personal life' (Hick, *EGL*, p. 302). We seem to be implying here that the protest atheist 'hands back his ticket' because the suffering and freedom in the universe are not worth the joy that is meant to be a recompense for earthly suffering when we attain to the eternal life. The question arises: how can it be known that they are not worth it? We would say, in reply, that the question of knowing this does not, or should not, even arise for the protest atheist, because for him it would be wrong even to look for a reward in a post-mortem existence, let alone to try and ascertain its worth. The ground of this refusal is ultimately the sense of moral outrage, the sheer injustice, felt by the protest atheist.

18 *EGL*, p. 311.

19 *EGL*, p. 313.

20 Or, to pursue our avian analogy: why do we have to bestow on the bird the freedom of its *cage*? Why not give it freedom *simpliciter*?

21 *The Destiny of Man* (London: Geoffrey Bles, 1937), p. 45.

22 *The Destiny of Man*, p. 32.

23 A truly impassible God, it would seem, can be on the side of neither victim nor executioner.

24 As Berdyaev points out in *The Destiny of Man*, p. 42.

25 *S*, p. 109.

26 A writer like John Cowburn goes so far as to say that the true nature of evil is a mystery even to God. Cf. *Shadows and the Dark*, chapter 8.

27 The story is quoted in *S*, p. 145; and *CG*, pp. 273–4.

28 *Proslogion*, trans. M. J. Charlesworth, as *St Anselm's Proslogion* (Oxford: Clarendon Press, 1965), chapter 8.

29 On this point and its relation to the views of Augustine, Anselm and Aquinas, cf. J. K. Mozley, *The Impassability of God* (Cambridge: Cambridge University Press, 1926), pp. 104–177.

30 See their respective works, 'Substance in Christology – a cross-bench view', *CFH*, pp. 279–300; and *HTRG*.

31 *S*, p. 86.

32 This essay, which was written in 1975, has been superseded by my *Theology and the Problem of Evil* (1986). The latter retains only three of the former's emphases: (i) its critique of the 'soul-making' theodicy; (ii) its acknowledgement that Christian reflection on the 'problems' of evil and suffering is most appropriately to be conducted under the rubric of the 'theology of the cross'; and (iii) its agnosticism on the question of the point and origin of evil and suffering. The argument of this chapter is defective in at least two major respects: (i) it evinces no recognition of the factitious nature of (post-seventeenth-century) 'philosophical theism', and in so doing takes it for granted that this 'theism' is what reflection on Christian faith is all about: and (ii) it makes too much of the notion of God as our 'co-sufferer' – it is now clear to me that this notion is *not* entailed by the proposition that God is 'involved' with the realities of human suffering.

5. Theodicy?

1 David Hume, *Dialogues Concerning Natural Religion*, part x, reprinted in Nelson Pike, ed., *God and Evil: Readings in the Theological Problem of Evil* (Englewood Cliffs, NJ: Prentice-Hall, 1964), pp. 22–3. On the ancestry of the problem of evil, see John Hick, *EGL*, p. 5.

2 For a magisterial survey of Christian responses to the problem of evil, see Hick, *EGL*.

3 Immanuel Kant, *CPR*, trans. N. Kemp Smith, p. 21. One is reminded too of Donald MacKinnon's stricture: 'where the treatment of "the problem of evil" is concerned, we reach an area in which in very various ways, theologians have allowed apologetic eagerness to lead them to suppose they had reached solutions, when in fact they had hardly begun effectively to articulate their problems.' See his *PM*, p. 124.

4 On Newton, see Charles Raven's 1951 Gifford Lectures, *Natural Religion and Christian Theology*, 2 vols. (Cambridge: Cambridge University Press, 1953), vol. 1, pp. 124–44, and Ian G. Barbour, *Issues in Science and Religion* (London: SCM Press, 1966), pp. 34–55; on Descartes, Leibniz and Spinoza, see W. von Leyden, *Seventeenth Century Metaphysics* (London: Duckworth, 1971); on Hume and Kant, see M. J. Charlesworth, *Philosophy of Religion: The Historic Approaches* (London: Macmillan, 1972), pp. 102–27; on Hegel, see Charles Taylor, *Hegel* (Cambridge: Cambridge University Press, 1975). These *Aufklärer* sought essentially to render morality and religious faith compatible with the exigencies of reason and sceptical empiricism. An alternative response to the thoroughgoing rationalism

and empiricism sponsored by the Enlightenment was to give morality and faith a basis in human subjectivity. Pascal and Kierkegaard took this alternative, in opposition to Descartes and Hegel respectively. See William Barrett, *Irrational Man: A Study in Existential Philosophy* (London: Heinemann, 1967), pp. 97–105 and 133–57; James Brown, *Subject and Object in Modern Theology* (London: SCM Press, 1955), pp. 11–82; and Robert C. Solomon, *From Rationalism to Existentialism: The Existentialists and Their Eighteenth-Century Backgrounds* (New York: Humanities, 1972). For a profound study of Pascal's response to the Enlightenment, see Lucienn Goldmann, *The Hidden God: A Study of Tragic Vision in the 'Pensées' of Pascal and the Tragedies of Racine*, trans. Philip Thody (London: Routledge & Kegan Paul, 1964). For a study of Kierkegaard in relation to Hegel, see Marc C. Taylor, *Journeys to Selfhood: Hegel and Kierkegaard* (Berkeley and Los Angeles: University of California Press, 1980). Charles Taylor's *Hegel* provides a lucid account of the way humankind's modern self-understanding emerged from the Enlightenment. See especially chapter 1.

5 Ernest Becker, *The Structure of Evil: An Essay on the Unification of the Science of Man* (New York: Free Press, 1976), p. 18.

6 *The Structure of Evil*, p. 18. It was Feuerbach who took the premises of post-Enlightenment anthropology to their logical conclusion by arguing that we should seek the absolute not in God but in human nature itself. Post-Enlightenment man, having expropriated God of his powers, thus makes himself into a man–god. Iris Murdoch has characterized this post-Enlightenment man–god in the following way:

> How recognizable, how familiar to us, is the man ... who confronted even with Christ turns away to consider the judgement of his own conscience and to hear the voice of his own reason.... this man is still with us, free, independent, lonely, powerful, rational, responsible, brave, the hero of so many novels and books of moral philosophy. (*The Sovereignty of Good* (London: Routledge & Kegan Paul, 1970), p. 80)

Murdoch maintains that this man–god is so depicted in Kant's *Grundlegung zur Metaphysik der Sitten*.

7 Becker, *Structure of Evil*, p. 17. Weber believes that the manipulability of the world (the principle on which bureaucracy operates) is a concomitant of the post-Enlightenment person's new-found identity as self-defining subject. Such a person regards the world, including the good and evil contained therein, as an object of control. The world for such a person is, in Weber's phrase, 'disenchanted' (*entzaubert*).

8 Frederick Sontag, as far as I know, is the only theodicist who makes a serious attempt to come to terms with the phenomenon of 'anthropodicy'. But even he does not seem to be really aware of the extent to which post-Enlightenment thought is likely to subvert the enterprise of theodicy. For Sontag's views, see his 'Anthropodicy and the Return of God' in Stephen T. Davis, ed., *Encountering Evil: Live Options in Theodicy* (Edinburgh: T. & T. Clark, 1981), chapter 5.

A referee of *The Harvard Theological Review* has noted that my argument about the connection between the Enlightenment and theodicy may in fact operate backwards, i.e., that perhaps it was the Enlightenment that made theodicy such an important problem. This is undoubtedly correct. The *Aufklärer*, and Kant in particular, discredited the notion that nature possessed an immanent teleology and thus made it less easy for theologians and philosophers to explain occurrences of evil and suffering in terms of a divine ordained creative process inherent in nature. Evil and suffering thus become more difficult to account for and explain away. The Enlightenment, it would seem, not only helped to deprive theodicy of its *prima facie* plausibility (which is what I have been arguing), but also served to make theodicy a *problem*, and an almost insoluble problem at that. I am grateful to this referee for suggesting this line of thought to me.

9 *God, Freedom and Evil* (London: Allen & Unwin, 1974), p. 29. John Hick upholds Plantinga's point of view when he says: 'a Christian theodicy ... offers an understanding of our human situation; but this is not the same as offering practical help and comfort to those in the midst of acute pain or deep suffering'. See his 'An Irenaean Theodicy' in Davis, ed., *Encountering Evil*, p. 68.

10 It is typical of the bureaucratic view of good and evil that it regards them in an abstract way, as something involving roles of office, administrative procedures, protocols, etc., but rarely personal guilt and responsibility. The evil bureaucrat *par excellence*, who rendered evil 'banal', was of course Adolf Eichmann. See Hannah Arendt, *Eichmann in Jerusalem: A Report on the Banality of Evil* (Harmondsworth: Penguin, rev. and enlarged edn, 1977). It is imperative therefore that the theodicist ask herself: am I operating with a conception of evil that, because of its abstract nature, effectively reduces evil to banality?

11 This quotation is taken from Nicholas Lash, *TDB*, p. 21, who in turn quotes from G. K. Chesterton's hymn 'O God of Earth and Altar'. Lash's book contains an admirably clear statement of the dangers involved in allowing theological reflection to degenerate into ideology by ignoring the particular social and political praxis mediated by such reflection. Relevant in this context is Isaiah Berlin's observation that 'if Kant had not discredited the God of the rationalist theologians, Robespierre might not have beheaded the king' (quoted in Bryan Magee, ed., *Men of Ideas: Some Creators of Contemporary Philosophy*, Oxford: Oxford University Press, 1982, p. 9). Berlin's quite plausible suggestion here is that in discrediting the God of rational theology, Kant effectively undermined (albeit indirectly) the notion that the monarchs of pre-revolutionary Europe ruled by divine right. Berlin goes on to say: 'the power of philosophical or metaphysical ideas ... can be very great – indirect, but far reaching ... philosophers [are] not harmless word-spinners, but a great force of good and evil, among the most formidable unacknowledged legislators of mankind' (p. 9).

12 To quote Sartre:
We have been taught to take [evil] seriously. It is neither our fault

nor our merit if we lived in a time when torture was a daily fact
....Dachau and Auschwitz have ... demonstrated to us that Evil
is not an appearance, that knowing its cause does not dispel it, that
it is not opposed to Good as a confused idea is to a clear one, that it
is not the effect of passions which might be cured, of a fear which
might be overcome, of a passing aberration which might be
excused, of an ignorance which might be enlightened. ...

We heard whole streets screaming and we understood that Evil
... is, like Good, absolute.

Perhaps a day will come when a happy age, looking back at the
past, will see in this suffering and shame one of the paths which led
to peace. But we were not on the side already made. We were, as I
have said, *situated* in such a way that every lived minute seemed to
us like something irreducible. Therefore, in spite of ourselves, we
came to this conclusion, which will seem shocking to lofty souls:
Evil cannot be redeemed. (*What is Literature?*, trans. Bernard
Frechtman (London: Methuen, 1950), pp. 160–2)

Sartre, in this passage, is reflecting on his experience as a member of the
war-time Resistance in France.

13 *Tales of Unrest* (Harmondsworth: Penguin, 1977), p. 100.
14 'The Hermeneutics of Symbols and Philosophical Reflection: I' in *The
Conflict of Interpretations*, trans. Don Ihde (Evanston: Northwestern
University Press, 1974), p. 312. See also p. 314, where Ricoeur argues
that theodicy is an expedient of false knowledge because it does not give
us an understanding of hope.
15 Namely, that of enabling us to come to terms not only with the mere
existence, but also with the *awfulness*, of evil and suffering; and not
only this, but in so doing for the theodicist also to address herself
directly to the plight of human sufferers.
16 That is, how coherent is the idea of an almighty and morally perfect
God who nevertheless creates a world that contains so much pain and
suffering? Herbert McCabe has argued that there is nothing incoherent
in the idea of a morally perfect God who permits the suffering caused by
sin to exist. To quote him:

it is one thing to say that sin is *not a manifestation* of God's goodness and quite another to say that sin is a manifestation that God is
not good. We do not know *why* the good God has made a world
which does not at all times manifest his goodness, but the notion is
not contradictory. Somehow the infinite goodness of God is compatible with his allowing sin. ('God: Evil', *NB*, 62 (1981), 17)

Even if we concede, for the purposes of argument, McCabe's claim that
there is no contradiction in the idea of a good God who allows sin to
exist, it seems to me that a problem remains if we accept that God is an
infinitely loving being: can an *infinitely loving* God permit the suffering
caused by sin to exist while he does nothing about it? It is one of the
main contentions of this essay that human suffering can be reconciled
with the existence of a God of love only if this God becomes a God of
salvation.

17 Of these two questions, (iii) is more important from the standpoint of theodicy than (iv). Even so, we are not justified in treating (iii) and (iv) as though they have no connection with each other; given the framework of Christian 'theism', (iv) is entailed by (iii).

18 Plantinga's and Hick's position on this issue can be inferred from the passages quoted on pp. 76–7 and in note 9 above.

19 *CG*, pp. 215–16.

20 To this extent, ours is not a theodicy in the traditional sense of the term. However, it seems to me that the point at issue for the theodicist is invariably the goodness and benevolence of deity – I have yet to come across a *Christian* theodicy which identifies divine omnipotence as the crux of the problem of evil.

21 For such a person there would be no point in doing theodicy: the 'solution' to the problem of evil will lie in altering the states of mind of individuals who are troubled by the fact of evil, and not in any need to justify God.

22 All references to *The Brothers Karamazov* will be to the translation by David Magarshack (Harmondsworth: Penguin, 1958). In discussing the case of Ivan Karamazov, I shall presuppose that the God of the problem of evil is the God worshipped by Christians (as indeed I have throughout this essay).

23 Stewart Sutherland, *Atheism and the Rejection of God: Contemporary Philosophy and 'The Brothers Karamazov'* (Oxford: Blackwell, 1977). See especially pp. 25–39.

24 I do not propose in this essay to consider Dostoyevsky's own answer to the problem of evil as it is posed by Ivan Karamazov – Sutherland does this more than adequately.

25 Thus Max Weber is able to distinguish between three forms of theodicy which he regards as consistent: (i) dualism; (ii) predestination; and (iii) 'virtuoso-like self redemption'. See his 'Three Forms of Theodicy' in *FMW*, pp. 358–9.

26 Brian Hebblethwaite, in a private communication, has also expressed the desirability of linking theodicy to an Irenaean picture of the world process in order to enhance the viability of theodicy.

27 Ivan, though, is in no way suggesting that man is worthy of the love of God. Thus he tells Alyosha: 'And what is so strange . . . is not that God actually exists, but that such an idea – the idea of the necessity of God – should have entered the head of such a savage and vicious animal as man' (p. 274).

28 It must be emphasized that Hick takes pains to distance himself from the position which regards the promised bliss of heaven as a compensation or reward for our earthly travails. As Hick says: 'The "good eschaton" will not be a reward or a compensation proportioned to each individual's trials, but an infinite good that would render worthwhile *any* finite suffering endured in the course of attaining to it' (p. 377). Admittedly, Ivan's outburst seems to be directed specifically against the idea of a compensatory heaven which Hick rejects. However, it seems to me that Ivan's strictures are just as applicable to Hick's claim that the

'good eschaton' would 'render worthwhile *any* finite suffering endured in the course of attaining to it'. For Ivan, not only can the principle of an eschatological transfiguration of innocent suffering *never* be morally justified; but (as he sees it) to adopt this principle is also to reduce the profoundest affirmations of the Christian faith to the status of empty chatter, idle speculation. A more detailed consideration of the 'soul-making' theodicy is to be found in chapter 4 above.

29 For this story, see Moltmann, *CG*, pp. 373–4; and Soelle, *S*, p. 145.
30 To use a phrase of Donald MacKinnon's. See his 'Order and Evil in the Gospel' in *Borderlands of Theology and Other Essays* (New York: Lippincott, 1968), p. 91. I am deeply indebted to this essay of MacKinnon's for several of the ideas developed in this chapter.
31 The principle that only a suffering God can help is elaborated in Kazoh Kitamori, *Theology of the Pain of God*, trans. M. E. Bratcher (Richmond: John Knox Press, 1965); and Geddes MacGregor, *He Who Let Us Be: A Theology of Love* (New York: Seabury, 1975). A valuable conspectus of recent discussions of the subject of divine suffering is to be found in Warren McWilliams, 'Divine Suffering in Contemporary Theology', *SJT*, 33 (1980), 33–53.
32 P. T. Forsyth, *The Justification of God* (London: Latimer House, 1948), p. 167. For a brief discussion of Forsyth's theodicy, see Hick, *EGL*, pp. 246–8.
33 Forsyth, *Justification of God*, p. 53.
34 Forsyth, p. 211 and p. 220. Relevant here too are the words of Donald MacKinnon:
> To suggest that Christianity deals with the problem of evil by encouraging the believer to view it from a cosmic perspective is totally to misunderstand both the difficulty and the consolation of its treatment. Rather Christianity takes the history of Jesus and urges the believer to find, in the endurance of the ultimate contradictions of human existence that belong to its very substance, the assurance that in the worst that can befall his creatures, the creative Word keeps company with those he has called his own. ('Order and Evil', p. 93)
35 It is precisely for this reason that John Hick rejects the 'classic' atonement doctrine, which, according to him, is inextricably bound up with the notion of the incarnation, effectively making christology the ground of soteriology. Hick rejects this incarnational christology because of the so-called 'scandal of particularity' which surrounds the incarnation. Salvation, thus conceived, says Hick, will *eo ipso* be confined to the adherents of an incarnational faith, and this is unacceptable in a world that is characterized by a plurality of faiths. See John Hick, 'Evil and Incarnation' in *IM*, pp. 77–84.
36 As will be indicated in the next section, sometimes silence is the *only* morally appropriate response to extreme suffering. The principle of redemptive incarnation is not one that can be vindicated by philosophical or systematic theology. That salvation should be proffered to humankind in and through a Nazarene who died on a cross at Golgotha

nearly two thousand years ago is a truth that can only be established by a theology of revelation based on the Word of God as given in Holy Scripture. If this is the case, then theodicy moves away from philosophical or systematic theology into the realm of dogmatic theology.

37 Theodicy hinges on the enormous presumption that evil is something that can be understood. It is this presumption which trivializes theodicy's treatment of evil and suffering, because they are reduced by it to humanly assimilable proportions. Theodicy would not 'get off the ground' if it heeded the words of a survivor of Auschwitz (Elie Wiesel): 'I who was there still do not understand.'

38 See his *Freedom and the Spirit*. This quotation is reproduced from Donald A. Lowrie, *Christian Existentialism: A Berdyaev Anthology* (London: Allen & Unwin, 1965), p. 41.

39 The content of this revelation, we have already argued, is to be articulated in terms of a *theologia crucis*: what God reveals to humankind, in the context of the problem of evil, is that he himself, through the Cross of Christ, endures the sufferings that afflict us. I have developed this point in chapter 8 below. In turning to the theology of revelation to provide a basis for a *theologia crucis* I am mindful of Wolfhart Pannenberg's formula that God is 'accessible ... by his own action'. Pannenberg makes this point in *Theology and the Philosophy of Science*, trans. Francis McDonagh (London: Darton, Longman & Todd, 1976), p. 310. Nicholas Lash rightly says that Pannenberg's formula is a necessary condition for the enterprise of critical theology. See his *TDB*, pp. 16–23. To quote Lash: 'unless God is accessible by his own action, Christian faith expresses only man's hope, and theology is rendered incapable of speaking of God' (p. 17).

40 Jürgen Moltmann, *Hope and Planning*, trans. Margaret Clarkson (New York: Harper & Row, 1971), p. 43.

41 'Theodicy' in this context refers primarily to the theoretical aspect of theodicy.

42 Such a person may even believe that it is possible to have an explanation which makes evil and suffering intelligible. (I happen to believe that it is not possible – in principle – to provide such an explanation.)

43 For Garfinkel's discussion, see *Forms of Explanation: Rethinking the Question in Social Theory* (New Haven: Yale University Press, 1981), chapter 1. See Hilary Putnam, *Meaning and the Moral Sciences* (London: Routledge & Kegan Paul, 1978), pp. 42–3, for another discussion of the 'interest-relativity' of explanation.

44 See note 34 above.

45 The 'mistake' of those who seek to acquire a cosmic perspective on the problem of evil is superbly depicted by R. S. Thomas in his poem 'The Prisoner' (in *The Critical Quarterly*, 17 (1975), 4):

> It is the same
> outside. Bars, walls
> but make the perspective
> clear. *Deus Absconditus!*
> We ransack the heavens, the distance between

stars; the last place we look
is in prison, his
hideout in flesh and bone.

46 As Hans Urs von Balthasar says: 'The key to the understanding of God's action lies exclusively in the interpretation which God gives of himself before man on the stage of human nature.... What God has done for man is "understandable" only in so far as it is *not* understandable or justifiable from a human, worldly point of view, and from the standpoint of our fragmentary knowledge: by these standards it is bound to appear "foolishness" and "madness"' (*Love Alone: The Way of Revelation*, ed. Alexander Dru, London: Burns & Oates, 1968, p. 58).

47 The position elaborated in this essay (which was written in 1981) has been modified somewhat in my book *Theology and the Problem of Evil* (1986). In particular, I am no longer wedded to the belief that the proponent of a *theologia crucis* needs to embrace the notion of God as a 'co-sufferer' of victims. God can be involved redemptively with the realities of human suffering without himself having necessarily to 'experience' these realities.

Parts of this essay were read to a meeting of the 'D' Society of Cambridge University, where it was penetratingly criticized by Nicholas Lash and Brian Hebblethwaite. The latter also kindly put some of his comments on paper in a way that helped with the production of the final draft.

6. Tragedy and the soul's conquest of evil

1 In G. N. A. Vesey, ed., *Talk of God* (London: Macmillan, 1969), pp. 86–99.

2 Quoted in Vesey, ed., *Talk of God*, p. 98. The original is to be found in C. G. Jung, *Memories, Dreams, Reflections* (London: Collins/Fontana, 1967), p. 362. Bartley expounds his position more fully in his *Morality and Religion* (London: Macmillan, 1971), especially pp. 49–65.

3 On Jägerstatter see the biography by the American sociologist Gordon Zahn, *In Solitary Witness* (New York: Holt, Rinehart & Winston, 1964).

4 *The Sovereignty of Good* (London: Routledge & Kegan Paul, 1970), pp. 67–8. A depreciation of the alleged value of self-knowledge is to be found in Coleridge's poem 'Self-Knowledge' in *The Golden Book of S. T. Coleridge* (London: Dent, 1906), p. 274:

What has thou, Man, that can be known?
Dark fluxion, all unfixable by thought,
A phantom dim of past and future wrought,
Vain sister of the worm – life, death, soul, clod –
Ignore thyself, and strive to know thy God!

5 Anyone familiar with the writings of Donald MacKinnon on the relation between ethics and tragedy will probably perceive how indebted I am to him. Cf. especially his *PM*, chapters 11 and 12; and 'Ethics and

Tragedy' in his collection of essays *Explorations in Theology* (London: SCM Press, 1979), pp. 182–95.

6 *Tragedy in the Victorian Novel* (Cambridge: Cambridge University Press, 1979), p. 107.

7 *The Return of the Native* (London: Macmillan, 1964), p. 371.

8 *The Return of the Native*, p. 115. I am indebted to King's book for several critical insights. I have also benefitted from reading R. P. Draper, ed., *Thomas Hardy (The Tragic Novels): A Selection of Critical Essays* (London: Macmillan, 1975).

9 *Morality and Religion*, p. 62.

10 Joseph Conrad, *Heart of Darkness* (Harmondsworth: Penguin, 1973), p. 100.

11 *Almayer's Folly* (Harmondsworth: Penguin, 1976), p. 123.

12 In referring to the work of Heidegger I am mindful of Edward Schillebeeckx's warning that theologians who use Heidegger's work inevitably dissociate the philosopher's thought from his distinctively philosophical sphere of questioning, so that we have what Heidegger himself has called a 'Christian misuse' of his philosophy. Cf. Schillebeeckx, *God the Future of Man* (London: Sheed & Ward, 1969), pp. 46–7. Schillebeeckx's warning does not really apply to us since we are not formulating a specifically theological argument.

13 *Morality and Religion*, p. 66.

14 *Principia Ethica* (Cambridge: Cambridge University Press, 1959), p. 224.

15 *Principia Ethica*, p. 188. Keynes said of the last chapter of *Principia Ethica* that 'The New Testament is a handbook for politicians compared with the unworldliness of Moore's chapter on the Ideal.' Cf. his *Two Memoirs* (London: Hart-Davis, 1949), p. 94.

16 In constructing this concluding argument I am indebted to several works. My skeletal outline of the 'moral realist' position is borrowed from the more substantial treatment in Mark Platts, 'Moral Reality and the End of Desire' in Platts, ed., *Reference, Truth and Reality* (London: Routledge & Kegan Paul, 1980), pp. 69–82; David Wiggins, 'Truth, Invention, and the Meaning of Life', *Proceedings of the British Academy*, 62 (1976), 331–78; and Iris Murdoch, *The Sovereignty of Good*. On the preexistence of evil I am indebted to Paul Ricoeur, ' "Original Sin": A Study in Meaning' in *The Conflict of Interpretations* (Evanston, Illinois: Northwestern University Press, 1974), pp. 269–86. An understanding of the atonement which accords with this theory of 'moral realism' is to be found in chapter 8 below.

7. Atonement and moral apocalypticism: *Sophie's Choice*

1 *God was in Christ: An Essay on Incarnation and Atonement* (London: Faber, 1961), p. 198. It should be stressed that we are not seeking to question the intrinsic coherence or plausibility of 'subjective' conceptions as such. Rather we shall be attempting to show that 'subjective' conceptions cannot stand on their own, that in addition to the 'persuasion in our hearts' that Baillie talks about, Christ's saving work must

be said to possess a dimension that is independent of the manner in which we appropriate this work. In other words: the saving efficacy of Christ's work can be guaranteed only if the atonement is conceived 'objectively', and not merely 'subjectively'.

2 The question whether it is possible to justify the shift away from 'objective' conceptions of the atonement is precisely the question that lies at the heart of the well-known Lampe–MacKinnon debate on the resurrection. Cf. G. W. H. Lampe and D. M. MacKinnon, *The Resurrection: A Dialogue* (London: Mowbray, 1966). For arguments in favour of detaching the doctrine of the atonement from an 'incarnational' christology, cf. Maurice Wiles, *The Remaking of Christian Doctrine* (London: SCM Press, 1974), chapter 4; and John A. T. Robinson, *The Human Face of God* (London: SCM Press, 1973), pp. 230ff.

3 *A Theology of Auschwitz* (London: SPCK, 1978), p. 71.

4 *Language and Silence: Essays 1958–66* (Harmondsworth: Penguin, 1969), p. 203.

5 Piet Schoonenberg, *Man and Sin: A Theological View* (London: Sheed & Ward, 1965), p. 21. Italics added.

6 *Christ: The Christian Experience in the Modern World*, trans. John Bowden (London: SCM Press, 1980), p. 203.

7 Eberhart Jüngel, *Death: The Riddle and the Mystery*, trans. I and U. Nicol (Edinburgh: The Saint Andrew Press, 1975), *passim.*

8 *Doctor Faustus* in Christopher Marlowe, *Complete Poems and Plays* (London: Dent, 1976), quoted in D. Z. Phillips, *Through a Darkening Glass: Philosophy, Literature, and Cultural Change* (Oxford: Blackwell, 1982), p. 90. I am deeply indebted to Phillips's masterly essay, 'Knowledge, Patience and Faust' in this volume, pp. 89–112, for several insights into the nature of the Faustian complex. It was Rowan Williams who drew my attention to the importance of Phillips's essay.

9 Phillips, *Through a Darkening Glass*, p. 90.

10 *Commentary on Romans*, trans. G. W. Bromiley (London: SCM Press, 1980), p. 104.

11 *The Theology of the New Testament*, trans. J. E. Steely (London: SCM Press, 1974), pp. 184–5.

12 *Theology of the New Testament: Volume One*, trans. K. Grobel (London: SCM, 1952), p. 290. Paul, of course, equates God's deed of salvation with the event of Christ's obedience on the cross. Cf. Philippians 2:8; and Romans 5:15–21.

13 *Theology of the New Testament*, p. 290.

14 *Grace and Personality* (Cambridge: Cambridge University Press, 1919), p. 206.

15 Von Niemand's realization represents a negation of the Pauline view that the ways of God are beyond all understanding (Philippians 4:7).

16 *Creon and Antigone: Ethical Problems of Nuclear Warfare* (London: The Menard Press, 1982), p. 26.

17 Cf. Käsemann, *Commentary on Romans*, p. 139, where Christ is described as being 'in person the irreversible "for us" of God'. My

understanding of the God of the future is deeply indebted to the writings of Paul Ricoeur. Cf. especially the essays in parts IV and V of his collection *The Conflict of Interpretations: Essays in Hermeneutics* (Evanston: Northwestern University, 1974). Ricoeur has, by the way, acknowledged his indebtedness to Jürgen Moltmann's *Theology of Hope*. It should be noted that the distinction between the God of the future and the God who is is not meant to be absolute – we use it simply to draw attention to the moral apocalypticist's rather one-sided affirmation of the God who is, which results in a failure on his part to recognize the importance of the God who is to come.

18 Goethe, *Faust/Part One*, trans. P. Wayne (Harmondsworth: Penguin, 1976), p. 91. Quoted in Phillips, *Through a Darkening Glass*, p. 111, which contains a splendid interpretation of this passage.

19 Cf. the quotation of Käsemann's cited in note 17 above.

20 On the fundamental dichotomy between salvation and our capacity to *comprehend* the true nature of this salvation, cf. Nicholas Lash, *TDB*, p. 93. The principal theme in our essay has been the denial that human beings can be the authors of their own salvation, and that our understanding of the atonement cannot therefore be merely 'subjective'. Simone Weil has shown exactly why it is that a purely 'subjective' interpretation of the atonement will never be really adequate to the true nature of our salvation: 'A hurtful act is the transference to others of the degradation which we bear in ourselves. This is why we are inclined to commit such acts as a way of deliverance.' Cf. her *Gravity and Grace* (London: Routledge & Kegan Paul, 1963), p. 65.

21 'On Free Will' in J. H. S. Burleigh, trans., *Augustine: Earlier Writings* (Philadelphia: The Westminster Press, 1963), p. 169.

8. Atonement and christology

1 See their respective works, *GS*; and *Jesus: An Experiment in Christology*, trans. Hubert Hoskins (London: Collins, 1979). It should be emphasized that although we distinguish between 'ontological' and 'functional' christologies, this distinction is not meant to be absolute. To regard it as such would be to simplify the christological question, and we are using this distinction merely to indicate that there are two fairly different ways of conceiving the nature and status of Jesus Christ.

2 'The Theology of the Humanity of Christ' in *CFH*, p. 62.

3 'Subjective and Objective Conceptions of Atonement' in *PFT*, pp. 169–82, p. 170. In this article MacKinnon attempts a reconciliation between 'objective' and 'subjective' conceptions of atonement. Roughly speaking, he regards the 'subjective' conception as involving fundamentally the moral consciousness of human beings, whereas the 'objective' conception has to do with the tragic ambivalence which seems inherent in the very fabric of the universe, and which therefore transcends the sphere of human moral powers. There is a difficulty with this attempted reconciliation, stemming from the fact that tragedy in its essence is outside the compass of our moral consciousness, and we will have to address ourselves to it later.

4 See, for instance, John Hick, 'Christology at the Cross Roads', in *PFT*, pp. 133–66; and 'Jesus and the World Religions', in *MGI*, pp. 167–85.

5 Thus Hick, in 'Christology at the Cross Roads', conceives of the incarnation not in terms of the *homoousion* but in terms of the identity between the *agape* of Jesus and the divine *agape*.

6 Thus the traditional Christian understanding of the atonement is explicitly rejected in Hick, 'Evil and Incarnation', in *IM*, pp. 77–84.

7 The inspiration for this argument comes from MacKinnon's contribution to the Farmer *Festschrift*; Stanley Cavell, 'The Avoidance of Love: A Reading of *King Lear*' in his *Must We Mean What We Say?* (Cambridge: Cambridge University Press, 1976), chapter 10, and his *CR*; and Sebastian Moore, *CNS*.

8 MacKinnon, 'Subjective and Objective Conceptions', p. 172.

9 MacKinnon, 'Subjective and Objective Conceptions', p. 181.

10 In saying this I am aware of the strictures which some theologians have expressed concerning the use of an abstract notion of human nature and human needs. For such strictures see, for instance, Sykes, 'The Theology of the Humanity of Christ'; Nicholas Lash, 'Up and Down in Christology' in S. Sykes and D. Holmes, eds., *New Studies in Theology*, vol. 1 (London: Duckworth, 1980), pp. 31–46; and Schillebeeckx, *Jesus*, p. 604. As we shall see later, one of the arguments of this essay will be that an 'ontological' christology is essential in order to avoid using an abstract conception of humanity in our typical salvation-scheme. For the moment, however, a degree of abstractness is unavoidable.

11 Likewise, it is not being implied here that MacKinnon's conception of the atonement typifies the anthropological approach. On the contrary, his position is more compatible with the theological approach as defined by Sykes.

12 MacKinnon, 'Absolute and Relative in History' in his *Explorations in Theology* (London: SCM Press, 1979), p. 67.

13 'The Appeal to Experience in Christology' in *CFH*, p. 272.

14 In discussion Hebblethwaite has denied that my objection is relevant. According to him, the 'reductionists' he has in mind are not 'full-scale reductionists' like van Buren, but those who are 'half-way' there, e.g. theologians such as Lampe and Robinson who regard Christ as purely human but who still wish to ascribe to this purely human figure the significance he has in the traditional affirmations of the Christian faith. However, it is not clear to me that Lampe (for example) takes a position which ascribes to Christ the significance he has traditionally been accorded – in his Bampton Lectures he holds the view that though God's revelation of himself through his Spirit in Christ is 'decisive', it is not 'final', and so God 'addresses all men everywhere at all times' (p. 180). Surely to deny the finality of God's revelation of himself in Christ is, effectively, to scale-down the 'weight of significance' we traditionally ascribe to Christ? We could not, for instance, uphold the traditional formula *extra ecclesiam nulla salus* without upholding the 'finality' of God's revelation in Christ. It seems to me, therefore, that

Lampe's position does involve a scaling-down of the 'weight of significance' we traditionally ascribe to Christ (*pace* Hebblethwaite).

15 This skeletal outline is entirely derivative, and I am deeply indebted to the works cited in note 7 in my presentation of it.

16 Rowan Williams, *WK*, p. 30.

17 Thus Sebastian Moore defines sin, in part, as the expression of fear in the form of hate. See *CNS*, p. 12.

18 Williams, *WK*, p. 10.

19 Moore, *CNS*, p. 14.

20 Moore, *CNS*, p. x.

21 'The Truth of Life: Observations on Truth as the Interruption of the Continuity of Life' in R. W. A. McKinney, ed., *Christ, Creation and Culture: Studies in Honour of T. F. Torrance* (Edinburgh: T. & T. Clark, 1976), p. 234.

22 I have argued more fully for the view that God's acceptance of humankind must take the form of a suffering *theophany* in chapters 4 and 5.

23 So much so that John Cowburn says that the true nature of evil is a mystery even to God. Cf. his *Shadows and the Dark: The Problems of Suffering and Evil* (London: SCM Press, 1979), chapter 8. The way evil exposes the inadequacy of our human moral powers is superbly depicted in Anthony Burgess's *Earthly Powers* (London: Hutchinson, 1980).

24 See Berdyaev, *The Destiny of Man* (London: Geoffrey Bles, 1937), p. 42. The substance of this objection was raised by Nicholas Lash when an earlier version of this paper was read to the Cambridge Christology Graduate Seminar.

25 In a sense, therefore, the two conceptions of the atonement are complementary (as MacKinnon rightly suggests).

26 *Theology of the Love of God* (London: Collins, 1980), p. 95. A similar point is made by Ray Anderson in his *HTRG*, p. 138.

27 A fuller treatment of a doctrine of creation which accords with the *imago Dei* is to be found in chapter 1.

28 I am indebted to Anderson, *HTRG*, p. 124, for this understanding of the function of the *imago Dei*, and have found his book very useful in formulating my views on this topic.

29 It is important to emphasize the need to preserve divine transcendence. As Herbert McCabe points out, we can justifiably claim *that* God is not impersonal, but it does not follow from this that we can specify *how* it is that he is personal. Cf. his 'God: I – Creation', *NB*, 61 (1980), 408–15.

30 *haer.*, v.1 and 10–23.

31 In thus appealing to Irenaeus we do not imply that his penal substitutionary doctrine of the atonement is entirely acceptable. As said, what we find most useful is his insistence on the *continuity* between the atonement and creation. For a similar insistence see Lampe, *GS*, pp. 14–24.

32 Newlands, *Theology of the Love of God*, pp. 59–60.

33 A view championed by Charles Moule in his 'Three Points of Conflict in

the Christological Debate' in *IM*, pp. 131–41, especially p. 138; and repeated in his valedictory lecture at Cambridge, 'The Holy Spirit and Scripture', delivered on 29 October 1980.

34 This point is made by Schillebeeckx in his *Jesus*, p. 169.

35 Newlands, *Theology*, p. 169.

36 For this proposal see MacKinnon, 'Substance in Christology' in *CFH*, pp. 279–300; and Schillebeeckx, *Jesus*, p. 549.

37 I am aware of the possibility that Schillebeeckx may be basing his claim on an untenable understanding of the New Testament.

38 P. F. Strawson, 'On Referring' in G. H. R. Parkinson, ed., *The Theory of Meaning* (Oxford: Oxford University Press, 1968), pp. 61–85.

39 Cf. his article cited in note 10.

40 As George Newlands puts it, 'If in Christ we have to do with the transcendent God, then our christology will always be in a sense from above, and since none of us can speak God's language, we must always work from below' (p. 161).

41 *Jesus: God and Man*, trans. L. L. Wilkins and D. A. Priebe (London: SCM Press, 1868), pp. 33–7.

42 See the works of Sykes, Lash and Schillebeeckx cited in note 10.

43 'Theology of the Humanity of Christ', p. 71.

9. Revelation, salvation, the uniqueness of Christ and other religions

1 *CD*, 1/2, p. 308. The italics are mine.

2 *Offenbarung, Kirche, Theologie*, p. 18. Quoted from H. R. MacKintosh, *Types of Modern Theology* (London: Collins/Fontana, 1964), p. 264.

3 This is the gist of the argument advanced in John Hick, 'Whatever Path Men Choose Is Mine' in *COR*, pp. 171–90. Cf. also his 'Jesus and the World Religions' in *MGI*, pp. 167–85. Also relevant in this context are Hick's 'Reply to Hebblethwaite' in *IM*, pp. 192–4; and several of the essays in Hick's collection *God and the Universe of Faiths* (London: Collins/Fount, 1977). Barth's position can also be criticized from a more specifically theological standpoint. The cornerstone of his dismissal of religion as 'unbelief' is his understanding of the place of revelation in theological speech, in particular, his belief that we can have no genuine knowledge of God apart from the revelation of God in Jesus Christ. This Barthian principle is emphatically rejected by Emil Brunner in his pamphlet *Nature and Grace* and in his later book *Revelation and Reason: The Christian Doctrine of Faith and Knowledge*, trans. Olive Wyon (London: SCM Press, 1947). Hendrik Kraemer endorses Brunner's protest in his *The Christian Message in a non-Christian World* (London: Edinburgh House, 1938), cf. especially p. 133. On p. 125 Kraemer argues that 'God is continuously occupying Himself and wrestling with man, in all ages and with all peoples.'

4 Barth, it seems to me, is perhaps less susceptible to the charge of triumphalism than some other Christian thinkers: he maintains, scrupulously, that Christianity, like all other religions, is still 'human' religion and therefore 'unbelief'.

5 For Rahner's notion, cf. his *Theological Investigations: vol. 5* (London: Darton, Longman & Todd, 1966), chapter 6. Cf. also *Theological Investigations: vol. 14* (London: Darton, Longman & Todd, 1976), chapter 17.

6 'The World Religions in God's Plan of Salvation' in J. Neuner, ed., *Christian Revelation and World Religions* (London: Burns & Oates, 1967), pp. 55–6. Küng's suggestion is hardly new – it was anticipated in the second century AD by Justin Martyr who, in his *Apologia* (I, xlvi), argued that those individuals born before the time of Christ 'who lived according to reason are Christians, even though they were classed as atheists. For example: among Greeks, Socrates, and Heraclitus; among non-Greeks, Abraham, Ananias, Azarius, and Misael, and Elias, and many others.' Extract taken from H. Bettenson, ed. and trans., *The Early Christian Fathers: A Selection from the Writings of the Fathers from St Clement of Rome to St Athanasius* (Oxford: Oxford University Press, 1969), p. 60.

7 'Christianity and the World Religions' in *COR*, p. 196. I have made a minor stylistic alteration to one of Moltmann's sentences.

8 *The Reality of God and Other Essays* (London: SCM Press, 1967), p. 173. Italics as an original.

9 'The Uniqueness of Christ' in *Truth Is Two-Eyed* (London: SCM Press, 1979), p. 124. Hereinafter referred to as *TT–E*.

10 Hick, 'Whatever Path Men Choose Is Mine', pp. 177–8.

11 'Christianity and the World Religions', p. 202. Moltmann derives the idea of Christianity as a 'critical catalyst' from Hans Küng, *On Being a Christian*, trans. Edward Quinn (London: Collins, 1976), pp. 110ff.

12 For the suggestion that the truths of the different faiths may not be mutually exclusive, but complementary, cf. John Hick, 'The Outcome: Dialogue into Truth' in Hick, ed., *Truth and Dialogue: The Relationship between World Religions* (London: Sheldon Press, 1974), pp. 152–3. Hereinafter referred to as *TD*. The idea of seeing Islam and Christianity as two complementary religious traditions vis-à-vis the notion of the incarnation is discussed in Kenneth Cragg, 'Islam and Incarnation' in *TD*, pp. 126–39.

13 *The Sense of the Presence of God: Gifford Lectures 1961–2* (Oxford: Oxford University Press, 1962), p. 199.

14 *The Sense of the Presence of God*, p. 200.

15 Cf. 'World Religions and Christian Theology' in Ernst's collection of essays, *Multiple Echo: Explorations in Theology* (London: Darton, Longman & Todd, 1979), pp. 28–40.

16 Quite simply, if we acknowledge the truth-claims of 'non-incarnational' faiths, then the incarnation – understood as the locus of God's self-revelation and saving activity – effectively becomes a dispensable explanatory 'myth'. We can see this principle at work in Hick's theology of world religions: Hick's understanding of the relationship between Christianity and the other world religions requires christology to be 'non-incarnational'. Cf. especially *God and the Universe of Faiths*, chapters 8–12. For the purposes of this essay I have overlooked the

arguments of Wilfred Cantwell Smith, who questions the propriety of notions like 'a religion', 'Christianity', 'Buddhism', etc., and who goes on to argue that the question of conflicting truth-claims is not a legitimate question because it involves a reification of notions like 'a religion', and so forth. Cf. *The Meaning and End of Religion* (London: SPCK, 1978). Cantwell Smith's views are cogently criticized in Ninian Smart, 'Truth and Religions' in *TD*, pp. 45–58; and John Hick, 'The Outcome: Dialogue into Truth' in *TD*, pp. 140–55. Cantwell Smith's reply to the strictures of Smart and Hick is to be found in 'Conflicting Truth-Claims: A Rejoinder' in *TD*, pp. 156–62. The dilemma just referred to can be bypassed by 'cultural-linguistic', as opposed to 'propositional', accounts of religion. For such accounts, cf. George Lindbeck's *TND*. Lindbeck's application of the 'cultural-linguistic' account to the theology of world religions is discussed in chapter 10 below.

17 *CD*, 1/2, pp. 301–2.
18 This, of course, is the 'positivism of revelation' that Bonhoeffer complained about. Cf. his *LPP*, pp. 286, 328. A valuable discussion of Bonhoeffer's criticisms of Barth's 'positivism of revelation' is to be found in Regin Prenter, 'Dietrich Bonhoeffer and Karl Barth's Positivism of Revelation' in *WCA*, pp. 93–130. This issue is further discussed in chapter 11 below.
19 I do not wish to dwell too long on Barth's disparagement of the way liberal theology treats the subject of revelation – this is too complex and important a question to be dealt with in a few paragraphs. I want only to suggest that a blanket condemnation of liberal theology might obscure the fact that, at a very fundamental level, liberal theology and 'neo-orthodoxy' are not as starkly antithetical as they are sometimes made out to be. *Both* 'neo-orthodoxy' and 'liberal theology' can be said to have arisen as (alternative) responses to the (*same*) challenge posed by Enlightenment (especially Kantian) thought for theology. Kant's significance for modern theology lies of course in his 'demonstration' that theological truths cannot be established by arguments based on 'pure reason'. Schleiermacher – Barth's *bête noire* – was mindful of Kant's stricture on rational theology, and sought as a consequence to ground theology in a phenomenology of human consciousness. 'Neo-orthodoxy', having found it easy to accept Kant's abjuration of rational theology, and having rejected as 'semi-pantheistic' the immanent theism of liberal theology (a rejection which naturally led 'neo-orthodoxy' to emphasize the discontinuities between the divine and human realms), had therefore to ground theology in revelation *simpliciter*. However, because 'neo-orthodoxy' and liberal theology *both* endorse the Enlightenment's prohibition on a rational 'theism', they have in common a desire to give the notion of *faith* a central place in their respective theologies. ('Faith' here being taken to be – virtually by definition – the antithesis of 'reason'.) However, while liberal theology explicates faith in terms of the phenomenology of Christian *experience*, 'neo-orthodoxy' understands faith as the human response to divine

revelation. Thus a deeper analysis of the underlying principles of 'neo-orthodoxy' and liberalism serves to confirm that these two approaches have some important things in common (e.g. the significance that both attach to the notion of faith, their mutual repudiation of *a priori* 'theism'), and that it is therefore somewhat misleading to view them as two totally incompatible forms of theological reflection. This somewhat lengthy excursus into the relationship between 'neo-orthodoxy' and theological liberalism is necessary because exponents of 'Christocentrism' tend usually to appeal to revelation when justifying their ascription of a unique status to the figure of Christ, whereas their opponents invariably argue that it is precisely this understanding of revelation which generates the so-called 'scandal of particularity' that lies at the heart of 'Christocentrism'. We shall be taking up this point later – cf. pp. 143ff below.

20 Thus Bonhoeffer seems to have certain aspects of Barth's understanding of revelation in mind when he says:

> In revelation it is less a question of God's freedom on the far side from us, i.e. his eternal isolation and aseity, than ... in his having freely bound himself to historical man, having placed himself at man's disposal. God is not free *of* man but *for* man. Christ is the Word of his freedom, God is *there*, which is to say: not in eternal non-objectivity but ... 'haveable', graspable in his Word within the Church. (*AB*, pp. 90–1)

Though, to be fair, it must be admitted that Barth scaled-down the 'diastasis' between revelation and human culture, and moved towards a position like Bonhoeffer's in his later writings (especially in his study of St Anselm, *Fides Quaerens Intellectum: Anselms Beweis der Existenz Gottes*, 1931), where he aligns himself with Anselm's view that faith's search for understanding *can* be a rational quest. For discussion of this issue. cf. chapter 11 below.

21 Prenter, 'Bonhoeffer and Barth' in *WCA*, p. 98. Prenter is here interpreting Bonhoeffer's criticism of Barth's failure to exclude 'any unrelatedness between revelation and the world'.

22 *MGI*, p. 182.

23 In the discussion which follows I shall be using ideas developed in chapters 4, 5, 6 and 7. The interested reader is recommended to consult these chapters for a more substantial treatment of issues involved in the argument I propose to develop in the remainder of this essay.

24 Donald MacKinnon, 'Subjective and Objective Conceptions of Atonement' in *PFT*, p. 181. Our 'model' is an 'ideal-typical' construction – indeed it cannot be anything else. However, as a 'model' it purports to depict what we crudely call 'reality' (in this case the 'reality' of the salvation that God brings to his creation); and it is also validated (or invalidated) by this 'reality'.

25 This 'anthropological concentration' is intended purely as a heuristic device, designed to ascertain, from an *anthropological* standpoint, the viability of the soteriologies of the various world religions. It does not in any way imply that the theology of God's saving work has to be *deduced*

from an anthropological statement of human needs – to do this would be to make theology subservient to anthropology. Barth, however, would maintain that in spite of this *caveat*, our procedure, precisely because it is lacking in 'christological concentration', is such that it cannot in principle tell us anything significant about God's gracious and saving activity:

> the covenant of grace which is ... the presupposition of the atonement ... is not amenable to any kind of human reflection or to any question asked by man concerning the meaning and basis of the cosmos or history.

(*CD*, II/1, p. 168)

It seems to me, however, that our purpose in delineating an anthropologically-based salvation-scheme is not strictly at odds with a theology which regards as paramount the free and sovereign work of God. For it may be that while the theology of salvation has to start from this gracious work of God, it is nevertheless true that our understanding of salvation (i.e. the '*epistemology*' of salvation) has an undeniable anthropological component. This anthropological component, however, is always subordinate to the notion of the outworking of divine grace.

26 Thus Sebastian Moore defines sin, in part, as the expression of fear in the form of hate. Cf. *CNS*, p. 12.

27 This moral 'realist' position is elaborated in chapter 6 above.

28 Rowan Williams, *WK*, p. 10. Williams, of course, makes this point in connection with a specifically Christian soteriology.

29 Thus, one such critic, Geoffrey Lampe, argues that God's identification with human beings in and through Jesus Christ is better construed in an 'inspirational', and not an 'ontological', sense. Cf. his *GS*.

30 Cf., e.g., the various essays in *MGI*.

31 This problem is traditionally referred to as the 'soteriological test' of christology. John Knox provides what is perhaps the most succinct formulation of this problem: 'How could Christ have saved us if he were not a human being like us? How could a human being like us have saved?' Cf. *The Humanity and Divinity of Christ* (Cambridge: Cambridge University Press, 1967), p. 52. Cf. also Charles Moule, 'Three Points of Conflict in the Christological Debate' in *IM*, pp. 139–40.

32 There is no necessary connection between 'exemplarism' and 'reductionist' christologies. Thus, it seems possible to adopt a 'reductionist' christology and to be able still to assert that Christ is *more* than just an exemplary figure – as Peter Baelz rightly points out, it is possible to say that the *man* Jesus is the supreme and unsurpassable instance of the divine self-giving, which would commit us to a 'reductionist' christology but seemingly not to 'exemplarism'. Cf. Baelz's critique of Maurice Wiles's influential paper, 'Does Christology Rest on a Mistake?', titled 'A Deliberate Mistake?' in *CFH*, pp. 13–34, especially p. 33. On the other hand, it is difficult to conceive of an 'exemplarism' that does not commit us to a 'reductionist' christology.

33 For Lampe's account, cf. his 'The Saving Work of Christ' in N. Pittenger, ed., *Christ for Us Today* (London: SCM Press, 1968), p. 149

34 *GS*, p. 116.

35 I would be doing Lampe a grave injustice if in raising this objection I imputed to him the belief that grace is an impersonal and mechanical force which 'invades' human beings. Lampe explicitly disowns this conception of grace. However, defining grace as the personal presence of God leaves him with the problem of accounting for those cases in which divine grace appears to be 'ineffective'. Can we ever say that the *personal presence* of God is not truly salvific? Lampe is mindful of this problem, and in addressing himself to it he says:

> Grace cannot be without effect. In the short term, at least, its effect may be two-edged, according as it is rejected or embraced by faith: the retention or the remission of sin. In the last resort, however, the Christian hope . . . must be that grace prevails, by the power of attraction. ('The Saving Work of Christ', p. 149)

But this only raises, but does not answer, the question: What is it that enables human beings to succumb to this power of attraction? And the answer, surely, is: salvation! So, again, it appears that the question of salvation is begged.

36 It is a corollary of our argument that the 'demythologized' (i.e. 'non-incarnational') christology of the authors of *The Myth of God Incarnate* is *not*, and indeed cannot be, the basis of a soteriology that describes a genuine salvation.

37 Unless, of course, soteriology is, from the outset, totally saturated with 'Christocentric' elements supplied by revelation. The stricture that 'Christocentrism' must ultimately rest *entirely* on revelation is of course quite congenial to neo-Barthians.

38 For our purposes the 'moderate Christocentrist' is the theologian who while maintaining that the incarnation of Christ is a unique and unsurpassable revelatory and salvific event, nevertheless allows that a measure of divine truth and salvation can be found in non-Christian faiths.

39 To use a term of H. H. Farmer's. Cf. his *Revelation and Reason* (London: Nisbet, 1954), pp. 195–6.

40 As has already been pointed out, the acceptance of this particular instantiation depends on a response of faith to a truth of revelation. It has to be emphasized that the locution 'God choosing to be incarnate', and its cognates, should always be regarded as a mere form of words – otherwise we will find ourselves employing a mode of christological discourse that is patently 'adoptionist'.

41 'Evil and Incarnation' in *IM*, p. 81.

42 For example, it would be axiomatic that Christianity is the only 'incarnational' faith if it were insisted that the incarnation be understood exclusively in terms of the categories employed by the New Testament writers and the Fathers of the early church.

43 Thus John Robinson says: '*Christos*, the Christ figure, can stand also for the broader notion of the "visibility of the invisible", the mystery of *theos*, of the ultimate reality of God, or *Brahman*, made manifest, embodied in history'. Cf. *TT–E*, p. 42.

44 Since syncretism lies at the centre of Hinduism's 'openness' to other faiths, any obstacles to the formulation of a coherent syncretism will obviously reduce the likelihood of a successful reconciliation between the *avatar* doctrine and the Christian doctrine of the incarnation.

45 Cf. *TT–E*, p. 44, where Robinson borrows these images from Lesslie Newbigin, *The Finality of Christ* (London: SCM Press, 1969), pp. 65ff.

46 In fairness, it should be pointed out that there is only one *avatar* in the *Bhagavad Gita* (viz., Krishna). However, the *Mahabharata* (the larger epic of which the *Gita* is a part) contains ten *avatars*, four of which are animal incarnations. After the *Mahabharata*, the principle of repetition enables the number of incarnations to increase, so that by the time of the *Bhagavad Purana* (ninth century AD) there are twenty-two *avatars*, including the Buddha. It should perhaps also be mentioned that although the *avatar* doctrine is present in the *Gita*, the word *avatar* (*avatara*, coming-down) is not actually to be found in the *Gita*, though it occurs in other sections of the *Mahabharata*. I am indebted to Geoffrey Parrinder's discussion of these matters in his 'The Place of Jesus Christ in World Religions' in N. Pittenger, ed., *Christ for Us Today*, pp. 13–28.

47 *The Message of Christ* (Bombay, 1940). Quoted in *TT–E*, p. 50.

48 *Essays on the Gita* (Pondicherry: Birth Centenary Library XIII, 1970), p. 12. Quoted in *TT–E*, p. 50.

49 *Works I* (Calcutta: Mayavatis Memorial Edition, 1955–62), p. 328. Quoted in *TT–E*, p. 50.

50 'Fragments of a Confession' in P. A. Schilpp, ed., *The Philosophy of Sarvepalli Radhakrishnan* (Cambridge: Cambridge University Press, 1952), p. 79. Quoted in *TT–E*, pp. 50–1. Radhakrishnan's passage bears illuminating comparison with the following words of Rudolf Bultmann: 'we must speak of God as acting only in the sense that He acts with me here and now. . . . The word of God is Word of God only as it happens here and now.' Cf. his *Jesus Christ and Mythology* (London: SCM Press, 1958), pp. 78–82. While Bultmann accepts the historicality of the cross-event, it is clear that his more systematic work is pervaded (some would say vitiated) by an undercurrent of the very idealism which afflicts Radhakrishan's characterization of Jesus Christ.

51 Having said this, it is necessary for us to acknowledge that it is open to question whether the doctrine of the 'unreality' of the world (*maya-vada*) does in fact underpin the core of Hindu thought. For an important debate in Hindu thought concerns the question of the relation between *Brahman* and the world of experience. Sankara (c. 788–820 AD), as a result of his insistence that only the *Brahman* is truly 'real', concluded from this that the world of ordinary experience is in some sense illusory. Ramanuja (died c. 1137 AD) rejected the unqualified monism of Sankara, and advocated instead a doctrine of 'qualified non-dualism' (*vishishtadvaita*), which led him to reject Sankara's principle that the ordinary world is devoid of 'reality'. Ramanuja agreed that there is only one 'Reality', but he maintained that within this one 'Reality' there can be gradations of 'reality', including the

'reality' of the ordinary world. The world-affirming doctrine of Ramanuja and his school must therefore be seen as a counterbalance to the
negative tendency of Sankara. But the temptation to use Ramanuja and
his school to enhance the mutual compatibility of Hinduism and
Christianity must be resisted. For Ramanuja, having spurned the
doctrine of the 'unreality' of the world (as adumbrated by Sankara),
had therefore to allow that the world could partake of the one true
'Reality'; however, since he remained a monist, he had no alternative
but to say that in some sense *Brahman* and the ordinary world were the
same 'Reality'. This he in fact did, in his teaching that the ordinary
world is 'the body of God' (though he did maintain that the world is
subordinate to God). It is easy to see why Ramanuja had to espouse
pantheism: if there is just one 'Reality', which is identified with the
being of God, then either the being of God encompasses everything
(pantheism), or else it does not, in which case that which exists apart
from the being of God can only be 'unreal' or illusory. Ramanuja
embraced the former, and Sankara the latter, horn of this dilemma.
The thought of Ramanuja and his school is ineluctably pantheistic (or
panentheistic), and this should dampen the enthusiasm of those participants in the Hindu–Christian dialogue who see in the thought of
Ramanuja the basis for a possible reconciliation between the two
religions. For an attempt to pave the way for such a reconciliation,
using essentially Ramanujan categories, cf. Santosh Sengupta, 'The
Misunderstanding of Hinduism' in *TD*, pp. 96–110, especially
pp. 102–4. Grace Jantzen's *God's World, God's Body* (London:
Darton, Longman & Todd, 1984) formulates a Christian understanding
of the God–world relationship which is interestingly similar in its thrust
to Ramanuja's position (though Jantzen sees herself as espousing a
'holism' that transcends the 'monism–dualism' dichotomy).

52 Sengupta, 'The Misunderstanding of Hinduism', p. 106.
53 It is of course quite misleading to use the language of atonement,
propitiation, expiation, etc., in connection with Hinduism – if such
language is to make sense the concept of *sin* must be presupposed, and
Hinduism has no place for this concept.
54 This essay was written in 1982. I am now (1987) less convinced that the
salvation-scheme delineated herein is as free from Christian and
christological elements as I made it out to be. In retrospect, the
argument of this essay can be seen to have been pulled in two quite
different directions. At times I appeared to take seriously the 'incommensurability' of the different religious paradigms. An unstinting
acknowledgement of this 'incommensurability' would have precluded –
in principle – the making of comparisons between 'incommensurable'
religious paradigms. And yet the whole thrust of my salvation-scheme
was precisely to facilitate the making of just such comparisons
(specifically in respect of the soteriological efficacy of the different
religious traditions). I have since decided to take 'incommensurability'
more seriously (and consistently!), and this has involved discarding the
salvation-scheme outlined here. The scheme continues to have a certain

heuristic value, inasmuch as it displays something of the nature of the kind of claim that the Christian has to make if he or she is to live in the world projected by the constitutive texts of the Christian faith. Chapter 10 provides an account more representative of my current thinking on the theology of religions.

10. 'Many religions and the one true faith': Lindbeck's chapter 3

1 *TND*. Hereinafter all page references to this work will be given in parentheses in the main text.

2 For a more extended discussion of the relation between 'intratextualism' and 'extratextualism', see chapter 12 below.

3 For a critique of this ideology, cf. my 'Towards a "Materialist" Critique of "Religious Pluralism": An Examination of the Discourse of John Hick and Wilfred Cantwell Smith' in Ian Hamnett, ed., *Proceedings of the 1987 Colston Symposium on Religious Pluralism* (forthcoming).

4 For Lindbeck's critique of this 'experiential-expressivist' assumption, cf. pp. 31ff. It should be noted that Lindbeck does not concern himself in any direct way with the 'pluralism' of Hick and Cantwell Smith. For surveys of 'religious pluralism', cf. Paul F. Knitter, *No Other Name?: A Critical Survey of Christian Attitudes Toward the World Religions* (London: SCM Press, 1985), *passim*; and Gavin D'Costa, *Theology and Religious Pluralism: The Challenge of Other Religions* (Oxford: Blackwell, 1986), chapter 1. Germane in this context is Knitter's charge, on pp. 44ff., that Cantwell Smith uses the notion of a universal faith as part of a reconstructed 'common essence' approach to the world religions. On faith as a 'generic' attribute of humanity, see Cantwell Smith's *Faith and Belief* (Princeton, NJ: Princeton University Press, 1979), pp. 129–72. John Hick endorses the broad outlines of Cantwell Smith's construal of 'faith' in his 'Foreword' to the latter's *The Meaning and End of Religion: A Revolutionary Approach to the Great World Religions* (London: SPCK, 1978). Cf. pp. xiv–xviii. In his contribution to the Cantwell Smith *Festschrift* Hick says that Cantwell Smith uses 'faith' to refer 'to the spiritual state, or existential condition, constituted by a person's present response to the ultimate divine Reality.... This ... is essentially the same within the different religious contexts within which it occurs....' Cf. John Hick, 'Religious Pluralism' in Frank Whaling, ed., *The World's Religious Traditions: Essays in Honour of Wilfred Cantwell Smith* (Edinburgh: T. & T. Clark, 1984), p. 148. In Lindbeck's scheme of things, therefore, Cantwell Smith and Hick are appropriately to be regarded as 'experiential-expressivists'.

5 Cf. especially pp. 63ff. It should be emphasized that the preceding discussion of unsurpassability derives its relevant context solely from Lindbeck's elaboration of the 'cultural-linguistic' model. What has been made available so far therefore is only the equivalent of a formal or uninterpreted 'syntax' for this concept. To furnish an interpretation or 'semantics' for 'unsurpassability' it will be necessary to scrutinize the 'intratextual' dimension of Lindbeck's programme.

6 Here I am mindful of Nicholas Lash's stress on the need for Christian

discourse to be self-reflexively and permanently 'iconoclastic'. Cf. his *A Matter of Hope: A Theologian's Reflections on the Thought of Karl Marx* (London: Darton, Longman & Todd, 1981), p. 132. Cf. also Lash's essays 'Should Christianity be Credible?' and 'The Church and Christ's Freedom' in his *TDB*, pp. 77–85 and 137–49 respectively. The need for such a Christian self-reflexive 'iconoclasm' in the context of Jewish–Christian dialogue is enjoined by Johann Baptist Metz in his essay 'Christians and Jews After Auschwitz' in his *The Emergent Church: The Future of Christianity in a Postbourgeois World*, trans. Peter Mann (London: SCM Press, 1981), pp. 17–33.

There is an ambiguity in Lindbeck's delineation of the 'unsurpassability' of a religion. When he likens a 'lived religion' to a 'gigantic proposition' (p. 51), Lindbeck indicates that what makes this proposition 'true' is 'the extent that its objectivities *are* interiorized and exercised by groups and individuals. . . . ' (my emphasis). However, on p. 52 he states that an unsurpassable religion is one which 'is *capable* of being rightly utilized. . . . ' (my emphasis). In the former case the 'utilization' in question is evidently deemed to be one that *is in fact* realized or which *has in fact to be* realized; in the latter it is clear that only a '*capacity*' for such 'utilization' is being talked about. Lindbeck is keen to stress that it is the *historical* practice of the community of faith which is determinative for the issue of truth, and this would favour the first reading of 'unsurpassability'. But this reading sits less easily with a 'prospective *fides ex auditu*' theory than the second one, and this must cause us to favour the latter gloss: the '*ex auditu*' theory, after all, is absolutely crucial for Lindbeck's theology of religions.

For a similar eschatological theology of religions, albeit a 'Catholic' one which does not invoke the patently 'Protestant' *ex auditu* notion, see Joseph A. DiNoia, 'Implicit Faith, General Revelation and the State of Non-Christians', *Th*, 47 (1983), 209–41; and 'The Universality of Salvation and the Diversity of Religious Aims', *Worldmission*, 32 (1981–2), 4–15.

7 Lindbeck's denial of the necessity of 'a primordial, prereflective experience of Christ's grace' is of course a criticism of a basic presupposition of Karl Rahner's theory of 'anonymous Christianity'. It should be noted that Lindbeck is careful to state that a 'prospective *fides ex auditu*' theory is only compatible with, and not implied by, the 'cultural-linguistic' model of religion (cf. p. 57).

8 In a trival sense, of course, our existence can be terminated only if it has first begun. Cf. Nicholas Lash, 'Eternal Life: Life "After" Death?' in *TDB*, pp. 164–80. Cf. especially pp. 169ff. I am deeply indebted to this essay for my subsequent remarks. Hereinafter all page references to it will be given in parentheses in the main text. A conception of the 'after-life' similar in outline to Lindbeck's is to be found in the articles of Joseph DiNoia cited in note 6 above.

9 Like Lash, Eberhard Jüngel is alert to the truth that 'death is just as much a social fact as life itself'. Cf. his *Death: The Riddle and the Mystery*, trans. Iain and Ute Nicol (Edinburgh: The Saint Andrew

Press, 1975), p. 31. On the body as a repository of social and cultural inscriptions, see Elaine Scarry, *The Body in Pain: The Making and Unmaking of the World* (New York: Oxford University Press, 1985), where it is argued, on pp. 118–19, that death empties the body of 'reference'. Cf. also Bryan S. Turner, *Religion and Social Theory* (London: Heinemann, 1983), chapter 5, for an account of the body as a repository of socio-religious inscriptions. On the body as a social product, see Pierre Bourdieu, *Distinction: A Social Critique of the Judgement of Taste*, trans. Richard Nice (London: Routledge & Kegan Paul, 1984), pp. 190ff. On the body as an object from which might be 'read' a history of power relations, see Michel Foucault, *Discipline and Punish: The Birth of the Prison*, trans. Alan Sheridan (New York: Vintage/Random House, 1979). Theologians who follow Lash in repudiating a 'subsequence' theory of the relation of time to eternity include Jüngel, Barth and Rahner. One consequence of Lindbeck's adherence to the 'subsequence' theory has been a quite evident (and extremely problematic) separation of salvation from creation – a feature of Lindbeck's 'cultural-linguistic' model rightly noted by Colman E. O'Neill, OP, in his 'The Rule Theory of Doctrine and Propositional Truth', *Th*, 49 (1985), 426–7. For an argument against this separation, cf. chapter 8 above; and Nicholas Lash, 'How Do We Know Where We Are?', *Theology on the Way to Emmaus* (London: SCM Press, 1986), pp. 67ff.

10 A possible clue as to how Lindbeck might approach our hypothetical case of the Jewish concentration-camp victim is provided by the following sentence from his earlier *The Future of Roman Catholic Theology* (London: SPCK, 1970): 'there is no salvation apart from Christ, for one day all the redeemed will confess that it is through him they are saved even though they may not have known it in this time between the times in which we live' (p. 36).

11 For a lucid conspectus of the history of the *extra ecclesiam nulla salus* doctrine, see Gavin D'Costa, '*Extra Ecclesiam Nulla Salus* Revisited' in Ian Hamnett, ed., *Proceedings of the 1987 Colston Symposium on Religious Pluralism* (forthcoming).

12 This further confirms my earlier claim, made on p. 169 above, that Lindbeck is properly to be regarded as an 'eschatological universalist' who is nonetheless wedded to the 'exclusivist' criterion of an explicit confession of Christ on the part of all who are candidates for deliverance. I use 'exclusivism' and 'inclusivism' purely as terms of art. In the essay cited in note 3 above I argue that these terms are entirely factitious, in as much as their deployment depends on an ideology – that of 'religious pluralism' – which obscures the material and historical conditions which generate and sustain the principles propounded by those who place themselves in the service of this ideology.

For further evidence of Lindbeck's 'quasi-universalism', cf. his *The Future of Roman Catholic Theology*, pp. 35 and 38. While, for reasons already indicated, the business of 'right utilization' cannot for Lindbeck have any bearing on the matter of Christianity's unsurpassability, it nevertheless remains the case that Christians will *themselves* need to continue to be interested in the 'right utilization' of their religion – in Lindbeck's 'meta-soteriology' such 'right utilization' will be consequential in determining whether they are truly for or against Christ. It is hard not to notice how this 'meta-soteriology' bears some of the traces of a characteristically Protestant 'decisionism'.

13 The above-mentioned contention that there can ultimately be only one candidate for the status of the 'categorially true' religion is compatible with both the stronger and the weaker versions of 'categorial unsurpassability' identified by Lindbeck. There is, it should be noted, a strong hint on p. 61 that Lindbeck's own preference is for the latter of these two versions of 'categorial unsurpassability'.

14 This passage seems to confirm that Lindbeck's overall inclination is to accept the weaker of the two senses of 'categorial unsurpassability' (as mentioned in note 13 above). Lindbeck's viewpoint is somewhat similar in its gist to that adopted by the late John Baillie in his Gifford Lectures:

we must not say that in the pagan religions [*sic*] there is no apprehension of God's healing and saving power and no measure of trustful acceptance of it. The ardent seeking which is there manifested bears witness to minds that have already been invaded by the presence of God, whom none can seek unless he has first been seeking them or even . . . unless they have in some measure found him. Each one of the pagan religions has some light in it, but it has also much darkness – and how great is that darkness! There is something in each that makes for spiritual health, but there is much also that makes for spiritual disorder and sickness. . . . I have thus no hesitation in reaffirming my conviction that only by following the Way of Christ is there any hope for the ultimate salvation of mankind. (John Baillie, *The Sense of the Presence of God: Gifford Lectures 1961–2*, London: Oxford University Press, 1962, pp. 199–200)

For further discussion of Baillie's position, cf. chapter 9 above.

15 Tracy's main criticism of Lindbeck is that the author of *The Nature of Doctrine* is insufficiently 'ecumenical' in his attitude to theologies. See David Tracy, 'Lindbeck's New Program for Theology: A Reflection', *Th*, 49 (1985), 460–72. Tracy is an advocate of what he calls 'revisionist theology'. William C. Placher, in contrasting this theology with Lindbeck's 'postliberal' theology, says that 'revisionist theologians tend to think that both theological language and Scripture symbolically convey a religious dimension of experience or a possibility for human existence'. Cf. his 'Revisionist and Postliberal Theologies and the Public Character of Theology', *Th*, 49 (1985), 392. For a discussion of the relation between these two theologies, especially with regard to the issues posed by 'textuality' for ecclesiology, see chapter 12 below.

16 It should again be noted that Lindbeck states clearly that an 'intratextual' theological method is 'compatible' with the 'cultural-linguistic' model of religion, and is not necessarily to be identified with the latter. Cf. pp. 113–14.

17 Interestingly, Lindbeck notes that 'Christians in the first centuries appear to have had an extraordinary combination of relaxation and urgency in their attitude toward those outside the church.... The early Christians both before and after the New Testament said too little about these matters to provide a basis for deciding between our two options or for some other alternative' (p. 58). One of the several possible historical reasons for this 'combination of relaxation and urgency' was that emergent Christianity only demarcated itself from *particular* Jewish groups in an *ad hoc* and unsystematic way. In his masterly survey of the beginnings of Christianity, Christopher Rowland studies the available historical evidence and concludes that early Christians were only in dispute with *certain* Jewish groups, and that it is therefore misleading to suggest that there was from the beginning a clearly-defined dispute between two '*religions*', namely, 'Judaism' and 'Christianity'. Rather, disputes between the early Christian movement and certain Jews focused on their respective interpretations of a common ancestral tradition – and in this respect Christianity was not unique among apostate Jewish groups. Cf. Christopher Rowland, *Christian Origins: An Account of the Setting and Character of the Most Important Messianic Sect of Judaism* (London: SPCK, 1985), pp. 299–308. It would seem that early Christianity could afford to be 'relaxed' in its attitude to non-Christians primarily because its adherents, while they were fairly uncompromising in their affirmation of the decisiveness of the Christ-event, did not (or were not able to) reify their faith into an 'essence' which could then be set over against competing alternatives in a neat and easily distinguishable way. I am suggesting, in other words, that the question of a religion's 'unsurpassability' only becomes urgent, or can only be perceived to be urgent, when that religion is presumed to have an 'essence' which can then be placed alongside other competing 'essences' and subjected to a 'good look'. It is most likely that early Christianity did not burden itself with this presumption. This view receives further support when attention is paid to the way the doctrinal structure of the early church functioned. Citing Irenaeus' *Adversus Haereses* and Tertullian's *Scorpiace*, R. A. Markus argues that for the early church 'criteria of orthodoxy ... seem to meet a more fundamental need. They enabled men to answer the question: "where, really, is the church to be found?", rather than the different question – closely related though it is – "what is the true teaching of the church?".... [W]hat mattered was not the precise shades of the true teaching but the identity of the Christian church....' Cf. R. A. Markus, 'The Problem of Self-Definition: From Sect to Church' in E.P. Sanders, ed., *Jewish and Christian Self-Definition: Vol. One (The Shaping of Christianity in the Second and Third Centuries)* (London: SCM Press, 1980), p. 5. If Markus is right, this doctrinal structure is not easily assimilable into any kind of essentializing discourse.

18 Thus Lindbeck says on p. 53 that '[religious] languages may be as different as Leibniz's calculus and Shakespeare's sonnets so that translation between them is impossible....'

19 T. S. Kuhn, *The Logic of Scientific Revolutions* (Chicago: University of Chicago Press, 2nd enlarged ed, 1970), p. 150. My espousal of the view that the religions are 'incommensurable' should not be taken to imply that no one religion can (in principle) be compared with another. A theological follower of Paul Feyerabend may be inclined to accept such an understanding of 'incommensurability', but it is not one which is intrinsic to my own position. Such rational comparisons, however, can only be made on a piecemeal and 'nonglobal' scale, that is, relative to a particular and historically-situated conceptual scheme.

20 For Rorty's definition of 'abnormal discourse', see his *Philosophy and the Mirror of Nature* (Oxford: Blackwell, 1980), p. 11, where he says that 'normal discourse ... is any discourse (scientific, political, theological or whatever) which embodies agreed-upon criteria for reaching agreement; abnormal discourse is any which lacks such criteria'. The state of affairs just sketched is of course gratuitously and even grotesquely speculative. We have no knowledge of what our language is being asked to do when we use it to speak about such matters, and one of the attendant drawbacks of the 'subsequence' theory is that it encourages theologians and philosophers to speak precisely when a chaste silence about such items as 'what goes on' in an 'after-life' is counselled. Lindbeck is very circumspect in his presentation of the 'eschatological *fides ex auditu*' theory, but it is hard to resist the thought that he has already said too much in mooting the ideas which underlie this theory. I am only too painfully aware that my discussion of this theory will give the impression that there is a language that can enable us to speak adequately about eternity. There is no such language, but I am compelled to speak in such terms simply in order to communicate my conviction that Lindbeck has spoken with too much clarity when he propounds his 'prospective *fides ex auditu*' theory – in such cases an interlocutor like myself has sometimes to speak in the language of the interlocuted subject (in this case Lindbeck's). The difficulty here is that such language about eternity must also be a language that is in some sense 'about' God, and such a language is difficult to conceive because God, as St Thomas Aquinas notes, is beyond any genus, even that of substance. On this, cf. St Thomas, *DePot* 7 3 and 3–5; *deT* 1 2 and 4. For this reason St Thomas insists that at the beatific vision we shall see God 'without a medium'. Cf. *CG*, III. 51. Those persuaded by St Thomas's analysis will therefore find it difficult to grant a basic operating condition for the '*fides ex auditu*' theory, namely, that we shall 'hear' the crucified and risen Lord in the 'after-life'. For it is hard to see what meaning can be attached to 'hearing' when no linguistic medium is available.

21 For a fuller discussion of Lindbeck's treatment of 'textuality', cf. chapter 12 below.

22 In a letter written in 1961 Barth gives the following statement of the position I am trying to adumbrate:
> Eternal life is not another, second life beyond our present one, but the reverse side of *this* life, as God sees it, which is hidden from us

here and now. It is this life in relationship to what God has done in Jesus Christ for the whole world and also for us. So we wait and hope – in respect of our death – to be made *manifest* with him (Jesus Christ who is raised from the dead).

Cf. Eberhard Busch, *Karl Barth: His Life from Letters and Auto-biographical Texts*, trans. John Bowden (London: SCM Press, 1976), p. 488. Quoted in Lash, 'Eternal Life', p. 173.

23 This, of course, is Aquinas's understanding of what is involved in accepting that God is Creator. On this, cf. the discussion in David B. Burrell, *A*, p. 139. Cf. also my 'Some Aspects of the "Grammar" of "Incarnation": Reflections Prompted by the Writings of Donald MacKinnon' in Kenneth Surin, ed., *Christ, Ethics and Tragedy: Essays in Honour of Donald MacKinnon* (Cambridge: Cambridge University Press, forthcoming).

24 On God's 'speaking' in both divine 'utterance' and human 'response', cf. Rowan Williams, 'Trinity and Revelation', *MT*, 2 (1986), 210. I am grateful to Gerard Loughlin for drawing my attention to this aspect of Williams's essay in his unpublished '"Audacious Yet Hopeless Dogmatism": Toward the Proper Autonomy of Religion and Doctrine'.

25 As Nicholas Lash puts it, the separation between 'creation' and 'salvation' is 'formal' rather than '*material*' in character. See his 'How Do We Know Where We Are?', p. 68.

26 It is hard to be sure whether Lindbeck's criticisms of Rahner's concept of 'anonymous Christianity' are entirely probative. In his review of *The Nature of Doctrine*, Nicholas Lash suggests that Lindbeck's assumption that what Rahner terms 'basic experience' is somehow 'categorial' leads him to misunderstand the theory of 'anonymous Christianity'. For this review, see *NB*, 52 (1985), 509–10. It may be that Rahner's theory can be attenuated in such a way that it is seen to imply no more (and no less) than what we have just accepted, namely, that the history of salvation and the history of the world are 'materially co-extensive'. Rahner argues for this 'material co-extension' in his 'History of the World and Salvation-History', *Theological Investigations V* (London: Darton, Longman & Todd, 1961), p. 102. But in any case our fairly strong assertion of the incommensurability of religious paradigms would seem on the face of it to preclude a full or unqualified acceptance of the theory of 'anonymous Christianity' as a corollary of the notion of an 'implicit faith', a notion which Rahner certainly does employ (and which therefore makes him susceptible to the criticisms of Lindbeck and DiNoia).

27 In this paragraph I have been guided by some ideas of Nicholas Lash's, to be found in his *A Matter of Hope* (cited in note 6 above), pp. 193 and 256.

28 I am deeply indebted to Gavin D'Costa, Greg Jones and Gerard Loughlin for their penetrating comments and criticisms of an earlier draft of this essay. They are not of course responsible for the mistakes that remain.

11. Bonhoeffer's 'discipline of the secret' and Adorno's 'strategy of hibernation'

1 Cf. Robert H. King, 'The Task of Systematic Theology' in Peter C. Hodgson and Robert H. King, eds., *Christian Theology: An Introduction to Its Traditions and Tasks* (Philadelphia: Fortress Press, 1982), chapter 1.

2 *The Cost of Discipleship*, trans. R. H. Ruller (London: SCM Press, rev. edn, 1959), p. 38. For other accounts which view the growth of monasticism as a response to the corrupt religiosity of the Constantinian state, see Louis Bouyer, 'Asceticism in the Patristic Period' in *Christian Asceticism and Modern Man*, trans. W. Mitchell and the Carisbrooke Dominicans (London: Aquin, 1955), pp. 15–29; and R. McCulloch, 'Monks, Bishops, Society in 4th and 5th Century Empire', *Tjurunga*, 17 (1979), 57–76.

3 *PESC*, p. 119.

4 For Weber's distinction between these two types of asceticism, see his *The Sociology of Religion*, trans. E. Fischer (London: Methuen, 1965), pp. 166–8.

5 *PESC*, p. 154.

6 *PESC*, p. 154.

7 For Weber's account of the routinization of charisma, cf. *The Theory of Social and Economic Organization*, trans. A. M. Henderson and Talcott Parsons (New York: The Free Press, 1947), pp. 363–86. Hereinafter referred to as *TSEO*. It is perhaps noteworthy that one of the best-known monks of this century – Thomas Merton – provides a characterization of *contemptus mundi* that is in virtual accord with Weber's delineation of Christian asceticism in a 'disenchanted' world. To quote Merton: 'True *contemptus mundi* is rather a *compassion* for the transient world and a humility which refuses arrogantly to set up the Church as an "eternal" institution in the world. But if we despise the transient world of secularism in terms which suggest an ecclesiastical *world* that is not itself transient, there is no way to avoid disaster and absurdity.' Cf. Thomas Merton, *Conjectures of a Guilty Bystander* (London: Sheldon Press, 1977), p. 52.

   So far only Weber's account of the historical development of Christian asceticism has been discussed. It will be necessary to consider his 'dialectic of social rationalization' later on: it will be one of the main contentions of this essay that Bonhoeffer's version of *contemptus mundi* – i.e. his conception of the 'discipline of the secret' (*Arkandisziplin*) – founders on the 'dialectic of social rationalization'.

8 *Ethics*, trans. N. H. Smith (London: Collins, 1964), p. 96. Weber, one imagines, would find little to quarrel with in this passage of Bonhoeffer's. Both Alfred and Max Weber were visitors to the Bonhoeffer household during Dietrich's childhood days in Berlin, and Bonhoeffer's attention had been drawn to Weber's work in his last year at school (1922). Furthermore, in a letter of 9 August 1924 he mentions having read Weber's 'interesting' *Sociology of Religion*. Cf. Eberhard Berthge, *Dietrich Bonhoeffer: A Biography*, trans. Eric Mosbacher *et al.* (London: Collins, 1970), p. 50. But it should be acknowledged that

Weber is never mentioned at any point in *The Letters and Papers from Prison*, even when Bonhoeffer is elaborating his idea of a world 'come of age'. In addition, Peter Berger has argued convincingly that the major weakness of *Sanctorum Communio* is Bonhoeffer's failure to come to terms with the thought of Marx and Weber – when Bonhoeffer needed a sociological framework for the ecclesiology of *Sanctorum Communio*, he turned to the representatives of the so-called formalistic school of systematic sociology (Tönnies, Vierkandt, Litt), and over-looked Weber. Cf. Peter Berger, 'The Social Character of the Question Concerning Jesus' in Martin E. Marty, ed., *The Place of Bonhoeffer* (London: SCM Press, 1963), p. 58. Tönnies's 'resigned romanticism' pervades the socio-ecclesiology of *Sanctorum Communio*, and much interesting work remains to be done on the romantic influences in Bonhoeffer's theology. On 'resigned romanticism', cf. Robert Sayre and Michael Löwy, 'Figures of Romantic Anti-Capitalism', *NGC*, 32 (1984), 42–92. Ernst Feil has shown that Bonhoeffer was acquainted with the writings of Dilthey (whose philosophy of history can be seen as an attempt to merge neo-Kantianism with a romanticist world-view). Cf. Feil, 'Der Einfluss Wilhelm Diltheys auf Dietrich Bonhoeffers "Widerstand und Ergebung"', *Evangelische Theologie*, 29 (1982), 662ff.

9 *LPP*, pp. 280–1. I have rendered *Arkandisziplin* as 'discipline of the secret' in preference to the more usual 'secret discipline'. The latter has connotations of an act of concealment, and it is fairly clear that Bonhoeffer did not intend this 'discipline' to be some kind of esoteric quasi-gnostic ritual.

10 *LPP*, p. 296.

11 Gerhard Ebeling has rightly pointed out that Bonhoeffer's treatment of Bultmann in *The Letters and Papers* is mistaken in several respects. Cf. his *Words and Faith*, trans. J. W. Leitch (Philadelphia: Fortress, 1963), pp. 103 and 139, footnote 2. A similar criticism of Bonhoeffer is made in Gerhard Krause, 'Dietrich Bonhoeffer and Rudolf Bultmann' in James M. Robinson, ed., *The Future of Our Religious Past: Essays in Honour of Rudolf Bultmann* (London: SCM Press, 1964), pp. 279–305. Bon-hoeffer had of course criticized Barth for his theological 'transcenden-talism' as early as his 1931 *Akt und Sein*. Cf. Bonhoeffer, *Act and Being*, trans. Bernard Noble (London: Collins, 1962), pp. 70f, 83f and 86f.

12 *The Free Man: Studies in Christian Anthropology* (London: Collins, 1969), p. 107. A similar interpretation of Bonhoeffer is to be found in John A. Phillips, *The Form of Christ in the World: A Study of Bonhoeffer's Christology* (London: Collins, 1967), p. 273. I do not accept Gregor Smith's claim that the 'existential dialectic' which he ascribes to Bonhoeffer is necessary because the Christian has to be both *for* the world (because God made it and loves it) and *against* it (because the world is sinful). *Pace* Gregor Smith, the tension in Bonhoeffer's theology of God's self-identification with the world (which leads Gregor Smith to posit this 'dialectic') arises not from any ontological or existential necessity, but from the very profaneness of the world. As

Weber shows, the world is 'disenchanted' (or 'dedivinized') because of the history of rationalization. Gregor Smith ontologizes, and therefore treats *ahistorically*, a tension in Bonhoeffer's thought whose provenance is essentially *historical*.

13 On Christ as the decisive revelation of God and as the community of believers, cf. Bonhoeffer's *Christology*, trans. E. Robinson (London: Collins, 1978), pp. 43–65 and 97; *Sanctorum Communio*, trans. R. Gregor Smith (London: Collins, 1963), pp. 103–55; and *Ethics*, pp. 188–213. There is a discussion of Bonhoeffer's two assumptions in Ray S. Anderson, *HTRG*, p. 96. Although Anderson's book is not an explicit discussion of Bonhoeffer's theology it is a profound and sustained attempt to resolve a theological problematic posed by Bonhoeffer's thought. Needless to say, I am much indebted to it. All future page references to *HTRG* will be given within the text.

14 For an illuminating discussion of Bonhoeffer's criticism of Barth, see Regin Prenter, 'Dietrich Bonhoeffer and Karl Barth's Positivism of Revelation', *WCA*, pp. 93–130. Bonhoeffer's strictures are somewhat surprising, given that he had expressed his approval of the shift in Barth's thinking represented by his book on Anselm. He conveyed his approbation to Barth himself in a letter of 19 September 1936, which makes it difficult to explain his reasons for continuing to accuse Barth of being a 'positivist'. For Bonhoeffer's letter to Barth, see Bonhoeffer, *Gesammelte Schriften: vol. II*, ed. E. Bethge (Munich: Kaiser Verlag, 1959), p. 285.

15 Bethge, *Biography*, p. 783.

16 As Bonhoeffer puts it: 'I should like to speak of God not on the boundaries but at the centre . . . The transcendence of epistemological theory has nothing to do with the transcendence of God. God is the beyond in the midst of life. The church stands, not at the boundaries where human powers give out, but in the middle. . . .' Cf. *LPP*, p. 283. Again it is possible to note Bonhoeffer's preference for a Hegelian, as opposed to a Kantian, approach to divine 'transcendence' – a Kantian approach would have delineated this 'transcendence' in terms of the noumenon-phenomenon distinction (i.e. *epistemologically*). Bonhoeffer's Hegelianism is attested to in Eberhard Bethge, 'The Challenge of Dietrich Bonhoeffer's Life and Theology', *WCA*, p. 28; and André Dumas, *Dietrich Bonhoeffer: Theologian of Reality*, trans. Robert McAfee Brown (London: SCM Press, 1971), pp. 31, 54 and 82f.; and Heinrich Ott, *Reality and Faith: The Theological Legacy of Dietrich Bonhoeffer*, trans. A. A. Morrison (London: Lutterworth Press, 1971), p. 221.

17 I am indebted to Prenter, 'Bonhoeffer and Barth', *WCA*, pp. 128ff. for his account of the difference between Barth's emphasis on act (i.e. cognition) and Bonhoeffer's stress on being (i.e. action).

18 *Ethics*, p. 195.

19 *Ethics*, p. 197. For an insightful discussion of Bonhoeffer's criticism of thinking in terms of two spheres, see Ebeling, pp. 115ff. See also Ernst Feil, *The Theology of Dietrich Bonhoeffer*, trans. Martin Rumscheidt (Philadelphia: Fortress Press, 1985), pp. 146ff.

20 This is Ebeling's own appraisal of the essence of Bonhoeffer's theological enterprise. Cf. p. 160.
21 Jürgen Habermas, 'The Dialectics of Rationalization' (Habermas interviewed by A. Honneth, E. Knödler-Bunte and A. Widmann), *T*, 49 (1981), 5–31.
22 *PESC*, pp. 54–181.
23 Weber, *TSEO*, p. 338.
24 Weber, *The Methodology of the Social Sciences*, trans. and ed. E. A. Shils and H. A. Finch (New York: The Free Press, 1949), p. 57.
25 Weber, *FMW*, p. 357.
26 *FMW*, p. 155.
27 *FMW*, p. 357.
28 In that it seemingly conceals the true extent and nature of the world's 'disenchantment' from the practitioners of the 'discipline of the secret'.
29 See, for example, his scathing dismissal of 'psychotherapists', in the letter of 8 June 1944, as people who 'wherever there is health, strength, security, simplicity, . . . scent fruit to gnaw or lay their pernicious eggs in' (*LPP*, p. 326). A similar position is taken up in the letter of 30 June 1944 (*LPP*, pp. 399–42). And if one considers that psychoanalysis is an integral constituent of any remotely plausible hermeneutics of 'suspicion', it is reasonable to believe that Bonhoeffer was not really in a position to acknowledge the need for such a hermeneutics. Unless, of course, he changed his mind. Bonhoeffer's ambivalent attitude towards the intellectual movements characteristic of modernity, and in particular his animus against the theories of Freud, is explored in G. Rothuizen, 'Bonhoeffer *Neuroticus*', *Gerereformeerd Theologische Tijdschrift*, 77 (1977), 120–32. In the same vein Hans Schmidt has made the pertinent remark that 'the problem of *history* in all its depth remained hidden from [Bonhoeffer]'. Cf. Schmidt, 'The Cross of Reality?', *WCA*, p. 219.
30 The incommensurability of paradigms is characterized thus by T. S. Kuhn:

> The proponents of competing paradigms are always at least slightly at cross-purposes. Neither side will grant all the non-empirical assumptions that the other needs in order to make its case. . . . Though each may hope to convert the other to his way of seeing . . . neither may hope to prove his case.
> . . . the proponents of competing paradigms will often disagree about the list of problems that any candidate for paradigm must resolve. Their standards or their definitions . . . are not the same.
> . . . the proponents of competing paradigms practice their trades in different worlds. . . . Practicing in different worlds, the two groups of proponents . . . see different things when they look from the same point in the same direction. Again, this is not to say they can see anything they please. Both are looking at the world, and what they look at has not changed. But in some areas they see different things, and they see them in different relations to one another. . . . The inevitable result is what we must call, though the

term is not quite right, a misunderstanding between two competing schools.

Cf. T. S. Kuhn, *The Structure of Scientific Revolutions* (Chicago and London: University of Chicago Press, 1962), pp. 147–9. Kuhn is of course talking about paradigms in natural science. But his views are, *mutatis mutandis*, also applicable to theological paradigms. The social and historical basis of paradigm shifts is lucidly discussed in Jeffrey Stout, *The Flight From Authority* (Notre Dame and London: University of Notre Dame Press, 1982).

31 Jacques Derrida, *Positions*, trans. Alan Bass (Chicago and London: University of Chicago Press, 1981), p. 6.

32 For a socio-historical critique of epistemological 'foundationalism', see the work by Stout cited in note 30 above. Cf. also Richard Rorty, *Philosophy and the Mirror of Nature* (Oxford: Blackwell, 1980).

33 *DE*, p. 3.

34 *DE*, pp. 3 and xi.

35 Some commentators on *Dialectic of Enlightenment* have mistakenly added the definite article to 'enlightenment', thereby implying that Adorno and Horkheimer take this term to designate the intellectual movement of the seventeenth and eighteenth centuries associated with the rise of modern science and philosophy. Adorno and Horkheimer, however, clearly use this term without the definite article, and take it to designate any attempt on the part of human beings to gain a *rational* domination over their surroundings.

36 *DE*, pp. 57–84.

37 According to Adorno, the 'reality' experienced by members of late capitalist society is necessarily distorted because 'no society which contradicts its very notion – that of mankind – can have full consciousness of itself'. Cf. his 'Cultural Criticism and Society' in his collection of essays *Prisms*, trans. S. and S. Weber (London: Spearman, 1967), p. 26. On this 'culture industry', see *DE*, pp. 120–67. See also Adorno's 'Culture Industry Reconsidered', *NGC*, 6 (1975), 12–19; and 'Culture and Administration', *T*, 37 (1978), 93–111.

38 T. W. Adorno, 'Society' in Robert Boyers, ed., *The Legacy of German Refugee Intellectuals* (New York: Schocken, 1972), pp. 144–53.

39 To quote Adorno: 'The superiority of objectification in the subjects not only keeps them from becoming subjects; it equally prevents a cognition of objectivity.' Cf. his *ND*, p. 171. Lacking this cognition of objectivity the modern individual becomes like 'the prisoner who loves his cell because he has nothing else to love'. Cf. Adorno, 'On the Fetish-Character in Music and the Regression in Listening' in A. Arato and E. Gebhardt, eds., *The Essential Frankfurt School Reader* (Oxford: Blackwell, 1978), p. 280.

40 T. W. Adorno, 'On the Historical Adequacy of Consciousness: An Interview with Peter von Haselberg', *T*, 56 (1983), 97–110.

41 Cf. Jürgen Habermas, 'Consciousness-Raising or Rescuing Critique' in his *Philosophical-Political Profiles*, trans. F. G. Lawrence (London: Heinemann, 1983), pp. 99–110.

42 Adorno, 'Commitment' in Robert Taylor, ed., *Aesthetics and Politics: Bloch, Lukacs, Brecht, Benjamin, Adorno* (London: Verso, 1977), p. 194.
43 Adorno, 'Die Aktualität der Philosophie' in *Gesammelte Schriften: Vol. 1* (Frankfurt: Suhrkamp Verlag, 1973), pp. 325–44.
44 Adorno, *ND*, p. 150.
45 Adorno, 'Schubert' in his *Moments Musicaux: Neugedruckte Aufsätze 1928 bis 1962* (Frankfurt: Suhrkamp Verlag, 1964), p. 26. At this juncture, Adorno's critique of reification reflects the profound influence exerted on him by Walter Benjamin. See Adorno, *Über Walter Benjamin* (Frankfurt: Suhrkamp Verlag, 1970). In view of Benjamin's undeniable influence on Adorno, Habermas's interesting attempt to differentiate clearly between an *Ideologiekritik* of the type favoured by Marcuse and Adorno and Benjamin's *Rettendekritik* is perhaps pressed too far. Cf. the essay by Habermas cited in note 41 above.
46 Adorno, *MM*, p. 73. In the same vein, Adorno says that 'Foolishness is the form in which truth strikes men when, surrounded on all sides by lies, they do not resist the truth.' Cf. his 'Bemerkungen über Politisch und Neurose' in *Kritik: Kleine Schriften zur Gesellschaft* (Frankfurt: Suhrkamp Verlag, 1971), p. 127.
47 Heiner Höfener, 'Sparks, Insanity and Fireworks', *T*, 46 (1980–1), 156.
48 Adorno, *MM*, p. 80.
49 Adorno, *MM*, p. 25. See also *ND*, p. 365, where Adorno says: 'if thinking is to be true – if it is to be true today, in any case – it must be a thinking against itself. If thought is not measured by the extremity that eludes the concept, it is from the outset in the nature of the musical accompaniment with which the *SS* liked to drown out the screams of its victims.'
50 Adorno, *MM*, p. 122.
51 Rowan Williams, in his valuable *WK*, speaks of the 'ironic sanity' which characterizes St Antony's renunciation of the worldly Christianity of the Constantinian Empire in favour of an *imitatio Christi* in the Egyptian desert. Williams discusses St Antony's saying, 'A time is coming when men will go mad, and when they see someone who is not mad, they will attack him saying, "You are mad, you are not like us"', and suggests that Antony's statement testifies to the 'intractable oddity of monasticism' (p. 92). Adorno would say that the time feared by Antony has indeed arrived, and that in today's totally administered society its arrival is indicated by a somnolent mass indifference to any attempted critique of society's reified fabric. The critic, who wants to rouse men and women from their sleep, risks being marginalized by society: he or she comes to be regarded as a nuisance, a fool, even a 'devil'. Jean-François Lyotard, who is generally critical of Adorno's 'negative dialectics', nevertheless acknowledges that Adorno's own marginalization was inevitable: 'once God fell mute . . . what place could Adorno assign himself, if not that of the devil? . . . When the Creation raves, it is the devil who risks being right. Nothing left to invoke, everything to revoke.' Cf. his 'Adorno as the Devil', *T*, 19 (1974), 127–37.

52 Adorno, *ND*, pp. 66–8.
53 Hans Schmidt suggests that Bonhoeffer inherited this problematic from Troeltsch. Cf. his 'The Cross of Reality?', *WCA*, pp. 217ff. See also Feil, *The Theology of Bonhoeffer*, p. 181.
54 Here Schmidt says that it is conceivable that Bonhoeffer might have substituted a 'positivism of the church' for Barth's 'positivism of revelation'. Cf. his 'The Cross of Reality?', *WCA*, p. 228.
55 Bonhoeffer, *Ethics*, pp. 198 and 201.
56 Cf. Paul Lehmann, 'The Concreteness of Theology: Reflections on the Conversation Between Barth and Bonhoeffer' in Martin Rumscheidt, ed., *Footnotes to a Theology: The Karl Barth Colloquium of 1972* (Waterloo, Ontario: Canadian Corporation for Studies in Religion), p. 67.
57 Bonhoeffer, *LPP*, pp. 328ff and 381ff.
58 Karl Barth, *Protestant Theology in the Nineteenth Century*, trans. John Bowden (London: SCM Press, 1972), p. 307.
59 Barth, *Protestant Theology*, pp. 306–12. There is an interesting exchange between Barth and Bultmann over the former's refusal to let theology have anything to do with philosophy. See their letters of 8 June 1928 (Bultmann) and 12 June 1928 (Barth) in Berndt Jaspert, *Karl Barth/Rudolf Bultmann: Letters 1922–1966*, ed. B. Jaspert (Edinburgh: T. & T. Clark, 1982), pp. 38ff.
60 Adorno, *ND*, p. 398. Translation slightly emended.
61 Richard Roberts has strongly criticized Barth for failing to relate revelation to the structures of human life. Cf. his 'Barth's Doctrine of Time: Its Nature and Implications' in S. W. Sykes, ed., *Karl Barth: Studies of His Theological Methods* (Oxford: Clarendon Press, 1979), pp. 88–146; 'The Ideal and the Real in the Theology of Karl Barth' in S. W. Sykes and D. Holmes, eds., *New Studies in Theology* (London: Duckworth, 1980), pp. 163–80; and 'Spirit, Structure and Truth in the Church', *MT* 3 (1986), 77–106. In his *MT* article Roberts uses Adorno to motivate an 'immanent critique' of Barth's 'transcendentalism', and rightly argues that the Barthian propensity to divorce the redeeming reality from the structures of human existence would be anathema to Adorno. However, it seems to me that in saying this Roberts overlooks Adorno's own espousal of a *diastasis* between the world (as it is presently constituted) and the sphere of redeemed life, a *diastasis* which, theology aside, has striking affinities with Barth's *diastasis*.
62 Joel Whitebook, 'Saving the Subject: Modernity and the Problem of the Autonomous Individual', *T*, 50 (1981–2), 95.
63 It is perhaps worth pointing out, as Rowan Williams does, that Barth himself, despite his reservations about monasticism, was in favour of *contemptus mundi*. Thus Barth says that this renunciation of the world may be regarded as 'a highly responsible and effective protest and opposition to the world, and not least to a worldly Church, and a new and specific way of combatting it' (*WN*, p. 92, quoting from *CD*, IV/2, p. 13).

It is possible to view this *diastasis* in christological terms. Barth had reservations about the monophysite tendency reflected in the *commu-*

nicatio idiomatum of Luther's christology, which (in his eyes) involved an exaltation of human nature and the human sphere. He therefore adverted to the *extra calvinisticum*, which denied a total and unreserved divine identification with human nature in Jesus Christ, to affirm the exalted Christ in a way that would not entail a corresponding exaltation of the human sphere. Bonhoeffer was more full-bloodedly Lutheran in this respect, and ended up by celebrating the human sphere when historical circumstances have demanded a far greater circumspection.

12. 'The weight of weakness': intratextuality and discipleship

1 John Howard Yoder, *The Priestly Kingdom: Social Ethics as Gospel* (Notre Dame, Indiana: University of Notre Dame Press, 1984), p. 188. My title is taken from a section heading in Yoder's book. Cf. p. 91. Josiah Royce, *The Problem of Christianity* (New York: Macmillan, 1913), vol. II, p. 270.
2 David H. Kelsey, *The Uses of Scripture in Recent Theology* (London: SCM Press, 1975), p. 208. Cf. also pp. 90–7 and p. 105.
3 The notion of such a biblical 'world depiction' is favoured by Paul Ricoeur, and the somewhat opposed idea of 'world rendition' (or 'world creation') is promoted by Hans Frei, George Lindbeck and Ronald Thiemann. For Ricoeur, cf. 'The Narrative Function' in *Hermeneutics and the Human Sciences*, trans. John B. Thompson (Cambridge: Cambridge University Press, 1981), p. 291; and *Time and Narrative*, trans. Kathleen McLaughlin and David Pellauer (Chicago: Chicago University Press, 1985), p. 176. For Frei, cf. *The Eclipse of Biblical Narrative* (New Haven and London: Yale University Press, 1974), p. 3; and 'The "Literal Reading" of Biblical Narrative in the Christian Tradition: Does It Stretch or Will it Break?' in Frank McConnell, ed., *The Bible and the Narrative Tradition* (New York: Oxford University Press, 1986), pp. 36–77. Cf. also George A. Lindbeck, *TND*, pp. 117ff; and Ronald F. Thiemann, *Revelation and Theology: The Gospel as Narrated Promise* (Notre Dame and London: University of Notre Dame, 1985), p. 143.
4 Stating the matter thus – that is, specifically in relation to the 'formation' of Christian *identity* – does not necessarily exclude the possibility that Christian witness involves, among other things, a 'decomposition' of the identity of the putative disciple. The question of such a 'decomposition' of the disciple's identity will feature later, in connection with the notion of being 'baptized' into the Christian narrative (cf. pp. 216ff below).
5 The locution 'the linguistic world of the Bible' is used here merely as a term of art. It is certainly not being suggested that the theologian is committed in any way to the assumption that 'language' is the only appropriate object of theological reflection; that he or she is behoved to accept something approximating to Roland Barthes's claim that ' "What takes place" in a narrative is . . . the adventure of language, the unceasing celebration of its coming. . . . "what happens" is language alone. . . . ' Cf. his 'Introduction to the Structural Analysis of Narrative'

Notes to pages 202–203

in *Image–Music–Text*, trans. Stephen Heath (London: Flamingo/ Fontana, 1977), p. 124. The principle that (literary) texts are to be understood as 'a kind of extension and application of certain properties of language' is also to be found in Tzvetan Todorov, *The Poetics of Prose*, trans. Richard Howard (Oxford: Blackwell, 1977), p. 19.

6 As far as I know, Lindbeck and Frei are the only ones of the above-mentioned individuals to have invoked publicly the notion of an intratextual or 'postliberal' theology. See Lindbeck, *TND*, especially chapter 6; and Frei, 'The "Literal Reading" of Biblical Narrative', especially pp. 71–2 (where reference is made to Lindbeck's book). However, while Lindbeck's is likely to remain the definitive account of intratextual theology, it is fairly clear that, important differences notwithstanding, the various approaches and formulations of the other above-named theologians can also be regarded as exemplars of this particular kind of theology. (The appropriate works of these theologians will be cited as our discussion proceeds.) A conspectus and tentative assessment of this 'postliberal' theology is to be found in William C. Placher, 'Revisionist and Postliberal Theologies and the Public Character of Theology', *Th*, 49 (1985), 392–416.

7 David Tracy, *Blessed Rage for Order: The New Pluralism in Theology* (New York: Seabury, 1978), p. 80. Cf. especially pp. 91–145, where Tracy elaborates this (at present) somewhat programmatic proposal. Tracy's extratextualism is criticized in Lindbeck, p. 120; and in Frei, 'The "Literal Reading" of Biblical Narrative', *passim*. Frei also has the hermeneutics of Paul Ricoeur as one of his primary targets. Lindbeck and Frei's rejection of any theological hermeneutics premised on a general anthropology can be seen to parallel Barth's strictures on 'naturalistic' or 'existentialist' anthropologies. Cf. Barth, *CD*, III/2, pp. 76–132; and IV/2, pp. 26–7. Tracy's own fairly critical assessment of Lindbeck's proposals for a 'cultural-linguistic' approach to theology is to be found in his 'Lindbeck's New Program For Theology: A Reflection', *Th*, 49 (1985), 460–72. There are striking affinities (and also undeniable divergences) between the Frei–Lindbeck–Thiemann critique of an extratextual hermeneutics and the argument, albeit of an entirely different philosophical provenance, for an 'immanent' analysis of texts to be found in Gilles Deleuze and Felix Guattari, *The Anti-Oedipus*, trans. R. Hurley, M. Seem and H. R. Lane (New York: Viking Books, 1977). Cf. especially pp. 25–8, 109–13, 305–8.

It may be argued that the notion of a 'common humanity' which features so prominently in *Blessed Rage for Order* is less in evidence in the later, more 'Gadamerian' *The Analogical Imagination* (London: SCM Press, 1981). This is perhaps true of the earlier, more obviously hermeneutical, sections of *The Analogical Imagination*, but in the Epilogue Tracy gives this notion a strategic place in his account of the relation that Christianity has to the other world religions. Is *The Analogical Imagination* therefore 'Gadamerian' in its characterization of 'the Christian classic', but 'Ricoeurian' in its understanding of the relations between the faiths? And, more importantly, would the

'Gadamerian' Tracy of *The Analogical Imagination* not have a conception of the text which is more in accord with the dialectical account of the text I shall be proposing later? These are matters which certainly merit discussion, but they involve issues of some complexity which are perhaps tangential to my subject, and this is therefore not the right place to address them.

8 *The Eclipse of Biblical Narrative*, p. 3. Cf. also 'The "Literal Reading" of Biblical Narrative', where Frei says that '[the] linguistic, textual world is in this case not only the *necessary* basis for our orientation within the real world, according to the Christian claims about this narrative, and this narrative alone, it is also *sufficient* for this purpose' (pp. 66–7. Frei's emphases). For the christological application of this principle, cf. Frei's *The Identity of Jesus Christ: The Hermeneutical Bases of Dogmatic Theology* (Philadelphia: Fortress Press, 1975), p. 138.

9 Thiemann, pp. 84–5. Cf. also p. 143 and p. 150. A similar understanding of the function of scriptural texts is implied by Kelsey's claim that '[to] call certain texts "scripture" is . . . to say that they ought to be *used* in the common life of the church in normative ways such that they decisively rule its form of life and forms of speech'. Cf. Kelsey, p. 94. The emphasis is Kelsey's. Also relevant here is Charles M. Wood, *The Formation of Christian Understanding: An Essay in Theological Hermeneutics* (Philadelphia: The Westminster Press, 1981); see especially p. 42 and p. 104. A more ecclesiologically-focused version of the thesis of the primacy of the Christian linguistic world is to be found in John Howard Yoder's *The Priestly Kingdom*. To quote Yoder: 'The church precedes the world epistemologically. We know more fully from Jesus Christ and in the context of the confessed faith than we know in other ways' (p. 11).

10 On this, cf. Lindbeck, p. 120ff; Frei, 'The "Literal Reading" of Biblical Narrative', pp. 37ff and pp. 68–73; Wood, p. 43; and Brevard S. Childs, 'The *Sensus Literalis* of Scripture: An Ancient and Modern Problem' in Herbert Donner, *et al.*, eds., *Beiträge zur Altestamentlichen Theologie: Festschrift Für Walter Zimmerli zum 70. Geburtstag* (Göttingen: Vandenhoeck & Ruprecht, 1977), pp. 80–93, cf. especially p. 92.

11 In this connection, cf. Lindbeck, pp. 120–1; Frei, *The Identity of Jesus Christ*, *passim*; Kelsey, p. 48; and Thiemann, pp. 84, 91 and 108.

12 The quoted phrase is from Lindbeck, p. 120. It should perhaps be noted that Brevard Childs distances his own position from the one espoused by Lindbeck and Frei when he insists that the New Testament speaks of realities which are external to the text. Childs says that 'it is far too limiting to restrict the function of the Bible to that of rendering an agent or an identity'. Cf. his *The New Testament as Canon: An Introduction* (London: SCM Press, 1984), p. 545.

13 Frei, *The Identity of Jesus Christ*, p. 159. This in fact approximates to Barth's construal of the *imitatio Christi*, which he articulates in terms of the notion of justifying faith, i.e. a faith which 'represent[s] an

immitation of God, *an analogy to His attitude and action*. It is the confidence of man which gives a corresponding and appropriate answer to the faithfulness of God as effective and revealed in His judgment and sentence. But in particular and concretely, it is an imitation of Jesus Christ, *an analogy to His attitude and action*', *CD*, IV/1, p. 634. My emphases. Implicit in Frei's statement is the entirely correct principle that the possibility of conformation to Christ is secured only through membership of the community of faith, i.e. through the Word and the Sacrament (as Frei avers on p. 159, the community is of course the body which is constituted by the Word and the Sacrament). A similar characterization of the community is to be found in Stanley Hauerwas, *A Community of Character: Towards a Constructive Christian Social Ethic* (Notre Dame, Indiana: Notre Dame University Press, 1981). To quote Hauerwas: '[the] most important social task [facing Christians] is nothing less than to be a community capable of hearing the story of God we find in the scripture and living in a manner that is faithful to that story' (p. 1). Hauerwas further develops this theme in 'The Church as God's New Language' in Garrett Green, ed., *Scriptural Authority and Narrative Interpretation* (Philadelphia: Fortress Press, 1987), pp. 179–98.

14 This is broadly in accord with Thiemann's remark that 'the discourse which functions within the text also functions between the text and the reader as an invitation to enter the world of the text'. Cf. Thiemann, p. 143. The 'discourse which functions within the text', *as it relates to the 'invitation to enter the world of the text'* can be seen as being in part the discourse of what Barth (following Calvin) terms the *participatio Christi*, that is 'the participation of the saints in the sanctity of Jesus Christ' (*CD*, IV/2, p. 518). It is the *participatio Christi* and the concomitant *conformitas Christi* which grounds the *analogia Christi* (understood in the manner of Frei), and so it is the *participatio Christi* – i.e. the truth that we are 'the people of Christ's possession' – which innervates the *imitatio Christi*. This grounding of biblical discourse in the *participatio Christi* implies that there is a sense in which the 'reader' has already to *be* in the world of the text (i.e. to be 'the possession of Christ') in order to be at all cognizant of the very 'invitation' to enter this world (i.e. to be a follower of Christ). In this respect and in this sense Thiemann's formulation is perhaps misleading. I am grateful to Christoph Schwöbel for getting me to think more clearly about these issues.

15 The potentially misleading designation 'new Yale Theology' is taken from Brevard Childs, *The New Testament as Canon*, p. 541.

16 Frei, *The Identity of Jesus Christ*, p. xvi. Cf. also 'The "Literal Meaning" of Biblical Narrative', p. 63, where Frei says that 'the text is a normative and pure "meaning" world of its own which, quite apart from any factual reference it may have, and apart from its author's intention or reader's reception, stands on its own with the authority of self-evident intelligibility'.

17 It should be noted, however, that Frei allows that '[the] reader's "interpretation" can, and indeed has to be, minimal, reiterative, and formal. . . . ' Cf. 'The "Literal Reading" of Biblical Narrative', p. 63.

18 The proposition that 'meanings' are 'interest-relative' is persuasively advanced in Jeffrey Stout's articles 'What is the Meaning of a Text?', *New Literary History*, 14 (1982), 1–12; and 'The Relativity of Interpretation', *The Monist*, 69 (1986), 103–18. It should, however, be stressed that Stout wants to follow Quine in dispensing with 'meanings' altogether: as he sees it, we are better-off talking about the 'interests' which – pragmatically – we bring to our readings of texts. In fairness to Frei, though, it has to be acknowledged that it is not *obvious* that he is committed to any theses about 'meanings' which are directly susceptible to Stout's strictures. In section III below I shall however sketch the basis for a 'church poetics' which pivots on a 'reader-response' theory of textual meaning, i.e., a variant of Stout's thesis. I am grateful to my erstwhile colleague Stephen Fowl for drawing my attention to Stout's articles.

19 This is clear from Frei's remark that 'realistic stories ... mean what they say, and that fact enables them to render depictively to the reader their own public world, which is the world he needs to understand them, even if he decides it is not his own real world'. Cf. *The Identity of Jesus Christ*, p. xv.

20 This identity-description is adapted, with minor stylistic alterations, from *The Identity of Jesus Christ*, p. 138.

21 *The Identity of Jesus Christ*, p. 15.

22 Gary Comstock, 'Truth or Meaning: Ricoeur versus Frei on Biblical Narrative', *JR*, 66 (1986), 117–40. References to this article will be cited parenthetically in the text.

23 Comstock says he is not absolutely certain whether Frei in fact subscribes to such a unity theory of the gospel's 'meaning', but, judging by what he says in footnote 23 on p. 125, Comstock seems convinced that the evidence to be gleaned from Frei's writings indicates a disposition on his part to conceive of the gospel's 'meaning' in precisely such unitary terms.

24 For Frei's invocation of the Strawsonian theory of reference, cf. his 'Theological Reflections on the Gospel's Account of Jesus' Death and Resurrection', *The Christian Scholar*, 49 (1966), 263–306; and *The Identity of Jesus Christ*, especially pp. 86–101 (though here Strawson is not mentioned by name). A similar, but more indirect, invocation is to be found in a discussion of Barth and Frei in Kelsey, pp. 46–50; and in Thiemann, pp. 82–91. Strawson's theory of reference is to be found in his *Individuals* (London: Methuen, 1959). Cf. pp. 18–20 for his espousal of Russell's dichotomy. For Russell's dichotomy, cf. Bertrand Russell, *The Problems of Philosophy* (Oxford: Oxford University Press, 1967), pp. 23–32, 62–3. My subsequent discussion owes a great deal to Gareth Evans's posthumous *The Varieties of Reference*, ed. John McDowell (Oxford: Oxford University Press, 1982). Cf. especially chapters 2, 3, 4, 5 and 9.

25 I am making a close paraphrase of Evans, p. 65, where he calls this conviction 'Russell's Principle'. On this, cf. Russell, *The Problems of Philosophy*, p. 58. For Strawson's version, cf. *Subject and Predicate in Logic and Grammar* (London: Methuen, 1974), p. 47.

26 Evans, p. 89. Cf. also p. 65.
27 This is a crude and much abbreviated rehearsal of Evans's characterization of 'description-based identification'. For this, cf. Evans,
pp. 132–7.
28 *The Identity of Jesus Christ*, p. 89. Cf. also pp. 5–9. This also supplies
the rationale for Frei's approving citation of Calvin's observation that
while 'our hearts and minds may need illumination, the text does not. It
is plain for all to read'. Cf. Frei, 'Theology and the Interpretation of
Narrative: Some Hermeneutical Considerations' (lecture delivered to
the Narrative Interpretation and Christian Theology Group of the
American Academy of Religion, December 1982), p. 22. Quoted in
Comstock, p. 126 note 24.
29 *The Identity of Jesus Christ*, p. 170.
30 *CD*, IV/2, p. 513. There is a trinitarian derivation for this community's
constitutive sociality: the community is what it is because it participates
in the life of God, and hence its 'grammar' is inescapably trinitarian
(i.e. social). A profoundly theological rendering of this derivation is to
be found in Ray S. Anderson, *HTRG*. Cf. p. 250, where Anderson
says: 'Through Word and Spirit, God entered human community to the
depths of its incapacity, and from that depth raised a response to God
which completed community through a union of man with God.'
Unfortunately, Anderson's discussion is conducted throughout in an
existential–ontological idiom, and he is thus unable to recognize that
reality 'speaks' because it has an inexpugnable rhetorical and linguistic
organization, and that it is therefore necessary to attend to this
organization before the project of formulating a viable *theo*-logic can be
advanced. Ingredient in this trinitarian derivation of the church's
constitutive sociality will be a pneumatology: the theologian has to
heed Bonhoeffer's warning that '[the] church does not come into being
through people coming together. . . . But it is in being through the Spirit
which is effective in the community.' Cf. his *Sanctorum Communio: A
Dogmatic Inquiry into the Sociology of the Church*, trans. R. Gregor
Smith (London: Collins, 1963), p. 116.
31 Karl Marx and Friedrich Engels, *The German Ideology*, ed. C. J.
Arthur (London: Lawrence & Wishart, 1974), pp. 50–1. For discussion, cf. John McMurtry, *The Structure of Marx's World-View* (Princeton, NJ: University Press, 1978), pp. 123–56. Cf. also p. 171 n. 27,
where McMurtry recognizes an affinity between Marx's acknowledgement of language's fundamental sociality and Wittgenstein's portrayal
of language as an activity rooted in shared 'forms of life'. This affinity is
also acknowledged in Sabina Lovibond, *Realism and Imagination in
Ethics* (Oxford: Blackwell, 1983), pp. 27ff. The quotation from Marx
and Engels is reproduced from Lovibond.
32 Lindbeck, p. 131. Cf. also Kelsey, pp. 47–8, 93 and 213; Thiemann,
p. 77; and Wood, pp. 19–21 and 75ff. Wood's is an excellent exposition
of the traditional interpretative procedure of *meditatio*, which he
defines as 'a quite active and strenuous discipline, namely, the discipline of endeavouring, by God's grace, to let the concepts found in the

Christian texts take root in one's life' (p. 79). The intratextual approach's insistence that *explicatio* only achieves completion in *meditatio* will be contested by Comstock: *meditatio* stresses that it is obedience, rather than 'belief', which is the path to knowledge. On this, cf. Wood's 'The Knowledge Born of Obedience', *Anglican Theological Review*, 61 (1979), 331–40. Comstock is keen that there should be a 'theoretical foundation for narrative theology', and my remarks summarize the line of argument taken by him in 'Truth or Meaning', pp. 129–30. The main thesis of 'Truth or Meaning' is that Christians will have to make truth-claims if they are to enter 'the game of rational argumentation', and that this desirable 'truth-theory' is more likely to be consonant with the principles of Ricoeur's biblical hermeneutics than it is with those of Frei's 'pure' narrativism.

33 *The Identity of Jesus Christ*, p. 8. Frei goes on to say that '[perhaps] it has very little to do with any kind of talk and much more with the eloquence of a consistent pattern of life that has seemingly suffered an inexplicably wounding and healing invasion. . . .' (*ibid.*). Frei is consistent in his avowal that the journey from unbelief to belief can take many routes, 'even the incongruous one that such a transition . . . occurs in the process of purely circular discourse concerning the unity of Christ's identity and presence' (pp. 8–9).

34 The *ceteris paribus* clause is in order because the 'understanding' in question here takes the form of an imputed knowledge which need not therefore be self-reflexive. The martyred Austrian peasant Franz Jägerstatter was certainly not the equal of Gerhard Kittel in the sphere of New Testament scholarship, but it is incontrovertibly true that it was Jägerstatter, and not Kittel (who supported the Nuremberg Racial Laws), whose life and death bespoke the conjunction of Christ's 'identity' and 'presence'. On Kittel, cf. Donald MacKinnon, 'Tillich, Frege, Kittel: Reflections on a Dark Theme' in his *Explorations in Theology* (London: SCM Press, 1979), pp. 129–37. On Jägerstatter, cf. the fully documented biography by Gordon Zahn, *In Solitary Witness* (New York: Holt, Rinehart & Winston, 1964). A more detailed specification of the differences between Jägerstatter and Kittel with regard to the question of 'understanding the truth of Holy Scripture' would require us to deal with this 'understanding' in the context of an adequate pragmatics.

35 I appropriate the concept of *semantic depth* from Mark Platts, *Ways of Meaning: An Introduction to a Philosophy of Language* (London: Routledge & Kegan Paul, 1979), pp. 261ff.; and Lovibond, *Realism and Imagination in Ethics*, pp. 31–6, 70, 160, 192 and 198. Both these accounts employ the concept as part of a characterization of the properties of moral discourse. I am especially indebted to Lovibond's presentation.

36 Lindbeck, p. 33. Cf. also p. 68 and p. 111 n. 25. Lovibond too cites Wittgenstein's correlation of judgement-making with participation in the life of a community, and quotes the following remark from his *On Certainty*: 'It is our *acting* which lies at the bottom of the language-

game.' Cf. Lovibond, p. 30; *On Certainty*, eds. G. E. M. Anscombe and G. H. von Wright (Oxford: Blackwell, 1969), section 204. Also germane to Lovibond's elucidation of the concept of 'semantic depth' is Wittgenstein's account, in *The Philosophical Investigations*, of what is involved in being a good judge of the genuineness of expressions of feeling: 'Can one learn this knowledge? Yes; some can. Not, however, by taking a course in it, but through "experience" ... What one acquires here is not a technique; one learns correct judgements. There are also rules, but they do not form a system, and only experienced people can apply them right.' Cf. Lovibond, p. 32; *PI*, II, p. 227. A similar emphasis on knowledge as 'praxological' because gained through, and manifested in, ritual is to be found in Theodore W. Jennings, 'On Ritual Knowledge', *JR*, 62 (1982), 111–27. Victor Turner, rather than Wittgenstein, is the *eminence grise* of Jennings's article.

37 Hence the point of St Thomas Aquinas's assertion that the 'content' of the articles of faith will only be grasped in the after-life. Cf. his *Summa Theologiae*, IIa, 4, 8. A similar eschatological stress lies at the heart of *The Nature of Doctrine*. Cf. especially pp. 57–63 and p. 125. Lovibond provides another, quite different, reason for affirming our fundamental inability to reach the absolute semantic depth of a concept, namely, the inevitability that 'our form of life will undergo further historical development in the future, so that the semantic depth of, for example, the concept of courage (as employed in our community) will be enhanced in ways that go beyond the experience of any existing speaker' (p. 35. Cf. also p. 192). Lindbeck will not be able to countenance all of Lovibond's historical perspectivalism because he wants to say that the 'grammar' of a religion is a communally authoritative, invariant and abiding categorical structure ranging over a 'vocabulary of symbols, concepts, rites, injunctions, and stories' that 'is in part highly variable' (pp. 80–1). Lindbeck's residual 'Kantianism' thus has the effect of casting into the ocean of historical change those items belonging to a religion's 'vocabulary' while keeping its 'grammar' strictly land-bound. David Ford has drawn attention to Lindbeck's 'Kantianism' in his review of *The Nature of Doctrine* in *JTS*, 37 (1985), 277–82.

38 To quote Lovibond: 'The phenomenon of "semantic depth" suggests ... that ... while a speaker may master the use of a ... word adequately for the purposes of participation in a certain limited range of language-games involving that word, yet the same word may also figure in various other language-games into which he has not so far been initiated' (p. 70).

39 Here I follow closely the line of argument developed in Lovibond, pp. 34–5.

40 Kelsey, p. 90. The emphases are Kelsey's. Cf. also p. 95.

41 For this understanding of the text, cf. Jonathan Culler, *On Deconstruction: Theory and Criticism after Structuralism* (London: Routledge & Kegan Paul, 1983), p. 35.

42 Lindbeck, p. 77. Cf. also pp. 16, 33, 84 and 114. Lindbeck does nothing to banish the suspicion that the Husserlian 'transcendental ego' is lodged deep in his discourse, that the critical thrust of his position is blunted by his failure to 'decentre' a certain kind of religious subject (and this despite his strictures on 'experiential-expressivism'). For such a 'decentring', cf. Fredric Jameson, 'Imaginary and Symbolic in Lacan: Marxism, Psychoanalytic Criticism, and the Problem of the Subject' in Shoshana Felman, ed., *Literature and Psychoanalysis: The Question of Reading – Otherwise* (Baltimore and London: Johns Hopkins University Press, 1982), pp. 338–95. Lindbeck does not even acknowledge the possibility of unconscious meaning, let alone its potentially disruptive effects, effects which displace or decentre this 'transcendental ego'. This criticism has been prompted by the following remark of Julia Kristeva's: 'logic and ontology have inscribed the question of *truth* within *judgement* (or sentence structure) and *being*, dismissing as *madness*, *mysticism* or *poetry* any attempt to articulate that impossible element which henceforth can only be designated by the Lacanian category of the *real*'. Cf. her essay 'The True-Real' in Toril Moi, ed., *The Kristeva Reader* (Oxford: Blackwell, 1986), p. 217. A similar criticism directed by Rainer Nägele at Habermas's 'ideal-speech situation' may also be applicable to Lindbeck. Cf. Nägele's 'The Provocation of Jacques Lacan', *NGC*, 16 (1979), 5–29.

43 Here I have to agree with the gist of the criticism made by John Milbank in his 'An Essay Against Secular Order' (paper presented to the Society for the Study of Theology Annual Conference, 1986), pp. 35–6, n. 5.

44 Fredric Jameson, 'On Magic Realism in Film', *CI*, 12 (1986), 304.

45 Lindbeck, p. 119.

46 Julia Kristeva, 'From One Identity to An Other', in her *Desire in Language: A Semiotic Approach to Language and Art*, ed. L. S. Roudiez (Oxford: Blackwell, 1981), pp. 124–47.

47 On filiative and affiliative relationships, cf. Edward W. Said, *The World, the Text, and the Critic* (London: Faber, 1984), *passim.*

48 Lindbeck, p. 78. Cf. also p. 127. For discussion cf. James J. Buckley's appropriately titled 'Doctrine in the Diaspora', *Th*, 49 (1985), 443–59.

49 Julia Kristeva, 'A New Type of Intellectual: The Dissident' in *The Kristeva Reader*, p. 298. Kristeva makes it clear that this passage is autobiographical.

50 Culler, *On Deconstruction*, p. 73.

51 For Bonhoeffer's distinction between the perfected and the developing communion of saints, cf. *Sanctorum Communio*, p. 116.

52 For Eco's distinction between 'open' and 'closed' works, cf. his *The Role of the Reader: Explorations in the Semiotics of Texts* (London: Hutchinson, 1979), pp. 8–11 and 47–66.

53 Fredric Jameson, *PU*, pp. 81ff.

54 For the notion of such an 'asymptotic' approach to the Real I am indebted to Fredric Jameson's 'Imaginary and Symbolic in Lacan', *passim.* Jameson of course identifies the Real with the material configurations of history (or 'History', to use his term).

55 Here I am indebted to Walter Benjamin's 'On Language as Such and on the Language of Man' in his collection of essays *One Way Street and Other Writings*, trans. E. Jephcott and K. Shorter (London: Verso, 1985), pp. 107–23.

56 I am indebted to David Ford for a number of valuable conversations which have helped put some of the above issues in a more adequate perspective. I owe a more general debt to John Milbank for continuing discussions on a whole range of topics. For their incisive written comments on an earlier draft, I am deeply grateful to Stephen Fowl, Stanley Hauerwas, Werner Jeanrond, Gerard Loughlin and Christoph Schwöbel. They are not of course responsible for any inadequacies that remain.

13. 'Theistic arguments' and 'rational theism'

1 For Hartshorne's formulation, see 'The Irreducibly Modal Structure of the Argument' in J. H. Hick and A. C. McGill, eds., *The Many-Faced Argument* (London: Macmillan, 1968), pp. 334–40. Malcolm's presentation is to be found in 'Anselm's Ontological Arguments', *The Philosophical Review*, 69 (1960), 41–62. For Plantinga's version, see his *The Nature of Necessity* (Oxford: The Clarendon Press, 1974), ch. 10.

2 See John J. Shepherd, *Experience, Inference and God* (London: Macmillan, 1975); and Germain Grisez, *Beyond the New Theism* (London: University of Notre Dame Press, 1975).

3 Richard Swinburne, *The Existence of God* (Oxford: Clarendon Press, 1979), chapter 8; and Brian Davies, 'Mackie on the Argument from Design', *NB*, 64 (1983), 384–90.

4 Oxford: Blackwell, 1982. Page references are given in parentheses in the text.

5 Ward presents his version of the ontological argument on pp. 24–35 of *Rational Theology*.

6 For Ward's claim that the root-principle of his argument is to be found in the *Proslogion*, see p. 26 of his book.

7 Thus, for example, Ward invokes the notion of a 'possible world'. As readers familiar with modal logic will know, the concept of a 'possible world' is characteristically employed as part of the apparatus used in explicating the semantics of modal logic. And since quantified modal logic was provided with its semantics as recently as the mid-1950s, it is difficult to resist the conclusion that any schematization of the ontological argument which hinges on the notion of a 'possible world' is purely and essentially a modern phenomenon.

8 See St Anselm, *Cur Deus Homo* in F. S. Schmitt, ed., *Sancti Anselmni Opera Omnia* (Rome: n.p., 1940), vol. II, 123.20; and *de Concordia praescientiae et gratiae Dei cum libero arbitrio* in Schmitt, ed., *Sancti Anselmni Opera Omnia*, vol. II, 246.27. But see also *Cur Deus Homo*, 125.1–13; and *de Concordia praescientiae*, where Anselm appears to introduce a *logical* sense of necessity. For discussion of this point, to which I am indebted, see Jonathan Barnes's fine study *The Ontological Argument* (London: Macmillan, 1972), pp. 22–6.

9 For an admirable discussion of the relation between St Anselm's general theory of physical dispositions and capacities and his modal complex, see D. P. Henry, *The Logic of St Anselm* (Oxford: Clarendon Press, 1967), pp. 134–80. Henry shows – convincingly in my opinion – that a faithful exegesis of Anselm's thought must come to terms with the neo-Platonic conceptuality of his time.

10 Anselm, *Cur Deus Homo*, 100.20–28, 100.3–8, 121.13–15.

11 Anselm, *Cur Deus Homo*, 123.11–124.2; and *de Concordia praescientiae*, 127.6–11. Anselm does not always distinguish between these two readings, as pointed out by Barnes in his *Ontological Argument*, pp. 24–5.

12 For an elucidation of this point, see Jonathan Bennett, *Kant's Dialectic* (Cambridge: Cambridge University Press, 1974), p. 234.

13 It is not being implied here that modern modal logic cannot accommodate notions of the type mentioned under (b). Certainly modern logic, especially modern 'action' logic, can accommodate notions like aseity and indestructibility. But the fact remains that the resulting axiomatizations of the notions in question are really the logical articulation of a set of specifically 'theistic' beliefs, and the abstract or formal *structure* of this articulation – the province of logic – should not be confused with the 'theistic' *content*, or underpinning, of these beliefs – the province of theology. Ward, I believe, makes this mistake because he believes that 'God exists' is a principle which must be presupposed if the ultimate intelligibility of the universe is to be affirmed.

14 Although Kant does rather bluntly assert that the cosmological argument 'is only a disguised ontological proof' (in *CPR*, p. 527), his actual treatment of the cosmological argument in *The Critique of Pure Reason* in no way suggests that this argument can be so easily reduced to the ontological argument. Complex issues of Kantian exergesis will have to be broached in any attempt to ascertain Kant's true position on the relation between these two 'theistic' arguments, issues which are not within the scope of this essay to pursue. The interested reader is referred to Peter Remnant's 'Kant and the Cosmological Argument', *The Australian Journal of Philosophy*, 37 (1959), 152–5, for a judicious account of Kant's view of the relation between these two arguments.

15 If we overlook, for the purposes of our argument, the possible justification for Ward's procedure adduced in (i) above, it is possible to appreciate just why it is likely that he would be somewhat less interested in isolating these arguments from each other in order to elucidate their purely intrinsic formal properties.

16 I owe the ensuing presentation of the notion of 'proof' to Robert Nozick's magisterial *Philosophical Explanations* (Oxford: The Clarendon Press, 1981), pp. 239–40.

17 It must be emphasized, where (2) is concerned, that the denial of q must be S's *reason* for not believing that p. After all, it is possible for (3) to obtain, while (2) does not. That is, p could entail q, and q be false (in which case p would be false as well), but the falsity of q must be S's reason for not believing p, because it is possible that S might not believe

p for a reason not in the least connected with the falsity of *q*. (Maybe *S* does not believe *p* because *p* is entailed by *r* (where *r* ≠ *q*), and *S* knows that *r* is false.) On this point, see Nozick, p. 239.

18 Nozick, p. 240. Nozick's account does not foreclose the possibility that the inference of *q* from *p* may beg the question for one person, but not for another, or that it may beg the question as a proof, but not as an argument.

19 In this context it is perhaps significant that Alvin Plantinga, whose account of the ontological argument Ward follows in essential outline, does himself admit that 'this argument is in some way question begging, or at least dialectically deficient'. Cf. Plantinga, p. 218.

20 'Can God's Existence Be Disproved?' in *NEPT*, p. 54. Findlay, before he changed his mind, was of course the exponent of the well-known ontological 'disproof' of God's existence, a 'disproof' based on the idea that the concept of God presupposed by the ontological argument is incoherent because it involves the logically untenable notion of necessary existence.

21 p. 43. Ward does not use the locution 'is necessarily false' – the term he actually uses is 'embodies a self-contradiction'. But since a self-contradictory proposition is one that is necessarily false, no harm is done by this substitution of expressions.

22 For an elaboration of the similarities and differences between the notions of *pragmatic futility* and *formal validity* where 'theistic arguments' are concerned, see James F. Ross, *PT*, chapter 1; and 'On Proofs for the Existence of God' in J. Donnelly, ed., *Logical Analysis and Contemporary Theism* (New York: Fordham University Press, 1972), pp. 1–19.

23 I suspect that it is perhaps the fear that the ontological arguer cannot avoid making use of such a stipulation which, in part, prompts Alvin Plantinga to say that this argument is 'dialectically deficient'. See note 19 above.

24 I am indebted to Plantinga, chapter 1, for these observations. Ward's identification of 'inconceivability' with 'impossibility' is even more unacceptable in view of his desire to locate his argument in the tradition alleged to have been inaugurated by Anselm. For Anselm did not, and indeed could not, make this identification between conceivability and (logical) possibility. In *Proslogion* 15 he states emphatically that the divine essence is beyond comprehension, although he acknowledges that God is conceivable, simply because we 'use' the concept 'God'. Consequently, if 'conceivability' is equated with '(logical) possibility', it would follow that for Anselm God is totally incomprehensible, since he believes that God surpasses the (merely) logically possible. On this and related matters, see Gareth B. Matthews, 'On Conceivability in Anselm and Malcolm', *The Philosophical Review*, 70 (1961), 110–11.

25 On this point I agree with the view expressed in Ninian Smart, *The Concept of Worship* (London: Macmillan, 1972), *passim*.

26 These reflections are suggested by the following passage in David Lewis's excellent 'Anselm and Actuality', *Nous*, 4 (1970), 183–8:

the ontological arguer needs to adopt standards of greatness so eccentric as to rob his conclusion of its expected theological import. If some mud in its mud-world is deemed to be as great as the greatest angel in his heavenly world, then it does not matter whether or not something exists in reality than which nothing greater – by *these* standards of greatness – can be conceived. . . . [The] ontological arguer who says that his world alone is the actual world is as foolish as one who boasts that he has the special fortune to be alive at a unique moment in history: the present. The actual world is not special in itself, but only in the special relation it bears to the ontological arguer. . . . The world an ontological arguer calls actual is special only in that the ontological arguer resides there – and it is no great distinction for a world to harbour an ontological arguer. Think of an ontological arguer in some dismally mediocre world – there are such ontological arguers – arguing that his world alone is actual, hence special, because a fitting place of greatest greatness, hence a world where something exists than which no greater can be conceived to exist. He is wrong to argue this. So are we.

Lewis's argument pivots on the principle that 'actual' is an indexical expression. For a generalization of this indexical interpretation of 'actual', see Bas van Fraassen, 'The Only Necessity is Verbal Necessity', *Journal of Philosophy*, 74 (1977), 71–85.

27 See above, p. 229.
28 For the construction of such a 'Platonist' account, albeit with specific reference to set-theory, see George Berry, 'Logic with Platonism', *Synthese*, 19 (1968), 215–49.
29 It is of course possible for x to exist in W^*, but x would not exist, in W^*, *as* the cause of y.
30 This essay was (in 1983) constructed entirely within the framework of a 'theistic metaphysics' of the kind so attractive to those who, like Ward, belong to the Anglo-American tradition of analytical philosophy. The practitioners of this philosophy have, invariably, been blind to the Cartesian–Lockean cognitive paradigm which underpins it. Critics of Ward who are heedful of the truth that historical circumstances may be such that they have now effectively dispelled the aura of irremovability which surrounds this paradigm, may regard the 'immanent critique' essayed in this chapter as superfluous. And they would not be wrong.

Index of names

Adorno, Theodor W. x, 180,
193–7, 199–200, 251n21,
290nn35, 37, 39, 291nn45, 46,
49, 51, 292n61, 292–3n63
Alston, William P., 42, 248n5
Anderson, Ray S., 17, 71, 186–8,
189, 240n30, 241n36, 242n42,
270nn26, 28, 288n13,
298n30
Anscombe, G. E. M., 237n6
Anselm, archbishop of Canter-
bury, xi, 70, 223–4, 258n29,
274n20, 302n8, 303nn9, 11,
304n24
Aquinas, Saint Thomas, xi, 16–17,
25, 57, 73, 163, 243nn8, 9,
254n36, 256n1, 258n29
on analogy, 1–19 *passim*,
237nn1, 4, 7, 238 nn8, 10, 13,
239n17, 241n34, 284n20,
285n23
on beatific vision, 16–17
on faith, 18, 241nn32, 35,
242nn40, 41, 300n37
Five Ways of, 4, 7, 15, 53, 229,
234, 253n31
on 'natural theology', 15–16, 19,
241n34
on 'revealed theology', *see* on
'natural theology'
Neo-Platonism of, 11, 239n21
on Trinity, 31, 246n20
Arendt, Hannah, 260n10
Athanasius, bishop of Alexandria,
29, 32, 239n18, 245n16

Augustine, bishop of Hippo, xi,
73, 175, 245n16, 258n29
on creation, 11–12
neo-Platonism of, 11–12,
239–40n22, 240n23
on Trinity, 29–32
Austin, J. L., 42
Ayer, A. J., 42

Baelz, Peter, 275–6n32
Baillie, Donald, 102, 266–7n1
Baillie, John, 139–40, 150, 281n14
Balthasar, Hans Urs von,
239nn17, 18, 241n38, 244n11,
265n46
Barnes, Jonathan, 302n8
Barth, Karl, 14, 176, 199–200, 210,
216, 240n30, 254n35, 271nn3,
4, 273n18, 273–4n19, 274n20,
274–5n25, 284–5n22, 287n11,
288nn14, 16, 292nn54, 49, 61,
293n63, 295–6n12, 296n14
on analogy, 8, 12, 17, 238n13,
239nn17, 18
his 'Christocentrism', 136–7,
141–3
on God, 26–7, 244n12
on 'natural theology', 18
on revelation, 141–3, 150–1,
181, 184, 186
undervaluation of *imago Dei*,
17–18
Barthes, Roland, 50, 175,
250nn17, 18, 253n29, 293–4n5
Bartley, W. W. III, 91–101

307

Index of subjects